"To Serve a Larger Purpose"

"TO SERVE
A LARGER PURPOSE"

*Engagement for Democracy and
the Transformation of Higher Education*

Edited by

JOHN SALTMARSH AND
MATTHEW HARTLEY

Temple University Press • Philadelphia

For Ira Harkavy and Edward Zlotkowski:
mentors, colleagues, friends

TEMPLE UNIVERSITY PRESS
Philadelphia, Pennsylvania 19122
www.temple.edu/tempress

Copyright © 2011 by Temple University
All rights reserved
Paperback edition published 2012

Library of Congress Cataloging-in-Publication Data

"To serve a larger purpose" : engagement for democarcy and the transformation
of higher education / edited by John Saltmarsh and Matthew Hartley.
    p. cm
  Includes Index.
  ISBN 978-1-4399-0506-7 (cloth : alk. paper) — ISBN 978-1-4399-0508-1 (e-book)
  1. Education, Higher—United States.   2. Democracy and education—United
States.   3. Educational leadership—United States.   4. Educational planning—United
States.   I. Saltmarsh, John A., 1957–   II. Hartley, Matthew, 1964–
  LA227.4.T6 2011
  378´.015—dc22   2010045074

ISBN 987-1-4399-0507-4 (paperback : alk. paper)

Printed in the United States of America

020112-P

CONTENTS

PREFACE

David Mathews

In the last decade, people in and around colleges and universities have been talking more and more about the civic role of their institutions as well as their disciplines or professions. Kettering Foundation research has tried to track what some call the "civic engagement movement" and look at its implications for two other phenomena. One is a serious problem for self-rule—that citizens have been pushed to the sidelines in our political system. The other is a problem of unrecognized potential—that communities and their societies of citizens could play a role in everything from economic development to educational and health care reform.

In studying these phenomena, the foundation concentrates on the problems *of* democracy, which are related to but distinct from the problems that occur *in* democratic countries—poverty, injustice, violence, and so on. Given our focus, we try to determine how various civic engagement projects in higher education understand the role of citizens. For example, are citizens treated as consumers of services or as producers of public goods? Do institutions of higher education see their mission as providing help and assisting people in becoming more informed "customers"? Or are academic institutions more concerned with developing people's capacity for collective action? Arguably, the problems *of* democracy are more likely to be solved in ways that preserve the values of self-government if we can make progress in addressing the problems *in* democracy.

Looking into the role of citizens inevitably and inescapably raises questions of power. What kind of power do institutions believe citizens need to have, we have asked in our research, and how do colleges and universities think citizens acquire such power? Must academic institutions empower people, or do people have their own sources of power?

Then there are issues of knowledge and education. Do citizens need to "be educated," as is often said, or do they have distinctive ways of knowing that need to be recognized and developed?

Higher education has a unique and significant role in addressing the problems of democracy. The foundation has a long history of recognizing and generating research to better understand higher education's role. A meeting was held in February 2008 at the foundation, and what emerged at the meeting, and in the subsequent report on the meeting captured in the "Democratic Engagement White Paper" (2009), was the critical understanding that, as Saltmarsh and Hartley write in their introduction to this book, "the dominant paradigm of civic engagement in higher education does not express or actively seek to fulfill a democratic purpose, and second, that colleges and universities, in the absence of this larger sense of purpose for their civic engagement work, have failed to pursue the kind of institutional change that is needed to realign the central premises and core work of the academy" (p. 1).

At the foundation, we welcome this book because it examines the purposes or goals of civic engagement initiatives and the kinds of institutional changes that are needed to advance democratic civic engagement. If these efforts are dedicated to serving democratic ends, what does that mean? Socially responsible institutions that address society's ills certainly serve democracy. Yet they may not address the problems of democracy. To do that, institutions would have to do more than serve and assist. They would have to take into consideration the role they play as political actors. Colleges and universities would have to account for the problems of democracy and address changes that would make their institutions and the education they provide more democratic— a central theme running though the chapters of this book. For instance, institutions of higher education would need to take more responsibility for the powerful control they exercise over what it means to know. As Harry Boyte argues in a Kettering Foundation white paper, "Civic Agency and the Cult of the Expert," the dominant concept of knowledge assumes that there are "atemporal standards of rationality" that can reveal the "universal truths" needed "to enlighten the masses" and solve their problems (2009, p. 11). This concept, Boyte argues, shapes the academic disciplines, structures research, and influences instruction. This epistemology also has political implications: it dominates everything from the standards for student academic progress in the No Child Left Behind legislation to the impact of evaluations conducted by both government programs and grant-making foundations. This epistemology privileges "objective," largely quantitative data, which is certainly one way to know but hardly the only way.

Perhaps recognition of the power of knowledge will gain some traction in one of the facets of the civic engagement movement—the emphasis on "public scholarship." It would seem important to know what the epistemology of this scholarship is. Does it do more than recognize that nonacademics have valid knowledge? Does it go further to recapture an appreciation for the ways of knowing that result in what the ancient Greeks called practical wisdom (*phronesis*), which is socially constructed in deliberative decision making?

The problem isn't that the social construction of knowledge is mysterious. It has been recognized as a valid source of wisdom since the fourth century B.C., when Isocrates provided one of the first accounts of *phronesis*. He clearly distinguished practical wisdom from scientific knowledge, philosophy, and popular opinion. Isocrates believed that humans had a particular mental faculty that they could use in making political decisions—the ability to distinguish between wise and unwise action. This ability doesn't come from the capacity for the rational analysis of objective data but, rather, from the capacity to weigh possible courses of action against what is most important to people and then arrive at sound judgments.

Another of the intriguing facets of the civic engagement efforts is the energy coming from faculty ranks. This is all the more interesting in light of what appears to be minimal trustee involvement. While the chapters by William Plater and John Presley address the importance of academic leadership for institutional change in addressing the problems of democracy, trustees are part of the citizenry that has been sidelined, and many undoubtedly live in communities that are trying to strengthen their civic powers. Why should they be almost invisible in the civic engagement movement, while the faculty is out in front?

At Kettering, we would also like to know if the faculty members who are leading civic engagement projects are different from those who have always been exemplary citizens involved in all manner of good causes. Are the leaders of the civic engagement initiatives driven by a desire to make their scholarly careers compatible with their public lives? Do they feel that academic culture isn't hospitable to their efforts? The chapters by KerryAnn O'Meara and Lorlene Hoyt are powerful contributions to our understanding of democratically engaged faculty.

Kettering is trying to find out how many faculty are like Marguerite (Peggy) Shaffer, director of American Studies at Miami University. In the 2008 *Higher Education Exchange*, Shaffer is quite articulate about her distress:

> I have joked with colleagues that I am in the midst of an academic midlife crisis—questioning every aspect of life in academe. In thinking about my future in the university, I have wondered whether my time will be well spent researching and writing a scholarly monograph that might well get me promoted, but that will be read by only a handful of like-minded scholars with similar intellectual interests. I have questioned the time I devote to teaching critical thinking skills to students who are socialized, both inside and outside the university, to care more about their final grades and potential career options than the knowledge they can share and the collective future they will create. (Brown, p. 24)

To sum up, it isn't clear what type of democracy the civic engagement movement will foster. But the strongest form of democracy (as noted in the first chapter of this book), one in which citizens create power through their ability to act collectively, is likely to be the most challenging for academe. There are a number of reasons why this may be the case; one reason, we suspect, is the difference between institutional politics and the politics of everyday democracy. Colleges and universities, being institutions, naturally relate more easily to institutional politics. Democratic politics seems to operate at two levels. The most obvious is the institutional level, which includes elections, lawmaking, and the delivery of services. The other level is less obvious and exists underneath the institutional superstructures. It is filled with informal gatherings, ad hoc associations, and the seemingly innocuous banter that goes on when people mull over the meaning of their everyday experiences.

What happens at the second level is much like what happens in the wetlands of a natural ecosystem. The wetlands of politics play roles similar to swamps and barrier islands. They may appear inconsequential when compared with what happens in elections, legislative bodies, and courts. Yet this pondering of the meaning of everyday experiences in grocery stores and coffee shops can be the wellspring of public decision making. Connections made in informal gatherings can become the basis for political networks; ad hoc associations can evolve into civic organizations.

Democracy in the political wetlands isn't perfect because there isn't such a thing. Still, ways of acting, generating power, and creating change occur that are unlike what occurs in institutional politics. Recently, we have been calling these characteristics "organic." Citizens are defined by what they do with other citizens rather than with the state. Their relationships are pragmatic or work-related rather than based on patronage or party loyalty. The names people give to problems in the political wetlands reflect the things they hold dear. They reflect their basic concerns—their deepest fears as well as their highest hopes as human beings: being safe from danger, being treated fairly, being free to act. These names are different from those that people use when they serve as experts in an institution or as politicians. For example, citizens want to feel that they are safe in their homes, a feeling that is less quantifiable but more compelling than the statistics professionals use to describe crime.

The knowledge needed to decide what to do about the problems citizens face is created in the cauldron of collective decision making. It is formed by the interaction of people with other people, by the comparison of experience with experience. This is different from the way scholarly knowledge is created, which is through rigorously disciplined science. As I said previously, this practical wisdom has to be socially constructed.

While institutions of higher education may have difficulty relating to the organic forms of wetlands democracy, this book provides some examples of ways in which those in higher education can assist in building and preserving the ecologically rich biodiversity of democracy on campus and in communities connected to campuses. These examples are excellent, but they aren't the only ones that could be cited, as the authors of this book know well. In fact, the growth in and diversity within the civic engagement movement is one of its most significant features. For instance, one of Kettering's most important discoveries is the number of academic centers that seem to have a unique potential to align their work with the work citizens do in everyday politics.

So far, we have located more than forty of these centers or institutes around the country. Their potential is based on how they approach democratic politics, which is through the decisions citizens have to make in order to reach sound resolutions on policy issues and act together effectively in solving community problems. These institutes concentrate on deliberative decision making and its ability to foster practical wisdom. Some institutes, such as the ones at Hofstra and Kansas State, are embedded in their universities. Others are freestanding, like the one in Alabama, but have ties to several universities. A number of institutes, including the one at the University of Hawaii, have strong connections to state legislatures. Still others are embedded in their communities but collaborate with a nearby university, as is the case for Penn State and the ad hoc Public Issues Forums of Centre County. These institutes and centers help complete the picture of the civic engagement projects and the various ways they serve democracy.

The objective of this collection of case studies is to help provide an even more complete picture of civic engagement projects, the various ways they serve democracy, and the kinds of changes that are taking place at institutions of higher education. This admirable book, with its focus on "the reclamation of the democratic purposes of civic engagement and an examination of the requisite transformation of higher education that would be required to achieve it" (p. 1), not only expands our understanding of what is happening on college and university campuses but also encourages us to draw as complete a picture as possible of the democratic potential of higher education.

REFERENCES

Boyte, H. 2009. "Civic Agency and the Cult of the Expert." Dayton, OH: Kettering Foundation.

Brown, D. 2008. "Changing Public Culture: An Interview with Marguerite S. Shaffer." *Higher Education Exchange*. Dayton, OH: Kettering Foundation.

ACKNOWLEDGMENTS

The origins of this book can be traced to a conversation that took place between John Saltmarsh and Ira Harkavy in the car on the way from the UMass Boston campus to the airport shortly after the publication of *Dewey's Dream*. From that conversation came the idea for a convening that would reflect on and analyze the state of the civic engagement movement, raise issues of democratic engagement, and challenge higher education institutions to confront the difficult issues on institutional change. Matt Hartley became the key collaborator on the project, and Derek Barker at the Kettering Foundation partnered with the New England Resource Center for Higher Education (NERCHE) to make possible the convening at the foundation. The convening led to the *Democratic Engagement White Paper*, written by John, Matt, and Patti Clayton. We want to acknowledge Patti's contribution to meeting and to the *White Paper*. The *White Paper* framed the thesis of the book, and participants from the meeting contributed chapters that address democratic engagement from varying perspectives within higher education. Ira Harkavy graciously hosted an authors' meeting at the Netter Center at the University of Pennsylvania, allowing for a critique of chapter drafts. Finally, our editor, Micah Kleit, at Temple University Press, saw the merit of the project and guided the book to publication.

None of this would have been possible without the support of NERCHE, the Kettering Foundation, the Bernard and Audre Rapoport Foundation, the Spencer Foundation, and the Netter Center for Community Partnerships at the University of Pennsylvania. We thank these organizations as well as all the participants at the February 2008 meeting at the Kettering Foundation.

In addition to Derek Barker, we also want to thank David Mathews, president of the Kettering Foundation, and John Dedrick, vice president of the Kettering Foundation, for their support of and participation at the meeting.

John would like to thank the staff at NERCHE, especially Brad Arndt, who worked on this project from its inception through to the final edits. John would also like to acknowledge the unwavering love and support and seemingly endless patience of his family: his wife, Jill, and his sons, Josh and Jay.

Matt would like to thank his colleagues at Penn GSE, who together have created a vibrant intellectual community seeking to ameliorate inequity and promote positive social change. He is deeply appreciative of the doctoral graduate assistants, David Soo and Laura Gorgol, who supported his research efforts during this time period. Matt would also like to thank John for bringing him on as an equal partner in the project and for modeling what it means to collaboratively and thoughtfully engage in inquiry about matters of first importance. Finally, Matt is sincerely thankful for the love and support of his wife, Jennie, and their children, Gib, Emma, and Samuel, whose enthusiasm, idealism, and engagement in the world is a source of tremendous inspiration.

INTRODUCTION

"To Serve a Larger Purpose"

JOHN SALTMARSH AND
MATTHEW HARTLEY

> But, at a deeper level, I have this growing conviction that what's . . .
> needed is not just more programs, but a larger purpose, a larger sense of
> mission, a larger clarity of direction in the Nation's life . . . creating a
> special climate in which academic and civic cultures communicate more
> continuously and creatively with each other.
>
> —Ernest L. Boyer, *The Scholarship of Engagement* (1996, pp. 32–33)

BACKGROUND AND CONTEXT

We conceived of this book with a sense of urgency that has emerged from reflections on civic engagement work in higher education— the current state of which points to fragmentation and drift. Seemingly, civic engagement efforts have not, in large part, fulfilled Ernest Boyer's call for higher education "to serve a larger purpose" (1996, p. 22). What Boyer was referring to was the democratic purpose of higher education, or what he called its "civic mandate" (1990, p. 16). Here, we are primarily concerned with two related dimensions of this deficit of purpose: first, that the dominant paradigm of civic engagement in higher education does not express or actively seek to fulfill a democratic purpose, and second, that colleges and universities, in the absence of this larger sense of purpose for civic engagement work, have failed to pursue the kind of institutional change needed to realign the central premises and core work of the academy. The focus of this book is the reclamation of the democratic purposes of civic engagement and an examination of the requisite transformation of higher education that would be required to achieve it.

The observation that the civic engagement movement in American higher education is adrift has been advanced by a growing number of civic engagement proponents over the past decade. In 1999, two influential documents pointing to significant challenges facing the movement were published. The "Wingspread Declaration on the Civic Responsibilities of Research Universities" (Boyte and Hollander 1999) admonished higher education institutions to reclaim their historic legacy and to again be "filled with the democratic spirit," a phrase from Harvard's Charles Eliot. A report from the Kellogg Commission, a group of university presidents, entitled "Returning to Our Roots" (1999) argued that land-grant universities ought to intentionally reclaim their public purposes.

In 2000, the "Presidents' Declaration on the Civic Responsibility of Higher Education"—signed by more than 500 college and university presidents—argued that civic engagement had failed to address the political disengagement of America's youth, pointing out that although volunteerism had increased, political understanding and engagement remained perilously low. Two years later, a report from the American Association of State Colleges and Universities (AASCU), representing over 400 public institutions, found that not only was there a lack of definition and clarity regarding civic engagement efforts, but

> many universities espouse the importance of public engagement but do little internally to align the institution to support its achievement. The result is that public engagement remains on many campuses very fragile and person-dependent. At most institutions, the idea of public engagement is not so deeply rooted in its culture that its emphasis would continue unabated after the departure of a committed CEO or other academic leader. (p. 8)

This candid report concluded that "there is considerable evidence that deep engagement is rare—there is more smoke than fire, more rhetoric than reality . . . Most [campuses] have some form of community interaction, but in the main it is piecemeal, not systemic, and reflects individual interest rather than institutional commitment" (p. 13).

In 2004, a group of movement leaders met at the Wingspread conference center to discuss the state of civic engagement in higher education (Brukardt et al. 2004). They concluded that while the movement had prompted some change, it had plateaued. Their report, provocatively entitled *Calling the Question*, inquired whether engagement should become a core value of the university of the twenty-first century—that is, a central feature informing the academic mission of higher education in generating and transmitting new knowledge. The report noted that "engagement has not . . . been embraced across disciplines, departments and institutions" (p. ii) and that "the momentum needed for engagement to become fully identified with the mission of higher education" was waning (p. 4). Echoing the concerns from the AASCU study, the Wingspread participants concluded that despite widespread evidence of innovative engagement activities across higher education, "few institutions have made the significant, sustainable, structural reforms that will result in an academic culture that values community engagement as a core function of the institution" (p. 5).

Beyond this troubling emergent consensus, there are important tangible factors that are also cause for concern. While there have been important gains, the dominant strategies advanced to promote civic engagement have hardly been universally embraced. For example, among Campus Compact members (institutions with a presidential commitment to civic and community engagement) the percentage of students engaging in service (both curricular and cocurricular "service") hovers a little below one-third (28 percent in 2001 and 32 percent in 2006). The average number of service-learning courses on these campuses (twenty-seven per campus in 2001 and thirty-five in 2006) suggests only a modest influence on the overall curricular offerings. When one considers what proportion of total courses that thirty-five represents, even at small liberal arts colleges, it is a sobering statistic.

The number of institutions committed both rhetorically *and* programmatically to civic engagement is relatively small. Over the first two application cycles (2006 and 2008), 196 campuses have received the elective classification for Community Engagement from the Carnegie Foundation for the Advancement of Teaching. As Gary Rhoades points out, this classification represents an effort on the part of the Carnegie Foundation "to inscribe in academic structures and in the consciousness of faculty" an emphasis on "the value of the local" (2009, p. 12). Yet the number of Community Engagement–classified campuses represents just over 4 percent of the more than 4,600 higher education institutions (campuses classified by the Carnegie Foundation) in the United States.

Additionally, external support for civic engagement efforts has declined. A number of key foundations that provided support in the 1990s (e.g., Pew, Ford, Kellogg, the Carnegie Corporation, Atlantic Philanthropies) have redirected their attention elsewhere.

Finally, like many movements, civic engagement efforts suffer from an absence of concerted action around a set agenda. A large network that reached broadly across sectors in higher education to advance civic engagement, the American Association for Higher Education (AAHE), faltered and failed in the late 1990s. No other network has stepped in to fill the void. A Wingspread meeting in 2006 that led to the formation of the Higher Education Network for Civic Engagement (HENCE) sought to enliven the movement through greater coordination. Yet it has been unable to articulate a powerful shared sense of purpose or advance a collective agenda.

FINDING A WAY FORWARD

What, then, is required to spur the deep change in institutional priorities and values needed to create the conditions for sustained civic engagement? As Benson, Harkavy, and Puckett pointedly observe, "for universities and colleges to fulfill their great potential and really contribute to a democratic . . . revolution, they will have to do things very differently than they do now. . . . To become part of the solution, higher eds must give full-hearted, full-minded devotion to the painfully difficult task of transforming themselves into socially responsible civic universities and colleges. To do so, they will have to radically change their institutional cultures and structures, democratically realign and integrate themselves, and develop a comprehensive, realistic strategy" (p. 84). In our view, the answer lies in reorienting the work from a vague emphasis on community involvement toward an agenda that seeks significant societal change. The movement must not only strive to encourage civic impulses and actions among students; it must assume a joint responsibility with the communities with which it works to confront problems and to enact change through every democratic means possible. It requires linking the pursuit of knowledge with the pursuit of a healthier society and a stronger, more robust democracy.

This sense of drift and stalled momentum in civic engagement work raises a number of important questions: Are current civic engagement efforts slowly transforming higher education or have they adapted in ways that foster legitimacy but ultimately fail to fundamentally challenge the dominant culture of higher education institutions and American society? How might the movement navigate the inherent tension between challenging the status quo and securing legitimacy through a measure of accommodation? How can colleges and universities cultivate caring and creative democratic citizens and advance democracy in schools, universities, communities, and society? What sort of institutional commitments are needed to foster civic engagement among students and among academics in order to advance participatory democracy on campus, in the community, and the wider society?

In an effort to explore these questions and others related to the democratic purposes of higher education, a group of thirty-one academic leaders[1] came together in February 2008 at the Kettering Foundation in Dayton, Ohio, for the purpose of critically examining the state of civic engagement in higher education and to determine ways to strategically promote democratic citizenship as a key institutional priority for American colleges and universities. The individuals were called together by the Kettering Foundation and the New England Resource Center for Higher Education (NERCHE) specifically because their ongoing work aligned with the original democratic purposes of the movement, which Frank Newman defined in 1985 as "[restoring] higher education [to] its original purpose of preparing graduates for a life of involved and committed citizenship" (1985, p. xiv). A significant catalyst for this dialogue was Lee Benson, Ira Harkavy, and John Puckett's book, *Dewey's Dream: Universities and Democracies in an Age of Education Reform* (2007). The premise of *Dewey's Dream* is that higher education in America has fundamental democratic purposes, both educating for democracy and creating educational institutions that foster the revitalization of democratic society.

We highlight an idea put forth by Benson and his colleagues: university-assisted community schools as one key strategy for achieving this aim. Such partnerships help university students understand the complex socio-political contexts in which social problems exist and encourage civic agency. They draw together partners with disparate strengths (faculty, community members, students) to resolve pressing real-world problems. The model also underscores the kind of institutional transformation that is required at universities for democratic engagement to be possible.

CHALLENGES TO ENGAGEMENT

At the Kettering meeting, two ideas met with near-universal agreement. The first was that *this nation faces significant societal challenges, and higher education must play a role in responding to them.* The imperative for higher education to respond to social injustice was readily seen in the persistent poverty of our inner cities ("rediscovered" by many in the aftermath of Hurricane Katrina), in the widening divide between the rich and poor, in our failure to have a meaningful dialogue about the wars in Iraq and Afghanistan, and in the emergent economic crisis. There was widespread agreement that colleges and universities have civic and public purposes, including the preparation of an enlightened and productive citizenry and engaging in scholarship that both addresses pressing problems and holds a mirror to society to allow for self-reflection and self-correction. The question was how to achieve these aims. A second point of agreement was that *the civic engagement movement has not realized its full potential.* While not everyone at the meeting characterized civic engagement in higher education as stalled, there was general agreement that the movement has unclear goals, fragmented efforts, and is met with a predominant ideology in the academy that acts contrary to overtly civic aims. Whatever the case, participants expressed the view that important work needs to be done in order to deepen existing work and to draw in others. A number of themes emerged from the Kettering meeting, which we offer here as (necessarily contestable) propositions.

An obligation for higher education to develop the civic agency of its students is not high on the public's agenda. Despite deeply troubling data regarding political knowledge and interest in public affairs, the ideals of promoting democracy are not pressing concerns for many people across the country. This prevailing view is reflected in student attitudes. As trend data from UCLA's survey of incoming freshman has shown, over the past two decades students have come to see higher education primarily as a ticket to a good job. Their interests in the more formative aspects of education (e.g., "developing a meaningful philosophy of life," one of the ideals of liberal education) have dramatically declined. As Caryn Musil noted, findings from focus groups conducted by the Association of American Colleges and Universities show that civic engagement remains a very low priority for many students.

Our inadequate conception of what effective democratic education might look like is reflected in the imprecise and even conflicting language by members of the movement. Currently, a wide variety of terms are used when discussing the public purpose of higher education—such as community engagement, civic engagement, engagement, democratic education, education for democracy, and so forth. This disparate language reflects substantive divisions within the broader movement. For example (and perhaps put a bit simplistically), there are faculty members who embrace service-learning as a superior means of conveying disciplinary knowledge, while others see it as a transformational pedagogy. This lack of clarity has the very real advantage of enabling a broad range of people to feel they are part of the movement. Vague language, however, also runs the risk of portraying a movement that stands for anything and therefore nothing. Can we find language that has wide "traction" but also inspires and conveys a core democratic purpose?

The movement is highly fragmented and compartmentalized. Perhaps because there is not a unifying vision, the "movement," such as it is, consists of many regional and national initiatives aimed at promoting a wide variety of activities (e.g., volunteerism, community service, service-learning, university/community partnerships, democratic deliberation, diversity initiatives) to various audiences. Some efforts are wholly disconnected from others. For example, we rarely see instances where democratic deliberation efforts help inform potential partnerships that then lead to rich service-learning opportunities. As the Association of American Colleges and Universities has pointed out, diversity efforts have too often remained divorced from civic engagement efforts. But it is not clear what efforts might profitably be advanced to address this fragmentation. Attempts to create umbrella networks (a "network of networks" as one calls itself) have met with negligible success.

The movement has largely sidestepped the political dimension of civic engagement. With only a few exceptions (the AASCU's American Democracy Project is a good example), institutional (and national) efforts do not explicitly link the work of engagement to our democracy. What has emerged is a remarkably apolitical "civic" engagement. As one participant put it, "We need a movement that puts the question of the democratic purpose of higher education on the table." There are pressures in certain sectors (e.g., some public institutions) against doing anything that is seen as "political"—in this sense, partisan activities and political awareness and agency are being confounded. A few participants at the Kettering meeting raised questions about the extent to which colleges and universities could meaningfully play such a role: Can our institutions of higher learning fulfill their various purposes (job preparation, economic development, knowledge creation, cultural resource provision) and also act to promote a strong democracy?

The dominant epistemology of the academy runs counter to the civic engagement agenda. The academy has established legitimacy within society in part through its widely recognized ability to convey expertise. Specialization has produced a great deal of new knowledge, but it has also produced a technocracy that places certain kinds of expertise above all others. One participant offered this critique: "We see no other warrant for our existence than the expert model." Excessive homage to a narrow disciplinary guild and the presumption of neutrality has robbed the academy of its ability to effectively challenge society and to seek change. How might a democratic epistemology be articulated? What kinds of knowledge and scholarly practices would it value and seek to support?

A significant thread that ran through the discussions addressed the significant challenges facing civic engagement efforts. The following represents reflections by Derek Barker, program officer at the Kettering Foundation, which were presented the second morning of the meeting. Barker thoughtfully and concisely captures the array of challenges raised at the meeting by participants, ones that must be addressed in order for the civic engagement movement to fulfill its potential.

Eleven Sticking Points: Priorities for the Future of Civic Engagement in Higher Education

By Derek Barker, The Kettering Foundation

One of the key objectives of the colloquium was to survey key leaders and practitioners in the civic engagement of higher education and solicit their frank assessments of the current state of the movement. This list brings together eleven sticking points that were mentioned during the first day of the colloquium. Some participants emphasized good news over bad news, while others used a variety of terms, such as "stalled," "plateaued," or "fragmented." Despite these differences, a number of key unresolved issues emerged as priorities for the next generation of civic engagement work in higher education.

1. Articulate a democratic epistemology. Higher education civic engagement must provide an alternative to the technocratic and expert model and show that citizens can play an active role in the production of knowledge. At present, the movement has developed a coherent critique of the limitations of positivism, expert knowledge, and the implied technocratic politics of excluding citizens from the production of knowledge. However, the democratic alternative has not been fully articulated. This would require more concrete examples of knowledge produced with the active participation of citizens.

2. Connect civic engagement of higher education institutions and professionals to larger civic politics. Higher education institutions and professionals often speak of civic engagement based on their perspectives and when it serves their interests. Wanting to serve the public is not enough if the public doubts that the institution serves the public good. Communities must have a reason to partner with institutions, but we do not know whether the civic engagement efforts currently supplied by universities are really in demand by citizens.

3. Diversify the civic engagement movement. Although both civic engagement and multiculturalism are each receiving attention in higher education, at present these efforts are largely independent of one another. However, civic engagement cannot serve democracy if it is not inclusive of diverse groups and perspectives. At the same time, diversity initiatives cannot have an impact outside of institutions if higher education is irrelevant to society. Proponents of both civic engagement and multiculturalism should recognize their interdependence and common aim to improve democracy.

4. Politicize civic engagement, especially beyond "service." The civic engagement movement has developed a coherent critique of the idea of service. It has shown that service tends to be interpreted apolitically and in ways that are consistent with expert or technocratic approaches. However, proponents of civic engagement must do more to articulate, document, and evaluate the political benefits of their work.

5. Connect local civic engagement to global issues. Citizens and college students are not currently prepared to engage politically on highly complex and large-scale social problems. Although civic engagement must begin locally, it must ultimately aim at the global level if citizens and students are to make a difference on the most pressing problems.

6. Make the democratic role of higher education explicit as the top institutional priority. Although many institutions have incorporated civic engagement rhetoric, established centers, or implemented projects, in most cases the democratic role of higher education is not infused throughout the institution. Individual projects and programs are not enough to generate culture change. Instead, colleges' and universities' commitments to civic engagement should integrate reforms in a variety of areas, including promotion and tenure, disciplinary norms, curriculum design, pedagogy, student life, and institutional governance.

7. Unify the language of civic engagement. Civic engagement reflects a diverse assortment of goals (diversity, social justice, citizenship) and methodologies (dialogue, deliberation, community organizing). However, there is a sense that the movement is fragmented as a result. Often programs adopting different labels compete with one another for funding and attention, giving the appearance of fundamental conflict. While proponents will rightly emphasize different aspects of democratic politics, the movement could make greater progress by articulating the common impulse unifying all the practices and constituencies of civic engagement.

8. Organize faculty for civic engagement. Faculty have led the way in innovating and promoting civic engagement. Despite being marginalized in their fields and discouraged by their institutional reward structures, their passion has been the key driving force behind the progress that has been made. However, a major obstacle to change is that faculty are trained to think as intellectuals, not as organizers. The next stage of civic engagement will require faculty to learn a new set of skills enabling them to transform their institutions.

9. Address the disconnect between theory and practice, rhetoric and reality. The basic principles of civic engagement are almost universally recognized. They have been reflected in the language of institutional mission statements and espoused by leaders at the highest levels. Although this is an important indicator of progress, the real practice of civic engagement does not always match the rhetoric. To show that they are serious about civic engagement, institutions must commit significant resources to match their rhetoric.

10. Resist the assimilation of civic engagement by bureaucratic institutions. Institutions and practitioners alike are talking about ways to enhance the legitimacy of civic engagement projects. This is in itself an important indicator of the progress that has been made. However, civic engagement initiatives are implemented in the context of institutions that have powerful incentives to copy "best practices" and meet evaluation criteria imposed from above rather than engage in genuine democratic experimentation. In order to move forward, civic engagement efforts will have to gain credibility in the eyes of institutions without losing their essential democratic character.

11. Model democratic politics in the internal governance of higher education institutions. Although some institutions have made conscious efforts to involve the community in their strategic planning, the democratic mission of higher education is in profound tension with the reality of hierarchical and bureaucratic governance. President-centered leadership continues to be the norm in higher education. Students and communities will not learn to take democracy seriously if universities do not model democracy in their own governance.

Democratic Engagement

The past two decades have witnessed the emergence of a host of activities aimed at advancing the civic and public purpose of American higher education. Dozens of new networks have been established involving tens of thousands of faculty members, administrators, and students. In many respects, civic engagement is flourishing; however, a central question has largely been sidestepped: Engagement for what, to what end? Increasingly, "civic engagement" is a term commonly used in higher education. The 2002 AASCU report referenced earlier noted that while engagement has become "shorthand for describing a new era of two-way partnerships between America's colleges and universities and the publics they serve . . . it also presents the risk that the term can say everything and nothing at the same time. . . . The lack of clear definition can leave some campuses and their leaders with the impression that they are 'doing engagement,' when in fact they are not" (p. 8). Engagement is often used as an umbrella term, connoting any campus-based activities that connect with or relate to something—issues, problems, organizations, schools, governments—outside the campus. It has a certain idealistic appeal as it relates to institutional mission—preparing socially responsible citizens as graduates—and speaks to the accountability of the college or university to the wider society and public interest.

This emphasis on activity and place is evident in the widespread use of the term "community engagement." Campuses that embrace the ideal of civic engagement create new courses, service opportunities, offices, and centers. Such activities, programs, and structures fit nicely into the existing norms of the academy. After all, campuses understand how to create new programs and are very interested in promoting learning. They are equally uncomfortable with the notion of encouraging activism among students or seeing their faculty members use their skills to challenge a problematic status quo.

As they are most often expressed, civic engagement activities rarely call on colleges and universities to fundamentally change the ways in which they operate, thus preserving underlying assumptions and institutional behaviors. Engagement defined by activity and place has provided a vitally important foundation for the civic engagement movement. Democratic engagement, however, requires something more—a larger sense of purpose and distinct processes to strengthen our communities and to build a participatory democracy. It also requires careful rethinking of the core work of the academy. It is this democratic imperative and the democratic dimension of engagement that we examine in this book.

The norms of a culture of democratic education are determined by values such as inclusiveness, participation, task sharing and reciprocity in public problem solving, and an equality of respect for the knowledge and experience that everyone contributes to education and community building. These democratic processes and purposes reorient civic engagement to what we are calling "democratic engagement." Democratic engagement presumes that the only way to learn the norms and develop the values of democracy is to practice democracy as part of one's education. Needless to say, applying democratic values to academic leadership, the scholarly work of faculty, the educational efforts of staff, and the leadership, personal development, and learning outcomes of students has significant implications for higher education—epistemological, curricular, pedagogical, research, policy, and cultural.

The infusion of democratic values into higher education also has implications for the civic engagement movement. Without an expressly democratic purpose, engagement efforts can be pursued for questionable aims (e.g., good public relations). Even more problematic, engagement runs the risk of being constrained and ultimately trapped by the dominant culture of the academy that privileges specialized expertise above all else. Expertise is important and has its place. The democratic dimension of engagement, however, is demonstrated by a capacity to also learn in the company of others. It embraces expert knowledge but is critical of expertise that claims an exclusionary position relative to other forms of knowledge and other knowledge producers. Academic culture also favors dispassionate inquiry and tends to look askance at any effort to openly challenge the status quo. It is perhaps no surprise that despite the originating ideal of producing enlightened and engaged citizens, what has emerged is a remarkably apolitical form of civic engagement. Indeed, as we explain in Chapter 1, the larger democratic purpose of the movement has been persistently sidelined such that the dominant framework of civic engagement in American higher education is largely lacking an intentional democratic purpose.

TRANSFORMING HIGHER EDUCATION WITH A LARGER SENSE OF PURPOSE

The chapters in this book provide examples in which a democratic flowering of civic engagement—what we call "democratic engagement"—is occurring, and they examine conceptually and practically what is needed to deepen democratic engagement to the extent that it becomes part of campus culture. Currently, the United States and the world are experiencing a financial catastrophe. Never has the imperative to strengthen participatory democracy for collective problem solving—at the institutional, local, state, and national levels—been greater. Now, more than ever, colleges and universities are being called upon—and in many cases held publicly accountable—to address localized community needs, to be socially responsive institutions. We believe that a democratic-centered civic engagement effort based on collaboratively addressing pressing real-world problems holds the promise of transforming not only the educational practice and the institutional identity of colleges and universities, but the larger public culture of democracy as well.

This book begins by addressing larger conceptual understandings of the state of civic engagement in higher education, with an introduction by the editors and an opening chapter drawing distinctions between engagement for democracy and what we argue has emerged as the dominant framework of civic engagement on campus today. Matt Hartley then explores, in Chapter 2, the historical contours of the civic engagement movement as a way of understanding the evolution of the movement and the current institutional commitments to engagement. Chapter 3 moves the focus of the discussion from the movement level to the campus, with Ira Harkavy, John Puckett, and Lee Benson examining the work at the University of Pennsylvania on university-assisted community schools as a model of democratic community and campus transformation. In Chapter 4, Harry Boyte and Eric Fretz reclaim the political dimensions of engagement as a key element in restoring its democratic dimensions. William Plater addresses, in Chapter 5, the ways in which deliberate creation of institutional structures can change institutional culture to sustain civic engagement work. In Chapter 6, former Provost John Presley reflects on the role of the Chief Academic Officer in embedding civic engagement in the core academic work of the campus. Chapter 7, by Nancy Thomas and Peter Levine, brings education for democracy into the curriculum, exploring the role of democratic deliberation as part of teaching and learning. This is followed in Chapter 8 with KerryAnn O'Meara's analysis of the implications of democratic engagement for faculty work. In Chapter 9, Rick Battistoni and Nick Longo assert the importance of student voice and leadership in advancing democratic engagement and catalyzing institutional change. Edward Zlotkowski then explores, in Chapter 10, what is needed to keep civic engagement vital as a core academic value and a vital form of academic work for the next generation of academic leaders and practitioners. In Chapter 11, Caryn Musil look at deficiencies in the civic engagement movement that have limited its democratic potential and chart a path to a more inclusive, richer, and deeper civic engagement movement. Lorlene Hoyt, in Chapter 12, explores and analyzes the promise and challenges surrounding campus community engagement and the implications that a shift in epistemology has for faculty work and institutional change. Finally, in the last chapter, the editors return to the key issues of democratic purpose and institutional transformation to offer recommendations for concrete, practical ways to shape civic engagement work in higher education.

NOTE

1. Meeting participants:

Derek Barker, Kettering Foundation
Rick Battistoni, Providence College
Harry Boyte, University of Minnesota
Barbara Burch, Western Kentucky University
Patti Clayton, North Carolina State University
Jeremy Cohen, Pennsylvania State University
Elizabeth Coleman, Bennington College
Julie Ellison, University of Michigan
Eric Fretz, University of Denver
Dwight Giles, Jr., University of Massachusetts–Boston
Ira Harkavy, University of Pennsylvania
Matthew Hartley, University of Pennsylvania
Beverly Hogan, Tougaloo College
Elizabeth Hollander, Tufts University
Lorlene Hoyt, Massachusetts Institute of Technology

Peter Levine, Tufts University
Nicholas Longo, Providence College
David Mathews, Kettering Foundation
George Mehaffy, American Association of State Colleges and Universities
Caryn McTighe Musil, Association of American Colleges and Universities
KerryAnn O'Meara, University of Maryland
Scott Peters, Cornell University
William Plater, Indiana University–Purdue University Indianapolis
John W. Presley, Illinois State University
John Puckett, University of Pennsylvania
John Saltmarsh, University of Massachusetts–Boston
Beverly Daniel Tatum, Spelman College
Nancy Thomas, Democracy Imperative
Byron White, Xavier University
Deborah Witte, Kettering Foundation
Edward Zlotkowski, Bentley College

REFERENCES

American Association of State Colleges and Universities. 2002. "Stepping Forward as Stewards of Place: A Guide for Leading Public Engagement at State Colleges and Universities." Washington, DC.

Benson, L., I. Harkavy, and J. Puckett. 2007. *Dewey's Dream: Universities and Democracies in an Age of Education Reform*. Philadelphia: Temple University Press.

Boyer, E. L. 1990. *Scholarship Reconsidered: Priorities of the Professoriate*. Princeton: Carnegie Foundation for the Advancement of Teaching.

———. 1996. "The Scholarship of Engagement." *Bulletin of the American Academy of Arts and Sciences* 49, no. 7 (April): 18–33.

Boyte, H., and E. Hollander. 1999. "Wingspread Declaration on Renewing the Civic Mission of the American Research University." Available at http://www.compact .org/initiatives/civic-engagement-at-research-universities/wingspread-declaration-on-the-civic-responsibilities-of-research-universities/.

Brukardt, M. J., B. Hollan, S. L. Percy, and N. Zimpher. 2004. *Calling the Question: Is Higher Education Ready to Commit to Community Engagement?* Milwaukee: Milwaukee Idea Office, University of Wisconsin. Available at http://servicelearning .org/filemanager/download/215/calling_the_question.pdf.

Ehrlich, T., and E. Hollander. 2000. "Presidents' Declaration on the Civic Responsibility of Higher Education." Providence: Campus Compact.

Eckel, P., B. Hill, and M. Green. 1998. "On Change: En Route to Transformation." Washington, DC: American Council on Education.

Kellogg Commission on the Future of State and Land-Grant Universities. 2001. "Returning to Our Roots: Executive Summaries of the Reports of the Kellogg Commission on the Future of State and Land-Grant Universities." Available at www.aplu.org/ NetCommunity/Document.Doc?id=187.

Newman, F. 1985. *Higher Education and the American Resurgence*. Princeton: Carnegie Foundation for the Advancement of Teaching.

Rhoades, G. 2009. "Carnegie, Dupont Circle and the AAUP: (Re)Shaping a Cosmopolitan, Locally Engaged Professoriate." *Change* 41, no. 1 (January–February): 8–13.

CHAPTER 1

Democratic Engagement

JOHN SALTMARSH AND MATTHEW HARTLEY

L ike all movements, the civic engagement movement has struggled to find conceptual and operational coherence. Disparate strategies have produced internal tensions. One key dilemma has been whether the movement should confront and challenge the dominant institutional culture or accommodate the status quo. For example, in the mid-1990s, a number of service-learning proponents argued that the surest means of anchoring it in the core work of the academy was to adhere to academic norms. While this helped engender widespread legitimacy of the practice, it also has come to mean that on many campuses the premise of service-learning is identical to that of field or clinical placements—the emphasis is squarely on the professional and disciplinary learning of students, and the community benefits are secondary. On many campuses what passes for "engaged scholarship" is largely indistinguishable from applied research. Even the language of recent declarations points to tensions. Should engagement be predicated on "academic neutrality,"[1] or should institutions foster the notion of faculty as moral agents whose "moral and civic imaginations" are directed at public work?[2] From an operational standpoint, the field is fragmented. Important efforts aimed at promoting civic learning such as diversity initiatives, democratic deliberation, global citizenship, and community-based learning and research operate in isolation from one another. Few campuses actively seek to integrate such efforts.

One of the key characteristics of a powerful movement is its conceptual and ideological coherence: Strong movements are propelled by compelling and clearly articulated purposes. Since movements develop in order to challenge the status quo, it is particularly important to identify what they are moving against. In the early 1990s, Page Smith bemoaned the emergence of "academic fundamentalism," which he defined as "the flight from teaching, the meretriciousness of most academic research, the disintegration of the disciplines, the alliance of universities with the Department of Defense, the National Aeronautics and Space Agency, etc., and, more recently, with biotechnology and communications corporations, and, last but not least, the corruptions incident to 'big time' collegiate sports" (1990, p. 1). Proponents of civic engagement have been pushing against a number of trends in higher education, providing a counterweight to forces that have undermined the democratic purposes of colleges and universities:

- **The persisting influence of the ivory tower:** "Disciplinary guildism" (Benson, Harkavy, and Hartley 2005)—the pressure for faculty to pursue narrow disciplinary specialization and seek knowledge for its own sake (the German university model) in order to advance professionally—has resulted in scholarly activity whose purpose is to advance theory but often does little to address pressing social problems.
- **The corporatization of the university:** The "management revolution" (Keller 1983) that embraced the notion of student-as-customer emphasized credentialing and de-emphasized the formative aspects of education. Fears of demographic shifts, a weak economy in the 1980s, and shifting values of students (toward a more-privatized view of higher education—a college education as a ticket to a good job) led many institutions to develop new professional and vocational programs, which produced dissonance on many campuses, where the larger historic purposes (e.g., a liberal arts education) were perceived as having been abandoned. Commercialization and commodification continue to shape campus practices (e.g., partnering with corporations, launching popular degree programs, expanding admissions and development offices into major administrative features of the university).
- **The crisis in undergraduate teaching and decontextualized learning:** The 1970s and 1980s saw a good deal of discussion about general education. Many felt the curriculum had lost coherence. The Banking Model of Education (as described by Paulo Freire in *Pedagogy of the Oppressed* [1970]), where faculty profess in lectures and place ideas into the heads of students, predominated. Learning also seemed decontextualized—uncoupled from the real world— and it remains so today. This is problematic since many students have grown up in middle class "bubbles" and never encountered others from different racial, ethnic, or socio-economic backgrounds.
- **Moral somnolence and civic disengagement:** The value neutrality of the German university model (in contrast to the character-building

emphasis of the English model and the earlier American models
[Reuben 1996]) raised questions of the relevance of higher education to address the pressing ethical and political challenges of our
times. This was particularly evident in the university's inability to
prepare students for lives of civic engagement, despite frighten-
ingly low levels of political engagement and widespread mistrust of
government. As Frank Newman (1985) put it, "If there is a crisis
in education in the United States today, it is less that test scores
have declined than it is that we have failed to provide the education
for citizenship that is still the most significant responsibility of the
nation's schools and colleges" (p. 31).

• **The politics of academic epistemology:** As David Mathews notes
in "Democracy's Megachallenges Revisited" (2008), the way in
which colleges and universities are engaged with local communities
"has implications for politics. . . . Colleges and universities have
an understanding of citizenship that is implicit in nearly everything
they do, including the kind of education they provide to undergraduates, the kind of leadership they champion in leadership programs,
and the services they offer to their communities" (p. 208). Expert-
driven, hierarchical knowledge generation and dissemination is not
only an epistemological position but also, as Harry Boyte (2008)
points out, a political one. Traditional academic epistemology, with
its embedded values, methods, and practices, signifies "pattern of
power" relationships and creates a "technocracy" and a particular
politics that is "the core obstacle to higher education's engagement."
Not only are the power and politics of expert academic knowledge
what he calls "the largest obstacle in higher education to authentic
engagement with communities"; they are also "a significant con-
tributor to the general crisis of democracy." Their "core negative
functions," he explains, "are to undermine the standing and to dele-
gitimate the knowledge of those without credentials, degrees, and
university training . . . conceiv[ing] of people without credentials
as needy clients to be rescued or as customers to be manipulated"
(p. 108). In this way of thinking and acting, he notes, genuine reciprocal learning is just not possible.

WHAT WE NEED ARE NOT MORE PROGRAMS

A 2008 article in the *Chronicle of Higher Education* profiled the efforts of
an urban university that, like many others, has made efforts to reconceptualize its mission around engagement with the city it is part of. The university has been sensitive to shifting demographics and has endeavored to
design learning environments where diverse students can thrive. The article
points to significant reform in the university's general education curriculum,
which now emphasizes experiential learning and has established courses and

programs with partners in the community as part of the students' educational experience. The curriculum now includes a number of community-based programs in areas including culture and the arts, legal aid, economic development, and support for small business. The article notes that the university's idea of "place-based learning" has been in practice for decades and that the campus's efforts are part of a larger national trend focused on urban-serving universities that advocates for greater collaboration between cities and higher education institutions. This example (at least as it is described by the *Chronicle*) is in many ways representative of what is happening at colleges and universities across the country: universities working together with their communities. Such efforts are laudable, as they move universities beyond the anachronistic role of the ivory tower. However, in our view, engagement that is defined solely by activities that occur in a particular place fall short unless there is clarity about the larger democratic purposes of the activities and a commitment to expressing this democratic ideal through institutional practices and policies. Without the intentionality of process and purpose, there is a diminution of democratic potential. Students may learn, and important service may be rendered. But rarely does such an approach to engagement result in actively contesting a problematic status quo or engender concerted action to challenge and change it by every democratic means possible.

To paraphrase John Dewey—who wrote in *Democracy and Education* (1916) that "mere activity does not constitute experience" (139)—mere activity in a community does not constitute civic engagement. Civic engagement defined by purpose and processes has a particular meaning in higher education and is associated with implications for institutional change. Purpose refers specifically to enhancing a public culture of democracy on and off campus and alleviating public problems through democratic means. The processes of engagement refer to the way in which those on campus—administrators, academics, staff, and students—relate to those outside the campus. Purpose and processes are inextricably linked—the means must be consistent with the ends, and the ends are defined by democratic culture. The norms of democratic education are determined by the values of inclusiveness, participation, task sharing and reciprocity in public problem solving, and an equality of respect for the knowledge and experience that everyone involved contributes to education and community building. Democratic processes and purposes reorient civic engagement to what we are calling "democratic engagement"—engagement that has significant implications for transforming higher education such that democratic values are part of the leadership of administrators, the scholarly work of faculty, the educational work of staff, and the leadership development and learning outcomes of students. Democratic engagement has epistemological, curricular, pedagogical, research, policy, and culture implications. It adheres to the shared understanding that the only way to learn the norms and develop the values of democracy is to practice democracy as part of one's education.

Without a democratic purpose, engagement efforts are often pursued as ends in themselves, and engagement becomes reduced to a public relations function of making known what the campus is doing in and/or for the community and providing opportunities for students to have experiences in the community. Engagement in this sense reflects the dominant academic culture of higher education, often characterized as "scientific," "rationalized," "objectified," or "technocratic," meaning that the approach to public problems is predominantly shaped by specialized expertise that is "applied" externally "to" or "on" the community, providing "solutions" to what has been determined to be the community's "needs."

The distinction we are making between civic engagement as it is widely manifested in higher education and what we are calling democratic engagement is not attributed to the kind of knowledge and expertise generated in the academy but to whether that knowledge and its use are inclusive of other sources of knowledge and problem solving. The measure of the democratic processes and purpose of engagement is demonstrated by a capacity to learn in the company of others and not to rely solely on the expertise of the academy. As Peter Levine (2007) has observed, "Technical expertise has evident value. No one can doubt that we are better off because of the specialized knowledge possessed by physicians, engineers, economists, and others. Expertise is such a fundamental organizing principle that we often overlook its drawbacks and limitations—especially for democracy" (p. 106). Democratic engagement is not dismissive of expert knowledge—on the contrary, it is expertise in solving social problems that is often sought by communities—but is critical of expertise that claims an exclusionary position relative to other forms of knowledge and other knowledge producers. Attention to process raises the question of how expertise is positioned and exercised. Attention to purpose defines the ways in which expertise can be exercised democratically.

The distinction that we are making between civic (or community) engagement as it is predominantly practiced in higher education and democratic engagement as an alternative framework, and the conceptual comparison of the two frameworks, recognizes that civic engagement on many campuses has elements of each of these frameworks, in some cases due to efforts to shift to a more democratic framing of engagement. Drawing these distinctions is intended to assist academic leaders and practitioners in the design and implementation of engagement efforts on campus with an intentionality of democratic purpose and an awareness of the kind of change in institutional culture needed to make civic democratic engagement a part of the institution's identity.

CIVIC ENGAGEMENT FRAMED BY ACTIVITY AND PLACE

The dominant framework of engagement in higher education is grounded in an institutional epistemology that privileges the expertise in the university and its application externally, through activities in the community. "This epistemology," William Sullivan (2000) has noted, "is firmly entrenched as the operating system of much of the American university." There exists, writes Sullivan, an "affinity of positivist understandings of research for 'applying' knowledge to the social world on the model of the way engineers 'apply' expert understanding to the problems of structures" (p. 29). Knowledge produced by credentialed, detached experts is embedded in hierarchies of knowledge generation and use, creating a division between knowledge producers (in the university) and knowledge consumers (in the community). In the positivist scheme, "researchers 'produce' knowledge, which is then 'applied' to problems and problematic populations." Academic expertise focuses "on building theory, being 'objective,' writing mainly for each other in a language of their own creation, building professional associations, and staying away from political controversies" (p. 29). Academic knowledge is valued more than community-based knowledge, and knowledge flows in one direction, from inside the boundaries of the university outward to its place of need and application in the community.

This framework of engagement locates the university as the center of solutions to public problems and educates students through service as proto-experts who will be able to perform civic tasks in and on communities that they work with because they will have the knowledge and credentials to determine what to do to help communities improve. In this framework, students, in their developing citizen roles, often will not be taught the political dimensions of their activities because questions of power typically are left out of the context of objectified knowledge production and the way that "service" is provided to communities. Civic engagement activities in community as an end in themselves perpetuate a kind of politics that rejects popularly informed decision making in favor of expert-informed knowledge application. Politics is something to be kept separate from the dispassionate pursuit of knowledge because it is understood in terms of competing partisan positions and opposing ideologies. It is thus not only avoided by academics who perceive such work as advocacy but also prohibited by federal mandate when community service programs are funded through federal agencies. What has emerged on many campuses are remarkably apolitical "civic" engagement efforts.

The dominant form of civic engagement that has emerged in higher education reflects interactions between those in colleges and universities with external entities in the community that are defined by partnerships (formal and informal relationships) and mutuality (each party in the relationship benefits from its involvement). Partnerships and mutuality allow the university to better meet its academic mission by improving teaching and learning and through community service and applied research opportunities. Communities benefit from the involvement of the university as students and faculty help in meeting unmet community needs. Engagement is enacted *for* the public, and because it entails the provision of a social service, it is understood by academics as "civic" in its aims and outcomes.

CIVIC ENGAGEMENT FRAMED BY PROCESSES AND PURPOSE

A democratic framework shaped by attention to processes and purpose is "based on both sides bringing their own experience and expertise to the project," noted Ernest Lynton (1994), and "this kind of collaboration requires a substantial change in the prevalent culture of academic institutions" (p. xii). It challenges leaders and practitioners of civic engagement on college and university campuses to reframe community-based teaching, scholarship, and service so that, as Davyd J. Greenwood (2008) explains, "The terms of engagement, the ways of studying the issues and the ownership of the actions and the intellectual products are . . . negotiated with the legitimate local stakeholders" (p. 333). Collaborative knowledge generation and discovery that brings together academic knowledge with the local knowledge of community stakeholders in defining the problem to be addressed, a shared understanding of the problem, and designing, implementing, and evaluating the actions taken to address the problem is what Greenwood (2008) calls "a democratizing form of content-specific knowledge creation, theorization, analysis, and action design in which the goals are democratically set, learning capacity is shared, and success is collaboratively evaluated" (p. 327).

Community partnerships in a democratic-centered framework of engagement have an explicit and intentional democratic dimension framed as inclusive, collaborative, and problem-oriented work in which academics share knowledge-generating tasks with the public and involve community partners as participants in public problem solving. As KerryAnn O'Meara and Eugene Rice (2005) point out, "The expert model . . . often gets in the way of constructive university-community collaboration" because it does not "move beyond 'outreach,'" or "go beyond 'service,' with its overtones of noblesse oblige" (p. 28). A shift in discourse from "partnerships" (relationships) and "mutuality" (shared benefit) to that of "reciprocity" (cocreation) is grounded in explicitly democratic values of sharing previously academic tasks with nonacademics and encouraging the participation of nonacademics in ways that enhance and enable broader engagement with and deliberation about major social issues inside and outside the university. Democratic engagement seeks the public good *with* the public, and not merely *for* the public, as a means of facilitating a more active and engaged democracy.[3] Reciprocity signals an epistemological shift that values not only expert knowledge that is rational, analytic, and positivist but also a different kind of rationality that is more relational, localized, and contextual and favors mutual deference between laypersons and academics. Knowledge generation and discovery is a process of cocreation, breaking down the distinctions between knowledge producers and knowledge consumers.

It further implies scholarly work that is conducted with shared authority and power with those in the community in all aspects of the relationship,
from defining problems to choosing approaches, addressing issues, developing the final products, and participating in assessment. "The design of
problem-solving actions through collaborative knowledge construction with
the legitimate stakeholders in the problem," writes Greenwood (2008), takes
place in

> collaborative arenas for knowledge development in which the profes-
> sional researcher's knowledge is combined with the local knowledge
> of the stakeholders in defining the problem to be addressed. Together,
> they design and implement the actions to be taken on the basis of their
> shared understanding of the problem. Together, the parties develop
> plans of action to improve the situation together, and they evaluate
> the adequacy of what was done. (p. 327)

Reciprocity operates to facilitate the involvement of individuals in the community not just as consumers of knowledge and services but also as participants in the larger public culture of democracy.

Democratic engagement locates the university within an ecosystem of
knowledge production, requiring interaction with other knowledge producers outside the university for the creation of new problem-solving knowledge
through a multidirectional flow of knowledge and expertise. In this paradigm,
students learn cooperative and creative problem solving within learning environments in which faculty, students, and individuals from the community
work and deliberate together. Politics is understood through explicit awareness and experiencing of patterns of power that are present in the relationship between the university and the community—politics is not reduced to
partisanship and advocacy. In the democratic-centered paradigm, academics
are not partisan political activists, but, as described by Albert Dzur (2008),
"have sown the seeds of a more deliberative democracy" in universities and
communities "by cultivating norms of equality, collaboration, reflection, and
communication" (p. 121). Civic engagement in the democratic-centered paradigm is intentionally political in that students learn about democracy by acting democratically. (See Table 1.1.)

Civic engagement without reciprocity (processes) and democratic
dimensions (purpose) is not the same as democratic civic engagement.
Civic engagement shaped by activity and place devoid of attention to processes and purpose represents what Greenwood (2008) calls "a tendency
for . . . engagement to become simultaneously fashionable and disengaged"
(p. 332). Civic engagement without an intentional and explicit democratic
dimension keeps academics and universities disengaged from participating
in the public culture of democracy. Further, it does not compel the same
kind of change in institutional culture that democratic civic engagement
requires.

TABLE 1.1   COMPARING CIVIC ENGAGEMENT FRAMEWORKS

	Civic Engagement (Focus on Activity and Place)	Democratic Civic Engagement (Focus on Purpose and Process)
Community Relationships	Partnerships and mutuality	Reciprocity
	Deficit-based understanding of community	Asset-based understanding of community
	Academic work done *for* the public	Academic work done *with* the public
Knowledge Production/ Research	Applied	Inclusive, collaborative, problem-oriented
	Unidirectional flow of knowledge	Multidirectional flow of knowledge
Epistemology	Positivist, scientific, technocratic	Relational, localized, contextual
	Distinction between knowledge producers and knowledge consumers	Cocreation of knowledge
	Primacy of academic knowledge	Shared authority for knowledge creation
	University as the center of public problem solving	University as a part of an ecosystem of knowledge production addressing public problem solving
Political Dimension	Apolitical engagement	Engagement that facilitates an inclusive, collaborative, and deliberative democracy
Outcome	Knowledge generation and dissemination through community involvement	Community change that results from the cocreation of knowledge

Institutional Change for Democratic Engagement

Civic engagement shaped by activities and place requires change in practices and structures and is associated with what Larry Cuban (1988) has described as "first-order change," which aims to improve "the efficiency and effectiveness of what is done . . . to make what already exists more efficient and more effective, without disturbing the basic organizational features, without substantially altering the ways in which [faculty and students] perform their roles. Those who propose first-order changes believe that the existing goals and structures . . . are both adequate and desirable" (p. 341). The dominant framework of civic engagement need not fundamentally alter the established organizational structures and culture of higher education. It does not require what Peter Eckel, Barbara Hill, and Madeline Green (1998) refer to as changes that "alter the culture of the institution," those that require "major shifts in an institution's culture—the common set of beliefs and values that creates a shared interpretation and understanding of events and actions" (p. 3). The dominant expert-centered framework of civic engagement does not compel change that transforms institutional culture. The pervasiveness of civic engagement, from this perspective, does not appear to have slowed down or stalled in any way. There is a proliferation of engagement activities and innovative community-based practice throughout the university and across higher education. Civic engagement appears to be flourishing.[4]

Civic engagement shaped by processes and purpose, with its explicit democratic value of reciprocity, points to change in the institutional culture of colleges and universities, or what Cuban (1988) identifies as "second-order changes" that "seek to alter the fundamental ways in which organizations are put together. These changes reflect major dissatisfaction with present arrangements. Second-order changes introduce new goals, structures, and roles that transform familiar ways of doing things into new ways of solving persistent problems" (p. 342). Second-order changes are associated with transformational change, which Eckel, Hill, and Green (1998) define as change that "(1) alters the culture of the institution by changing select underlying assumptions and institutional behaviors, processes, and products; (2) is deep and pervasive, affecting the whole institution; (3) is intentional; and (4) occurs over time" (p. 3). Cultural change focuses on "institution-wide patterns of perceiving, thinking, and feeling; shared understandings; collective assumptions; and common interpretive frameworks," which work as "the ingredients of this 'invisible glue' called institutional culture" (p. 3). From this perspective, the civic engagement movement seems to have hit a wall: innovative practices that shift epistemology, reshape the curriculum, alter pedagogy, and redefine scholarship are not being supported through academic norms and institutional reward policies that shape the academic cultures of the academy. There are limits to the degree of change that occurs institutionally, and the civic engagement work appears to have been accommodated to the dominant expert-centered framework. Democratic engagement is not embedded in the institutional culture. It remains a marginalized activity, and its sustainability is questionable. (See Table 1.2.)

While the analysis provided here points to a dominant form of civic engagement that has emerged in higher education that is largely devoid of both long-term democracy-building values and higher education's contribution to the public culture of democracy, our aim is to demonstrate that an alternative framework is possible and can contribute to the re-shaping of higher education to better meet its academic and civic missions in the twenty-first century. As Sullivan (2000) reminds us, "Campuses educate their students for citizenship most effectively to the degree that they become sites for constructive exchange and cooperation among diverse groups of citizens from the larger community" (p. 20). It is this democratic-centered framework of civic engagement that holds the promise of transforming not only the educational practice and institutional identity of colleges and universities but our public culture as well.

TABLE 1.2   TRANSFORMATION THROUGH CHANGE IN
INSTITUTIONAL CULTURE

First-Order Change	Second-Order Change
Aims to improve the efficiency and effectiveness of what is done—to make what already exists more efficient and more effective.	Aims to alter the fundamental ways in which organizations are put together. These changes reflect major dissatisfaction with present arrangements.
Does not disturb the basic organizational features or substantially alter the ways in which faculty and students perform their roles. Those who propose first-order changes believe that the existing goals and structure are both adequate and desirable.	Introduces new goals, structures, and roles that transform familiar ways of doing things into new ways of solving persistent problems.
Does not require changes that alter the institution's culture—the common set of beliefs and values that creates a shared interpretation and understanding of events and actions.	Is associated with transformational change, defined as change that (1) alters the culture of the institution by changing select underlying assumptions and institutional behaviors, processes, and products; (2) is deep and pervasive, affecting the whole institution; (3) is intentional; and (4) occurs over time.
	Focuses on institution-wide patterns of perceiving, thinking, and feeling; shared understandings; collective assumptions; and common interpretive frameworks as the ingredients of the "invisible glue" of institutional culture.

Adapted from L. Cuban, "A Fundamental Puzzle of School Reform," *Phi Delta Kappan* 69, no. 5 (1988): 341–344; P. Eckel, B. Hill, and M. Green, *On Change: En Route to Transformation* (Washington, DC: American Council on Education, 1998); and G. D. Kuh and E. J. Whitt, *The Invisible Tapestry: Culture in American Colleges and Universities*, ASHE-EPIC Higher Education Report No. 1 (Washington, DC: Association for the Study of Higher Education, 1988).

NOTES

1. Kellogg Commission on the Future of State and Land-Grant Universities 2001, p. 15.

2. Boyte and Hollander 1999, p. 10.

3. There is a growing body of literature that addresses the democratic dimensions of civic engagement in higher education that includes the work of Harry Boyte, William Sullivan, Albert Dzur, Michael Edwards, David Mathews, Ira Harkavy, Scott Peters, Donald Schön, Ernest Lynton, Ernest Boyer, Michael Gibbons, Mary Walshok, and Eugene Rice, among others. See in particular Benson, Harkavy, and Hartley 2005; Boyer 1990, 1996; Boyte 2008a, 2008b; Dzur 2008; Edwards 2006; Greenwood 2008; Gibbons 1994; Schön 1995; Sullivan 2000; Van De Ven 2008; Walshok 1995.

4. The literature on institutional change in higher education is considerable and growing. Our analysis of institutional culture, institutional transformation, and institutionalization draws heavily on Cuban 1988. Cuban's distinctions are drawn from Watzlawick, Weakland, and Frisch 1974. They describe first-order change as change that occurs within an existing system, which itself remains unchanged. Second-order change results from a change in the system itself. See also Eckel, Hill, and Green 1998; Kuh and Whitt 1988; and Tierney 1988.

REFERENCES

Benson, L., I. Harkavy, and M. Hartley. 2005. "Integrating a Commitment to the Public Good into the Institutional Fabric." In *Higher Education for the Public Good: Emerging Voices from a National Movement*, ed. A. J. Kezar, T. Chambers, and J. Burkhardt, 185–216. San Francisco: Jossey-Bass.

Boyer, E. 1990. *Scholarship Reconsidered: Priorities of the Professoriate*. Princeton, NJ: Carnegie Foundation for the Advancement of Teaching.

———. 1996. "The Scholarship of Engagement." *Journal of Public Service and Outreach* 1 (1): 11–20.

Boyte, H. 2008a. "Against the Current: Developing the Civic Agency of Students." *Change* 40, no. 3 (May/June): 8–15.

———. 2008b. "A New Civic Politics." [Review of the book *Dewey's Dream: Universities and Democracies in an Age of Education Reform*, by L. Benson, I. Harkavy, and J. Puckett.] *Journal of Higher Education Outreach and Engagement* 12 (1): 107–112.

Boyte, H., and E. Hollander. 1999. "Wingspread Declaration on Renewing the Civic Mission of the American Research University." Available at http://www.compact.org/initiatives/civic-engagement-at-research-universities/wingspread-declaration-on-the-civic-responsibilities-of-research-universities/.

Cuban, L. 1988. "A Fundamental Puzzle of School Reform." *Phi Delta Kappan* 69 (5): 341–344.

Dewey, J. 1944/1916. *Democracy and Education*. New York: Free Press.

Dzur, A. 2008. *Democratic Professionalism: Citizen Participation and the Reconstruction of Professional Ethics, Identity, and Practice*. University Park: Pennsylvania State University Press.

Eckel, P., B. Hill, and M. Green. 1998. *On Change: En Route to Transformation*. Washington, DC: American Council on Education.

Edwards, M. 2006. "Looking Back from 2046: Thoughts on the 80th Anniversary of the Institute for Revolutionary Social Science." (Keynote Address, 40th Anniversary of the Institute for Development Studies, University of Sussex, UK). *IDS Bulletin* 38, no. 2 (March): 40–45.

Freire, P. 1970. *Pedagogy of the Oppressed*. New York: Continuum.

Gibbons, M., C. Limoges, H. Nowotny, S. Schwartzman, P. Scott, and M. Trow. 1994. *The New Production of Knowledge: The Dynamics of Science and Research in Contemporary Societies*. London: Sage.

Greenwood, D. J. 2008. "Theoretical Research, Applied Research, and Action Research: The Deinstitutionalization of Activist Research." In *Engaging Contradictions: Theory, Politics, and Methods of Activist Scholarship*, ed. C. R. Hale, 319–340. Berkeley: University of California Press.

Keller, G. 1983. *Academic Strategy: The Management Revolution in Higher Education*. Baltimore: Johns Hopkins University Press.

Kellogg Commission on the Future of State and Land-Grant Universities. 2001. "Returning to Our Roots: Executive Summaries of the Reports of the Kellogg Commission on the Future of State and Land-Grant Universities." Available at www.aplu.org/netcommunity/document.doc?id=187.

Kuh, G. D., and E. J. Whitt. 1988. *The Invisible Tapestry: Culture in American Colleges and Universities*. ASHE-EPIC Higher Education Report 1. Washington, DC: Association for the Study of Higher Education.

Levine, P. 2007. *The Future of Democracy: Developing the Next Generation of American Citizens*. Medford, MA: Tufts University Press.

Lynton, E. A. 1994. "Knowledge and Scholarship." *Metropolitan Universities: An International Forum* 5, no. 1 (Summer): 9–17.

Mathews, D. 2008. "Democracy's Megachallenges Revisited." In *Agent of Democracy: Higher Education and the HEX Journey*, ed. D. W. Brown and D. Witte, 207–223. Dayton, OH: Kettering Foundation.

Newman, F. 1985. *Higher Education and the American Resurgence*. Princeton, NJ: Carnegie Foundation for the Advancement of Teaching.

O'Meara, K., and R. E. Rice, eds. 2005. *Faculty Priorities Reconsidered: Encouraging Multiple Forms of Scholarship*. San Francisco: Jossey-Bass.

Reuben, J. 1996. *The Making of the Modern University: Intellectual Transformation and the Marginalization of Morality*. Chicago: University of Chicago Press.

Schön, D. 1995. "The New Scholarship Requires a New Epistemology." *Change* 27, no. 6 (November/December): 26–35.

Smith, P. 1990. *Killing the Spirit: Higher Education in America*. New York: Viking Press.

Sullivan, W. M. 2000. "Institutional Identity and Social Responsibility in Higher Education." In *Civic Responsibility and Higher Education*, ed. T. Ehrlich, 19–36. Phoenix: Oryx Press.

Tierney, W. G. 1988. "Organizational Culture in Higher Education: Defining the Essentials." *Journal of Higher Education* 59 (1): 2–21.

Van De Ven, A. 2008. *Engaged Scholarship: A Guide for Organizational and Social Research*. New York: Oxford University Press.

Walshok, M. 1995. *Knowledge Without Boundaries: What America's Research Universities Can Do for the Economy, the Workplace, and the Community*. San Francisco: Jossey-Bass.

Watzlawick, P., J. H. Weakland, and R. Frisch. 1974. *Change: Principles of Problem Formation and Problem Resolution*. New York: W. W. Norton.

CHAPTER 2

Idealism and Compromise and the Civic Engagement Movement

MATTHEW HARTLEY

INTRODUCTION

The civic roots of American higher education can be traced back to its beginnings. The first institutions, colonial colleges, were established soon after European settlers arrived in order to ensure a continuity of religious and civic leadership. The founders of the college that is now Harvard University explained:

> After God had carried us safe to New England, and we had built our houses, provided necessaries for our livelihood, reared convenient places for God's worship, and led the civil government, one of the next things we longed for and looked after was to advance learning and perpetuate it to posterity; dreading to leave an illiterate ministry to the churches, when our present ministers shall lie in the dust.[1]

Yale, too, is described in its earliest documents as an institution "wherein youth may be instructed in the arts and sciences, who through the blessing of Almighty God, may be fitted for public employment, both in Church and civil State."[2] This commitment to promoting civic leadership grew in the aftermath of the American Revolution as hundreds of new colleges were established. As the historian Frederick Rudolph (1962) aptly put it, "A commitment to the republic became a guiding obligation of the American college" (p. 61).

This commitment to upholding the democracy continued unabated throughout the nineteenth century. It found expression in the land-grant movement launched by the Morrill Act of 1862, which established colleges and universities dedicated to the public good. The trustees of the Ohio Agricultural and Mechanical College (now Ohio State University) in 1873, for example, said that they intended not just to educate students as "farmers or mechanics but as men, fitted by education and attainments for the greater usefulness and higher duties of citizenship" (qtd. in Boyte and Kari 2000, p. 47). The Wisconsin Idea, launched in 1903 by Charles Van Hise, president of the University of Wisconsin, and Governor Robert La Follette (a former classmate of Van Hise's) sought to make "the boundaries of the university . . . the boundaries of the state" (University of Wisconsin–Madison 2006). The salient idea was that universities should be committed to addressing pressing societal problems and fostering enlightened civic and political leadership.

A Contested Purpose

Despite this rich legacy, the democratic purpose of higher education has been a contested ideal, struggling with other societal imperatives and purposes for ascendancy (Hartley and Hollander 2005). In contrast to the above examples, the Brown brothers, Nicholas Jr., John, and Moses, for whom the institution in Providence, Rhode Island, was named after a large gift was given by Nicholas Jr., did so for another (very pragmatic) "civic" reason—to make money. They argued that "building a college here will be a means of bringing great quantities of money into the place, and thereby greatly increasing the markets for all kinds of the country's produce, and consequently increasing the value of estates to which the town is a market" (Cochran 1972, p. 35). Of greater importance was the shift in higher education that occurred in the latter half of the nineteenth century with the ascendancy of the German university model and its emphasis on research and specialization. The search for new knowledge for its own sake became the overriding purpose of many institutions. The ideological underpinnings of the German university model, with its "value-free" ethos, deemphasized higher education's role as a civic actor in shaping students' values (Reuben 1996). This prevailing view was powerfully reinforced in the mid-twentieth century as the Cold War brought unprecedented governmental spending on research, which fueled the growth of the modern research university.

It must also be noted that despite the rhetoric espousing a higher purpose, American higher education has historically served the interests of men of European descent. It was not until the twentieth century (and the latter half) that the doors of many colleges and universities began to swing open in earnest for women and people of color—hardly a history to support a strong, diverse democracy (Schneider 2005b).

A Crisis of Purpose

As noted in the introductory chapter of this volume, the early 1980s brought a host of concerns about the "larger purpose" of higher education. Some of the pressures were external to the academy. A faltering economy produced intense fiscal pressures (Thelin 2004). A projected demographic decline in the number of 18- to 22-year-olds threatened tuition-dependent institutions (Crossland 1980). Many colleges and universities responded by adopting a market-centered mind-set (student-as-customer), and what the customer wanted was jobs (Bloom, Hartley, and Rosovsky 2006). There was an explosion of preprofessional and occupational programs, which proved popular with students (Breneman 1994; Delucchi 1997; Knox, Lindsay, and Kolb 1993). David Breneman (1994) noted, "For all colleges, professional degrees awarded rose from 33 percent in 1972 to 54 percent in 1988" (p. 139). This shift in academic mission, however, exacted a price. Faculty morale on many campuses suffered. Ernest Boyer, in the prologue of his influential 1987 book *College: The Undergraduate Experience in America,* pointedly observed, "Scrambling for students and driven by marketplace demands, many undergraduate colleges have lost their sense of purpose" (p. 3).

Over the next two decades, a large number of initiatives were launched, aimed at re-enlivening the civic and public purpose of American higher education (Astin 1995; Boyer 1990; Boyte and Kari 2000; Colby et al. 2003; Gutmann 1987; Newmann 2000). Some were sponsored by existing associations such as the Association of American Colleges and Universities (AAC&U), the American Association for Higher Education, and the American Council on Education. Many new organizations and associations—ones with expressly civic purposes—were also formed.

The scope of these activities has led some scholars to liken them to a movement (Brukardt et al. 2004; Hollander and Hartley 2000; Kezar, Chambers, and Burkhardt 2005). Like a social movement, the civic engagement movement has sought to challenge and change a problematic status quo (often defined as political disaffection and civic apathy.) The vehicle for collective action has been networks that play a key role in coordinating and supporting movement members (Della Porta and Diani 2006). Networks organize action, communicate information, and channel resources to members. They also aid in the formation of a common identity (Melucci 1989). In sum, effective networks convey both the material means and the ideological rationale to sustain a movement.

The account that follows describes the emergence and activities of several key networks. It is necessarily a partial accounting since numerous networks have advanced this movement. Even a full accounting of the ones presented here is not possible in the scope of this discussion. My intent, rather, is to point to the kinds of initiatives that occurred in three stages in the movement. I pay particular attention to one network, Campus Compact, which is one of the oldest national networks and arguably the largest one focusing on promoting civic engagement in American higher education. The evolution of the networks described here underscore the challenges of establishing the legitimacy of the engagement agenda and the tensions inherent in appealing to wider groups at the expense of a more-transformative agenda.[3]

TRACING THE TRAJECTORY OF THE CURRENT MOVEMENT

Origins

The 1980s were difficult times for American higher education: Some experts predicted that within a decade as many as one-third of all colleges and universities would merge or close (Keller 1983). Many institutions attempted to compete for students by significantly reshaping their academic programs to appeal to a more pragmatic and career-minded student body. There had been a significant shift in student attitudes regarding higher education (Bloom, Hartley, and Rosovsky 2006). In 1969, 80 percent of incoming freshmen indicated that developing a meaningful philosophy of life (the chief aim of a liberal education) was an important goal; by 1996, that value had fallen to 42 percent. Between 1971 and 1991, the percentage of students indicating that they were attending college "to be able to make more money" increased from 49.9 to 74.7 percent (Astin 1998). Many colleges and universities began altering their curriculums to emphasize preprofessional programs (Breneman 1994; Brint 2002), a strategy that triggered a kind of existential crisis on some campuses (Hartley 2002).

Another major concern that surfaced during the 1980s was the political disaffection of America's youth. The media continually made unfavorable comparisons between the career-minded students of the 1980s and the idealistic students of the sixties (Clifford 1982; Taylor 1980). A front-page article in the *Miami Herald* in 1983, typical of the time, described college students as "optimistic about themselves but cynical about the world, concerned about their careers and involved with the care of their bodies. Competitive, well-groomed, they are also practical and status-conscious" (Veciana-Suarez 1983, p. 1A). The American Political Science Association's Task Force on Civic Education (1998) concluded:

> We take as axiomatic that current levels of political knowledge, political engagement, and political enthusiasm are so low as to threaten the vitality and stability of democratic politics in the United States. We believe political education is inadequate across the board.

The impetus for reasserting the civic purposes of colleges and universities seemed clear.

The Stirrings of Collective Action

A host of new civic initiatives began to emerge. Some were led by existing organizations. Although the National Society of Internships and Experiential Education (later renamed the National Society of Experiential Education, or NSEE) was small (in 1985 it had 3 staff members and 600 members), its annual and regional conferences drew hundreds of faculty and staff members interested in experiential education. NSEE was an important incubator for conceptual work on combining service and learning, which found fruition in three seminal volumes in 1990 (Kendall 1990). In 1982, the Association of American Colleges and Universities (AAC&U), in partnership with the Kettering Foundation, sponsored a special issue of *Liberal Education* whose articles laid out the argument for a return to civic education in the postsecondary years and described how that might be achieved at different types of institutions, themes that were taken up in its annual conference.

In some instances, existing organizations sponsored particular initiatives. AAC&U's influential project American Commitments: Diversity, Democracy, and Liberal Learning began in 1993 and drew together 160 colleges and universities engaged in initiatives aimed at examining their role in promoting a diverse democracy. The Kellogg Commission was established by the National Association of State Universities and Land-Grant Colleges (NASULGC, now the Association of Land-Grant Universities, or APLU) in 1996 in order to reimagine the land-grant tradition and enliven its public purposes. In 2004, the American Association of State Colleges and Universities, in partnership with the *New York Times*, launched the American Democracy Project to help enliven debate on contemporary issues on more than 220 state college and university campuses.

Beginning in the 1980s, a number of new organizations were established as well (see Table 2.1). Some focused on particular constituencies. For example, the Campus Outreach Opportunity League (COOL) sought to support student-led efforts while the Invisible College brought together faculty members interested

TABLE 2.1   NETWORKS ESTABLISHED TO PROMOTE COMMUNITY
AND CIVIC ENGAGEMENT

Network	Founding Year
National Society of Experiential Education (NSEE)	1978
International Partnership for Service-Learning and Leadership	1982
National Youth Leadership Council	1983
Campus Outreach Opportunity League (COOL)	1984
Campus Compact	1986
Bonner Scholars Program	1990
Integrating Service and Academic Study (an initiative of Campus Compact)	1991
Breakaway	1991
Invisible College (renamed Educators for Community Engagement)	1993
American Commitments (an initiative of AAC&U)	1993
Corporation for National and Community Service	1994
Associated New American Colleges	1995
Community–Campus Partnerships for Health	1996
Kellogg Commission (an initiative of NASULGC)	1996
Partnering Initiative	1997
Imagining America	1999
Project Pericles	2000
American Democracy Project (an initiative of AASCU)	2004
Talloires Network	2005
Higher Education Network for Community Engagement (HENCE)	2006
The Research University Civic Engagement Network (TRUCEN)	2008

in community-based teaching and research. Some of these networks emphasized the work of particular types of institutions—for example, the Talloires
Network and TRUCEN worked with representatives from research universities.
The Associated New American Colleges aimed to advance Ernest Boyer's vision
of the New American College—one dedicated to a formative education whose
institutional ethos emphasized teaching over research. Project Pericles, a group
of twenty-two institutions, required each member to demonstrate institutional
commitment to civic engagement through the appointment of a director and the
formation of a committee by the governing board. The common denominator
for all these groups is that they functioned as networks supporting the work of
the members and encouraging others to embrace these efforts.

It is important to note that the work of many of these groups evolved over
this two-decade period. Some networks (NSEE and Campus Compact) sought
to promote volunteerism in the 1980s and then shifted their efforts toward service-learning in the 1990s. Networks formed later tended to focus on the needs
and interests of particular types of institutions. Finally, a few networks formed
in later years (the Partnering Initiative and HENCE) sought to draw together
representatives from many networks in order to advance their collective aims.
Also, a few networks (most notably, COOL and the Invisible College) were
not able to remain viable entities as they were originally conceived.

Campus Compact

Campus Compact, one of the earliest networks, focused its efforts in the
1980s on promoting student volunteerism and advocating for governmental
support of public service. In 1989, it shifted its emphasis decisively toward
service-learning with the launch of the Integrating Service with Academic
Study (ISAS) initiative, funded by the Ford Foundation. Over the next few
summers, ISAS worked with faculty and administrative teams from more than
60 institutions. It also provided 120 faculty grants and funded 130 service-
learning workshops nationwide. In 1994, ISAS launched a series of regional
Institutes that introduced over 1,000 participants to service learning and
encouraged its institutionalization. ISAS also developed written materials and
gathered syllabi from a wide range of disciplines. Campus Compact's membership swelled in the first half of the 1990s in part because of its growth
strategy, which was the establishment of state compacts—offices dedicated to
serving the needs of colleges and universities in a particular state by bringing
together presidential leaders on a board and providing training and support
for staff members responsible for overseeing civic and community engagement
efforts and faculty interested in service learning. By 1997, three-quarters of all
Campus Compact members were in states with a state compact. By 2006, the
percentage had risen to 90.

In every instance, the formation of a state compact resulted in the significant growth of Campus Compact membership. For example, Massachusetts
had fourteen members prior to the formation of a state compact in 1995;

by 1996, that number had grown to thirty and was at sixty-five by 2006. Pennsylvania saw its membership grow from three members to thirty-seven in 1991 and, by 2006, sixty-one. Michigan's membership grew from four to fifteen in 1991 and by 2006 the state had forty-four members. By contrast, all of the other states with Campus Compact members experienced modest growth—only one (of fifteen) had more than ten members in 2006— eleven had five or fewer members. At the end of 1989, Campus Compact had 202 members. Within five years, thirteen new state compacts had been formed and the number of Compact members more than doubled to 520.

The Roles of Networks in Establishing the Movement

What did the formation of this widening web of network activity accomplish? The benefits of networks fall into several broad areas. Networks increased awareness of civic engagement within the academy, conveyed resources, and established civic engagement as a legitimate activity. Yet as the analysis below suggests, the role the networks played differed somewhat among various stages of the movement.

Stage 1: The (re)formation of the movement. The early civic engagement networks sought to rekindle efforts to promote civic engagement by identifying early adapters who could form the nucleus of a broad-based effort and by developing a compelling rationale for the movement given the context of the time. In 1980, a small band of "pioneers" had already been seeking to combine education and social action (Stanton, Giles, and Cruz 1999). Many of these individuals had been involved in efforts to promote civic engagement in the 1970s. The NSEE was a vulnerable organization in 1980 (its staff had been reduced from nine to two). But it also was an important link to earlier efforts. Among its small membership was a group of individuals who had been involved in community-based learning and research in the 1970s. Jane Kendall, NSEE's executive director, recalled, "A lot of what I did was listen to people's stories and connect them to other stories. In some ways that's what NSEE was—a storytelling community—telling stories to keep it alive during some of the leaner times" (qtd. in Stanton, Giles, and Cruz 1999, p. 158). These networks helped keep the embers of an earlier movement alive.

Implicit in Kendall's statement and reflected in the experiences of others is the notion that networks provided a kind of home for early adaptors who were laboring in obscurity at (and often at odds with) their institutions. Even as late as 1997, those involved in this work represented only a small proportion of faculty and staff at the vast majority of institutions, residing in "enclaves" (Singleton, Burack, and Hirsch 1997). The accounts of many individuals who became actively involved in the movement reveal their astonishment (and satisfaction) at discovering that other individuals and institutions were engaging in similar work and organizing themselves to advance it further. As a staff member from one campus center put it, "Several of us were doing all this work in the community, and then I heard about this service-learning meeting. I went and I said, 'Oh, so this is what it's called. Look at all the other people struggling with this, too.'"[4] Such networks enabled like-minded individuals to find, learn from, and support one another.

Networks identified individuals with a preexisting inclination to the cause of civic engagement. The latent interest proved considerable. COOL, through its work on more than 400 campuses and annual conferences, helped raise the visibility of burgeoning student-led volunteer efforts. It played a key role in dispelling the prevailing myth of student apathy. In fact, there were students on many campuses anxious to express their idealism in tangible ways. At its founding in 1986, the three presidents of Campus Compact voiced a bold vision of establishing a coalition of 100 college and university presidents. They achieved that goal less than a year later. These early successes demonstrated the resonance of a civic agenda.

Network forums (such as meetings and conferences) enabled proponents of civic engagement to determine how best to advance the cause. Part of this entailed making the case for civic engagement, as in a special issue of AAC&U's Liberal Education in 1982, which included a bold manifesto arguing for a "counterrevolution" reshaping American higher education and reclaiming its democratic purposes (Cawallader 1982). Despite a fair amount of rhetorical idealism, many early discussions centered on a more pragmatic project: promoting volunteerism. The virtue of this approach was that such activities were widely viewed as valuable and legitimate. Several state legislatures and some members of Congress discussed potential legislation that might support public service (which later found expression in the National Community Service Act of 1993). Volunteerism was by far the most prevalent form of service on college and university campuses in the 1980s. It was a safe strategy. According to a former board member of NSEE, Campus Compact cofounder Frank Newman liked the idea of curriculum-based service but felt it would never be widely embraced by faculty on college campuses. A group of service-learning proponents, however, lobbied Campus Compact's Director, Susan Stroud, and its board chair (and cofounder), Stanford president Donald Kennedy, and slowly that attitude began to shift. By 1990, the notion of combining service with academic study became a principal emphasis of Campus Compact and the wider movement.

In sum, the early years of the movement were a time of drawing together small but committed groups of individuals (e.g., presidents with Campus Compact, students with COOL, faculty pioneers with NSEE) who were personally committed to the cause of civic engagement and testing the attractiveness of the idea to broader audiences. The other key activity involved finding actual projects or activities that could be advanced in the name of civic engagement. A tension that began to emerge was that the pragmatic strategies for achieving civic engagement (e.g., promoting volunteerism) seemed ill suited to achieving the transformative agenda that many of the early proponents hoped to enact.

Stage 2: Midlife expansion. The midlife of the movement was characterized by the expansion of membership through material and technological support and the formation of an agenda with broad-based appeal.

Once established, networks sought to support their members and encourage others to participate. One strategy was the creation of national and regional conferences and regional and local workshops. These enabled participants to come together and learn from one another, showcased promising practices, and oriented and equipped newcomers to the movement. These meetings took several forms. Some, such as the Summer Institute developed by Campus Compact's ISAS program, convened teams of individuals who were interested in promoting service-learning on their campuses. This strategy was employed by a number of state compacts as well. Regional workshops such as those sponsored by Campus Compact provided groups of faculty with basic tools in order to get started—essentially, "service-learning 101."

Initiatives also did a great deal of important conceptual work, helping members think deeply about their civic responsibilities. AAC&U's American Commitments project, funded by the Ford Foundation, sought "to address fundamental questions about higher education in a diverse democracy and to provide resources for colleges and universities willing to engage those questions as dimensions of institutional mission, campus climate, and curricular focus."[5] The project produced a series of reports that explored the role of college and universities in a pluralistic democracy (AAC&U 1995a, 1995b). Such association initiatives proved invaluable for establishing an intellectual rationale for civic engagement activities. Involvement in association initiatives helped validate and legitimize efforts on individual campuses.

National conferences also conveyed useful, practical information. Moreover, with high-profile speakers and the presence of several thousand individuals who cared passionately about changing the academy, these events also conveyed the sense that the movement was achieving a critical mass. This was particularly important for those individuals who had labored long and alone on their own campuses.

A cadre of experts, many of whom were frequent presenters at conferences and/or participants in various association initiatives, began to emerge. In this regard, the associations served as incubators of talent. They were called on to consult on hundreds of campuses. These experts provided a measure of external validation for fledgling institutional efforts and were able to speak with authority about best practices at other institutions. Validation also occurred as associations held up certain campuses as models. Throughout the 1990s, few issues of the *Compact Currents* quarterly newsletter failed to include a profile of one or more member campuses. Campus Compact also served as a conduit for grant monies, another critical means for encouraging efforts on campus and validating particular kinds of activities. The network received a number of large grants in the 1990s that it used to support initiatives on many campuses.

In the early 1990s, Campus Compact began encouraging the formation of state compacts. An early prototype already existed in Minnesota. Mark Langseth, who had helped found the organization based at the University of Minnesota, recalled that there had been an initial discussion about forming a state compact in the late 1980s that had been aborted. A few years later, another concerted effort was made by Frank Newman (president of the Education Commission of the States, which had provided administrative support to Campus Compact in its early years) and several others to revive the idea. This effort was met with a measure of skepticism, in part because of the ill-fated earlier attempt. There were also concerns about autonomy: To what extent would the local organization have to subvert its interests to that of the national office? In the end, the factor that tipped the scale was greater legitimacy for the cause.

State compacts put local legs on the movement by forming the infrastructure to support campus engagement efforts. The formation of new state compacts provided a powerful means for galvanizing the efforts of people around engagement. A small group of presidents (often with explicit attention paid to those at flagships or elite privates) along with a staff member served as the nucleus of the group. They, in turn, identified other prospective presidential members for the founding board. Over the next several years, many hundreds of presidents were thus able to note with satisfaction that they were "founding members" of a state compact. The organizations established a peer group of presidents who supported the cause of engagement and who had made a personal commitment to the cause. State compacts had the additional benefit of incubating a variety of initiatives and innovations that took into account local needs. They proved to be an essential engine of growth. In states that formed compacts, membership jumped dramatically within a year. The vast majority of Campus Compact's growth occurred through the formation and work of state compacts.

The growth during the 1990s was significantly aided by support from external funding. A number of foundations—Kellogg, Pew, Kettering, Ford—provided significant funds to fuel various initiatives under the auspices of higher education associations. Another major funder was the Corporation for National Service (formed in 1993), which provided as much as $10 million per year in grants to colleges and universities under its Learn and Serve America program. Learn and Serve also awarded monies to Campus Compact and to some state compacts for various projects, often involving sub-granting to members. The promise of grant funding (and the requirement that institutions provide matching funds) spurred conversations on many campuses about the potential uses of service-learning. The very fact of governmental support lent credibility to the effort on campuses. Funders, however, often had specific ideas about how they wanted their funds spent. Learn and Serve focused its efforts squarely on service-learning. Understandably, because it was a governmental program, it expressly forbade the money to be used for political activities to avoid partisan entanglements. Such constraints, however, exacted a price. A service-learning project in a business course addressing the logistical challenges of serving an intransigent population fit well under these guidelines, while helping a community-based group gather information on fair housing practices to pressure local politicians to act did not.

By the mid-1990s Campus Compact was experiencing growing pains. In 1995, the network reached a landmark 500 members. At a board meeting, Frank Newman posed the questions: What do we gain from growing further? Should we continue to focus our energies on expansion or work closely with a subset of institutions to promote significant change? During her interview for the executive director position, Elizabeth Hollander recalled the board posing the question this way: "Should we go for growth or deepen the work with who we have?" Her answer was, essentially, both. It would prove a difficult charge.

One of the significant challenges for Campus Compact was the tension between centralization and decentralization. When Hollander scheduled her first meeting with state compact directors, she found considerable division. State compacts questioned the added value of the national office (to whom they paid a portion of their membership revenues), and in a couple of cases, there was talk of secession. Some state compacts had even obtained independent 501(c)(3) status. Hollander began a discussion about the roles of state compacts and the national office. There emerged a consensus that individual state compacts ought to be able to pursue their own initiatives but that the national office played a vital role in coordinating the network and communicating to external constituents (particularly the leadership of other associations) the impact of the entire network. Hollander insisted on creating a common logo, a symbolic act that communicated solidarity. Ultimately, state compact directors were persuaded that being linked collectively through a national office provided them a measure of legitimacy for their collective actions.

The pull between quantity and quality—breadth and depth—proved a persistent one. Growth meant drawing more and more colleges and universities to the cause. But in some cases this occurred at the cost of lowering the bar. In stark contrast to the early years when presidents had to make a personal commitment before joining, a significant number of state compacts no longer required this commitment. In some instances, high-profile institutions were allowed to join with only a very perfunctory nod of the president (often at the urging of a staff member). In many states, Compact was becoming an organization that primarily served service-learning and community-engagement staff members rather than functioning as a presidential coalition. Further, despite some discussions about instituting quality measures, none ever materialized.

By the end of this period, association efforts had evolved from supporting a small band of true believers to spurring a full-fledged movement, one largely committed to promoting engaged scholarship and service-learning. Through the support of foundations and the federal government (through Learn and Serve and programs designed to encourage activities on campus (such as the

American Association for Higher Education's forum on faculty roles and rewards), the issue of engagement was beginning to gain more widespread acceptance.

Stage 3: Maturity and seeking a second act. By the mid-1990s, the landscape had significantly changed for the movement. Some early networks faltered. One important early effort, COOL, which had drawn thousands of students to its national conference on volunteerism, could no longer sustain its work and shut down. Other venues, including the Points of Light foundation, provided competition. Perhaps more relevant was the notable turn in the 1990s away from volunteerism toward curricular-based service-learning as a principal strategy. Because of its direct impact on the curriculum, proponents hoped that service-learning would institutionalize a commitment to civic engagement in the core work of the academy.

It is important to note that a number of important efforts that might have potentially contributed to a wider civic engagement movement remained isolated from one another. With the exception of AAC&U's American Commitments project, which sought to integrate diversity work with other civic engagement efforts, many campus-based diversity initiatives remained wholly separate from service-learning initiatives. Similarly, activities like democratic deliberation—promoting debate and dialogue on difficult community and societal issues—rarely informed service-learning partnerships and placements. A larger, more ambitious democratic purpose was set aside for a more focused and practical effort aimed at promoting service-learning.

The project appealed widely. However, ideological tensions began to emerge among service-learning adherents. This is perhaps most notable in a project that was originally an off-shoot of Campus Compact, the Invisible College. Founded by John Wallace, a professor of philosophy at the University of Minnesota, the group was intended to bring together a cohort of experienced service-learning practitioners who could deepen the work—move it beyond "service learning 101." What quickly emerged after the first few meetings was a significant ideological rift in the group. Some of its members had viewed service-learning as a strategy for establishing reciprocal partnerships and working with the local community for the common good. Many had a clear social justice emphasis. Some had been community organizers; the endgame for them was transforming the academy. Another group of members had entered service-learning from a very different avenue: They saw it primarily as a superior pedagogy and were uncomfortable with the social justice message.[6] This group openly questioned whether service-learning could establish broad-based legitimacy without accommodating the norms of the academy. Some felt it untenable to make community impact a desired outcome— service-learning ought to primarily benefit students (Liu 1996). One of the most thoughtful advocates for a less ideologically grounded service-learning was Edward Zlotkowski. He argued:

Until very recently the service-learning movement has had an "ideological" bias; i.e., it has tended to prioritize moral and/or civic questions related to the service experience. Such a focus reflects well on the movement's past but will not guarantee its future. What is needed now is a broad-based adjustment that invests far more intellectual energy in specifically academic concerns. Only by paying careful attention to the needs of individual disciplines and by allying itself with other academic interest groups will the service-learning movement succeed in becoming an established feature of American higher education. (Zlotkowski 1995)

This pragmatic stance would prove so successful that by the end of the 1990s, one pioneer, Naddine Cruz, noted the discouragement of having to defend social justice as a *possible* desirable outcome of service-learning at an association meeting (Stanton, Giles, and Cruz 1999). There were good reasons for taking such an approach. Despite its increasing use, service-learning was still not widely known (or well understood) by the professoriate. Many still confused it with the earlier volunteer community service efforts and were concerned about the propriety of granting credit for what they saw as charitable acts. As with any educational initiative, faculty contested its academic rigor.

A number of efforts were made to legitimize service-learning. In 1995, members of the Invisible College began to discuss the possibility of a monograph series focusing on the use of service-learning as a means of advancing disciplinary knowledge. AAHE agreed to support the work (eventually twenty-one volumes were produced) under the editorial leadership of Edward Zlotkowski. The wildly successful series demonstrated how service-learning could be creatively used by many faculty members in a range of disciplines. Campus Compact's Engaged Department initiative in 2000 furthered these efforts by working with groups of disciplinary colleagues to reorient their curricular offerings through service-learning, internships, capstone courses, and community-based research to promote greater engagement.

There was progress on the research front as well. A growing number of studies on the impact of service-learning on students provided important empirical confirmation of its efficacy as a pedagogy (Astin 1998; Astin, Sax, and Avalos 2000; Eyler and Giles 1999). In addition, several outlets for research on engaged teaching and scholarship emerged during the 1990s. These included the *Metropolitan Universities Journal* (1990), published by the Coalition of Urban and Metropolitan Universities, which focuses on upholding the mission of member institutions, including the imperative to "educate students to be informed and effective citizens, as well as capable practitioners of professions and occupations";[7] the *Michigan Journal for Community Service Learning* (1994), which seeks "to widen the community of service-learning educators to sustain and develop the intellectual vigor of those in this community, encourage research and pedagogical scholarship related to service-learning, [and to] contribute to the academic legitimacy of service-learning";[8] and the *Journal of Higher Education Outreach and Engagement* (1996), which aims "to advance theory and practice related to all forms of outreach and engagement between higher education institutions and communities."[9]

Finally, in the late 1990s, Campus Compact, with support from the Pew Charitable Trusts, attempted to influence academic disciplines directly. A survey of twelve learned societies conducted in the early 1990s by AAC&U found that only the American Sociological Association and National Women's Studies Association had statements referring to the advancement of civic engagement (qtd. in Schneider 2005a p. 133). As one senior staff member from Campus Compact (who, like many sources interviewed for this chapter, preferred to remain anonymous) explained,

> The effort was explicitly designed to impact the culture of the disciplinary associations, because we knew that's where faculty were going when they wanted resources and information. They weren't going to Campus Compact. So we did sub-contracts to fourteen discipline associations over a five-year period, and you see the results. For example, if you go to the American Psychological Association website, they now have tremendous service-learning resources, which were created through the sub-grant we gave them.[10]

For a time, service-learning became not a means to some democratic end, but an end in itself. Despite important inroads made in promoting service-learning, these initiatives appealed far more to the growing cadre of center directors on campuses than Campus Compact's presidents. Executive Director Liz Hollander struggled with identifying an issue that would animate her presidential members. In 1997, the directorship of Campus Compact's ISAS opened up. John Saltmarsh, a faculty member who had spearheaded an innovative service-learning program at Northeastern University, was approached about applying for the position. He agreed to speak with Campus Compact's leadership: "I pretty much said to them, 'Let's stop talking about service-learning. It's not that it's not important. But let's talk about reforming American higher education. That's what the Compact should be doing. That's what ISAS should be doing.'"[11] Hollander had been thinking along similar lines (1998), and she prevailed upon Saltmarsh to help advance this effort.

A key event that reanimated the discourse on the civic purposes of higher education was the work of the National Commission on Civic Renewal (cochaired by William J. Bennett and Senator Sam Nunn), which pointed to the decline in political and civic participation, as well as the "stirrings" of "a new movement." The Commission's final report, "A Nation of Spectators: How Civic Disengagement Weakens America and What We Can Do About It" (1998), stated:

Within the neighborhoods, the towns, the local communities of America are the stirrings of a new movement of citizens acting together to solve community problems. It is a nonpartisan movement that crosses traditional jurisdictions and operates on a shoestring. It is a movement that begins with civic dialogue and leads to public action. It has gone largely unnoticed, unappreciated, and unsupported. (p. 9)

In the fifty-seven-page document, no mention was made of higher education. This slight galvanized Campus Compact leaders. In a letter from the executive director published in *Compact Currents*, Elizabeth Hollander pointed to the oversight and argued that a wide range of efforts being undertaken by colleges and universities remained unrecognized: "We need to do a better job in spreading the word about the good work campuses are doing in educating students about their civic responsibilities. . . . When was the last time you saw a major article in the *Chronicle of Higher Education* on this topic?" (1998, p. 2). Hollander, however, also pointed to recent research by Alexander Astin that suggested the impact of community-based learning on the "social conscience and political activism" of students was "not encouraging" (p. 2). Service-learning, though a powerful pedagogy, tended to be directed at goals other than political awareness and civic consciousness. This was an oversight that needed to be addressed.

The American Council on Education established the ACE Forum on Higher Education in cooperation with several other associations, including the Association of American Universities, AAHE, AAC&U, Campus Compact, and the New England Resource Center for Higher Education. The first conference was held in 1998 at Florida State University in Tallahassee, Florida. ACE president Stanley O. Ikenberry explained its purpose: "The quality of civic life in our country, and the strength of our democracy, is in some trouble. . . . We have a role to play in improving it, through the opportunities we offer our students and the service we render to the community" (ACE 1998). In December of that year, a group of university presidents, provosts, deans, faculty members, and representatives of foundations and associations met at the Wingspread conference center in Racine, Wisconsin; they convened again in July 1999. The product of those two meetings was the "Wingspread Declaration on Renewing the Civic Mission of the American Research University," written by Harry Boyte and Elizabeth Hollander. Evoking the words of Charles Eliot, the declaration provocatively asked, How might students, faculty, staff, and administrators become "filled with the democratic spirit?" The statement asserted that faculty members ought to

take responsibility for a vibrant public culture at their institutions. Such a public culture values their moral and civic imaginations and their judgments, insights, and passions, while it recognizes and rewards their publicly engaged scholarship, lively teaching, and their contributions through public work. (Boyte and Hollander 1999, p. 10)

This was a call for colleges and universities to kindle the civic imaginations of students and to reimagine their own civic roles.

In addition, Campus Compact convened fifty-one university presidents at the Aspen Institute in July 1999 to establish an agenda to promote civic engagement. What resulted was the "Presidents' Declaration on the Civic Responsibility of Higher Education," drafted by Thomas Ehrlich, a senior scholar at the Carnegie Foundation for the Advancement of Teaching, and Elizabeth Hollander. As the work was disseminated over the next few months, the document was signed by 539 college and university presidents. Of particular note is the following passage:

> We are encouraged that more and more students are volunteering and participating in public and community service, and we have all encouraged them to do so through curricular and co-curricular activity. *However, this service is not leading students to embrace the duties of active citizenship and civic participation.* We do not blame these college students for their attitudes toward the democracy; rather, we take responsibility for helping them realize the values and skills of our democratic society and their need to claim ownership of it. (Ehrlich and Hollander 1999, p. 2; original emphasis)

The Declaration underscored the failure of many community engagement or service-learning efforts to demonstrate any impact on civic outcomes such as voting or knowledge of political issues. It was a call for radical restructuring of the engagement movement around the formation of civic skills. Sadly, a follow-up project for which ACE agreed to take the lead never got off the ground.

That same year, another important document on engagement, "Returning to Our Roots: The Engaged Institution," was published by the Kellogg Commission on the Future of State and Land-Grant Universities, a group of 24 land-grant presidents. Pointing to "enrollment pressures . . . [and] a growing emphasis on accountability and productivity from trustees, legislators, and donors," the document defines engagement as redesigning core functions "to become even more sympathetic and productively involved with their communities, however community may be defined" (Kellogg Commission 1999, p. 9). The document outlines seven principals of engagement: responsiveness to communities, respect for partners, academic neutrality, accessibility, interdisciplinary work, coordination of institutional efforts, and the commitment of resources.

This conception of "engagement" stands in stark contrast to the Declaration's. There is no call here for a renewal of the "democratic spirit." Rather, the aim is to create a more responsive, less "ivory tower-ish" university. "Value neutral" engagement is an advantageous stance for avoiding messy entanglements in contentious local issues. It is also a markedly different vision than the Declaration's notion that faculty and administrators should step up as moral agents involved in public work. Indeed, the "engaged university" (as expressed in "Returning to our Roots") looks surprisingly like the traditional university. It is also the prevailing conception of "engagement" on many campuses today (Hartley and Soo 2009).

FROM CIVIC TO DEMOCRATIC ENGAGEMENT

The above account points to the significant role that networks have played in promoting the civic purposes of colleges and universities at the movement's inception and during its period of growth and eventual maturity. A central concern at each stage has been the issue of legitimacy. In the early years, the movement focused its attention on identifying and supporting early adopters, individuals inclined to lead the way with an innovation (Rogers 1995). This small group of individuals was passionately committed to transforming the academy. Drawing together like-minded individuals (who were often marginalized on their own campuses) helped establish an internal legitimacy among movement members. As the movement grew, this vanguard had to contend with greater challenges to its legitimacy. In doing so, it sought to promote engaged scholarship and service-learning, which had several advantages. First, both of these activities have counterparts long familiar to the academy—applied research and field placements, respectively. Second, foundations and the Corporation for National Service saw them as useful (and noncontroversial) innovations to support. As it reached maturity, the movement began distancing itself from more transformational efforts, as was evident in the shift from service-learning as a transformational project to service-learning in the service of the academic disciplines. As it softened the more radical edge of the movement, however, the question arose: Engagement for what? In a real sense, service-learning had moved from being the means of promoting civic engagement to an end in and of itself. (See Table 2.2.)

This is a pattern common to many social movements. Their ideals adapt and evolve in order to draw more people to them. Social movement theorists Della Porta and Diani explained: "An important precondition for the success of movements lies in their activists' ability to reformulate their own values and motivations in order to adopt them in the most efficient manner to the specific orientation of the sectors . . . which they wish to mobilize" (Della Porta and Diani 2006, p. 73). The advantage of pitching a large tent is that many people can fit inside. David Mathews, President of the Kettering Foundation, commented on civic engagement efforts: "Anyone who wants to join in seems welcome; there are few definitional barriers" (2005, p. 81). Without barriers, a movement will offend few; however, it risks inspiring no one.

Powerful movements balance the impulse to accommodate an ever-widening circle of participants with a clear conception of its purpose. This preserves a sense of identity for its core members, precisely the group most likely to expend energy for the cause (Marwell and Oliver 1993). This precise concern was highlighted at a recent Wingspread meeting that pointed to cultivating

TABLE 2.2   ROLE OF NETWORKS AT DIFFERENT STAGES

(Re)formation of the Movement	Struggle for Broad-Based Support	Maturity/Renewal
• Keeping the story alive • Identifying existing proponents and early adopters • Establishing internal legitimacy of the movement among supporters • Serving as a support group for individuals laboring in obscurity on their campuses • Forging a political coalition (around the issue of public service legislation) • Establishing a vanguard • Clarifying which activities might be undertaken in support of the goal	• Broadening support through disseminating information and training • Profiling best practices • Creating experts • Growth through local networking (state compacts) • Supporting institutional efforts through recognition • Demonstrating a "critical mass" through national conferences • Focusing on institutionalization of efforts in the core work of the academy • Providing multiple entry points and different rationales with which individuals could commit • Securing external support (e.g., foundations)	• Winnowing of the field (e.g., the demise of COOL) • Weeding out the "fringe" • Appealing to disciplines with service-learning (monograph series) • Using research to confirm efficacy of engagement • Alienating members of the transformational wing of the movement • Searching for a second act (e.g., *Calling the Question*; Kettering Meeting on the Future of Engagement) • Confronting difficulty in bridging networks to spur significant change • Bureaucratizing • Witnessing emergence of a mainstream conception of engagement

a new generation of engagement "champions" as a key task (Brukardt et al. 2004). The question before the movement now is whether an often ill-defined and rather conventional—even bland—conception of engagement will be adequate to the task of inspiring people to undertake the difficult transformational change our democracy needs.

What is required now is a return to first principles, with a fuller and more creative response to the question: What are the responsibilities of college and universities in our democracy? It is this question that in part inspired the meeting at the Kettering Foundation and gave rise to this book. The capacity for us to imagine a larger, democratic purpose is evident in the accounts of the authors represented here. But what is required is a movement beyond first-order change (the championing of discrete strategies) toward a richer and fuller conception of the academy in which multiple initiatives are directed at building an academy whose work strengthens our diverse democracy. That vision, discussed in detail in our concluding chapter, requires more than a collection of programs.

The ultimate measure of legitimacy of the civic engagement movement, as in any movement, comes from its ability to inspire people to collectively challenge a problematic status quo. This means more than the advancement of specific pedagogies. It means more than the maintenance or even proliferation of university-community partnerships. It means building strategic initiatives that confront injustice and relentlessly seek change through every democratic means possible. It means looking more broadly to work with people who are advancing issues that are of central importance to our democracy—efforts that seek to alleviate the legacies of racism and classism in order to forge a strong, diverse democracy—including student political activists (Rhodes 2009) and faculty members whose courses many not contain service-learning but that are intentionally designed to grapple with pressing real-world problems and advance critical thinking that leads to action. That is the kind of democratic civic engagement that will help the movement progress beyond the complacency of maturity toward renewal. It is what is required to inspire the active support of a new and ever-widening circle of people eager to join this important work.

NOTES

1. "New England's First Fruits" 1640.
2. http://www.yale.edu/about/history.html.
3. The data informing the account of the movement are two-fold: first, an analysis of periodic and archival materials from several associations and networks (American Association of Colleges and Universities, Campus Compact, Campus Outreach Opportunity League); and second, interviews with 123 individuals who led civic engagement efforts both nationally and on campuses.
4. Unattributed quotes are from interviews with movement leaders conducted by the author.
5. http://www.aacu.org/american_commitments/index.cfm.
6. Such debates continue today. As Denson observes, "There is not agreement within the service learning field that social justice ought to be an intended outcome of service learning participation" (Denson, Vogelgesang, and Sanchez 2005).
7. http://ualr.edu/about/index.php/home/history-and-mission/metropolitan.
8. http://quod.lib.umich.edu/m/mjcsl/about.html.
9. http://openjournals.libs.uga.edu/index.php/jheoe/about/editorialPolicies#focus AndScope.
10. Interview with Campus Compact senior staff member, September 8, 2006.
11. J. Saltmarsh, interview by the author, October 2, 2006.

REFERENCES

AAC&U. 1995a. *American Pluralism and the College Curriculum*. Washington, DC: American Association of Colleges and Universities.

———. 1995b. *The Drama of Diversity and Democracy: Higher Education and American Commitments*. Washington, DC: American Association of Colleges and Universities.

ACE. 1998. "ACE Conference Explores the Role of Colleges in Promoting Civic Responsibility." *Higher Education and National Affairs* 47, no. 1 (July): 3.

American Political Science Association. 1998. "A Call for Reactions and Contributions." Available at http://h-net.msu.edu/cgi-bin/logbrowse.pl?trx=vx&list=APSA-CIVED &month=9806&week=b&msg=HmrIsfd31GbBGXJ904AP6g&user=&pw.

Astin, A. W. 1995. "The Cause of Citizenship." *The Chronicle of Higher Education* (October): B1–B2.

———. 1998. "The Changing American College Student: Thirty-Year Trends, 1966–1996." *The Review of Higher Education* 21 (1): 115–135.

Astin, A. W., L. J. Sax, and J. Avalos. 2000. *Long-Term Effects of Volunteerism During the Undergraduate Years*. Los Angeles: Higher Education Research Institute, University of California.

Bloom, D., M. Hartley, and H. Rosovsky. 2006. "Beyond Private Gain: The Public Benefits of Higher Education. " In *International Handbook of Higher Education*, ed. P. G. Altbach and J. Forrest, 293–308. Dordrecht, The Netherlands: Kluwer Press.

Boyer, E. 1987. *College: The Undergraduate Experience in America*. New York: HarperCollins.

———. 1990. *Scholarship Reconsidered*. Princeton: Carnegie Foundation for the Advancement of Teaching.

Boyte, H., and E. Hollander. 1999. "Wingspread Declaration on Renewing the Civic Mission of the American Research University." Available at http://www.compact .org/initiatives/civic-engagement-at-research-universities/wingspread-declaration-on-the-civic-responsibilities-of-research-universities/.

Boyte, H. C., and N. N. Kari. 2000. "Renewing the Democratic Spirit in American Colleges and Universities." In *Civic Responsibility and Higher Education*, ed. T. Ehrlich, 36–59. Phoenix: Oryx Press.

Breneman, D. W. 1994. *Liberal Arts Colleges: Thriving, Surviving, or Endangered?* Washington, DC: Brookings Institution.

Brint, S. 2002. "The Rise of the 'Practical Arts.'" In *The Future of the City of Intellect*, ed. S. Brint, 231–259. Stanford, CA: Stanford University Press.

Brukardt, M. J., B. Holland, S. L. Percy, and N. Zimpher. 2004. *Calling the Question: Is Higher Education Ready to Commit to Community Engagement?* Milwaukee: Milwaukee Idea Office, University of Wisconsin.

Cawallader, M. L. 1982. "A Manifesto: The Case for an Academic Counterrevolution." *Liberal Education* 68 (4): 403–420.

Clifford, T. 1982. "Norman Campus Quiet, Students Differ from '60s Generation." *The Daily Oklahoman*, February 9.

Cochran, T. C. 1972. *Business in American Life: A History*. New York: McGraw-Hill.

Colby, A., T. Ehrlich, E. Beaumont, and J. Stephens. 2003. *Educating Citizens: Preparing America's Undergraduates for Lives of Moral and Civic Responsibility*. San Francisco: Jossey-Bass.

Crossland, F. E. 1980. "Learning to Cope with a Downward Slope." *Change* 12 (5): 18–25.

Della Porta, D., and M. Diani. 2006. *Social Movements: An Introduction* (2nd ed.). Oxford: Blackwell Publishing.

Delucchi, M. 1997. "'Liberal Arts' Colleges and the Myth of Uniqueness." *Journal of Higher Education* 68 (4): 414–426.

Ehrlich, T., and E. Hollander. 2000. "Presidents' Declaration on the Civic Responsibility of Higher Education." Providence: Campus Compact.

Eyler, J., and D. E. Giles Jr. 1999. *Where's the Learning in Service-Learning?* San Francisco: Jossey-Bass.

Gutmann, A. 1987. *Democratic Education*. Princeton: Princeton University Press.

Hartley, M. 2002. *A Call to Purpose: Mission-Centered Change at Three Liberal Arts Colleges*. New York: RoutledgeFalmer.

Hartley, M., and E. Hollander. 2005. "The Elusive Ideal: Civic Learning and Higher Education." In *Institutions of Democracy: The Public Schools*, ed. S. Fuhrman and M. Lazerson, 252–276. Oxford: Oxford University Press.

Hartley, M., and D. Soo. 2009. "Building Democracy's University: University-Community Partnerships and the Emergent Civic Engagement Movement. In *The Routledge Handbook of Higher Education*, ed. M. Tight, K. H. Mok, J. Huisman, and C. C. Morphew, 397–408. New York: Routledge.

Hollander, E. 1998. "Civic Education: Is Higher Ed Losing?" *Compact Currents* 12 (October–November): 2.

Hollander, E., and M. Hartley. 2000. "Civic Renewal in Higher Education: The State of the Movement and the Need for a National Network." In *Civic Responsibility and Higher Education*, ed. T. Ehrlich, 325–366. Phoenix: Oryx Press.

Keller, G. 1983. *Academic Strategy: The Management Revolution in Higher Education*. Baltimore: Johns Hopkins University Press.

Kellogg Commission on the Future of State and Land-Grant Universities. 1999. "Returning to Our Roots: The Engaged Institution." Washington, DC: National Association of State Universities and Land-Grant Colleges. Available at http://www.cpn.org/topics/youth/highered/pdfs/Land_Grant_Engaged_Institution.pdf.

Kendall, J. C. 1990. "Combining Service and Learning: An Introduction." In *Combining Service and Learning: A Resource Book for Community and Public Service* 1, ed. C. Kendall, 1–33. Raleigh, NC: National Society for Internships and Experiential Education.

Kezar, A. J., T. Chambers, and J. Burkhardt, eds. 2005. *Higher Education for the Public Good: Emerging Voices from a National Movement*. San Francisco: Jossey-Bass.

Knox, W. E., P. Lindsay, and M. N. Kolb. 1993. *Does College Make a Difference? Long-Term Changes in Attitudes and Activities*. Westport, CT: Greenwood Press.

Liu, G. 1996. *Community Service in Higher Education: A Decade of Development*. Providence: Providence College.

Marwell, G., and P. Oliver. 1993. *The Critical Mass in Collective Action: A Micro-Social Theory*. Cambridge: Cambridge University Press.

Mathews, D. 2005. "Listening to the Public." In *Higher Education for the Public Good: Emerging Voices from a National Movement*, ed. A. J. Kezar, T. Chambers, and J. Burkhardt, 71–86. San Francisco: Jossey-Bass.

Melucci, A. 1989. *Nomads of the Present: Social Movement and Individual Needs in Contemporary Society*. Philadelphia: Temple University Press.

National Commission on Civic Renewal. 1998. "A Nation of Spectators: How Civic Disengagement Weakens America and What We Can Do About It." College Park: University of Maryland.

"New England's First Fruits." 1640/1792. From the Collections of the Massachusetts Historical Society 1, 242–248.

Newmann, F. 2000. *Saving Higher Education's Soul*. Providence: The Futures Project: Policy for Higher Education in a Changing World.

Reuben, J. 1996. *The Making of the Modern University: Intellectual Transformation and the Marginalization of Morality*. Chicago: University of Chicago Press.

Rhodes, R. 2009. "Learning from Students as Agents of Social Change: Toward an Emancipatory Vision of the University." *Journal of Change Management* 9 (3): 309–322.

Rogers, E. 1995. *Diffusion of Innovations* (4th ed.). New York: Free Press.

Rudolph, F. 1962. *The American College and University: A History*. New York: Alfred A. Knopf.

Schneider, C. G. 2005a. "Liberal Education and the Civic Engagement Gap." In *Higher Education for the Public Good: Emerging Voices from a National Movement*, ed A. J. Kezar, T. Chambers, and J. Burkhardt, 127–145. San Francisco: Jossey-Bass.

———. 2005b. "Making Excellence Inclusive: Liberal Education and America's Promise." *Liberal Education* 91 (2): 6–17.

Singleton, S., C. A. Burack, and D. J. Hirsch. 1997. *Faculty Service Enclaves: A Summary Report*. Boston: University of Massachusetts.

Stanton, T. K., D. E. Giles Jr., and N. I. Cruz. 1999. *Service-Learning: A Movement's Pioneers Reflect on Its Origins, Practice, and Future*. San Francisco: Jossey-Bass.

Taylor, B. 1980. "Few Passions Now Stirred in Once-Radical Madison." *Boston Globe*, March 28.

Thelin, J. R. 2004. *A History of American Higher Education*. Baltimore: Johns Hopkins University Press.

Veciana-Suarez, A. 1983. "On Campus, Students Eye Bottom Line Materialism, Status Take Hold at Colleges." *Miami Herald*, October 5: 1A.

University of Wisconsin–Madison. 2006. "The Wisconsin Idea." Available at http://www.wisconsinidea.wisc.edu/history.html.

Zlotkowski, E. 1995. "Does Service-Learning Have a Future? *Michigan Journal of Community Service Learning* 2, no. 1 (Fall): 123–133.

CHAPTER 3

Democratic Transformation through University-Assisted Community Schools

LEE BENSON, IRA HARKAVY, AND JOHN PUCKETT

It is not possible to run a course aright when the goal itself is not rightly placed.

—Francis Bacon, *Novum Organum* (1620)

The philosophers have only *interpreted* the world, in various ways; the point is to *change* it.

—Karl Marx, *Theses on Feuerbach* (1845–1846; original emphasis)

In conception, at least, democracy approaches most nearly the ideal of all social organization; that in which the individual and the society are organic to each other.

—John Dewey, *The Ethics of Democracy* (1888)

Democracy must begin at home, and its home is the neighborly community.

—John Dewey, *The Public and Its Problems* (1927)

Democracy has been given a mission to the world, and it is of no uncertain character. I wish to show that the university is the prophet of this democracy, as well as its priest and its philosopher; that in other words, the university is the Messiah of the democracy, its to-be-expected deliverer.

—William Rainey Harper, *The University and Democracy* (1899)

Nothing is more conducive to innovation in social theory than collaboration on a complex practical problem.

—Paul Lazarsfeld and Jeffrey G. Reitz,
An Introduction to Applied Sociology (1975)

This chapter is based on four propositions. First, the radical democratic transformation of colleges and universities is crucial to the democratic transformation of America into a genuinely democratic society. In the opening decade of the twenty-first century, it seems to us nearly axiomatic that universities are the most influential institution in advanced societies. As William Rainey Harper, John Gardner, Ernest Boyer, and Derek Bok, among others, have noted, universities possess enormous resources (most significantly human resources), play a leading role in developing and transmitting new discoveries and educating societal leaders, and basically shape the schooling system.

Second, as it currently operates, the American higher educational system does not contribute to the development of democratic communities and schools. Among other deficiencies, American universities significantly contribute to a schooling system that is elitist and hierarchical.

Third, as John Dewey emphasized, participatory democratic schooling is mandatory for a participatory democratic society. Simply put, unless the schooling system, from pre-K through 20, is transformed into a participatory democratic schooling system, America will continue to fall far short of functioning as a decent, just, participatory democracy. The transformation of higher education is crucial to the transformation of the entire schooling system and the education of creative, caring, contributing democratic citizens.

Fourth, the key question is about implementation, that is, "What is to be done to create an effective, creative, progressive university civic engagement movement dedicated to the democratic transformation of American higher education, schooling, and society in general?" Needless to say, this is an exceedingly complex question, but unless we attempt to answer it—along with the even harder question of *how* to create such a movement for participatory democracy—the university civic engagement movement could become mired in endless disputation and academic (in the pejorative sense) debate, mirroring the dominant current academic culture.

In our book, *Dewey's Dream*, we proposed, through historical analysis and illustrations from more than twenty years of work with West Philadelphia schools and neighborhoods, that university-assisted community schools constitute the best practical means for democratically transforming universities, schools, and communities in order to develop participatory democracy. We discussed how these schools need to be developed democratically, involving community, school, and university partners within a university's local ecological system, as a means to develop neighborly, democratic, face-to-face communities.[1]

We also sketched how local efforts of this kind can be—and, in our case, have been—connected to national and global organizations and emerging movements. We offered these proposals primarily to stimulate democratic dialogue and generate counterproposals as to *how* to develop and advance a participatory democratic movement in order to develop a participatory democratic society. In this chapter we build on those arguments and also discuss some of the impediments to creating and sustaining effective uni-versity-assisted community schools. Providing a concrete example from our work, we suggest *how* those impediments might be reduced so that universi-ties can eventually realize what we view as their basic mission of contributing to an optimally democratic society through research, teaching, learning, and service.

UNIVERSITIES, DEMOCRATIC SCHOOLING, DEMOCRATIC COMMUNITIES, AND DEMOCRATIC SOCIETIES

Plato was the philosopher John Dewey most liked to read. Though Dewey admired Plato, their worldviews differed radically. We need only note two basic differences: Plato's worldview was aristocratic and contemplative, whereas Dewey's was democratic and activist. Despite their many differences, Dewey saw the great value of the basic ideas Plato had developed in *The Republic* concerning the complex relationships between education and society. To sum-marize Dewey's views on education after 1894, we quote a leading philoso-pher of education, Steven M. Cahn. According to Cahn, Dewey believed that

> philosophy of education was the most significant phase of philosophy. Charles Frankel once noted that for Dewey "all philosophy was at bottom social philosophy implicitly or explicitly." I would extend this insight and suggest that for Dewey all social philosophy was at bot-tom philosophy of education implicitly or explicitly. As he put it, "it would be difficult to find a single important problem of general philo-sophic inquiry that does not come to a burning focus in matters of the determination of the proper subject matter of studies, the choice of methods of teaching, and the problem of social organization and administration of the schools." [2]

Noting that other philosophers also emphasized the importance of edu-cation, Cahn quotes Kant's proposition that "the greatest and most difficult problem to which man can devote himself is the problem of education." Cahn then observes that he knows of

> only two major philosophers who exemplified this principle in their philosophical work: one was Dewey, the other was Plato. He too found it difficult to discuss any important philosophical problem without reference to the appropriateness of various subjects of study, methods of teaching, or strategies of learning. But while Dewey's philosophy of education rested on his belief in democracy and the power of scientific method, Plato's philosophy of education rest-ed on his belief in aristocracy and the power of pure reason. Plato proposed a planned society, Dewey a society engaged in continuous planning. Plato considered dialectical speculation to be the means

toward the attainment of truth; Dewey maintained that knowledge is only acquired through intelligent action. . . . Suffice it to say that John Dewey is the only thinker ever to construct a philosophy of education comparable in scope and depth to that of Plato.[3]

Like the ancient Greek philosopher, Dewey theorized that education and society were dynamically interactive and interdependent. It followed, therefore, that if human beings hope to develop and maintain a particular type of society or social order, they must develop and maintain the particular type of education system conducive to it; that is to say, if there is no effective democratic schooling system, there will be no democratic society.

It is critically important to emphasize another radical difference between Plato and Dewey. To implement his aristocratic philosophy of education and society, Plato created what can arguably, if loosely, be viewed as the world's first university: the remarkably influential Academy, whose elitist, idealist philosophy of education continues to dominate Western schooling systems to this day. Surprisingly, Dewey never saw what Plato saw so clearly, that universities invariably constitute by far the most strategic component of a society's schooling system.

Perhaps Dewey's greatest contribution was his emphasis on the primacy of the schooling system, not the economic, political, or media systems, during the twentieth century. Put another way, Dewey powerfully theorized that the schooling system would function as the strategic subsystem of the increasingly complex industrial and "postindustrial" societies produced by the post-1800 economic and communication revolutions. To use the term now in vogue, Dewey predicted that the school-based operations of "civil society" would become more important than the traditional functions performed by the state in solving "the difficult problems of life." Just as Dewey saw citizenship expanding to take on functions that were beyond the capacity of the state in an advanced capitalist society, he saw an expanded role for the school in preparing citizens to assume these functions.

Extending Dewey's observations, particularly in the twenty-first century, we contend that it is not the judicial, legislative, and administrative state, but rather the complex schooling system of American society—from early childhood centers to elite research universities—that (1) must function as the strategic subsystem of the society; (2) has performed that function poorly—in the past and present—at all levels; (3) must radically improve its performance, at all levels, if we hope to solve the problems of American life in the twenty-first century; and (4) can only be radically reformed if questions about its performance—in the past, present, and likely future—are given the highest priority by action-oriented researchers and administrators dedicated to advancing knowledge for "the relief of man's estate,"[4] which Francis Bacon long ago specified as the goal of science.

Higher educational institutions are, in our judgment, the strategic agent for the effective and democratic transformation of a society's schooling system. Simply put, the path toward effective democratic schooling and large-scale, significant, ongoing systemic change must run through American higher education, particularly the American research university. The research university's significance derives in part from its status as a particularly resource-rich and powerful local institution. More fundamentally, universities have arguably become the most influential institutions in the world. In 1990, Derek Bok, then president of Harvard, highlighted the growth in importance of universities since World War II:

> All advanced nations depend increasingly on three critical elements: new discoveries, highly trained personnel, and expert knowledge. In America, universities are primarily responsible for supplying two of these three ingredients and are a major source of the third. That is why observers ranging from Harvard sociologist Daniel Bell to editorial writers from the *Washington Post* have described the modern university as *the central institution in post-industrial society* [emphasis added]. . . .[5]

Bok did not explicitly emphasize, however, what we regard as the most critical reason for higher education's leadership role. As stated above, we think it axiomatic that the schooling system functions as the core subsystem—the strategic subsystem—of modern information societies. More than any other subsystem, it now influences the functioning of the societal system as a whole; it is the subsystem that, on balance, has the greatest "multiplier" effects, direct and indirect, short- and long-term. We think it equally axiomatic that universities function as the primary shapers of the overall American schooling system. The powerful role of research universities stems not only from their enormous prestige and power—they serve, in effect, as the reference group that defines and shapes the entire schooling system—but also from their role in educating teachers. In short, what universities do and *how* they do it, and what they teach and *how* they teach, have enormously complex, enormously far-reaching impacts on the entire schooling system and on society in general.

The idea that universities play the central role in shaping the schooling system, and therefore American democracy, inspired William Rainey Harper when he served as the first president of the University of Chicago (1892–1906). For Harper, the university was the "prophet," "the Messiah of the democracy." To realize in practice the promise of American democracy, Harper worked tirelessly to develop pedagogy as a university discipline of distinction and to make teaching at all levels a profession "equal to any other." In 1896, the year Dewey began the Laboratory School at Chicago, Harper enthusiastically proclaimed his "desire to do for the Department of Pedagogy what has not been undertaken in any other institution." Even more telling, when criticized by a university trustee for sponsoring a journal focused on pedagogy in precollegiate schools, Harper emphatically proclaimed, "As a university we are interested above all else in pedagogy."[6] Harper's devotion to pedagogy logically derived from two propositions central to his vision for the University of Chicago in particular and for American universities in general:[7]

1. "Education is the basis of all democratic progress. The problems of education are, therefore, the problems of democracy."[8]
2. More than any other institution, the university determines the character of the overall schooling system: "Through the school system, the character of which, in spite of itself, the university determines and in a larger measure controls . . . through the school system every family in this entire broad land of ours is brought into touch with the university; for from it proceeds the teachers or the teachers' teachers."[9]

The societal, indeed global, reach of universities also makes them particularly important partners in school-system and community-wide reform. In this era of global information and communication, local school systems are powerfully affected by the larger national and global schooling systems. But local changes cannot be sustained if they remain only local and unconnected to broader national and global developments. Significant systemic change not only must, therefore, be locally rooted and generated; it must also be part of a national/global movement for change. For that to occur, an agent is needed that can simultaneously function on the local, national, and global levels. Universities are that agent. They are simultaneously the preeminent local (they are embedded in their communities) and national/global (they operate within an increasingly interactive worldwide network) institutions.

William Rainey Harper brought John Dewey from the University of Michigan to Chicago in 1894. While Dewey was at the University of Chicago, Harper significantly helped him see the crucial role the schooling system must play in the development of a democratic American society. Unfortunately, Dewey's work on schools suffered severely from his failure to see what Harper saw so clearly, namely that the research university must constitute the primary component of a highly integrated (pre-K–post 16) schooling system that could potentially function as the primary agent of democracy in the world and in the United States in particular. As we noted earlier, Harper envisioned the university as the "prophet of democracy, its priest and its philosopher . . . the Messiah of the democracy, its to-be-expected deliverer."[10]

Democracy is the soul of America—its charter myth, its ultimate end-in-view. The American university, alas, has never played anything like the messianic democratic role Harper optimistically envisioned for it. But "the times they are a-changin'," and our work since 1985 has been strongly influenced by our own optimistic belief that Harper's vision may yet be realized. Does our optimistic belief show that we simply are suffering from a bad case of the delusional utopianism long characteristic of American progressives and leftists? As we hope to show, this is not the case.

Following Donald Kennedy's provocative lead in his book *Academic Duty*, we view American higher education today as in the early stages of its third revolution.[11] The first revolution, of course, occurred in the late nineteenth century. Beginning at Johns Hopkins in 1876, the accelerating adoption and uniquely American adaptation of the German model somewhat revolutionized American higher education. By the turn of the century, the American research university had essentially been created. The second revolution began in 1945 with Vannevar Bush's "endless [research] frontier" manifesto and rapidly produced the big science, Cold War, entrepreneurial university.[12] We believe that the third revolution began in 1989. The fall of the Berlin Wall and the end of the Cold War provided the necessary conditions for the "revolutionary" emergence of the democratic, cosmopolitan, engaged, civic university— the radically new type of "great university" that William Rainey Harper had prophesized would advance democratic schooling and achieve the practical realization of the democratic promise of America for all Americans.

The emergence of the new type of university a century after Harper had first envisioned it can be credibly explained as a defensive response to the increasingly obvious, embarrassing, and immoral contradiction between the status, wealth, and power of American higher education—particularly its elite research university component—and the pathological state of American cities. To paraphrase Oliver Goldsmith's late eighteenth-century lament for "The Deserted Village," while American research universities flourished in the late twentieth century as never before, "ill-fared the American city, to hastening ills a prey."[13]

If American research universities really were so great, why were American cities so pathological? After the Cold War ended, the contradiction became increasingly obvious, troubling, indefensible, and immoral. The manifest contradiction between the power and the performance of American higher education sparked the emergence of the truly (not simply rhetorically) engaged university and the growing acceptance of the proposition that power based on a great capacity for the integrated production and use of knowledge should mean responsible performance. In the aftermath of the Cold War, accelerating external and internal pressures forced research universities to recognize (very reluctantly) that they must—and could—function as moral/intellectual institutions simultaneously engaged in advancing universal knowledge, learning, and improving the well-being of their local geographic communities (i.e., the local ecological systems that powerfully affect their own health and functioning). We believe that after 1989, the combination of external pressure and enlightened self-interest spurred American research universities to recognize that they could, indeed must, function simultaneously as universal and local institutions of higher education—institutions not only *in* but *for* their local communities.

To reduce, if not avoid, misunderstanding, we emphasize that we view the "third revolution" as still in its very early stages. As the old academic joke has it, American universities constitute such remarkably fragmented, self-contradictory, internally competitive, and conflicted institutions that they tend to move with all the speed of a runaway glacier. But things are changing in the right direction. One indicator of positive change is the accelerating number and variety of universities and colleges (i.e., "higher eds," a less cumbersome term than "higher educational institutions" or "postsecondary institutions") that now publicly proclaim their desire to collaborate actively with their neighboring public schools and local communities. Predictably, to date, public proclamations of collaboration far surpass tangible, interactive, mutually respectful, and beneficial collaboration, but progress is being made.

To help accelerate progress to the point where major changes become firmly institutionalized and produce significant results, we call for action-oriented acceptance of this radical proposition: all higher eds should explicitly make solving the problem of the American schooling system a very high institutional priority; their contributions to its solution should count heavily both in assessing their institutional performance and in responding to their requests for renewed or increased resources and financial support. Actively helping to develop an effective, integrated, genuinely democratic pre-K through higher education schooling system, we contend, should become a primary mission of American universities and colleges.

Primary mission does not mean sole mission. Obviously, American higher eds now have—and will continue to have—important missions other than collaboratively helping to solve the problems of the American schooling system. If we had unlimited space, we would try to show in great detail how those other missions would benefit greatly from successful collaborative work on the schooling problem. Here we restrict ourselves to a barebones statement of two corollary propositions:

1. Solving the overall problem of the schooling system must begin with changes at the higher education level.
2. Solving the overall schooling-system problem would, in the long run, both directly (e.g., increased governmental and philanthropic support) and indirectly (e.g., more diverse and able student body and faculty) give higher eds much greater resources than they now have to carry out *all* of their important missions.

We concede that, in the short term, our proposed mission change would require higher eds to experience the trauma entailed by any attempt to radically change academic priorities, structures, and cultures. We are calling on these institutions to reallocate a very large share of their intellectual (among other) resources to the immediate improvement of their neighboring public schools and communities. Given their ferociously competitive "pure research" orientation, how in the world can we possibly expect universities to answer our call positively rather than contemptuously? Until the recent economic recession began to affect them, higher eds were not experiencing any real crisis. Why then should self-congratulatory, increasingly rich, prestigious, powerful, "successful" American research universities undertake the difficult job of trying to transform themselves into engaged civic institutions that accept reciprocal and mutually respectful collaboration with their local schools and communities as a priority for the new millennium? Particularly in light of the worsening global recession, they should try to do so for strong institutional reasons. If they succeed, they will be much better able than they are now to achieve their self-professed, traditional missions of advancing, preserving, and transmitting knowledge; and they will help produce the well-educated, cultured, truly democratic citizens necessary to develop and maintain a genuinely democratic society.[14]

To restate two core propositions that undergird our argument: We think it axiomatic that universities—particularly elite research universities with highly selective arts and sciences colleges—function as the primary shapers of the overall American schooling system. We think it equally axiomatic that, in the global era, the schooling system increasingly functions as the core subsystem—the strategic subsystem—of modern information societies. Contrary to the position taken by orthodox Marxist ideologists, for example, more than any other subsystem, it now influences the functioning of the societal system as a whole. Viewed systemically, the schooling system has the greatest "multiplier" effects, direct and indirect, short and long term.

To understate the case, developing the democratic, cosmopolitan, civic university dedicated to, actively engaged in, and pragmatically capable of solving the problem of the overall American schooling system will be extraordinarily hard. There is a great deal to think about and do. Among many other things, to fully develop that new type of American university will require countering and displacing the now-dominant big science, Cold War, entrepreneurial university strategy with a more compelling, morally inspiring, and intelligent one. Since 1985, we have been trying to contribute concretely to the complex process of developing such a strategy by following brilliant leads provided by William Rainey Harper, John Dewey, and many others. We have stood on their shoulders and consciously tried to integrate, realize, and progress beyond their combined visions.

University-Assisted Community Schools as a Practical Strategy to Achieve a Democratic Devolution Revolution

Since 1985, the University of Pennsylvania has engaged itself with its local public schools in a comprehensive school-community-university partnership that was initially known as the West Philadelphia Improvement Corps (WEPIC). In its nearly 25 years of operation, the project has evolved significantly, spawning a variety of related projects that engage Penn with public schools in West Philadelphia. From its inception, we designed Penn's work with WEPIC to forge mutually beneficial and respectful university-school-community partnerships. In recent years, we have begun to conceptualize that work in much broader terms, namely as part of a radical attempt to advance a "democratic devolution revolution."[15] It is from that lofty perch that an overview of Penn's work—and the work of many other higher educational institutions engaged with their local public schools—is best comprehended.

For nearly a generation, John Gardner, arguably the leading spokesperson for the "New Democratic, Cosmopolitan Civic University" (our term for it), thought and wrote about organizational devolution and the university's potential role. For him, the effective functioning of organizations required the planned and deliberate rather than haphazard devolution of functions:

> We have in recent decades discovered some important characteristics of the large-scale organized systems—government, private sector, whatever—under which so much of contemporary life is organized. One such characteristic—perhaps the most important—is that the tendency of such systems to centralize must be countered by deliberate dispersion of initiative downward and outward through the system. The corporations have been trying to deal with this reality for almost 25 years and government is now pursuing it. . . . What it means for government is a substantially greater role for the states and cities. And none of them are entirely ready for that role. . . . Local government must enter into collaborative relations with nongovernmental elements. . . . So how can colleges and universities be of help?[16]

Gardner powerfully extended the Harper-Dewey vision by proposing a multisided involvement in "contemporary life" for higher eds, including initiating community building, convening public discussions, educating public-spirited leaders, offering continuing civic and leadership seminars, and providing a wide range of technical assistance. The effective, compassionate, democratic devolution revolution we call for requires much more than practicing new forms of interaction among federal, state, and local governments and among agencies at each level of government; it requires, to use Gardner's phrase, "the deliberate dispersion of initiative downward and outward through the system." For Gardner, government integration by itself does not make meaningful change. New forms of interaction and alignment among the public, for-profit, and nonprofit sectors are also mandatory. Government must function as a collaborating partner, effectively facilitating cooperation among all sectors of society, including higher educational institutions, to support and strengthen individuals, families, and communities.[17]

To extend Gardner's observations about universities and colleges (and similar observations by such highly influential thinkers as Ernest Boyer, Derek Bok, Lee Shulman, and Alexander Astin), we propose a democratic devolution revolution.[18] In our proposed "revolution," government serves as a powerful catalyst and largely provides the funds needed to create stable, ongoing, effective partnerships. But government would function only as a second-tier deliverer of services, with higher eds, community-based organizations, unions, churches, other voluntary associations, school children and their parents, and other community members functioning as the first-tier operational partners. That is, various levels and departments of government would guarantee aid and significantly finance welfare services. Local personalized-care services, however, would actually be delivered by the third tier (private, nonprofit, voluntary associations) and fourth tier (personal—family, kin, neighbors, friends) of society. Government would not be primarily responsible for the delivery of services; it would instead have macro-fiscal responsibilities, including fully adequate provision of funds.

The strategy we propose requires creatively and intelligently adapting the work and resources of a wide variety of local institutions (e.g., higher eds, hospitals, faith-based organizations) to the particular needs and resources of local communities. It assumes, however, that universities and colleges, which simultaneously constitute preeminent international, national, and local institutions, potentially represent by far the most powerful partners, "anchors," and creative catalysts for change and improvement in the quality of life in American cities and communities.

Of course, for universities and colleges to fulfill their great potential and really contribute to a democratic devolution revolution, they will have to do things very differently than they do now. To begin with, changes in "doing" will require recognition by higher eds that, as they now function, they— particularly universities—constitute a major part of the problem, not a significant part of the solution. To become part of the solution, higher eds must devote themselves to the difficult task of becoming socially responsible, responsive, civic universities and colleges. To do so, they will have to radically change their institutional cultures and structures, democratically realign and integrate themselves, and develop a comprehensive, realistic strategy.

The major component of the neo-Deweyan strategy now being developed and slowly implemented by Penn focuses on developing university-assisted community schools designed to help educate, engage, activate, and serve all members of the community in which the school is located. The strategy assumes that community schools, like higher eds, can function as focal points to help create healthy urban environments, and that both universities and colleges function best in such environments. More specifically, the strategy assumes that, like higher eds, public schools can function as environment-changing institutions and can become the strategic centers of broadly based partnerships that genuinely engage a wide variety of community organizations and institutions. Since public schools "belong" to all members of the community, they should "serve" all members of the community. (No implication is intended that public schools are the only community places where learning and social organization take place; other "learning places" include libraries, museums, private schools, etc., and ideally, all of these places would collaborate.)

We contend that, more than any other institution, public schools are particularly well suited to function as neighborhood "hubs" or "centers" around which local partnerships can be generated and developed. When they play that innovative role, schools function as community institutions par excellence. They then provide a decentralized, democratic, community-based response to rapidly changing community problems. In the process, they help young people learn better, at increasingly higher levels, through action-oriented, collaborative, real-world problem solving.

For public schools to actually function as integrating community institutions, however, local, state, and national governmental and nongovernmental agencies must be effectively coordinated to help provide the myriad resources community schools need to play the greatly expanded roles we envision them playing in American society. How to conceive that organizational revolution, let alone implement it, poses extraordinarily complex intellectual and social challenges. But as Dewey argued, working to solve complex, real-world problems is the best way to advance knowledge and learning, as well as the general capacity of individuals and institutions to do that work.

We argue, therefore, that American universities should give the highest priority to solving the problems inherent in the cultural and organizational revolution we have sketched above. If universities were to do so, they would demonstrate in concrete practice their self-professed theoretical ability to simultaneously advance knowledge, learning, and societal well-being. They would then satisfy the critical performance test proposed in 1994 by the president of the State University of New York at Buffalo, William R. Greiner, namely that "the great universities of the twenty-first century will be judged by their ability to help solve our most urgent social problems."[19]

Since 1985, to increase Penn's ability to help solve America's most urgent social problems, we have worked to develop and implement the idea of university-assisted community schools. We emphasize "university-assisted" because community schools require far more resources than traditional schools and because we have become convinced that, in relative terms, universities constitute the strategic sources of broadly based, comprehensive, sustained support for community schools.

The idea we have been developing at Penn since 1985 essentially extends and updates John Dewey's theory that the neighborhood school can function as the core neighborhood institution—the neighborhood institution that provides comprehensive services, galvanizes other community institutions and groups, and helps solve the myriad problems communities confront in a rapidly changing world. Dewey recognized that if the neighborhood school were to function as a genuine community center, it would require additional human resources and support. But to our knowledge, he never identified universities as the (or even a) key source of broadly based, sustained, comprehensive support for community schools.

It is critical to emphasize, however, that the university-assisted community schools now being developed have a very long way to go before they can effectively mobilize the powerful, untapped resources of their communities, and thereby enable individuals and families to function as community problem solvers, as well as deliverers and recipients of caring, compassionate local services.

ACADEMICALLY BASED COMMUNITY SERVICE, THE NETTER CENTER, AND PENN'S DEVELOPMENT OF UNIVERSITY-ASSISTED COMMUNITY SCHOOLS IN WEST PHILADELPHIA

Following the brilliant leads provided by Harper, Dewey, Gardner, and others, we believe that, as is true of all American universities, Penn's highest, most basic, and most enduring responsibility is to help America realize in concrete practice the egalitarian promise of the Declaration of Independence: America will become an optimally democratic society, the path-breaking democratic society in an increasingly interdependent world, the exemplary democratic model for the improvement of the human condition. Once that proposition is granted, the question then becomes how can Penn best fulfill its democratic responsibility? We believe it can best do so by effectively integrating and radically improving the entire West Philadelphia schooling system, beginning with Penn but including all schools within West Philadelphia, the university's local geographic community.

Admittedly, the history of Penn's work with West Philadelphia public schools has been a process of painful organizational learning and conflict; we cannot overemphasize that we have made many mistakes and our understanding and activities have continually changed over time.[20] Moreover, Penn is only now beginning to tap its extraordinary resources in ways that could mutually benefit both Penn and its neighbors and result in truly radical school, community, and university change. Significantly, we have come to see our work as a concrete example of Dewey's general theory of learning by means of action-oriented, collaborative, real-world problem solving. Conceptualizing our work in terms of schools as the strategic components of complex urban ecological systems represented a major advance for us.

When we first began work on university-community relationships in 1985, we did not envision schools or universities as highly strategic components of urban ecological systems. What immediately concerned us was that West Philadelphia was rapidly and visibly deteriorating, with devastating consequences for Penn. Given that "present situation" (as Dewey would have phrased it), we asked, what should the university do? Committed to undergraduate teaching, we designed an Honors Seminar aimed at stimulating undergraduates to think critically about what Penn could and should do to remedy its "environmental situation." For a variety of reasons, the president of the university, Sheldon Hackney, himself a former professor of history, agreed to join us in hosting that seminar in the spring semester of 1985. The seminar's title suggests its general concerns: Urban University-Community Relationships: Penn–West Philadelphia, Past, Present, and Future as a Case Study.

When the seminar began, we didn't know anything about Dewey's community school ideas. We literally knew nothing about the history of community school experiments and had not given any thought to Penn working with public schools in West Philadelphia. For present purposes, we need not recite the process of trial, error, and failure that led us—and our students—to see that Penn's best strategy to remedy its rapidly deteriorating environmental situation was to use its enormous internal and external resources to help radically improve both West Philadelphia public schools and the neighborhoods in which they are located. Most unwittingly, during the course of the seminar's work, we reinvented the community school idea.

Put another way, during the seminar, we developed a strategy based on this proposition: universities can best improve their local environment if they mobilize and integrate their great resources, particularly the "human capital" embodied in their students, to help develop and maintain community schools that function as focal points for creating healthy urban environments.

As noted above, by their very nature, community schools engage in far more activities and serve far wider constituencies than do traditional neighborhood schools. To do all that successfully, however, a community school, serving a specific neighborhood, requires far more resources (broadly conceived) than does a traditional school serving the same neighborhood.

Once that problem was recognized, the service-learning that students had been performing in West Philadelphia schools helped us to see that the solution was to actively mobilize the great resources of universities like Penn to assist the transformation of traditional neighborhood schools into innovative community schools. And once that was seen, the concept of university-assisted community schools followed logically. From then on, the seminar concentrated on helping to develop and implement that concept in real-world practice. In effect, the highly complex problem that the seminar concentrated on solving became the problem of effectively mobilizing and integrating Penn's resources to help transform the traditional public schools of West Philadelphia into innovative community schools.

Over time, as students continually worked to develop and implement the concept of university-assisted community schools, the seminar evolved into an innovative service-learning program. Briefly, the program was based on collaborative, action-oriented community problem solving, which provided both Penn students and teachers, and students in West Philadelphia schools, "with a real motive behind and a real outcome ahead," to quote John Dewey's proposition about the conditions most likely to permit effective learning.[21]

Observing the work of our students and our partners in West Philadelphia community schools over a number of years led us to develop a key principle that has guided their thinking and practice in a wide variety of ways and situations. That principle can be formulated as follows: at all levels (K through 16 and above), collaborative, community-based, action-oriented service-learning projects, which by their nature innovatively depart from customary, teacher-dominated school routines, allow and encourage both teachers and students to participate democratically in school and classroom governance and functioning. Put another way, such projects create spaces in which school and classroom democracy can grow and flourish.

In our judgment, that general principle can be instrumental in inspiring and developing effective programs for democratic citizenship in a wide variety of schools (at all levels) and communities. It warrants careful consideration, we believe, by everyone engaged in trying to solve the complex problems inherent in education for democratic citizenship.

Over time, the seminar's increasingly successful work stimulated an accelerating number of "academically based community service" (ABCS) courses in a wide range of Penn schools and departments, developed and implemented under the auspices of the university's Netter Center for Community Partnerships. (For historical reasons that are unique to Penn, "academically based community service" is the term the university uses for what elsewhere is called "service-learning.") ABCS courses focus on action-oriented, community problem solving and the integration of research, teaching, learning, and service, as well as reflection on the service experience and its larger implications (e.g., why poverty, racism, and crime exist).

To date, approximately 160 such courses, working with schools and community organizations to solve strategic community problems, have been developed at Penn. Fifty-nine courses, across eight schools and twenty-one departments, involving over 1,500 Penn undergraduate and graduate students were offered during the 2007–2008 academic year. Over the past fifteen years, an increasing number of faculty members, from a wide range of Penn schools and departments, have revised existing courses, or have created new courses, to offer innovative curricular opportunities for their students to become active learners, creative real-world problem solvers, and active producers (as opposed to passive consumers) of knowledge. That relatively rapid growth has resulted largely from the organizational innovation described below.

In July 1992, the president of the university, Sheldon Hackney, created the Center for Community Partnerships. (The Center was renamed the Barbara and Edward Netter Center for Community Partnerships in 2007 in recognition of the generous term and endowment support provided by Barbara and Edward Netter.) To highlight the importance Hackney attached to the Center, he located it in the Office of the President and appointed Ira Harkavy as its director, while Harkavy continued to serve as director of the Penn Program for Public Service, created in 1988 in the School of Arts and Sciences. Symbolically and practically, the Center's creation constituted a major change in Penn's relationship with West Philadelphia and the city as a whole. In principle, by creating the Center, the university formally committed itself, as a corporate entity, to finding ways to use its enormous resources (e.g., student and faculty "human capital") to help improve the quality of life in its local community—not only in respect to public schools but also to economic and community development in general.

The Netter Center is based on the assumption that one highly effective and efficient way for Penn to simultaneously serve its enlightened institutional self-interest and to carry out its academic mission of advancing universal knowledge and educating students is to function as a truly democratic, cosmopolitan, engaged, civic university. It assumes that Penn's research and teaching should strongly focus on strategic universal problems—such as schooling, health care, and economic development—as these universal problems manifest themselves locally in West Philadelphia and the rest of the city. By focusing on strategic universal problems and effectively integrating general theory and concrete practice, as Benjamin Franklin advocated in the eighteenth century, Penn would improve symbiotically both the quality of life in its ecological community *and* its academic research and teaching.

The Netter Center is also based on the proposition that when Penn is creatively conceived as a community-engaged civic university, it constitutes, in the best sense, both a universal and a local institution of higher education. As we optimistically envisioned it functioning, the Center for Community Partnerships would constitute a far-reaching innovation in university organization. To help overcome the remarkably competitive fragmentation that had developed after 1945, as Penn became a very large research university, the Center would identify, mobilize, and integrate Penn's vast resources that could be used to help transform traditional West Philadelphia public schools into innovative community schools.

The emphasis on partnerships in the Center's name was deliberate: it acknowledged that Penn could not try to go it alone in West Philadelphia as it had been long accustomed to do. The creation of the Center was also significant internally. It meant that, at least in principle, the president of the university would have—and use—an organizational vehicle to strongly encourage all components of the university to seriously consider the roles they could appropriately play in Penn's efforts to improve the quality of its off-campus environment.

Implementation of that strategy accelerated after Judith Rodin became president in 1994. A native West Philadelphian and Penn graduate, Rodin was appointed in part because of her deeply felt commitment to improving Penn's local environment and to transforming Penn into *the* leading urban American university.[22]

IMPEDIMENTS TO DEVELOPING AND SUSTAINING UNIVERSITY-ASSISTED COMMUNITY SCHOOLS IN WEST PHILADELPHIA

Amy Gutmann, Penn's current president, is a distinguished political philosopher whose scholarly work has explored the role public schools and universities play in advancing democracy and democratic societies. In her inaugural address on October 15, 2004, President Gutmann unveiled a comprehensive Penn Compact designed to advance the university "From Excellence to Eminence." Although the compact's first two principles—increased access to a Penn education and the integration of knowledge—have significant implications for our discussion, the third principle is particularly relevant:

> The third principle of the Penn Compact is to engage locally and globally. No one mistakes Penn for an ivory tower. And no one ever will. Through our collaborative engagement with communities all over the world, Penn is poised to advance the central values of democracy: life, liberty, opportunity, and mutual respect. Effective engagement begins right here at home. We cherish our relationships with our neighbors, relationships that have strengthened Penn academically while increasing the vitality of West Philadelphia.[23]

Penn as an institution is now strongly oriented to advancing democratic, civic work.[24] Penn, of course, cannot become an institution dedicated to preparing a moral, engaged democratic citizenry with a set of disconnected programs, no matter how extensive. It must become a central organizing principle of the institution, embedded in its DNA, so to speak—and that is a primary goal of Gutmann's Penn Compact.

Even with partnerships dating back over twenty years with schools and communities in West Philadelphia, a developing and expanding critical mass of faculty and students involved in academically based community-service teaching and learning, and visible and sustained support from the Netter Center and from President Gutmann, serious impediments have prevented Penn from realizing the potential of university-assisted community schools in practice. These impediments have also had the general impact of slowing Penn's development as a truly democratic, cosmopolitan, engaged, civic university dedicated to realizing Franklin's original vision for the university to educate students with "an *Inclination* join'd with an *Ability* to serve Mankind, one's Country, Friends and Family [original emphasis]."[25] The impediments are not unique to Penn. To the contrary, they affect nearly all higher eds in the United States to some significant extent, and, therefore, need to be significantly reduced if the university civic engagement movement is to make progress and move to the next level in the years ahead.

In our judgment, the forces of Platonization, commodification, and disciplinary ethnocentrism, tribalism, and guildism stand as powerful impediments to the development of democratic university-school-community partnerships, particularly university-assisted community schools.

Platonization

Plato's elitist, idealist theory of schooling has had, and continues to have, incalculable day-to-day impacts on education and society. In part, the continuing extraordinary impact of Plato's antidemocratic theory on American democracy can be explained by John Dewey's failure to translate his own ideas into practical action.

Like Plato, Dewey theorized that education and society were dynamically interactive and interdependent. But their aims differed radically. Plato's philosophy of education aimed to achieve aristocratic order; Dewey's, to achieve democratic community. For Dewey, then, it followed that if human beings hope to develop and maintain a participatory democratic society, they must develop and maintain a participatory democratic schooling system.

Ironically, however, it was the philosophical idealist Plato who pragmatically created an influential Academy to implement his aristocratic philosophy of education and society, while the philosophical activist Dewey failed to work pragmatically to institutionalize his democratic philosophy of education and society, except by "lay preaching." That is, despite the historical example of Plato's Academy, Dewey flagrantly violated his own general theory of thinking and action. Perhaps too simply stated, as a result of Dewey's astonishing error, Plato's general theory of learning and knowledge—which argued for the great superiority of elegant "pure theory" and "pure science" compared to "inferior" real-world practice—and his elitist theory of governance are deeply embedded in the culture and structure of American colleges and universities.[26]

Indeed, the "dead hand" of Plato continues to shape American higher education, and through American higher education it shapes the entire schooling system. Yet, as we argue, the development of genuinely democratic community-university partnerships through democratic, collaborative, community problem solving can be an effective strategy for releasing the vise-like grip of Plato's dead hand.[27] "Overthrowing" Plato, however, would only achieve a partial victory. A clear and present danger to the democratic mission of higher education and to American democracy in general also comes from the forces of commodification (i.e., education for profit, students as customers, syllabi as content, academics as superstars).

Commodification

To discuss systematically the history of commodification in American higher education would require much more space than we have in this chapter. We merely note, therefore, that it was the Cold War and its extraordinarily complex consequences, direct and indirect, short and long term, that "redefined American science" and accelerated and deepened the commodification of American universities in powerful and, in our judgment, deeply disturbing ways.

To place that highly complex development in historical perspective, we cite Stuart Leslie's analysis that during the Second World War, to a far greater extent than during the First World War, universities had

> won a substantial share of the funds [going into wartime mobilization], with research and development contracts that actually dwarfed

those of the largest industrial contractors. . . . Vannevar Bush, the chief architect of wartime science policy and a strong advocate of university research, was the man behind the change.[28]

Bush engineered that change as director of the powerful wartime Office of Scientific Research and Development. Late in 1944, President Roosevelt, highly impressed by its accomplishments, asked Bush to draft a long-term plan for postwar science. Bush delivered his famous report *Science: The Endless Frontier* in 1945. General agreement exists that since 1945, that report has profoundly influenced America's science policy.[29] For our purposes, the chief importance of Bush's "Basic Science Manifesto" (our sardonic term for it) is that it rapidly produced what we have previously characterized as the big science, Cold War, entrepreneurial, commodified American research university system. Derek Bok brilliantly stigmatized this development in his book *Universities in the Marketplace* as the "commercialization of higher education."[30]

Perhaps the most important consequence of the commercialization of higher education is the devastating impact it has on the values and ambitions of college students. When universities openly and increasingly pursue commercialization, their behavior legitimizes and reinforces the pursuit of economic self-interest by students and contributes to the widespread sense that they are in college primarily to gain career skills and credentials. It would only belabor the argument to comment further on how student idealism and civic engagement diminish strongly when students see their universities abandon academic values and scholarly pursuits to function openly and enthusiastically as entrepreneurial, competitive, profit-making corporations. Commercialization also powerfully stimulates faculty members to celebrate and practice disciplinary ethnocentrism, tribalism, and guildism.

Disciplinary Ethnocentrism, Tribalism, Guildism

Disciplinary ethnocentrism, tribalism, and guildism strongly dominate American universities today and work against their efforts to implement what they promise rhetorically to do.[31] A few years ago, the postmodern literary theorist Stanley Fish provided us with a marvelous case in point. In his monthly column in the *Chronicle of Higher Education* (May 16, 2003), Professor Fish caustically attacked

> the authors of a recent book [Anne Colby, Thomas Ehrlich, Elizabeth Beaumont, and Jason Stephens], *Educating Citizens: Preparing America's Undergraduates for Lives of Moral and Civic Responsibility* (Jossey-Bass 2003). A product of the Carnegie Foundation for the Advancement of Teaching, the volume reports on a failure that I find heartening.[32]

The failure, according to the authors of *Educating Citizens*, is that under-graduate education does not provide "the kind of learning [college] graduates need to be involved and responsible citizens."[33] Why was that failure "heart-ening" to Professor Fish? Because, he insisted unequivocally, professors can-not possibly provide that kind of learning; nor should they attempt it. Their job is simply to teach what their disciplines call for them to teach and to try to make their students into good disciplinary researchers. Professors can't make their students "into good people and . . . shouldn't try." Indeed, for Fish, "emphasis on broader goals and especially on the therapeutic goal of 'per-sonal development' can make it difficult to interest students in the disciplinary training it is our job to provide."[34]

In effect, Professor Fish not only called on American academics to repudi-ate John Dewey and his democratic adherents, he called on them to repudi-ate Plato and his antidemocratic elitist adherents. Since Plato's philosophy of education, like Dewey's, gives its highest priority to making good citizens, according to the Fish doctrine of professorial responsibility, they both were completely wrong. As teachers, according to Fish, the only duty of professors is to teach their discipline; it emphatically does not require or permit them to try to make their students "into good people."

In a perverse way, Fish's attack on the authors of *Educating Citizens* actu-ally performed a valuable function. It splendidly illuminated what might be called the "disciplinary fallacy" afflicting American universities, namely the fallacy that professors are duty-bound only to serve the scholastic interests and preoccupations of their disciplines and have neither the responsibility nor the capacity to help their universities keep their longstanding promises to pre-pare "America's Undergraduates for Lives of Moral and Civic Responsibility." In effect, Professor Fish baldly asserts what most professors now believe and practice but tend not to admit openly. This belief and practice also tend to produce disciplinary isolation, or "siloization," which severely inhibits the interdisciplinary cooperation and integrated specialization necessary to solve significant, highly complex, real-world problems.[35]

REDUCING IMPEDIMENTS TO DEVELOPING AND SUSTAINING UNIVERSITY-ASSISTED COMMUNITY SCHOOLS IN WEST PHILADELPHIA

Having briefly identified the impediments that prevent Penn and other higher eds from developing democratic university-assisted community schools, we turn now to the really hard, really significant, question: What is to be done to release higher education from the dead hand of Plato and the live hands of commodification and the disciplinary fallacy? More specifically, what is a prac-tical strategy to reduce these impediments and help American higher education overthrow Plato and institute Dewey, reject commodification and disciplinary guildism, and practically realize its democratic mission? In our view, the first step is to clarify and even redefine the purpose of undergraduate education.

Refocusing the Ends of Undergraduate Education

In the foreword to *Educating Citizens*, Lee Shulman, President of the Carnegie Foundation for the Advancement of Teaching (the book's publisher) emphasized the crucial role colleges play in the development of the virtues and understanding vital for democratic citizenship. Observing that a democratic society requires an "educated citizenry blessed with virtue as well as wisdom," Shulman hailed the book's demonstration that achieving the requisite

> combination of moral and civic virtue accompanied by the development of understanding occurs best when fostered by our institutions of higher education. It does not occur by accident, or strictly through early experience. Indeed, I argue that there may well be a critical period for the development of these virtues, and that period could be the college years. During this developmental period, defined as much by educational opportunity as by age, students of all ages develop the resources needed for their continuing journeys through adult life.[36]

Shulman's astute observation helps us see the important, diverse roles that colleges play in the lifelong, all-encompassing development of the different types of personnel who directly and indirectly control and operate the American schooling system. If their formative years at college neither contribute to their own development as democratic citizens nor concretely demonstrate to them how schools can function to produce democratic citizens, they will necessarily reproduce what they have learned—more precisely, failed to learn—in college. As a result of that disastrously flawed reproductive process, the schooling system will be incapable of developing an effective program for democratic citizenship. Put another way, we agree with Schulman that American colleges constitute the strategically important component of American universities when their goal is to help develop an American schooling system capable of producing students who possess the set of attributes necessary to function as democratic citizens.

We have, for example, devoted lots of thought and hard work to the question of *how* best to create a democratic classroom. Besides trying to function more "as a guide on the side" than a "sage on the stage," each of us has encouraged our students to work in collaborative groups with community members on community-identified and societal problems that are of deep personal interest. In effect, we have been trying to put into practice Dewey's insight that individuals learn best when they are driven by "a real motive behind and a real outcome ahead." Moreover, Lee Benson and Ira Harkavy have organized their seminars, including a seminar on University-Community Relationships they have cotaught since 1985, so that relatively early in the semester students and faculty in the seminar collaboratively design the syllabus and take an increasing (and, over time, the primary) responsibility for the organization and operation of the seminar itself. We cannot describe here the detailed steps, both useful and "false," we and our colleagues have taken to help advance genuinely democratic learning at Penn, including in the seminars we teach. Suffice it to say that, although we believe we have made progress, particularly during the past five or so years, we have a very long way to go to realize Dewey's democratic vision in practice.

What more specific steps might help engage Penn, as well as other universities, to embrace this goal actively as well as rhetorically? Two of these steps are described below.

Act Locally and Democratically

In her edited volume *Building Partnerships for Service-Learning*, Barbara Jacoby and her associates emphasize that creating effective, democratic, mutually beneficial, mutually respectful partnerships should be a primary, if not *the* primary, goal for service-learning in the first decades of the twenty-first century. Jacoby calls on colleges and universities to focus their attention on improving democracy and the quality of life in their local communities.[37] Here she is echoing one of John Dewey's most significant propositions: "Democracy must begin at home, and its home is the neighborly community."[38] Democracy, Dewey emphasized, has to be built on face-to-face interactions in which human beings work together cooperatively to solve the ongoing problems of life. In effect, Jacoby and her associates have updated Dewey and advocated this proposition: Democracy must begin at home, and its home is the engaged neighborly college or university and its local community partner.

The benefits of a local community focus for college and university civic engagement programs are manifold. Ongoing, continuous interaction is facilitated through work in an easily accessible local setting. Relationships of trust, so essential for effective partnerships and effective learning, are also built through day-to-day work on problems and issues of mutual concern. In addition, the local community also provides a convenient setting in which a number of service-learning courses, community-based research courses, and related courses in different disciplines can work together on a complex problem to produce substantive results. Work in a college or university's local community, since it facilitates interaction across schools and disciplines, can create interdisciplinary learning opportunities. And finally, the local community can function as a democratic real-world learning site in which community members and academics pragmatically determine whether the work is making a real difference, and whether both the neighborhood and the institution are better as a result of common efforts.

Since our work began more than twenty-five years ago, we have devoted particular attention to developing democratic, mutually beneficial, mutually respectful partnerships between Penn and schools and communities in

West Philadelphia/Philadelphia. Over time we have come to conceptualize the Netter Center for Community Partnerships' work to develop university-assisted community schools as an ongoing, communal, participatory action research project designed to contribute simultaneously to the improvement of West Philadelphia and to Penn's relationship with West Philadelphia, as well as to the advancement of learning and knowledge. As an institutional strategy, communal participatory action research differs significantly from traditional action research. Both research processes are directed toward problems in the real world, are concerned with application, and are participatory; but they differ radically in the degree to which they are continuous, comprehensive, and beneficial both to the organization or community studied and to the university.

For example, traditional action research is exemplified in the efforts developed by the late William Foote Whyte, Davydd Greenwood, and their associates at Cornell University to advance industrial democracy in the worker cooperatives of Mondragón, Spain.[39] Its considerable empirical and theoretical significance notwithstanding, the research at Mondragón is not at all an institutional necessity for Cornell. By contrast, the University of Pennsylvania's enlightened self-interest is directly tied to the success of its research efforts in West Philadelphia—hence its emphasis on, and continuing support for, communal, participatory action research. In short, proximity to an easily accessible site and a focus on problems that are institutionally significant to the university encourage sustained, continuous research involvement. Put another way, strategic community problem-solving research tends strongly to develop sustained, continuous research partnerships between a university and its local community.

Given its fundamental democratic orientation, the Netter Center's participatory action research project has worked toward achieving higher levels of participation by community members in problem identification and planning, as well as in implementation. To put it very euphemistically, this has not been easy to do. Based on decades of Penn's destructive action and inaction involving the local community, university-community conflicts take significant effort and time to reduce.[40] The Center's work with university-assisted community schools has focused on health and nutrition, the environment, conflict resolution and peer mediation, community performance and visual arts, school and community publications, technology, school-to-career programs, and reading improvement. Each of these projects almost inevitably varies in the extent to which it engages and empowers public school students, teachers, parents, and other community members in each stage of the research process. Though it has a long way to go before it actually achieves its goal, the Center's overall effort has been consciously democratic and participatory—to genuinely work *with* the community, not *on* or *in* it.

As university-assisted community schools and related projects have grown and developed, and as concrete positive outcomes for schools and neighborhoods have continued to occur, community trust and participation have increased. It would be terribly misleading, however, if we left the impression that town-gown collaboration has completely—or even largely—replaced the town-gown conflicts that characterized Penn-community relationships before 1985. It has not.

Penn's engagement with West Philadelphia schools and neighborhoods has certainly come a long way since 1985. But Penn still has a far distance to travel before it radically changes its hierarchical culture and structure and truly uses its enormous resources to help transform West Philadelphia into a democratic, cosmopolitan, neighborly community and multidimensional asset for a major university. Stated directly, we do not think we have largely solved the problem of developing and implementing the practical means needed to realize Dewey's theory of participatory democracy. We are well aware that we are a long way from having done so. As noted above, however, we have found that working with the community to solve strategic community-identified problems is a powerful means for advancing ongoing, increasingly democratic relationships between Penn and schools and communities in West Philadelphia.

Focus on Significant, Community-Based, Real-World Problems

To Dewey, knowledge and learning are most effective when human beings work collaboratively to solve specific, strategic, real-world problems. "Thinking," he wrote, "begins in . . . a *forked road* situation, a situation which is ambiguous, which presents a dilemma, which poses alternatives [original emphasis]."[41] A focus on universal problems (such as poverty, unequal health care, substandard housing, hunger, and inadequate, unequal education) as they are manifested locally is, in our judgment, the best way to apply Dewey's brilliant proposition in practice. To support our position, we turn to a recent example from Penn's work with West Philadelphia.

REDUCING IMPEDIMENTS AND DEVELOPING UNIVERSITY-ASSISTED COMMUNITY SCHOOLS IN PRACTICE: A BRIEF CASE STUDY

In a number of other publications, the three of us and our colleague Matthew Hartley have described how a focus on the problem of improving health care in a specified school and community resulted in a comprehensive integration of Penn resources and the development of the most successful university-assisted community school in West Philadelphia, Sayre High School.[42] The work with the Sayre school and its community to create and operate a large-scale health promotion and disease prevention program continues to be a particularly powerful example of the benefits that can result when a university and its neighbors work together to solve a complex, real-world, community-identified problem.[43] For the purposes of this chapter, however, we think it best to briefly describe another example: our work to help improve community planning and design with West Philadelphia High School (WPHS) students and with community members residing within the boundaries of the school's catchment area.

Since the summer of 2005, West Philadelphia residents from diverse backgrounds, including John Puckett and Elaine Simon, director of the university's Urban Studies Program, have organized to establish a new West Philadelphia High School, to be composed of small theme-based academies located on a quiet green-space campus. This organizing effort has led to the School District of Philadelphia's designation of a site and completion of an architectural plan for a new facility, which is scheduled to open in the fall of 2011.

Each semester Puckett and Simon teach a seminar on "Schools and Community Development," which engages Penn undergraduates and WPHS students and teachers in collaboratively planning and implementing an urban studies academy. The academy is now being developed at the existing high school for transfer to the new high school in 2011. The seminar's joint activities are defined as "public work," as they engage groups from different social and economic backgrounds to accomplish shared goals for neighborhood planning and design, a decidedly public purpose.[44] For the high school students these activities are also academic, involving higher-order analytic and communication skills needed to solve the problem of what West Philadelphia should be and do in the future. In the process, the students contribute to the construction of the high school as a "community-centered school," a goal advocated by the Philadelphia Student Union and the community organizing team. For the university, this initiative produces not only tangible intellectual benefits for Penn undergraduates—for example, "a first-hand contact with actualities" (to use John Dewey's apt phrase) and a set of theoretical lenses to interpret that experience—but also centers on a real-world universal problem whose resolution activates interschool, interdepartmental, and interdisciplinary cooperation at Penn—and advances the idea of "One University."

Penn is perhaps the only major American university where all of its schools and colleges are located on a contiguous urban campus. In the early 1970s, Martin Meyerson, then the newly appointed president of the university, emphasized the extraordinary intellectual and social benefits that would result if the university took optimum advantage of the ease of interaction that a single campus location provides. To realize those benefits, he called for implementation of a "One University" organizational realignment—in which Penn would be characterized by intellectual collaboration and synergy across departments, divisions, colleges, and schools that would result in significant advances in knowledge and human welfare.

That kind of radical realignment, of course, is much easier said than done. In practice, overcoming Penn's disciplinary fragmentation and conflict, narrow specialization, bureaucratic barriers, and what Benjamin Franklin stigmatized in 1789 as "ancient Customs and Habitudes,"[45] proved enormously difficult to achieve; the "One University" idea essentially remained an idea, not a program of action. We are convinced, however, that it is possible to resurrect and realize the "One University" idea in practice through working to implement solutions to highly complex community-identified problems (such as improving community health care and designing and developing an effective urban high school) that require interschool and interdisciplinary collaboration.

The following chronology briefly explains the progress of the high school planning initiative and the immediate background of the seminar.

Meeting throughout the late summer and fall of 2005, a large citizens' group called the "Plenary," which included some 180 West Philadelphia residents, teachers, and students, deliberated democratically (and often heatedly!) to draft a proposal to create a "new" West Philadelphia High School. The new school would replace the existing antiquated structure at Forty-sixth and Walnut streets, a neo-Gothic edifice that has been in continuous operation since 1912, and since the 1970s has been racially segregated and neglected by the city. Eric Braxton, founding director of the Philadelphia Student Union, and a small cadre of WPHS students gave informed presentations to the Plenary regarding small theme-based high schools they had visited in cities such as New York, Oakland, and Hartford. The Plenary subsequently backed the idea of replacing "the old West" with a set of small high schools or academies, each to be organized around a particular theme.

Completing the initial community-side planning for the new high school in December 2005, the Plenary then designated a smaller working group named the "Sustainability Circle" (later renamed the "West Philadelphia High School Community Partners") to fine-tune the general proposal and to work out the themes for each academy. Suggested by the Student Union and endorsed by a vote of the Sustainability Circle, an urban studies academy became part of the proposal in the summer of 2006. Throughout 2006 and into 2007, the Sustainability Circle worked on the final proposal and vigorously lobbied School District CEO Paul Vallas and the city's School Reform Commission (the School District's appointed governing board); the high school's neighboring community associations in Walnut Hill, Spruce Hill, and Garden Court; and the area's local politicians—Councilwoman Jannie Blackwell, State Representative Jim Roebuck, and Congressional Representative Chaka Fattah.

In the spring of 2007, the longstanding crisis of malign neglect at West Philadelphia High School erupted in student assaults on teachers, incidents of arson, and other building-clearing disruptions, underscoring the virtual collapse of education in this under-resourced, badly failing comprehensive high school. To stabilize the situation, Vallas removed the principal and brought in an interim leadership team. Next, responding to heavy pressure from the Sustainability Circle, Vallas's staff appointed an "executive committee" with a twofold charge: (1) to launch concrete plans to support the implementation of four theme-based "academies" at the existing high school in the fall of

2007, and (2) to interview principal candidates and to recommend up to three names to the School District's chief academic officer. This executive committee was broadly representative, including the School District, the Walnut Hill and Garden Court community associations, the Student Union at WPHS, two teachers, community members, the Home and School Association, and a Penn faculty member (John Puckett). The committee was chaired by the head of the Secondary School Division and facilitated by a consultant to the School District. In June 2007, at the end of this process, Saliyah Cruz, a dynamic African American applicant, was appointed the new principal of West Philadelphia High School. Puckett, Simon, and Richard Redding, director of community planning at the Philadelphia City Planning Commission, with the approval of the Sustainability Circle and Principal Cruz, organized EDUC 410/URBS 327, an academically based community service seminar to provide on-site planning support and implementation strategies for the new Urban Studies Academy (URBSA).

In the fall of 2007 three new academies opened at WPHS: URBSA, CAPA (Cultural and Performing Arts), and Business/Technology. (A previously existing entity, the Automotive Academy, is located in a separate building on Hansen Street, a block west of WPHS; "Auto" will remain on Hansen Street after the new high school opens in 2011.) URBSA start-up projects in 2007–2008 included, among others, the publication and public presentation of a plan to redesign and rehabilitate a vacant lot at Forty-ninth and Chancellor Streets. For this project, the Penn students in EDUC 410/URBS 327 taught their high school counterparts principles of scale-modeling, which the West students applied to produce mathematically precise designs for a vest-pocket park on the site. At a celebratory picnic held with the Penn students at the end of the spring semester, the West students voted on the best design features of their collective work to be incorporated into the final plan. This project was advised by Michael Nairn, a landscape architect who teaches in the Urban Studies Program and lives in West Philadelphia, and it was carried out in conjunction with the West Philadelphia Enterprise Center Community Development Corporation (TEC-CDC), which served as a "client" for the West students. (Exemplifying the web of school-community-university cooperation supporting this effort, Gabe Mandujano, director of the TEC-CDC, a 2005 Penn graduate with a dual degree from Wharton and Urban Studies, a former Marshall Scholar, and a former student of ours, mediated the seminar's relationship with the Walnut Hill neighborhood, where the project was based.) The West students wrote and digitally designed the booklet that includes the final plan for the project, which Nairn produced professionally, based on the students' own drawings. Residents of the two blocks adjacent to the vacant lot have embraced the project, which puts a benign, neighborly face on the high school after years of nonengagement.

It is important to note the problem-focused orientation of EDUC 410/ URBS 327: Its commitment is to provide a continuous flow of new ideas and resource support to the URBSA. In addition to the activities just described,

Penn students located and annotated resources (books, articles, and curriculum guides) for three new courses that were introduced in the URBSA in fall 2008: The American City, Urban Sociology, and Neighborhood Planning and Design. In fall 2008, the seminar assisted a project in the new Neighborhood Planning and Design course, taught by Neil Geyette, the new URBSA coordinator and the teacher with whom the Penn team had worked previously; this was a research and community organizing project to address the problem of a vacant, delinquent, blighted apartment building adjacent to the high school. With Puckett and Simon, John Landis, chair of Penn's Department of City and Regional Planning, and Domenic Vitiello, an assistant professor in the department, provided a summer institute to help the URBSA teachers plan the components of Geyette's course and to brainstorm interdisciplinary activities that would link their own courses to Geyette's.[46]

To briefly summarize, the West Philadelphia High School initiative stands on a foundation of school, community, and university cooperation. The community problem-solving orientation of the EDUC 410/URBS 327 seminar, and the interschool/interdepartmental/ interdisciplinary relationships (Graduate School of Education, School of Arts and Sciences, School of Design) the seminar activates, illustrate fundamental propositions of the idea and strategy of "One University."

CONCLUSION

Although we have focused on the efforts at Penn, we believe this strategy holds promise for all institutions of higher learning. Indeed, many have already made significant commitments to developing university-assisted community schools, including the University of Dayton, University of New Mexico, Indiana University–Purdue University Indianapolis (IUPUI), and University of Oklahoma–Tulsa. We have learned, and continue to learn, a great deal from these and other universities and their school and community partners that we have applied to our work in West Philadelphia.

When institutions of higher learning give very high priority to actively solving strategic, real-world, community-identified problems in their local communities, a much greater likelihood exists that they will significantly advance learning, research, teaching, and service and thereby simultaneously reduce the dysfunctional "ancient Customs and Habitudes" that impede the development of mutually beneficial, democratic university-school-community partnerships. More specifically, by focusing on solving universal problems that are manifested in their local communities, institutions of higher learning will be better able to realize what we view as their basic mission of contributing to an optimally democratic society. Even more specifically, they will be able to translate the theoretical advantages of the "One University" idea into practical action and help create the university-assisted community schools, which, as this chapter contends, is one of the best ways to help develop democratic students, K through age twenty, and thereby significantly contribute to the development of democratic schools, democratic universities, and a democratic American Good Society in the twenty-first century.

NOTES

1. Benson, Harkavy, and Puckett 2007.
2. See Cahn 1981, pp. xvi–xvii. Cahn quotes from John Dewey's "The Determination of Ultimate Values or Aims through Antecedent or A Priori Speculation or through Pragmatic Inquiry."
3. Cahn 1981, pp. xvii–xviii.
4. For an insightful analysis of Bacon's conception of science, see Rossi 1996, pp. 25–28.
5. Bok 1990.
6. Quoted in White 1977, p. 15. For our views on the Harper-Dewey relationship at the University of Chicago, see Benson and Harkavy 2000, pp. 174–196; and Benson and Harkavy 1999, pp.14–20.
7. For Harper's view of the university as the "Messiah" of democracy, see his 1899 address in Harper 1905, pp. 1–34. See also the highly insightful study of Harper and the University of Chicago in Wind 1987.
8. Harper 1905, p. 32.
9. Ibid., p. 25.
10. Ibid., p. 12.
11. Kennedy 1997, pp. 265–288, 299.
12. For a highly perceptive, devastatingly critical analysis of Bush's report *Science: The Endless Frontier*, see Stokes 1997.
13. Goldsmith 1910, p. 24.
14. For an illuminating discussion of the American university's democratic mission, see Anderson 1993 and Anderson 1997, pp. 111–130. See also Harkavy 1999, pp. 7–24.
15. Discussion of the concept of a democratic devolution revolution is found in testimony by Harkavy (U.S. Congress 1997).
16. Gardner 1998.
17. Ibid.
18. See Astin 1997, pp. 207–223; Bok 1990, passim; Boyer 1994, p. A48; and Schulman 1997, pp. 151–173.
19. Greiner 1994, p. 12.
20. For an illuminating discussion of the concept of organizational learning, see Whyte 1991, pp. 237–241.
21. Dewey 1991, p. 12.
22. Rodin 2007.
23. Gutmann 2004.
24. Benson, Harkavy, and Puckett 2007.
25. Franklin, "Proposals Relating to the Education of Youth in Pennsilvania [*sic*]," reprinted in Best 1962, pp. 150–151.
26. Benson and Harkavy 2000, pp. 174–196.
27. Harkavy and Benson 1998, pp. 11–19.

28. Leslie 1993, p. 6.

29. Leslie 1993.

30. Bok 2003.

31. The discussion of disciplinary ethnocentrism, tribalism, and guildism, as well as the sections that follow, were initially developed in Benson and Harkavy 2003.

32. Fish 2003, p. C5.

33. Colby, Ehrlich, Beaumont, and Stephens 2003, p. 7.

34. Fish 2003, p. C5.

35. In its 1982 report, *The University and the Community*, the Organization for Economic Development (OECD) describes the inhibiting impacts of university "siloization" and narrow "departmentalism" on fostering the interdisciplinary scholarship necessary for solving real community problems. The following epigraph, which begins part 3, chapter 2, neatly captures the report's argument: "Communities have problems, universities have departments." See Center for Educational Research and Innovation 1982, p. 127.

36. Schulman 2003, p. viii.

37. Jacoby 2003.

38. Dewey 1954, p. 213.

39. Greenwood and Santos 1992; W. F. Whyte and K. K. Whyte 1988.

40. Harkavy and Puckett 1991, pp. 10–25.

41. Dewey 1990, p. 11.

42. See, for example, Benson, Harkavy, and Hartley 2005, pp. 185–216; Benson, Harkavy, and Puckett 2007; Harkavy 2006, pp. 5–37.

43. The benefits for Sayre High School included achieving Adequate Yearly Progress (AYP), according to No Child Left Behind (NCLB) measures, by meeting thirteen out of thirteen AYP targets in 2006–2007. For example, student attendance increased from 75 percent to 85 percent from the 2005–2006 to 2006–2007 school year. Sayre is one of only five neighborhood high schools (of a total of more than thirty citywide) that made AYP in 2007. The Sayre-Penn Partnership also received recognition for its work, including a School District of Philadelphia Best Practices for Effective Community Partnerships Award (May 2008) and the Coalition for Community School's National Award for Excellence (June 2007). Also, Penn State nurse practitioners and Sayre students received first prize in the research poster category at the 24th Annual Pediatric Nursing Conference in June 2008 for their work assessing growth and diabetes risk factors in the school and the community.

44. For public work theory and citizenship, see Boyte 2004; and Boyte and Kari 1996.

45. See Reinhold 1968, p. 224.

46. During the more than two years when this chapter was under review and later in press, the Schools and Community Development seminar, in conjunction with an undergraduate class in the Penn School of Design, provided technical support for a branding project inside the high school, for which Geyette's students, on the basis of schoolwide surveys, designed the logos and banners for each academy. The most recent project is a plan submitted by Geyette's students for the partial rehabilitation of a large vacant property that stands in the shadow of the city's newly renovated Market Street Elevated station at Forty-sixth and Market streets. Two-thirds of the CDC-controlled lot is already under development for community and commercial gardening. The West students' contribution is a digitally rendered landscape design—supported by their historical, marketing, and stakeholder research—for a park that would front the gardening components on the site.

REFERENCES

Anderson, Charles W. 1993. *Prescribing the Life of the Mind.* Madison: University of Wisconsin Press.

———. 1997. "Pragmatism, Idealism, and the Aims of Liberal Education." In *Education and Democracy,* ed. Robert Orrill, 111–130. New York: College Board.

Astin, Alexander W. 1997. "Liberal Education and Democracy: The Case for Pragmatism." In *Education and Democracy,* ed. Robert Orrill, 207–223. New York: College Board.

Benson, Lee, and Ira Harkavy. 1999. "University-Assisted Community Schools as Democratic Public Works." *Good Society* 9 (2): 14–20.

———. 2000. "Integrating the American System of Higher, Secondary, and Primary Education to Develop Civic Responsibility." In *Civic Responsibility and Higher Education,* ed. T. Ehrlich, 174–196. Phoenix: Oryx.

———. 2003. "Informal Citizenship Education: A NeoPlatonic, NeoDeweyan, Radical Program to Develop Democratic Students, K–16." Discussion paper, University of Pennsylvania, July.

Benson, Lee, Ira Harkavy, and Matthew Hartley. 2005. "Integrating a Commitment to the Public Good into the Institutional Fabric." In *Higher Education for the Public Good: Emerging Voices from a National Movement,* ed. J. Burkhardt, T. Chambers, and A. Kezar, 185–216. San Francisco: Jossey-Bass.

Benson, Lee, Ira Harkavy, and John Puckett. 2007. *Dewey's dream: Universities and Democracies in an Age of Education Reform.* Philadelphia: Temple University Press.

Bok, Derek. 1990. *Universities and the Future of America.* Durham, NC: Duke University Press.

———. 2003. *Universities in the Marketplace: The Commercialization of Higher Education.* Princeton: Princeton University Press.

Boyer, Ernest L. 1994. "Creating the New American College." *Chronicle of Higher Education* (March): A48.

Boyte, Harry C. 2004. *Everyday Politics: Reconnecting Citizens and Public Life.* Philadelphia: University of Pennsylvania Press. .

Boyte, Harry C., and Nancy N. Kari. 1996. *Building America: The Democratic Promise of Public Work.* Philadelphia: Temple University Press.

Cahn, Steven M. 1981. Intro. to *The Later Works of John Dewey, 1925–1953,* vol. 13, ed. Jo Ann Boydston, ix–xviii. Carbondale: Southern Illinois University Press.

Center for Educational Research and Innovation. 1982. *The University and the Community: The Problems of Changing Relationships.* Paris: Organization for Economic Development.

Colby, Anne, Thomas Ehrlich, Elizabeth Beaumont, and Jason Stephens. 2003. *Educating Citizens: Preparing America's Undergraduates for Lives of Moral and Civic Responsibility.* San Francisco: Jossey-Bass.

Dewey, John. 1899/1991. *The School and Society.* Chicago: University of Chicago Press.

———. 1910/1990. *How We Think.* Boston: D.C. Heath.

———. 1927/1954. *The Public and Its Problems.* Denver: Alan Swallow.

Fish, Stanley. 2003. "Aim Low." *Chronicle of Higher Education* (May): C5.

Franklin, Benjamin. 1749/1962. "Proposals Relating to the Education of Youth in Pennsilvania [sic]." Reprinted in *Benjamin Franklin on Education,* ed. John Hardin Best. New York: Teachers College Press.

Gardner, John W. 1998. Remarks to the Campus Compact Strategic Planning Committee. San Francisco, February 10.

Goldsmith, Oliver. 1910. "The Deserted Village." In *Oliver Goldsmith's Poems and Plays*, 24. London: J.M. Dent and Sons.

Greenwood, Davydd J., and José Luis Gonzáles Santos. 1992. *Industrial Democracy as Process: Participatory Action Research in the Fagor Cooperative Group of Mondragón*. Assen/Maastricht, The Netherlands: Van Gorcum.

Greiner, William R. 1994. "In the Total of All These Acts: How Can American Universities Address the Urban Agenda?" *Universities and Community Schools* 4 (1–2): 12.

Gutmann, Amy. 2004. "Inaugural Address." In [University of Pennsylvania] *Almanac Supplement* 51, no. 8 (October). Available at http://www.upenn.edu/almanac/volumes/v51/n08/inaug_ag_speech.html.

Harkavy, Ira. 1999. "School-Community-University Partnerships: Effectively Integrating Community Building and Education Reform." *Universities and Community Schools* 6 (1–2): 7–24.

———. 2006. "The Role of Universities in Advancing Citizenship and Social Justice in the 21st Century." *Education, Citizenship and Social Justice* 1 (1): 5–37.

Harkavy, Ira, and Lee Benson. 1998. "De-Platonizing and Democratizing Education as the Bases of Service Learning." In *Academic Service-Learning: Pedagogy and Research*, ed. Robert A. Rhoads and Jeffrey P. F. Howard, 11–19. San Francisco: Jossey-Bass.

Harkavy, Ira, and John Puckett. 1991. "The Role of Mediating Structures in University and Community Revitalization: The University of Pennsylvania and West Philadelphia as a Case Study." *Journal of Research and Development in Education* 25 (1): 10–25.

Harper, W. R. 1905. *The Trend in Higher Education*. Chicago: University of Chicago Press.

Jacoby, Barbara, ed. 2003. *Building Partnerships for Service-Learning*. San Francisco: Jossey-Bass.

Kennedy, Donald. 1997. *Academic Duty*. Cambridge, MA: Harvard University Press.

Leslie, Stuart W. 1993. *The Cold War and American Science: The Military-Industrial-Academic Complex at MIT and Stanford*. New York: Columbia University Press.

Reinhold, Meyer. 1968. "Opponents of Classical Learning in America During the Revolutionary Period." *Proceedings of the American Philosophical Society* 112 (4): 224.

Rodin, Judith. 2007. *The University and Urban Revival: Out of the Ivory Tower and into the Streets*. Philadelphia: University of Pennsylvania Press.

Rossi, Paolo. 1996. "Bacon's Idea of Science." In *The Cambridge Companion to Bacon*, ed. Markuu Peltonen, 25–46. Cambridge: Cambridge University Press.

Schulman, Lee. 1997. "Professing the Liberal Arts." In *Education and Democracy*, ed. Robert Orrill. New York: College Board.

Schulman, Lee S. 2003. Foreword to *Educating Citizens: Preparing America's Undergraduates for Lives of Moral and Civic Responsibility*, ed. T. Ehrlich, E. Beaumont, and J. Stephens, vii–viii. San Francisco: Jossey-Bass.

Stokes, Donald E. 1997. *Pasteur's Quadrant: Basic Science and Technological Innovation*. Washington, DC: Brookings Institution Press.

U.S. Congress. 1997. House. Subcommittee on Housing and Community Opportunity, Committee on Banking and Financial Services. 105th Cong., 1st sess.

White, Woodie Thomas. 1977. "The Study of Education at the University of Chicago: 1892–1958." PhD diss., University of Chicago.

Whyte, William F., ed. 1991. *Participatory Action Research*. Newbury Park, CA: Sage.

Whyte, William F., and Kathleen K. Whyte. 1988. *Making Mondragón: The Growth and Dynamics of the Worker Cooperative Complex*. Ithaca, NY: ILR Press.

Wind, James P. 1987. *The Bible and the University: The Messianic Vision of William Rainey Harper*. Atlanta: Scholars Press.

CHAPTER 4

Civic Professionalism

HARRY C. BOYTE AND ERIC FRETZ

INTRODUCTION

We believe that higher education has a significant role to play in the reinvigoration of American democracy. We also believe that narrow specialization of academic interests and technocratic practices throughout colleges and universities cramps the work and learning within them, while dramatically limiting the contributions of higher education to the work of democracy and the collective redress of the challenges of a new century. Overspecialization and technocracy thwart our institutions' capacities to interact in fluid and respectful ways with citizens and civic institutions outside higher education in generating the knowledge needed in a flourishing democratic society.

Others outside the civic engagement movement in higher education make some similar points. For instance, in her collection of essays, *The Death of Adam* (1998), the novelist Marilyn Robinson notes that while we depend on universities to produce knowledge and teach future generations, "it was never intended that the universities should do the thinking, or the knowing, for the rest of us. Yet this seems to be the view that prevails now inside and outside the academy" (p. 7). Robinson goes on to accuse universities of becoming simultaneously "hermetic" and lacking in "confidence and definition," describing the issue as "*something about the way we teach and learn* [emphasis added] that makes it seem naïve to us to talk about these things outside of a classroom, and pointless to return to them in the course of actual life" (p. 8).

We believe that the civic engagement movement has something very important to say about "the way we teach and learn" in higher education, because it seeks to redress patterns of narrow specialization and technocratic practices, especially in the humanities and social sciences, where these practices have resulted in a drift away from humanistic inquiry, understanding, and democratic engagement. The civic engagement movement has the potential to return higher education to its roots of preparing people to work with others to solve problems and build thriving communities in ways that enhance democratic capacity. In the process, those in higher education may also relearn to work with others in the broader society to generate useful and usable knowledge.

Other scholars also argue for changing faculty (and sometimes staff) roles in order to realize higher education's commitment to civic engagement (Bringle, Hatcher, and Clayton 2006; Rice and O'Meara 2005; Saltmarsh 2010; Ward 2005). Our argument adds a focus on the ways that theories and practices of *community organizing* and attention to the *public meanings and qualities of work* will be central to reshaping faculty roles and identities and to infusing a robust, transformative civic mission throughout higher education.

CONFRONTING INDIVIDUALISM AND ISOLATION

Leaders in the civic movement in higher education must engage in an ongoing critical examination of cultural practices within the university and within the movement itself. In our view, the civic engagement movement has all too often been framed by and infused with a culture of individualism, privatization, and isolation—the very norms and practices that organize higher education itself. In its efforts to mainstream itself, to institutionalize service-learning pedagogy and other forms of civic engagement, and to justify the movement to suspicious onlookers, the engagement movement has ghettoized activities in discrete programs or centers and, in the case of service-learning, oftentimes isolated efforts of single faculty members within academic departments. This model is proving unsustainable. This rigidity dramatically limits the movement's potential.

The everyday practices of higher education work against the collaborative practices that are the heart of engaged scholarship, service-learning, and reciprocal, fluid, respectful partnerships with communities. The way faculty members are educated and rewarded encourages working in isolation or primarily with colleagues within their own academic disciplines, and seeing their own knowledge as qualitatively superior to other forms of knowledge and knowledge-making. This set of received practices conflicts with the fundamental sensibility of the engaged scholarship movement, which, as Saltmarsh (2010) writes, is "localized, relational, practice-based, actively collaborative, experiential, and reflective." Moreover, faculty members work in a way that reflects the larger social trends of an increasingly consumer society, as described by writers such as Susan Faludi (1999). Public purposes of work have been replaced to a significant degree by celebrity cultures and the pursuit of individual achievement and financial reward (Boyte 2004).

To progress, the civic engagement movement will need to confront this culture of individualism, isolation, and the instrumentalization of work into private pursuits. Specifically, institutions that take their engaged mission seriously will need to employ a number of practices and concepts that come from community organizing and its adaptation to efforts at institutional culture change. These include understanding self-interests; building public relationships across lines of difference; working with and understanding power as an ability to act rather than an oppressive, unidirectional force; creating spaces where people can work with power and confidence in a freer, more public fashion; addressing questions of work incentives and routines, as well as purposes and cultures of work and the workplace; understanding and embracing the messiness of change; and, overall, retrieving and practicing politics in the older tradition of constructive encounters with those who are different, rather than the mass mobilizing politics of the twentieth century, which treats people solely as members of limited categories (e.g., liberal or conservative, Republican or Democrat). We need a politics of Aristotle and Ella Baker, not of George Bush and Ralph Nader.

As we see it, the overarching task of the civic engagement movement is to engender civic professionals who will renew a robust sense of the public purposes of their work and will develop and sustain a far more public culture for collaborative, visible, open work. We all live and act in a professional and symbolic world, so making our work public goes far beyond developing new programs, creating new courses, or writing articles for publication. The current state of higher education can make such advances appear difficult or even impossible. We hold a more optimistic view.

John Dewey intimated these points many years ago, observing that technocratic and commercial dynamics undermine the habits of participatory and productive democracy. In response to the pretensions of credentialed intellectuals and academics, Dewey made action—not detached thought—the foundational experience of human beings who create meaning in the world. As Alan Ryan (1995) has put it, "One reason why Dewey was never able to accept the orthodox argument of stimulus-response was the fact that it made the organism whose behavior was supposed to be built up out of endless stimulus-response circuits too passive, too spectatorial, and too much a creature of the environment." Rather, the person "makes sense *of* the world for the sake of acting productively *on* the world" (p. 127; original emphasis). This focus led Dewey to a critique of detached intellectuals who assume the primacy of their own thought. "The depreciation of action, of doing and making, has been cultivated by philosophers," Dewey wrote in 1937 (1981, p. 357), attacking the idea that inquiry can be separated from social contexts. Dewey observed the aura of infallibility that those armed with "expertise" could assume. "The dogma worked out practically so as to strengthen dependence upon authority," he wrote. "Just as belief that a magical ceremony will regulate the growth of seeds to full harvest stifles the tendency to investigate . . . so acceptance of dogmatic rules as bases of conduct in education, morals, and social matters lessens the impetus to find out about the conditions which are involved in forming intelligent plans" (1981, p. 382).

Yet habits—including our own—are not blind repetitions but rather learned patterns that create predispositions for action in unexpected circumstances. Habits can be changed and developed through "intelligent action." This has proven a fertile theory for educational innovation in other settings. Thus Deborah Meier, the great democratic educator, founder of the Central Park East schools in East Harlem and the Mission Hill School in Boston, demonstrated the fruitfulness of the concept of relational habits in bringing about education for democracy. She wrote, "The real crisis we face is not a threat to America's economic or military dominance but the ebbing strength of our democratic and egalitarian culture." Meier recalled the "traditional public function of schools: to pass on the skills, aptitudes, and habits needed for a democratic way of life," observing that these "are hard to come by; they are not natural to the species. They are as hard to teach as relativity. Democratic culture needs citizens with very strong habits" (2003, p. 16).

As the civic engagement movement in higher education progresses, leaders and practitioners should intentionally learn from such civic innovators elsewhere in education and in other fields in order to develop and practice relational habits of democracy within institutions of higher education. Nan Kari, describing one of the earliest examples of adapting organizing to higher education in a multiyear experiment at the College of St. Catherine in St. Paul, Minnesota, observed that "civic design and institutional renewal are rarely if ever brought together" (1999, p. 50). But here and there one can see examples emerging. They often have significant impact.

Organizing at the College of St. Catherine

In the late 1980s, Nan Kari and her colleagues at the College of St. Catherine joined Project Public Life (PPL), a confederation of teams from diverse institutions that was organized as part of the early work of civic engagement at the University of Minnesota's Humphrey Institute (Project Public Life was the precursor to the Center for Democracy and Citizenship). PPL included ARC, a community group made up mainly of low-income parents, Augustana Nursing Home, Minnesota Cooperative Extension Service, local schools such as St. Bernard's in St. Paul, the Metropolitan Regional Council government group, and others interested in experimenting with community organizing approaches to bringing about institutional change. PPL initially used the notion of "citizen politics" to describe organizing methods and concepts.

At St. Catherine's, the Citizen Politics faculty group began meeting each week as a strategy team, involving a mix of different interests and disciplines.

They responded to long-standing institutional conflicts and crises: Discontent and fragmentation within the faculty ranks created an unpleasant institutional culture that spilled outward and affected the larger community of students, staff, and community partners (Kari 1999).

They looked for strategic openings. The chair of the faculty senate was a member of the Citizen Politics group, so one strategy involved changing the culture and practice of faculty meetings, notorious for their unproductive, whiny qualities. Another strategy, broader in ambition, sought to lay groundwork for far-ranging revision of the college's core curriculum. For years, the faculty had sought to create curricular change, but turf wars and disciplinary jealousies had repeatedly stymied all previous attempts.

The Citizen Politics faculty group decided to create a molecular process of relationship building across disciplinary silos. Kari secured external funding to develop Faculty Study Groups (FSGs)—interdisciplinary, self-selecting groups that were designed to examine issues of interest to all group members and to produce a tangible public project by the end of the academic year. Over several years, the FSGs involved a majority of the faculty in a zany mix of projects (from writing a novel to examining the Twin Cities as a learning text to going to Italy), and, in the process, produced dramatic change in the culture at the institution. Because they thought and acted like community organizers—not technocrats—they showed how weighty, contentious projects like curriculum revision, when approached from a community organizing and civic renewal framework, hold the possibility of pulling people together, energizing professional passions, and integrating the disparate and oftentimes conflicting elements of institutions. Thomas Ehrlich and his colleagues highlight the successes of the college in their now-classic work in our movement, *Educating Citizens* (Colby et al. 2003)—though this account leaves out the community organizing that brought it about.

Faculty Study Groups were founded upon community organizing principles of building public relationships across lines of difference, creating spaces for people to work freely and publicly with others, and understanding and embracing the messiness of change. Participating faculty were challenged to perform cultural work that was collaborative, based in intellectual, symbolic work, and aimed at the development of a public project. Large numbers of participants—far more than would have described themselves as "civic renewers"—became self-directed agents of cultural change within their institutions (not passive receptors as so often happens in task forces and committees), greatly multiplying the available energies and talents. The St. Catherine's experiment was not only successful but also enjoyable to participants primarily because it pushed back powerfully against pervasive privatizing tendencies of work in higher education: self-interest was an important element in making faculty members' work "more public." (Indeed, St. Catherine's proved a seedbed for early development of the Center for Democracy and Citizenship's public work–based conceptual framework of citizenship and civic action.)

Faculty and staff prioritized and came to value immensely the public dimensions of their work. As William Myers, chair of the faculty senate and coordinator of the curriculum process, observed, "When we make our discussions public, we can accomplish difficult and potentially divisive goals without acrimony. The key is to create a spirit of openness, and constantly to keep the common work of the whole college community in view" (qtd. in Kari 1999, p. 42). Additionally, faculty participants engaged in the older understanding of politics as negotiation, exchange, and deliberation rather than the hardscrabble and often ideological struggle for scarce resources that often becomes the default mode of doing business in higher education. Such older "citizen politics" does not do away with conflict; the work at St. Catherine's often surfaced conflicts that had been submerged. But it allows conflicts to be addressed constructively.

Faculty were engaged by their own self-interests, rather than pulled together by high-level administrators and exhorted to participate in task forces or committees for an abstract "common good." Project Public Life used a working understanding of self-interest drawn from developments in the field of community organizing. In the language of community organizing, self-interest is about "the self among others." Organizers know how to identify and work with the self-interests of a large group of constituents, and how to tie people's immediate self-interests to salient community issues and long-term community projects or challenges.

A number of lessons can be drawn from the St. Catherine's experience: institutional change requires open, flexible, and dynamic ways of dealing with conflict; it entails a self-conscious commitment to fostering public cultures and integrating and negotiating the wide variety of self-interests that populate our institutions. The focus on values, tied to individual faculty members' stories and life experiences, rather than a narrow issues focus, proved essential as an organizing method at St. Catherine's. Finally, the faculty members thought deeply and effectively about the public meanings and possibilities of their own work, bridging the customary divide in civic theory and practice alike, which have long seen civic engagement as a function of "off-hours" voluntary and associational life. This is the kind of organic, pragmatic, iterative, public, conceptual, and also messy process that is fundamentally different from the technocratic practices common in our institutions.

The successes at St. Catherine's, however, did not simply continue to expand unaided. The organizing work depended on the strong support of the president, Anita Pampusch. When she left, and after a turbulent succession fight, some of the democratic gains were eroded, though not the core architecture of curricular changes. But the experiences signaled strongly the importance and potential of bringing organizing into higher education, while the concept of public work that developed at St. Catherine's proved a fruitful foundation for subsequent institution-wide civic engagement efforts at the University of Minnesota (Boyte 2004, p. 145).

Community Organizing at the University of Denver

Our work at the Center for Community Engagement and Service Learning at the University of Denver has similarly sought to translate community organizing principles, concepts, and methods into a higher education setting. We see community organizing as occupying the middle ground between 1960s-inspired protest politics and indifference to social and political issues. This translation includes approaches to faculty and student development. Like that of our predecessors at the College of St. Catherine, our work is rooted in cultural and transformative change, and the organizing skills we teach are tools that we use to move our stakeholders into civic action.

Our operational principles are some of the core concepts of the community organizing model, including understanding and working with power, practicing accountability, and understanding self-interests. For instance, like the Faculty Study Groups at St. Catherine's, we design our faculty development offerings in a way that honors and encourages the self-interests of our faculty participants. Thus, our Service Learning Pods are faculty development offerings designed to provide opportunities for faculty members to work together in issues-based cohort groups or in disciplinary teams identified by participants. Our Community-Based Writing group is designed to help faculty members write peer-reviewed journal articles about their community-based work.

These same operating principles are at work in our curricular offerings. Our Spectator to Citizen three-course sequence is designed to help University of Denver students develop a set of public skills that will allow them to actively participate in the public life of their communities. In this course sequence, students come to understand community not as a homogeneous group of like-minded people but as a heterogeneous group striving for collective self-interest in order to better their communities. In the first course, Community Organizing, students learn the very same elements of community organizing we defined at the beginning of this piece. They define their self-interest and individual public lives, build consensus across multiple perspectives, become experts on a community issue, and develop partnerships in the community that aim for dialogue and action. The second course, Denver Urban Issues and Policy, allows students to investigate important Denver-based issues by employing a community organizing model that includes research, immersion, and basic knowledge—of powers, structures, and stakeholders—necessary for understanding root causes of social problems. The third course, School-Based Civic Engagement, provides students opportunities to engage with a Denver Public School (or urban youth organization) in a meaningful way that challenges them to think about how our public schools are preparing students to be effective citizens.

One of the organizing techniques we frequently employ with our faculty partners and students is The World As It Is and The World As It Should Be. It is a simple exercise in which a facilitator writes "The World As It Is" on the left side of a whiteboard and "The World As It Should Be" on right. The left side is the real world, including all the things that we rub up against every day and that create friction and problems in our lives. The right side is the ideal—what we would like our world to look like, what we are aspiring toward. Usually, the discussion is modified for the audience, so for a group of Greek-life students or Resident Assistants, the discussion would be narrowed to the context of the Greek-life or Resident Assistant system. The facilitator then asks participants to identify and talk about issues that come up for them. Always, the facilitator probes, questions, and challenges participants to think deeply about the issues they are generating and to begin to take responsibility for the parts of their world they don't like. Our goal is to create an ethic and a mind-set within our students that allow them to work and live on the tension lines between The World As It Is and The World As It Should Be. As Ed Chambers notes in *Roots for Radicals* (2004), effective community organizers operate on this tension line and understand that living entirely in The World As It Is equals a life of supporting the status quo, while living entirely in The World As It Should Be is the equivalent of being stuck in romantic idealism (p. 22).

One of the primary ways we teach community organizing is through Public Achievement, a youth civic engagement initiative originally developed by the Center for Democracy and Citizenship that trains undergraduates to act like community organizers in schools and to engage in consequential, productive public work that has an impact on the world. The following reflections of Sarah McCauley, a University of Denver (DU) alum and a former Public Achievement coach, illustrate how DU students practice community organizing.

The half-block schoolyard at Bryant Webster middle school in Northwest Denver was a gravel field, both unsafe and unpleasant for students. Parents and teachers had tried for four years to raise funds to buy playground equipment and build athletic fields, but had failed.

When I arrived at Bryant Webster, I began working with a group of nine seventh grade [students] who were upset that they didn't have a playground and that no one was doing anything about it.

Our first step was identifying our reasons for wanting a playground. The students told me how they felt unsafe and bored during their recesses. Next, we started to research what had been tried to address the issue in the past. We held interviews with students, parents and teachers at the school. Next, the students were ready to make an action plan. They decided that the Denver Public School district was the party responsible for helping them to improve the condition of their schoolyard. They called the school board and requested to present at their monthly public meeting. Then, the students took the information they had gathered from their peers and teachers and created a presentation. They divided the presentation so that each of the seventh grade students would get a chance to talk.

At the school board meeting, the students explained why they needed the playground, why the school board was responsible, and what they expected the board to do for their school. They fielded questions from the board and the other attendees gracefully. When we left, the students were eager to know if they had succeeded. Three weeks later, I received a call from the principal of Bryant Webster informing me that the school board had decided to allocate funds to the school to build a Learning Landscape, a playground designed for educational recreation. Today this school has a functional playground that serves both the students and the surrounding neighborhood.[1]

This story of students accomplishing public work through organizing includes two especially noteworthy points. First, the public action the students staged went beyond simple protest politics. The students' work was done in the open. The seventh grade students clearly articulated their concerns and their requests in a public forum and defended their position against critical questions. Second, this story illustrates how understanding and working with power, one of the primary techniques of community organizers, works even in the most challenging of institutions. Most of us are afraid of power, either because it is held by the "enemy" or because we see it as an oppressive force in our lives. Community organizers and civic professionals redefine power as "an ability to act." McCauley helped students understand power as relational. They learned that ordinary people, whatever their age, race, wealth, or formal credentials, can create trusting, public relationships with the right people, and can generate change.

The Problem That Cannot Be Named

As it grows and develops, the civic education movement in higher education bumps up against a set of long-standing cultural practices that are so pervasive and deep-seated that they can hardly be named; they are taken for granted as parts of the dominant culture. A consumerist, hypercompetitive, and privatized philosophy governs higher education as it does much of American cultural and institutional life. It is assumed as a matter of course that "the best and brightest" should govern, that the most important measure of achievement is victory in competitive activities, and that work is pursued largely for private ends rather than public ones. This pervasive understanding and set of practices informs the way students and faculty members do their work and play their roles in our nation's higher education institutions. It values an intense focus on individual success rather than on collaborative work that adds to our commonwealth. This approach, which might be described as a soft technocracy, renders most people not only marginal to real decision making but also needy and deficient. It generates what might be called "credentialitis"—excessive reliance on formal degrees and officially authorized marks of recognition. It also radically devalues other forms of knowledge and knowledge-making: knowledge gained through experience, local knowledge, spiritual knowledge, and wisdom passed down from elders in rooted cultural communities. This pattern of exalting one particular approach to knowledge-making (academic) and devaluing others has become pervasive through the ecology of higher education and the professional systems of our society.

An unconscious assumption of the superiority of academic knowledge operates among many higher education leaders who call for reengagement with society, generating a "service" approach that sees others as in need of rescue. Thus, in "Mandate for a New Century," the David Dodds Henry Lecture at the University of Illinois Chicago campus in 1989, Donna Shalala, then chancellor of the University of Wisconsin, made an impassioned plea for public service and social justice, for struggles against racism and sexism, for environmentalism and peace. She called for public universities to engage the world, and she wed these calls explicitly to meritocracy. For her, "the ideal [is] a disinterested technocratic elite" fired by the moral mission of "society's best and brightest in service to its most needy." The imperative is "delivering the miracles of social science" to fix society's social problems, "just as doctors cured juvenile rickets in the past" (p. 17).

The unnamed problem we are identifying has a stultifying effect on a wide range of actors and constituencies. Higher education bears an important measure of responsibility for this problem, which is among the underlying causes for many students' feeling that they cannot significantly affect the larger world. In the November/December 2007 issue of *Change* magazine, Parker Palmer described the weak sense of civic agency that often results from students' experiences in higher education: "The hidden curriculum of our culture portrays institutions as powers *other* than us, over which we have marginal control at best" (p. 6; original emphasis). One day while walking across the University of Denver campus, Eric Fretz overheard three undergraduates talking about their classes. "We debate these issues in class," one of them exclaimed, "but we don't *do* anything about it! Everything just remains the same!" This is a common chorus among undergraduate students. It is our hope that in the months and years to come, we will begin to overhear conversations among students that are sparked with the energy and wisdom of the work they are doing in communities to deepen democratic traditions, and to open democratic possibilities.

RETRIEVING THE CIVIC POPULIST TRADITION

In the face of these very large challenges, a pressing task for practitioners is to recover methods of practicing their crafts in public life and in public ways, using their academic skills to create powerful public relationships, and becoming culture-workers and facilitators of meaning-making in the public sphere. We call this kind of work the work of civic professionals, heirs to a long-standing tradition of community organizing in American culture and a less visible but vital tradition of civically engaged professionalism. Retrieving these traditions is crucial.

The organizing tradition, rooted in the earlier practices of mutual aid, community action, and associational life that Tocqueville found so remarkable in the United States, was translated into the world of big cities and large institutions in the twentieth century by figures like Jane Addams at Hull House, James Weldon Johnson in the Harlem Renaissance, and Liberty Hyde Bailey in land-grant universities. The organizing tradition reemerged and flourished on an enormous scale in the movements of the Great Depression, especially among such figures as Saul Alinsky, Ella Baker, Bayard Rustin, A. Philip Randolph, Myles Horton, and others who reveled in the popular organizing of the time but did not like the left-wing and Leninist distinction between scientific "vanguard" and "mass." The organizing tradition resurfaced once again in the civil rights movement through the work of the Highlander Folk School, the Citizenship Education Program of the Southern Christian Leadership Conference, the Student Nonviolent Organizing Committee, and other efforts. It continues today through the work of the Gamaliel Foundation (Barack Obama's formative experience), the Industrial Areas Foundation (IAF), and related community-organizing institutions.

The tradition of community organizing continued, albeit less visibly, through the 1960s and gained new foundations and promoters. In the early years of the decade, a group of community organizers in the Deep South effectively began to use organizing tactics. This story is told in Charles Payne's *I've Got the Light of Freedom* (1995), a book that distinguishes between the protest politics of the movement (the march on Selma, the Freedom Rides) and the grassroots organizing approaches promoted by Septima Clark and Ella Baker to develop the citizenship schools. Payne's analysis of the civil rights movement uncovers a largely ignored layer of grassroots community organizing that developed alongside the protest movements (the sit-ins, the protest marches, and the boycotts): "If people like Amzie Moore and Medgar Evers and Aaron Henry tested the limits of repression, people like Septima Clark and Ella Baker and Myles Horton tested another set of limits, the limits on the ability of the oppressed to participate in the reshaping of their own lives" (p. 68). Thousands of activists and community leaders learned these skills at the Highlander Folk School and later at the citizenship schools across the South. The vision, articulated in Highlander's statement of purpose, which, as Payne notes, was drafted by Septima Clark, was to "broad[en] the scope of democracy to include everyone and deep[en] the concept to include every relationship" (qtd. in Payne 1995, p. 68). As Highlander director Myles Horton noted when he described the philosophy of citizenship education, "We're into people who can help other people develop and provide educational leadership and ideas, but at the same time, bring people along" (qtd. in Payne 1995, p. 71). All had what Payne called an "expansive" concept of democracy. As Payne summarized, "Above all else . . . they stressed a developmental style of politics, one in which the important thing was the development of efficacy of those most affected by a problem." This meant that "whether a community achieved this or that tactical objective was likely to matter less than whether the people in it came to see themselves as having the right and the capacity to have some say-so in their own lives" (1995, p. 68).

In the late 1960s, key bridging figures translated the freedom movement's organizing themes into a larger politics of organizing. Among these figures was Monsignor Geno Baroni, arguably the most important architect of modern organizing. The son of an immigrant coal mining family in Pennsylvania, Baroni became a Catholic priest in 1956, served in working-class parishes in Altoona and Johnstown, Pennsylvania, and then was transferred to an inner-city African American parish in Washington. He became involved in the freedom movement, served as Catholic coordinator for the 1963 March on Washington, and led the Catholic delegation to the 1965 Selma-to-Montgomery March.

The enormous ferment among ethnic-minority Americans in the late 1960s inspired many intellectuals to move sharply in a conservative direction, forming the basis for neoconservatism. But a key group of ethnic leaders and intellectuals forged a third way, neither mass politics liberalism nor neoconservatism. For these leaders, Baroni was a pivotal figure, a courageous and inspiring organizer of a new ethnic movement with immense democratic potential (Boyte 1980, pp. 42, 62–63; Krickus 1976, pp. 272–274).

Baroni and others sought to develop a larger political project, called the new populism, that could bring together African Americans, and other ethnic minorities, through organizing. Baroni saw the new populism as an alternative to both "universalist liberalism" and neoconservatism. In this politics, the values of diversity, equality, and justice combine with a deep commitment to people's agency and appreciation of the immense *particularity* of American communities.

New populism represents a clear alternative to the "mobilizing" politics that perceives the citizen largely as a consumer—a view now flourishing in higher education's redefinition of the student as customer. Mass politics, which has roots dating from the early twentieth century, emphasizes universal claims, distributive justice, a consumer view of the citizen, and individual rights. It is organized around a conception of the person as concerned primarily with individual, material acquisition and fulfillment of needs, not with questions of purpose or civic contribution. As the philosopher Michael Sandel (1996) has put it, "A politics based on consumer identities . . . asks how best—most fully, or fairly, or efficiently—to satisfy [needs and wants]" (p. 225).

Mass politics, operating within the world as it is, has won substantial gains for poor and marginal groups against enormous concentrations of wealth and power. However, it is important to recognize the sharp distinction between organizing and the mass politics of a consumer society. The conception of the person as an immensely complex, dynamic, and generative agent of one's own life, and a shaper of one's environments, is at the heart of organizing, a dramatically different conception from the citizen as an uprooted consumer.

In some respects, civically engaged work at the university thus functions more as a reclamation project than a trendy and ephemeral movement within higher education. In order to perform this work, we need not only methods and concepts of organizing in order to make the changes required in our cultures but also a bold, theoretically grounded, and deeply public conception of our work in the world. For this, it is important to surface a work tradition that melds powerfully with, and is informed by, the community organizing tradition: the history, concept, and practice of civic professionalism.

CIVIC PROFESSIONALISM

Thomas Bender (1993) has detailed an older university culture, which was open to engagement with a variety of publics, and which cultivated the rise of "civic" (not mainly "disciplinary") professionalism among students. "Before the rise of modern professionalism," Bender argues, "there were identifiable audiences that judged and affected the work of American thinkers" (p. 4). The emergence in the early twentieth century of a discipline-based academic professionalism was, in many ways, the result of the early academic freedom struggles inspired by industry, government, and religious pressure to use academic knowledge for ideological and market-driven purposes. This dynamic, while providing a relatively safe space for faculty members to accomplish their research agendas free from public influence, also paved the way for the intellectually isolated, jargon-ridden, and un-public-minded academic departments of the twenty-first century. In other words, the academy responded to legitimate threats posed by demands to create knowledge that served private and selfish interests by folding in on itself; creating structures, products, and texts that were impenetrable to outsiders; and creating an intellectual culture that isolated and barred entry to a large sector of the population.[2] Bender is not nostalgic for a past where intellectual inquiry and public needs were in peaceful harmony. A healthy tension, rather than a great divide, between the pursuits of the academy and the needs of publics, may be a useful way of thinking about how universities in the twenty-first century will relate to their publics. We all know the stories of fringe legislators and right-wing ideologues set on privatizing higher education by portraying the academy's esoteric knowledge and identity politics as outside the mainstream of American thought. Intentional and strategic attempts to include a variety of publics in the processes of American higher education would serve to demystify an academic culture that has related to increasingly narrow audiences.

The philosophical foundations of civic professionalism found early expression in the work of John Dewey (1937/1981), who stressed—against the grain of conventional democratic political theory traceable to ancient Greece—the educative dimensions of "all callings [and] occupations" (p. 334). He especially focused on professions, doubtless having in mind the examples of popular citizenship education and educators such as Jane Addams and others at Hull House, who saw their work as catalytic and energizing. Thus, professionals, he said, needed to become more conscious of their educative roles and responsibilities. "The professions . . . not merely require education in those who practice them but help to form the attitudes and understanding of those who consult their practitioners," Dewey wrote (1937/1981, p. 336). "As far as science is humanized, it educates all the laymen. Artists, painters, musicians, architects, and writers are also an immense educative force" in potential, though "at the present time . . . this educative function is hampered and distorted" (p. 334).

For Dewey, education should be practiced as a dynamic engagement with the world, its problems, and its work. Education for democracy—education's highest and most important goal—had to self-consciously cultivate the habits that once were generated through young people's involvement in the life and work of families and communities. "There was always something which really needed to be done, and a real necessity that each member of the household should do his own part faithfully in co-operation with others," Dewey argued. Everyday work taught habits of cooperation, responsibility, and productive outlook. It also meant a deep connection with the world; or, as Dewey wrote, "We cannot overlook the importance for educational purposes of the close and intimate acquaintance got with nature at first hand." Everyday work had once connected young people "with real things and materials, with the actual processes of their manipulation and the knowledge of their social necessities and uses. In all this there was continual training of observation, of ingenuity, constructive imagination, of logical thought, and of the sense of reality acquired through first-hand contact with actualities" (1937/1981, p. 457).

Scholars such as William Sullivan (2004) and Albert Dzur (2008) have recently further developed the concept of civic professionalism. Sullivan, for instance, charts the historical trajectory of the American professional from the colonial period to the twentieth century and concludes by identifying one of the central tensions of professionalism in the United States:

> The most constant tension, as we have seen, has been between a technical emphasis which stresses specialization—broadly linked to a utilitarian conception of society as a project for enhancing efficiency and individual satisfaction—and a sense of professional mission which has insisted upon the prominence of the ethical and civic dimension of the enterprise. (p. 28)

In contrast with practitioners applying a technical emphasis, civic professionals are those who work *with* citizens, rather than acting *on* them. Our collaborator, Bill Doherty (Doherty, Mendenhall, and Berge, forthcoming), and his students and colleagues at the Citizen Professional Center have pioneered in showing what this can mean. They have drawn on the theory of public work and the experiences at the College of St. Catherine in a series of initiatives that show how public work can be translated into a powerful

wellspring of democratic change in which family and health professionals function as catalysts and coaches rather than as service providers. In the
Families and Democracy initiatives associated with their Center, professionals work as citizen professionals with families on a host of issues to tame the
forces of a degraded, hypercompetitive, hyperindividualistic culture that tend
to overwhelm families. Their citizen professional model recognizes that solving the complex problems we face today requires many sources and kinds of
knowledge. The families and communities themselves are the main source of
energy and action.

This methodology is in sharp contrast with the dominant professional
development approach, which teaches professionals to look at people in terms
of their deficiencies rather than their assets, and to be detached from the civic
life of communities. Here are the central premise and core principles that the
Citizen Professional Center offers instead of dominant approaches:

> **Central premise:** The greatest untapped resource for improving health
> and social well-being is the knowledge, wisdom, and energy of indi-
> viduals, families, and communities who face challenging issues in their
> everyday lives.

CORE PRINCIPLES

1. See all personal problems as public ones too: the I and the We.
2. Look to family and community resources first.
3. See families and communities as producers, not just clients or
   consumers.
4. See professionals as citizens and partners, not just providers.
5. Let citizens drive programs rather than programs service
   citizens.
6. Make sure every initiative reflects the local culture.
7. Grow leaders, then more leaders.
8. Make all decisions democratically.
9. Go deep before taking action.
10. Think big, act practically, and let your light shine (Doherty,
    Mendenhall, and Berge, forthcoming).

The partnerships of the Citizen Professional Center are diverse and
wide-ranging, suggesting the immense civic energy and power waiting to be
"unlocked" by professionals who shift from substituting their own agency for
broader civic agency. They include, among others, several suburban movements of families seeking to tame overscheduled, hypercompetitive, consumerist lives; an African American Citizens Father Project seeking to foster
positive fathering models and practices; a new project with Hennepin County
to change civil service practice into public work; a pilot with Health Partners
Como Clinic, called the Citizen Health Care Home, which stresses personal
and family responsibility for one's own health care, and opportunities for

patient leadership development and co-responsibility for the health mission of the clinic; and FEDS (Families, Education and Diabetes Series), a project that engages low-income, urban American Indians and their families to improve the health and well-being of American Indian people through diabetes education, fellowship, and support in a manner that embraces their heritage, values, and culture.

Democratic professionals in this vein are facilitators of the creation of public knowledge. They seek out common interests that link professional inquiry and local knowledge, and they work to develop systems of communication and knowledge production that involve laypeople in the solution of public problems. As Dzur (2008) observes, democratic or citizen professionals refuse to "dominate discussion" and are capable of "stepping back and allowing laypeople the chance to take up responsibilities" (p. 41).

Civic professionalism directly challenges higher education's dominant credentialing practices, which are embodied in conventional promotion and tenure guidelines. Across the ecology of higher education, these guidelines reflect the positivist assumptions of research universities, a pattern that remains in place despite a rapidly growing body of theory—beginning with Ernest Boyer's (1991) landmark *Scholarship Reconsidered*, and most recently detailed in Imagining America's *Scholarship in Public* (Ellison and Eatman 2008)—which has demonstrated the impoverishment of knowledge-creation that results. An organizing perspective points to the need for a broad campaign across our institutions to challenge and diversify the current privatized, self-referential credentialing norms and practices that hold sway. Faculty, as well as students, staff, and the larger public environment, have much to gain from such a campaign by "breaking our chains," the technocratic standards that now have us all in thrall.

LESSONS FROM THE FIELD

Citizen professionals as well as community organizers acknowledge their own interests in creating a good society. They develop unique styles grounded in local civic cultures. They learn respect for the insights of those without formal credentials. They recognize that they have much to learn from communities where populist values of cultural roots, community vitality, and equality are alive. They also build collaborative public work skills that help energize and activate broad civic energies. Where do these skills come from? What do they look like? How are they practiced?

We conclude with an example of a citizen professional in the world beyond higher education, since we are convinced that higher education and organizing approaches have an enormous amount to learn from others outside the university's walls.

Mike Kromrey has served during the past twenty-five years as the executive director of Metro Organizations for People (MOP), a Denver organization that strives to engage ordinary people in the democratic process to fight for living wages, to secure health care for children and the working poor, to work toward educational reform, and to fight for the rights of immigrants. For Kromrey, the key component of the practice of civic professionalism is rooted in the iron rule of community organizing: never do for others what they can do for themselves (Mike Kromrey, interview by Eric Fretz, April 10, 2009).

Indeed, the iron rule is MOP's "truth barometer." When it is being practiced, Kromrey believes, MOP is forwarding its mission of "teaching ordinary people to do extraordinary things." But when the iron rule is violated—that is, when Kromrey and his MOP colleagues speak, write, or *do* for their constituents what they could very well do on their own—Kromrey believes their mission and function as organizers are compromised.

The question that hangs over Kromrey's head every day is not how he and his staff can help the working poor and their metro Denver constituents but how they can find ways to help these people develop skills to engage in the democratic process—using their own voices, personal skills, and capacities. "Most other professionals don't have to worry about this," he notes. Activists, mobilizers, groups engaged in protest politics, and advocacy groups ground their professional stance in their expert knowledge to speak and do for others. This certainly has its place in society. Yet, as Kromrey says, "The unique quality of what we try to do well is to teach other people how to think on their feet and how to engage the democratic process in a meaningful and powerful way" (Kromrey, interview).

Kromrey draws bold lines between the community organizing work of MOP and advocacy groups that speak for others: "No one is losing sleep over whether they have volunteer leaders in the community prepared to lead the way. Most of the time it's paid staff speaking for others." The culture that MOP and other community organizing groups develop is one that is constantly reflecting on the roles that the "experts" are playing and attempting to perform. For Kromrey, an effective organizer works in the background, training, encouraging, and even exhorting ordinary people to develop their public voices, develop powerful public relationships, and bring about change with a broad base of constituents (Kromrey, interview).

Practicing this style of professionalism takes a lot of work. Hours and hours of education, practice, dialogue, and analysis go into every MOP-trained citizen who engages in the democratic process—whether those activities involve speaking at a public meeting, writing a letter to a city official, or participating in a press conference.

For Kromrey, technocracy threatens the essence of a democratic culture because it is constantly violating the iron rule of organizing. When professionals and experts consistently set themselves up as the solution to our problems, the problem-solving, asset-based culture of ordinary people doing extraordinary things gets whittled away. Kromrey names John McKnight's *The Careless Society* (1995) as an important text about the detrimental effects of meritocracy in a democracy. "My experience with professionals who work in communities—health care clinics, schools, medical profession-als, teachers, social workers, clergy—is that they view the community as a client to be fed and that engaging ordinary people to come up with their own conclusions and use their own skills is a foreign concept. It's just easier to speak for others, or write a check or give advice" (Kromrey, interview). Kromrey notes that this notion is so deeply pervasive in the culture of profes-sionalism in America that it is hard to talk about and identify. He describes his work as "lifting up this way of thinking" of ordinary people as agents of change in communities. "It's shocking to me that this way of practicing my profession is radical. To me, it's deep, it's the way I was taught, and it's hard to do because it's scary—I have to let go of the control in these relationships" (Kromrey, interview).

CONCLUSION

Today, higher education is caught in a cycle of complaint and apathy regard-ing civic engagement, our students, our own lives, and the state of our democ-racy. Those faculty who advocate for change nonetheless often complain about students' and citizens' lack of civic imagination and involvement in a way that puts us outside the problem being addressed. We also fail to pro-vide our students with meaningful and sustained opportunities to develop the very civic skills that will foster a strong democracy. To break out of this cycle, those invested in the civic mission of higher education will need to reconstitute and shift received roles, and learn to practice their profession as a craft that engages public life on multiple fronts and in myriad ways. The stories from St. Catherine, the Public Achievement initiative at the University of Denver, and the partnerships of the Citizen Professional Center all suggest the growing, but still largely untapped, potentials of translating organizing methods and concepts, and public-work approaches into the higher education civic engage-ment movement.

We are convinced that faculty and staff, like our students, will need to practice community organizing, both on campus and in their surrounding communities, if they are to see much change. Higher education professionals will also need to make their work more public, in multiple ways—more inter-active with and respectful toward those outside higher education, more open and visible, more infused with robust democratic and public purposes. Faculty members, staff, and students will need to engage with the community as equals and pursue solutions to community issues, not as a theoretical exercise but as a path to becoming agents and architects of a flourishing democracy.

NOTES

This essay was previously published in the *Journal of Higher Education Outreach and Engagement* 14, no. 2 (2010): 67–90.
The authors are indebted to Sarah McCauley for her editorial work on this paper.

1. This reflection was written by Sarah McCauley for the purposes of this paper.

2. For a full treatment of the early history of tenure and the formation of the American Association of University Professors, see Menand 2001, Chapter 15.

REFERENCES

Bender, T. 1993. *Intellect and Public Life: Essays on the Social History of Academic Intellectuals in the United States*. Baltimore: Johns Hopkins University Press.

Boyer, E. L. 1991. *Scholarship Reconsidered: Priorities of the Professoriate*. San Francisco: Jossey-Bass.

Boyte, H. C. 1980. *The Backyard Revolution: Understanding the New Citizen Movement*. Philadelphia: Temple University Press.

———. 2004. *Everyday Politics: Reconnecting Citizens and Public Life*. Philadelphia: University of Pennsylvania Press.

Bringle, R. G., J. A. Hatcher, and P. H. Clayton. 2006. "The Scholarship of Civic Engagement: Defining, Documenting, and Evaluating Faculty Work." *To Improve the Academy* 25: 257–279.

Chambers, E. 2004. *Roots for Radicals: Organizing for Power, Action and Justice*. New York: Continuum International Publishing.

Colby, A., T. Ehrlich, E. Beaumont, and J. Stephens. 2003. *Educating Citizens: Preparing America's Undergraduates for Lives of Moral and Civic Responsibility*. San Francisco: Jossey-Bass/Carnegie Foundation for the Advancement of Teaching.

Dewey, J. 1937/1981. *The Philosophy of John Dewey*, ed. J. McDermott. Chicago: University of Chicago Press.

Doherty, B., T. Mendenhall, and J. Berge. Forthcoming. "The Families and Democracy and Citizen Health Care Project." *The Journal of Marital and Family Therapy*.

Dzur, A. 2008. *Democratic Professionalism: Citizen Participation and the Reconstruction of Professional Ethics, Identity, and Practice*. University Park: Pennsylvania State University Press.

Ellison, J., and T. K. Eatman. 2008. *Scholarship in Public: Knowledge Creation and Tenure Policy in the Engaged University*. Syracuse, NY: Imagining America.

Faludi, S. 1999. *Stiffed: The Betrayal of the American Man*. New York: HarperPerennial.

Kari, N. 1999. "Political Ideas: Catalysts for Creating a Public Culture at the College of St. Catherine." In *Creating the Commonwealth*, ed. H. C. Boyte, 30–54. Dayton, OH: Kettering Foundation.

Krickus, R. 1976. *Pursuing the American Dream: White Ethnics and the New Populism*. Garden City, NY: Doubleday.

McKnight, J. 1995. *The Careless Society: Community and Its Counterfeits*. New York: Basic Books.

Meier, Deborah. 2003. "So What Does It Take to Build a School for Democracy? *Phi Delta Kappan* 85 (September): 15–21.

Menand, Louis. 2001. *The Metaphysical Club*. New York: Farrar, Straus and Giroux.

Palmer, Parker. 2007. "A New Professional: The Aims of Education Revisited." *Change* (November/December): 4–9.

Payne, Charles. 1995. *I've Got the Light of Freedom: The Organizing Tradition and the Mississippi Freedom Struggle*. Berkeley: University of California Press.

Rice, E., and K. O'Meara. 2005. *Faculty Priorities Reconsidered: Rewarding Multiple Forms of Scholarship*. San Francisco: Jossey-Bass.

CIVIC PROFESSIONALISM • 101

Robinson, M. 1998. *The Death of Adam: Essays on Modern Thought*. New York: Picador.

Ryan, A. 1995. *John Dewey and the High Tide of American Liberalism*. New York: W. W. Norton.

Saltmarsh, J. 2010. "Changing Pedagogies." In *Handbook of Engaged Scholarship: Contemporary Landscapes, Future Directions* 1, ed. H. Fitzgerald, D. L. Zimmerman, C. Burach, and S. D. Seifer. East Lansing: Michigan State University Press.

Sandel, M. 1996. *Democracy's Discontent: America in Search of a Public Philosophy*. Cambridge, MA: Harvard University Press.

Shalala, D. 1989. *Mandate for a New Century*. David Dodds Henry Lecture, University of Illinois–Chicago. Available at http://www.uic.edu/depts/oaa/ddh/ddhlectures/Lec11.pdf.

Sullivan, W. 2004. *Work and Integrity: The Crisis and Promise of Professionalism in America*. San Francisco: Jossey-Bass.

Ward, K. 2005. "Rethinking Faculty Roles and Rewards for the Public Good." In *Higher Education for the Public Good: Emerging Voices from a National Movement*, ed. A. J. Kezar, T. C. Chambers, and J. Burkhardt, 217–234. San Francisco: Jossey-Bass.

CHAPTER 5

Collective Leadership for Engagement

Reclaiming the Public Purpose of Higher Education

WILLIAM M. PLATER

After nearly a quarter of a century of effort by several thousand presidents, chancellors, and chief academic officers, America's colleges and universities appear to be no closer to a consensus about the role of higher education in ensuring a sustained and committed role for the academy in preparing civic-minded graduates, generating and applying knowledge about community engagement, and taking leadership in the exercise of democratic processes for the benefit of the common good than they were at the height of their work in 2000. Beyond individual actions, these leaders have formed organizations to support ideals based on community engagement, directed many of their national membership associations to establish programs for student, faculty and institutional development, and supported each other in taking public stands on behalf of civic engagement. Why has what was once thought to be a "movement" become routine, if not ritualized? No one is opposed to civic engagement for colleges and universities, but who is actually engaging?

Did the events following 9/11 sap the energy and drive of the movement, which may not have responded to the national crisis with the clarity of purpose and the effective strategies that the moment demanded? Have responses to natural disasters, including Hurricane Katrina, been more individualistic than institutional? Did the generation of leaders who began the movement simply move on to other things—new issues, satisfaction in having done enough, retirement—without having prepared their successors to continue the work as their own? Is there something inherent in the concept of democratic civic engagement for colleges and universities that leads to banality and routinization? Did the movement actually succeed, and the sense of stasis experienced by some actually become evidence of success for others? Or is there something in the nature of leadership for engagement itself that is, as yet, insufficiently examined or critiqued?

Without question there have been extraordinary achievements led by individual presidents and provosts. Some institutions have literally recast their missions in the language of civic engagement. We are approaching a quarter century of activism that has had an impact on at least two generations of students; thousands of faculty, including many younger faculty whose idealism has drawn them to higher education instead of other, less civic-minded professions; and quite arguably the self-awareness of a nation that has elected its first African American president. Despite the apparent health of democratic action and the fresh energy of activism, a vague malaise nonetheless haunts the academy and the expectations of those who imagined that there would be more.

Yet, is it possible that instead of waning, the collegiate civic engagement movement is actually pausing at a transition point, much as a car shifts gears, so it can move to a different, higher level of engaged leadership—one more suited for a long-distance effort? Is it worth considering whether a form of collective leadership may be capable of succeeding the individual leaders who have defined the civic engagement movement until now?

LEADERSHIP ON HOLD: HAVE SENIOR COLLEGE AND UNIVERSITY LEADERS CONTRIBUTED TO STASIS IN CIVIC ENGAGEMENT?

As a hallmark of service-learning specifically and academic civic engagement more broadly, reflection has entered into the habits as well as the vocabularies of teachers, researchers, and administrators alike. Progress and continuous improvement are due as much to the consequences of reflection and self-assessment as anything else; yet reflection individually or collectively has seemingly not led to inspirational and continuous innovation, enthusiasm, or even renewal at the collective institutional level. If we *are* in a transition period, do we recognize it?

As the movement toward the democratic civic engagement of higher education has matured, there have been several major nationwide, shared efforts to move institutions toward self-studies, formal assessments of engagement, and collective action toward common goals such as those articulated by Campus Compact (e.g., the Presidents' Declaration and self-assessment), the American Association of Colleges and Universities (e.g., projects on Educating Students for Personal and Social Responsibility or Liberal Education and America's Promise), the American Association of State Colleges and Universities (e.g., the American Democracy Project and the Political Engagement Project), Imagining America: Artists and Scholars in Public Life (e.g., "The Tenure Team Initiative on Public Scholarship"), the Association of Public and Land-Grant Universities[1] (e.g., "Statement on Engagement"), and the Association of American Community Colleges (e.g., America's Promise). Those committed to engagement began several new associations, including those now focusing on global issues of civic engagement, such as the Talloires Network, which requires presidents or chancellors to commit their institutions only after a self-reflection on institutional purpose (Tufts 2008). More recently, the Carnegie Foundation has created a new voluntary classification for community engagement that also is based on self-assessment and reflection. There are tool kits and tools aplenty to stimulate aid in and use of reflection as an intentional process to improve institutional practice and to shore up resolve. Given the available apparatus, we might have indeed expected more.

So, where has leadership gone? One of the most obvious answers is that it has simply moved on—literally. Many of the earlier advocates of democratic civic engagement as an institutional priority have retired or moved on to other positions, often at other colleges or universities. Retirees might understandably be forgiven for not meddling in the affairs of their successors by advocating or agitating for a continuation of their engagement agenda. And those who moved on might understandably believe that their new posts and, perhaps, new institutions need something beyond the transplantation of an old idea from their former campuses or former roles, no matter how successful or beloved that work might have been.

For provosts who become presidents, there is the opportunity to continue prior commitments to civic engagement but, in general, not much of an incentive to earmark a new era or to generate excitement by reprising the last act of their respective professional dramas. They may maintain without enhancing engagement, but—most likely—they will offer new ideas beyond engagement to attract followers and to win support in their new roles. So, one question for the structure of leadership is how to deal with succession.

An important corollary to the inevitable changes in leadership that occur naturally is the duration of leaders in a key position or role. How many presidents, chancellors, or provosts remain in office long enough to actually change the cultures, practices, and perhaps missions of their institutions to embed the principles of democratic civic engagement so deeply that they endure beyond the personal commitment of the leaders? One of the most commonly told stories of successful transformation is that change occurred over a long period of time because at least one leader at a campus was persistent over so many years that a generation or more of faculty and staff matured their own professional careers on the outlines of the senior leader's interests that, in turn, became imprinted on their own sense of purpose and professionalism. In essence, the long-distance leader was able to change the infrastructure as a key to changing the culture. How much time is actually required to implement "second-order" changes? And is there an alternative to longevity as a factor in successful lasting change?

Even when a change in leaders within an institution is not a factor (and surely there are examples of effective leadership moving toward substantive change in only a few years), leaders can be distracted from the priority of civic engagement by local, national, and global issues. If the civic engagement agenda is doing well enough, what president or provost or dean would not be motivated to expend time, energy, and resources on more pressing matters brought about by enrollment shifts, reduced revenues, increased costs, demands for accountability and transparency in matters such as student learning outcomes, rankings that have now gone global, and a host of other local, potentially toxic issues that preoccupy leadership, like high tuition hikes, binge drinking, athletic problems, economic development, reduced federal research funding, and enrolling undocumented immigrants?

But perhaps nothing causes a president to shy away from civic engagement as much as explicitly linking community service to action—especially democratic action—that might have consequences. "Democracy" has been politicized and polarized so that any action under that label is likely to lead to results that some constituents will find objectionable or divisive. While surely not the sole or even leading reason, trepidation over the consequences of democratic action may have contributed to a sense that the civic engagement movement is stalled as presidents seek cover in the safer, more banal language and public purposes of civic engagement.

As this volume tries to make clear, there is a distinction between civic engagement and engaging higher education in building democratic community or in developing the capacity for democratic action. In the former, well-intended action may suffice, whereas in the latter, action for consequence is the intention. Because of its very qualities of inclusiveness, respect for the contributions of all participants, and group decision making, the outcomes of democratic engagement are uncertain and occasionally unwelcome; civic engagement, on the other hand, can have defined limits and presumed results. An anecdote from the American Democracy Project (ADP) is illustrative.

For the provost, it may be relatively safe to approve students' requests for a public space where anyone could express views on any subject and exercise constitutionally guaranteed rights of speech and assembly. Known as Democracy Plaza on one campus, this space also included chalkboards where passers-by could write a message free from censorship and subject only to personal dictates of taste and responsibility. For the provost, this space manifests academic principles and goals, encouraging students especially to put into practice theoretical or hypothetical ideas and conclusions. In such a setting, "Democracy" not only has a positive connotation but its existence as a physical space where interaction occurs affirms the role of the university as the place where differences can be discussed, understood, and, if not reconciled, tolerated. For the president, however, "democracy" may instead be thrown up as a license for indecency, indecorum, and indiscretion irrespective of constitutional guarantees or the opportunities for learning because anything might be said—or written.

The very word "democracy" is laden with undertones that imply intentional action with consequence in a way that another label, such as "free speech area," may not. What might pass for bad judgment or poor taste in the latter is seen as deliberate, even irresponsible provocation in the former simply because it is considered to be "democratic"—outside predictability and the authority of hierarchy and expertise. In merely sanctioning a Democracy Plaza, the institution and the leaders accept a responsibility for actions they might otherwise be able to disavow or avoid. There are ways to finesse this dilemma, as happened at the ADP campus in question, but the need to be institutionally self-aware and to negotiate unstated fears makes the issue of embracing democracy much more complicated than it might appear. It is safer to be civically engaged than democratically engaged.

This distinction is crucial to the purpose of this volume, but for the purpose of this chapter the issue of whether engagement is democratic is secondary to understanding how leadership can itself be transformed from the personal (and thus hierarchical) to the collective (and thus democratic). It is enough simply to understand first how civic engagement can be transformative. Then, democratic engagement can follow.

While civic engagement may offer ways to address difficult public issues, it is unlikely to attract the attention, interest, or use of leadership unless the applications are fresh, focused, and fast. Few leaders can make civic engagement adequately inviting year after year even if they are undaunted in their commitment, and pursuing democratic change may be too risky. Is there a difference between the movement's having stalled or merely reached a plateau in the estimation of a president with budget cuts looming or a provost wondering how to begin one more fall faculty convocation with an engaging theme of civic opportunities?

And whether budgets are actually being reduced or merely not increasing with the demands for new activities and higher levels of quality, resource constraints may make it more difficult to form a new center, hire a service-learning coordinator, authorize workshops for civic-minded departments, or offer an annual prize for exemplary engagement. Even when earlier allocations are preserved in the face of budget cuts, civic engagement can seem to lose steam if new funding is not added to expand successes or to reward innovations.

Undoubtedly there are many other reasons—some personal or idiosyncratic—for leadership's putting civic engagement on hold at any particular institution, but limited time horizons, distractions, and resource constraints are surely at the top of the list—and they are all understandable. The story might end there, with a shrug of regret, except for the fact that not all of these conditions are likely to affect so many leaders or institutions at the same time. Why have so many engines of change lost steam concurrently, just when the needs are even more pressing—no less because of the now critical need to prepare graduates who are globally competent citizens as well as intelligently engaged local participants? One possible answer is that all of us, from presidents to students, from association executives to neighborhood nonprofit activists, have compartmentalized leadership too hastily and too easily and have become over-reliant on a few individuals.

MOVING ON: FROM PRESIDENTS TO A CONSPIRACY OF THE CONCERNED

Of course, leadership occurs at many different levels of an organization, and the least of us can be a leader among our peers. Civic engagement depends on this reality to succeed, and the growing recognition and respect for community-based reciprocal expertise and leadership has been one of the most rejuvenating factors of the past decade for higher education.

Nonetheless, the early success of Campus Compact has been attributed to its presidential membership and the implication of presidential commitment as the key to institutional involvement and sustained practice. For the first president of a college or university to champion engagement, this may well be true. But is it for the next or third president, whose sense of legacy may extend well beyond making good on a predecessor's promise? The commitment and buy-in of the president or chief executive officer (CEO) is nearly universal as the first premise of a civically engaged campus. Even the new Carnegie Classification—voluntary as it is—asks a foundational question of all would-be classified institutions: "Does the executive leadership of the institution . . . explicitly promote community engagement as a priority?" (Carnegie Foundation 2010). Although an equivocal answer to this leading question may not disqualify an institution, it is clearly a deficit to be made up by some other countervailing force that can compensate for the missing president.

While this seeming lack of buy-in may have nothing to do with the implied conditions of the presidential ennui or inattention to succession commitments (as a function of strategic planning) noted in the preceding paragraphs, there is another intriguing anecdote. One of the most successful and dynamic community engagement projects of a national scope in recent years (i.e., since 2005) is the previously mentioned American Democracy Project sponsored by the American Association of State Colleges and Universities. While this project is limited to public comprehensive universities, it has attracted enormous interest from students, faculty, media, community leaders, and, yes, even presidents. But it is an activity principally of provosts—that is, provosts guide it, energize it locally, and connect it nationally. Why has this activity been such a countervailing force to the general perception of stagnation of the overall civic engagement movement? One answer is that it is succeeding simply because provosts, not presidents, are leading it.

Having once been a provost for a long time, I like this answer. But I also know that as capable, talented, and innovative as they are as a group, provosts have even fewer cards to play than presidents when it comes to committing an institution as a whole to a course of action. Thus, it may be that provosts have been leading engagement efforts only because they are filling the vacuum left by presidents who are preoccupied or who have moved on, literally or figuratively. And the next question will be, can a provostial project be sustained any longer than a presidential one? Will the same conditions apply to provosts as those suggested for presidents?

My guess is that these same conditions will drain the energy out of this effort, exemplary as it is. When the originating provost moves on, who will become the project's champion? Experience suggests that most succeeding provosts will put the American Democracy Project, along with other signature efforts of their predecessors, into maintenance mode. Some may find new expressions of civic engagement, focusing on neglected or under-supported dimensions of faculty work, student learning outcomes, or community involvement. But most won't stake their reputation as provost on following up on the work of the last incumbent, no matter how successful.

So, where do we turn next for energy and innovation—deans, department chairs, center directors, exemplary faculty? How long do we wait to cycle back to presidents to provide the drive and energy for a movement that has not yet succeeded? And can we think of projects with enough scale and appeal to restart the civic engagement movement, if it is indeed stalled?

The Carnegie classification for engaged campuses contains an intriguing hint of a possibility. In addition to the prominent question about the senior leadership's commitment, the instrument also asks, "Does the institution have a campus-wide coordinating infrastructure to support and advance community engagement?"(Carnegie Foundation 2010). Maybe the answer to leadership is not individuals. Instead, maybe the answer to revitalizing the movement is collective leadership of a particular kind—organized, intentional, and sustainable.

Conspiracies are not usually regarded kindly by those in power, since they imply doing something clandestine that would be unlikely to succeed if everyone were in the know. But what if there were a conspiracy of the concerned, operating not in secret but below the level of policy or official approbation, assuming that civic engagement is already in place but neglected? The Carnegie Foundation asks about infrastructure, which suggests committees, offices, and routine, not leadership. Perhaps the collective action of those involved in the operations and actions of an infrastructure might assume the form of leadership if there were a tacit but not necessarily sanctioned or officially charged commitment to identify and achieve defined and measured goals, regardless of the current president's or provost's level of interest. When an institution can sustain a movement—any movement perhaps, but especially that of civic engagement—independent of who occupies the role of president or provost, does that signal that the institution itself has been transformed?

Every institution is distinct in its collective personality. History, location, mission, resources (as well as their sources), and values all combine in richly varying patterns to create a culture. Individuals contribute to the culture, though rarely does any one person lead a personality change, and this reality may account for the possibility that presidential or provostial leadership alone cannot effect institutional transformation. Instead, over time, procedures, policies, practices, and precedents emerge as an infrastructure of roles, rules, and offices that determine the capacity of individuals, including presidents and provosts, to act. (Just ask any president who has tried to initiate a change in faculty governance or a provost who has prepared new policies for promotion and tenure.) It is this culture and its formal properties that give rise to the necessity of a broad range of individuals working across the institution in consort to achieve common objectives. Reciprocally, when the infrastructure is changed, not only can the culture be changed; change can be sustained independent of individual leadership, much as when a paradigm shifts, because the whole pattern of interactions is viewed from a new and different perspective. But is there a way to change infrastructure through collective leadership?

Leadership is tricky and uncertain business. Based on the hundreds of books and thousands of articles and essays on leadership of just the past decade, we know that individual leadership is, in fact, critically important to organizational success. And we even have scholarship on collective organizational leadership—especially teams, where many people can be leaders. This scholarly research and the experiential anecdotes published in commercial media should all be considered and applied to developing strategies for collective leadership to support the transformation of whole institutions as permanently and significantly engaged with society. But maybe, just maybe, we also need to be a little more deliberate, in a quiet sort of way, in thinking about how to structure leadership that draws on the conventional and on symbolic leadership but does not depend on them.

If the civic engagement movement has indeed stagnated at university after university, college after college, then it must have once been dynamic and ambitious. Almost always, initial progress required the active participation and leadership of the president or chancellor—and if not the CEO, then the chief academic officer, who was given license to articulate engagement in some form as an institutional priority. Axiomatically, stagnation and stasis are the consequence of the neglect or loss of interest of one or both of these senior leaders. On campuses where stagnation has not occurred because activity has never gained enough momentum to approach a movement, there is a different diagnosis and a different starting point for remediation.

The Anatomy of Leadership

To undertake the design of collective leadership, we should consider the full range of players, beginning with senior, or executive, leadership. Certainly the president, chancellor, or CEO, by whatever title, is of paramount importance as suggested by Campus Compact's and the Carnegie Foundation's processes for classifying community-engaged institutions. There is no substitute for a committed and effective president in moving an institution forward and leading change toward a sustained culture of engagement. As will be noted in the next section, there is a model with stages of leadership that best defines what the CEO does.

As already suggested, however, this model contains its own inherent limitations because once the CEO does what is expected, what next? It is not in the nature of presidential duties to be a maintainer and sustainer. Few presidents seek to make their mark by dealing with infrastructure, for example. (In some settings where there are multiple campuses of a university, one ought also to consider the role of the chancellor or president in leading civic engagement. A system head might well provide the same leadership as a campus CEO, just on a broader scale, but more typically the system head is the person to encourage campus CEOs and to hold them accountable instead of actually leading institutional change.)

Equally understood is the role of the chief academic officer (CAO), again named by a variety of titles including provost, vice chancellor or vice president for academic affairs, dean of faculties, or executive dean. Chapter 6 of this volume explores in detail the role of this critical senior leader, and little more needs be said here except perhaps to note that the CEO and CAO can work together as a well-coordinated team with differentiated duties directed toward a common end, or they can work in countervailing ways with one compensating for the inattention or avoidance of the other—and everything in between. Whatever the rapport, there is a necessary relationship between the two, and this relationship has a profound impact on what happens among other leaders and within the infrastructure. The example of the Democracy Plaza cited earlier offers an example of how important managing the relationship actually is. In some instances, the counterpart to the CEO is not actually the CAO; instead, this responsibility is entrusted either to a vice president for community relations or external affairs, or to a vice president for student affairs or student life. In either case, the CEO leads by setting forth the goals or vision, and the CAO (or alternate) leads by implementing. The individual roles and the interplay of the roles of the CEO and CAO, therefore, must be the first order of business in diagnosing stasis. But there are other defined leadership roles to consider. For simplicity, these might be grouped as external and internal leaders.

External leaders include trustees (classified here as external because they are responsible for ensuring the broader interests of the public, the alumni, and other constituencies and not for leading the institution, although the Carnegie Foundation includes trustees in its definition of executive leadership), community leaders, alumni leaders, state coordinating councils or commissions (for public institutions), directors of accrediting bodies, and heads of national organizations that are particularly important to institutional identity. These external leaders are important because of their direct and indirect influence over the CEO and, in turn, the CAO, and they can exercise enormous short-term authority over the direction of an institution by the way they engage the senior leadership of the institution. (Consider the current emphasis being placed on economic development as engagement and the ways the civic or public good is recast in economic terms.) Under the best of or even normal circumstances, these external leaders are concerned about civic engagement and the institution's involvement with the public. They need to be considered in any infrastructure of collective leadership. The point is not to delineate all the possible roles external leaders might play in creating a new model of collective leadership. Instead, it is to note that such leadership must be considered and engaged.

Beyond the CAO, internal leadership necessarily includes other senior campus officers who report to the CEO or CAO and who might have some role in engagement. As noted, this might be the senior student affairs officer, the person responsible for community relations (public, government), or a special assistant. The provost might have an associate responsible for engagement, and there may be others who report directly to the CAO including the director(s) of the center(s) for service-learning, community engagement, teaching and learning, or similarly named entities. Other leaders who exercise authority out of title or role include deans of schools (and especially those for whom community-based learning is an essential component of pedagogy, including most of the professional degree programs), department chairs, and the chairs of standing committees or councils whose charge touches on community or civic engagement. And surely there are more titles and roles that can be identified as leaders in civic engagement, according to the preferences and histories of colleges and universities. These leadership roles are named, identified, and authorized with some formal reporting relationship in a hierarchy. They are, in large part, the agents of infrastructure and the people whose coordination the Carnegie classifiers are most interested in understanding.

Not so easily named are all of the others who exercise leadership because of their interests, actions, or commitment, not because of their titles or administrative duties. Most notably, these are the faculty whose teaching or research involves them in the several communities of which any college or university is a part, beginning with the geographic community where the campus is located. There are student affairs personnel, human resources staff, office support staff, and students who also play key leadership roles out of interest instead of duty. Several chapters of this volume address the leadership of faculty, staff, and students.

It is important to note here that these leaders are self-motivated and act largely out of genuine interest instead of duty, and they are accountable—if at all—only because civic engagement may fall within rewardable definitions of responsibilities, as is the case for many faculty where service is explicitly recognized (along with teaching and research) for advancement or salary considerations. These are the people whose collective actions define civic engagement but who are, in most instances, led by others. Their personal leadership manifests itself in the actions and deeds that eventually define transformation. Yet without the authority to allocate resources, to speak for and to commit the institution, and to hold others accountable for performance, they cannot launch or sustain a movement, let alone manage the transformation of a campus, unless they are acting as collective leaders.

Among the three broad groupings used here, it is the internal leaders below the level of CEO and CAO who offer the greatest potential for untapped leadership when the senior executives are disinterested, preoccupied, or otherwise not engaged.

So, what is the model of collective leadership through some type of conspiracy of the concerned that might compensate for the seeming doldrums of executive leadership and the stagnation of institutional transformation? How can collective leadership overcome the inherent and structural deficits that typically follow changes in the CEO or CAO or both? And even when the senior leaders don't change, how can transformative progress occur when the once exciting and leading ideals of engagement become stale?

IMPLEMENTING COLLECTIVE LEADERSHIP

The formalization of collective leadership is most likely to be found in defining the infrastructure of civic engagement on a campus, as implied by the Carnegie Foundation's second question. Identifying and naming the offices, functions, and recurring activities of which civic engagement is comprised are surely the starting points for rethinking leadership in collective terms. Actions that are repeated year after year, offices that have budgets to do things, and people who have titles are the formal elements of infrastructure and thus the custodians of culture. But people with ideas, commitments, and a will to act are, above all else, the basis of leadership.

The basic concept is not only obvious and commonplace; it can be a part of stagnation when merely defined as infrastructure instead of leadership. Even a comprehensive and competent infrastructure can contribute to stagnation when its sense of leadership is dependent on the CEO or CAO. When only one of these senior leaders loses interest in civic engagement (or never develops it) as a matter of personal passion and institutional priority, the infrastructure can carry on admirably if the other leader is committed. Progress toward transformation and cultural change may be slowed—even irritatingly so—but it can and often does continue under such a circumstance. Progress can be invigorated and renewed by collective leadership, but the real need for collective leadership occurs when neither the CEO nor the CAO is personally involved or committed to civic engagement as an institutional priority.

As the driving force for institutional transformation and sustained institutionalization of civic engagement processes and goals, collective leadership emerges out of infrastructure when one or more of the infrastructure participants set goals and define strategies without waiting for or asking the permission of the CEO or CAO. It is in this sense that collective leadership is a "conspiracy" of the concerned individuals because it is unauthorized or unrecognized. It does not depend on the formal leadership to proceed or to succeed. It does not ask permission out of a realization that a negative response would preclude or limit the range of action. It is collective because success depends on the participation—witting or unwitting—of many, if not all, of the people who are the infrastructure. It is democratic because its legitimacy depends on the consent and the participation of the constituents of the infrastructure itself. While certainly not a rebellion or even a critique of the senior leadership, collective leadership is also most likely to succeed when it is neither known about nor sanctioned by the senior leaders.

It should be quickly noted, however, that collective leadership can also succeed without being conspiratorial when the CEO or CAO either explicitly or tacitly acknowledges the role of the infrastructure in acting on its own. If the president or provost has no interest in civic engagement but is willing to let others engage publicly, there is no need to act surreptitiously. Leaders need to conspire only when there is a worry about being shut down. In either case, the point is that the potential for leadership and institutional advancement in civic engagement exists even when presidents and provosts are not leading. It's a lot like democracy.

Put directly, one or more people who are recognized as having legitimacy and authority in a defined role, and are thus in a position to act on behalf of the institution to advance the civic engagement role, can compensate for the indifference, inadequacy, or distractions of the CEO and CAO. Faculty, staff, other administrators, and students can all participate in collective leadership when they have such roles, whereas otherwise they would have limited capacity to act on behalf of the institution. No matter how effective and how well-known a faculty member might be for using service-learning, for example, this colleague needs to overcome putative self-interest by acting out of a role recognized by the academic community as communal, as based on the common good. For similar reasons, collective and compensating leadership has to come from within the internal leadership group. External leaders may contribute to collective action in effective ways, but they can neither instigate nor lead without posing a risk to the senior leadership. Members of the internal leadership group are presumably in their assigned roles with the explicit or tacit approval of the CEO and CAO, and thus their legitimacy and basis of acting is not inherently a threat.

Put even more directly, at some point in the life of almost every college and university that is on the path to making civic engagement a defining characteristic and to asserting a public purpose for higher education in perpetually renewing democratic actions and processes, someone other than the president and provost must literally seize leadership and articulate a strategy for achieving what may have been a senior leader's vision—but a vision still in the making. It would be the rare CEO or CAO who could so transform a whole institution as to ensure continuity of commitment regardless of who might occupy the position in the future. Such an action may occur without fault or blame, but when stagnation is diagnosed, something has to be done. It may be done by more than a single catalyst, but however many are engaged in acting against a vacuum, they must do so with self-awareness, intentionality, deliberate organization, and a plan for sustainability. Where to begin?

LEADING WHEN LEADERS WON'T

In our essay "Leading the Engaged Institution," Lorilee Sandmann and I identified four stages of leadership focused principally on the CEO and, to a lesser extent, the CAO and others:

1. Interpreting institutional mission to reflect engagement with multiple communities beginning with the local geographic community
2. Defining specific objectives and goals to implement the mission
3. Articulating the means and priorities to achieve the goals
4. Manifesting the commitment through personal interaction (Sandmann and Plater)

If collective leadership is to compensate for the absence of executive leadership, it must find other ways to address each of these four stages. Alternately, if the senior leaders have already gone through these stages and the movement is now faltering for whatever reason, there needs to be a fifth stage, in which others assume responsibility for supplanting the senior leaders' roles.

Interpreting Mission

The CEO is positioned best to interpret and articulate the mission of an institution—and, when necessary, revise it—by connecting the institution's current activities and priorities to its constituencies and by offering a vision for the future that extends the mission and includes both "old" and new constituents. Interpretation is a powerful means of effecting change, and CEOs especially are assigned a ritual function by virtue of their position to be the chief spokespeople and interpreters of the institutions' past, present, and future. The narrative told to relate these three phases of identity is the rationale for current action. The CAO can play a similar but lesser role on behalf of the CEO in speaking, principally, to the internal constituencies.

When the concept of civic engagement, and engagement with the local community in particular, has dropped from the rhetoric of the senior leadership, however, there are ways that others can pick up lapsed promises or create new implications. With a consistent, repeated message to a variety of community leaders, organized and intentional center directors, associate provosts, committee chairs, and individual faculty engaged in community-based research and teaching can create the impression of mission-driven involvement to match their activities. In time, the expectations of community leaders will mirror this commitment back to the senior leadership and to other external leaders such as trustees, government officials, and media, with the net result that there is an obligation on the part of the institution to make good on the implied mission. As long as this strategy does not contradict or violate directives of the president or provost, it can overcome or revitalize the inattention of the senior leaders in time. And it becomes transformative when the community's expectations are high.

There are other ways for collective leadership to compensate for silence on mission and vision. One is to take advantage of periodic accreditation, a time when representative committees of the campus community necessarily must conduct a self-study and set forth statements of mission and vision supported by examples. Most regional accreditors and many specialized accreditors have standards or criteria that call for the institution to articulate its goals with regard to mission; civic engagement can be introduced into the self-study even when it is not a formal part of mission. As supplements to the mission statement itself, vision and values statements are more malleable.

In contributing to these documents, those committed to civic engagement have a fair and equitable chance to suggest both language and concrete objectives that advance the civic engagement mission of the campus. Since relatively few faculty will volunteer for such committees or task forces, it is a good opportunity to gain influence—even suggesting that renewal of civic engagement or some specific necessary advancement within civic engagement becomes the centerpiece of a self-study or a thematic or focused visit. If incorporated into the reports and documents on which accreditation is based, there is then a solid foundation on which to build further action for the duration of the accreditation. For good reason, missions are difficult to change—but interpreting mission can take many forms and have more than one voice.

When senior leadership has actively embraced the civic engagement agenda and related it to mission, they ordinarily set forth specific goals to implement their interpretation. Presidents do this in their speeches to the community and to national audiences. Provosts do it in their presentations to faculty assemblies, councils of deans, and committees. They both do it when they allocate resources. This is when vision is given shape and meaning, often in the specific expectations for the new academic year—an ideal time to inspire and to elevate. Although their titles and positions bestow presidents and provosts with ritualistic authority as the managers of symbolic interactions, others can play decisive roles in redirecting attention and activity toward the engagement agenda when its bloom has faded—or fails to blossom.

Implementing Mission and Inspiring

Presidents and provosts have special opportunities for leadership by defining objectives for the whole institution and linking these to mission in ways that have meaning and significance for the campus constituents. A proactive president who is still energizing civic engagement might join with the mayor of the city to announce a multiyear project to improve K–12 education through articulated service projects that involve students in community service. Or a provost might set forth goals for reforming the tenure and promotion process to recognize service as a valid basis for advancement, equal in status to research or teaching. In setting objectives both for the year and long term, senior executives are exercising a familiar trait of effective leadership. They are implementing mission in tangible ways and using the actions and results to innovate and to inspire. When faculty, staff, students, and external constituents can see value in the proposed actions, they will not only work toward them but in the process begin institutional transformation.

When leadership from the top has stagnated, however, others can also set goals. Usually they must be more modest, and often they must be attained without the benefit of a resource allocation. But if they are intentional and organized, small steps can have a similar cumulative impact in time. A dean or center director may not have the media coverage of a president, but these leaders, when working together across organizations and offices, can set their own goals with local school superintendents or other community groups and achieve much the same result. The goal in this instance may not be heightened awareness as much as substantive change. Faculty committees, led by one or two committed and well-regarded public scholars, can undertake reforms in the promotion and tenure process. Almost always, a department or school can adopt more specific criteria for advancement than the institution. As long as they are not inconsistent with the campus goals, they can privilege civic engagement at the unit level. In all such cases, collective leadership must depend on organization, communication, shared objectives, and intentional actions to achieve cumulative results equal to or greater than the singular actions of the CEO or CAO.

But one of the most effective ways for collective leadership to act when senior officials have not is to participate in a regional or national project on civic engagement that matches a need or opportunity for the institution. Few presidents or provosts will decline to accept participation in a project that might have prestige, and even funding, attached to it. As national organizations announce opportunities for campus involvement, a few keepers of the infrastructure can develop a proposal that, if accepted, will enable the institution to make progress on a specific goal or set of goals. While the American Democracy Project is sponsored largely by provosts, a small group of faculty, for example, could easily request that their provost join the project, or similar projects that may emerge in the future. It would be the rare provost that would deny such a request, even if the provost's personal participation is nominal and resource commitments are nil.

And there are always opportunities for innovation and reshaping the familiar in a novel approach. When the president or provost is advocating internationalization and study abroad, for example, creative organizational leaders can respond with proposals and ideas for international service-learning. Or when presidents are struggling to explain why such a large portion of institutional resources are going into merit-based as opposed to need-based scholarships, creative organizational leaders can recast merit to include community service in addition to SAT scores, high GPAs, and athletic or musical prowess.

Perhaps the most simple and direct means to act when the symbolic leaders do not is to propose that the institution seek the Carnegie designation as a community-engaged institution. Most of the work can be done within the infrastructure, requiring the CEO and CAO to do little but sign off. If neither rushed nor presented with an ultimatum, most CEOs will gladly and gratefully accept the work of an individual, committee, or office if it adds positively to the campus's image and costs little or nothing, even when they do not initiate the request for an application. Moreover, once classification is attained, one or two of the collective leaders can easily make the case for the value of maintaining the classification, even as CEOs and CAOs are replaced or change their focus. If the application is not accepted, this decision can then become the case for increased attention for senior leadership—along with resource allocations to ensure future acceptance.

Articulating the Means (i.e., Allocating Resources)

Presidents and provosts have a more tangible means of demonstrating leadership in their ability to articulate the means of implementing mission and related strategic objectives by setting priorities, both annual and long term. While establishing the specific steps to be taken and the priority order are important, the actual leadership comes in allocating resources to achieve the goals and priorities—that is, making choices about where to spend time and money. In the early years of presidential leadership for civic engagement, impressive commitments were made for faculty and staff positions; centers; departmental and school grants for engagement; award and recognition programs for faculty, students, and staff (and even community organizations that collaborated with universities and colleges); scholarships, attendance at conferences and summer institutes; data collection and analysis; and special initiatives of all kinds. Many of these investments have remained in place and even grown annually proportionate to overall gains in institutional budgets. But in some institutions, budgets have been cut and programs, projects, and positions eliminated. Even when there is a steady-state budget, the early enthusiasm and sense of innovation may have given way to maintenance and routine. The answer to renewal and to reinvigorating the civic engagement movement cannot always be more money.

Whether the president or provost has merely lost enthusiasm or has diminished resources to invest, others can step in to help overcome the inertia. The most obvious way to sustain or restart momentum is through an external grant. While grants rarely provide funds for sustaining a new initiative, presidents or provosts may be willing to commit sustaining funds if the grant is successful; the time to secure this a priori commitment is as a part of the grant application, not later, when the grant funding has been exhausted.

A few institutions have been successful in attracting external support in the form of an endowment—for a center, for service scholarships, or for other engagement activities. Almost always, the donors' interest comes through their involvement with faculty, center directors, and students—the people actually engaged in the community or in generating community-based knowledge. Wise and prudent members of the collective leadership will ensure a prominent place for the president in managing the gift, and no president or provost should be surprised by a major contribution in support of civic engagement even when it has been cultivated over months and years without their prior knowledge.

But the greatest power of collective leadership comes when important gains are made without new resources—by changing practices, by reusing existing resources, and by changing goals. Service-learning has been one of the most important instruments of institutional transformation. While it requires some investment of time to adapt a new pedagogy and some investment in workshops and orientations for faculty to learn about the pedagogy, the costs are minimal to the institution and the gains are impressive in terms of increased retention, student satisfaction, alumni loyalty, and so forth. Some of these gains can be reframed as savings to the institution (e.g., because of enhanced retention) and a request made for a reinvestment of savings to improve quality and success.

The most effective means of transforming an institution and repurposing it to address meaningfully and permanently the goals of civic engagement is not adding on something new without discontinuing something existing; it is replacing or redefining existing goals in new ways. Faculty committees, individual faculty, and offices or centers focused on engagement have a special asset they can use to great advantage, one that is beyond the means of presidents and most provosts. Faculty retain responsibility for the curriculum, and to the extent to which they can define student learning outcomes in ways that use the power of engagement and community-based learning to both enhance documented learning and explicitly address learning objectives in terms and concepts that draw on community engagement, they can—literally— transform their institutions.

The costs are minimal because the fundamental activity of teaching and learning is being changed, not the resources being committed to it. With the reauthorization of the federal Higher Education Act, national attention has been fundamentally redirected toward assessing actual student learning. While the means of such assessment may go through many trials and tests, there is no doubt that accreditation and qualification for federal financial support will depend to some extent on institutions' having defined learning objectives and the means of assessing actual student achievement. This is an ideal time for faculty, center directors, and others committed to civic engagement to ensure that learning outcomes for the institution as a whole include some form of engagement.

Perhaps the most exciting prospect is turning the soft and mushy catalog copy of "preparing graduates for citizenship" into meaningful learning objectives with assessable means of documenting whether a graduate is, in fact, not only ready for citizenship but also a globally competent and responsible citizen. Presidents, and especially provosts, can play a role in encouraging faculty and their many councils, committees, informal networks, and colleagues in staff roles to move toward more meaningful learning objectives and procedures for assessing actual attainment, but this opportunity for institutional transformation belongs truly to the collective leadership of committed faculty and administrators.

Manifesting Commitment

There really is no substitute for a president's manifesting institutional commitment to civic engagement through personal interaction. A provost can augment and reinforce the presidential involvement and even add substance when the president's interactions are superficial. But the opportunities for these senior leaders to demonstrate personal commitment—passion even—generate a level of trust and investment by others that gives energy and scope to a movement. It's not easy to imagine alternatives to senior leadership actually "being there."

But when collective leadership must compensate for disengaged CEOs and CAOs, the idea of conspiracy may play a role. Organizational leaders can, in fact, maneuver senior leaders into more visible roles by inviting them to participate in media events, by securing the participation of external leaders (e.g., the mayor, a CEO of a significant corporation, the head of a national organization, a trustee or two, a prominent donor) in an engagement activity, by inviting them to present awards or scholarships to students, and with a dozen other activities that place them before an audience, media, or both. If the idea of manipulating senior leaders is unappealing, then there are alternative conceptual frameworks throughout the leadership literature, such as those suggested by Peter Senge, for example, in roles of "facilitator" or "designer" (Senge 1990).

Even when a president or provost does not manifest personal commitment, an institution can. One of the newest and most important ways to demonstrate institutional commitment is through recognition in the relatively new Carnegie Classification of Community Engagement, developed in 2006. As already noted, one of the leading and key qualifying questions asks for evidence of the president's commitment. While the purpose of the question is meaningful, there are levels of evidence and levels of commitment; with a minimal response about the CEO, other areas of commitment through collective organizational leadership can compensate for a marginally involved CEO. This is not an argument for deception or misrepresentation, but it is a strategy for maneuvering the CEO into threshold conditions of engagement while a strong organizational leadership—perhaps with the active or tacit support of the CAO—demonstrates that the institution is committed even if the president is not—or not yet.

There are other ways for a whole campus to demonstrate its commitment and interaction. As already noted, some of the new voluntary associations devoted to civic engagement require a president's approbation and statement of institutional commitment. But when the president is not the one actively seeking such association with like-minded presidents, others can propose affiliation and ask the president to commit the institution to the principles or the declaration on behalf of all those who are engaged.

SECOND-ORDER LEADERSHIP

The premise of this volume is that there is a need to address what Larry Cuban has called "second-order changes" (1988) in institutional practice because of the stagnation of first-order changes—that is, changes the editors of this volume have labeled as improvements to existing practices without fundamental "reconceptualization or transformation of organizational purposes, roles, rules, relationships, and responsibilities—dimensions of institutional culture and policy" (Hartley and Saltmarsh 2008). As outlined in this chapter, one response is the emergence of a second-order leadership—not second-class or derivative in any sense, but a leadership that can compensate for the absence of first-order leaders—those who are first-order in the sense of having had the greatest initial impact of creating a national movement among higher educational institutions and first-order in occupying the key roles prescribed by title, authority, and ritual.

The basic premise has been that when first-order leaders flag, there is a need for a new order of leadership born of the organizational infrastructure and manifesting itself in collective responsibility instead of a singular figurehead or two. This premise is based on the need to compensate for the diminished role of the principal leaders, the CEO and the CAO. But there are at least three other reasons to begin considering second-order leadership by thinking ahead instead of looking back on the stagnation and a diminishment of enthusiasm in first-order leaders.

Conspiring to Act by Setting Learning Outcomes

Decades of popular literature and scholarly research alike have given us multiple schemes for defining leadership and constructing pathways to improve it. One of the most repeated, albeit in many different guises, is to divide leaders into two types: (1) those who lead by listening to what their constituents *want* and then by acting out the four stages identified above in a manner that builds consensus and (2) those who lead by imagining what their constituents *need* and then by acting out the four stages in a manner that inspires and motivates. (Most leaders, of course, would say they both listen and imagine, creating leadership in a combination of consensus and inspiration. But in my experience, leaders tend to lean in one direction or another.)

While not all organizations may be ready for a view that provides an alternative to traditional ways of characterizing leadership in dichotomies and contrasting strengths, higher education is prepared to do so because there is a basic stability to institutions below the level of CEO and CAO that perseveres and perpetuates itself. Ordinarily, this might be a problem since such structures tend to preserve the status quo—the very issue being addressed in this volume—but there is an opportunity to use this historical tendency as a strength, because informed individuals are in key positions where their actions can cumulatively transform the institution.

The following are needed to turn maintenance into action: (1) self-awareness and the practiced capacity for reflection; (2) an intention to act through the infrastructure on the part of at least one or two of its key members who can initiate collective leadership (i.e., people whose opinions would be respected because of past actions if not because of title or position); (3) an understanding that persistence and a long-term horizon are assets, not detriments (in contrast to most senior leaders, who understand that their advantage is in relatively quick action given the average time in office); and (4) the capacity to use data, benchmarks, and concrete goals to take incremental steps toward larger objectives, including, ultimately, overall institutional transformation.

The principal distinction between this approach to the leadership of the dichotomous consensus-builder or the visionary-activist is that in both of these instances (and most other models of leadership discussed within the context of civic engagement) the focus is on the individual as actor. (In the most cynical characterization, presidents or provosts have to prove themselves with notable deeds in order to move on.) This model distributes the capacity and opportunity for action across both time and the infrastructure itself. Yes, this model does depend on one or more individuals to be the catalyst and, in that sense, the "leader" to initiate collective leadership, but once the capacity for group reflection is established, collective leadership has the potential to persist beyond any individual, so members of the infrastructure itself can change while the collective action continues. Put bluntly, there has to be at least one person who will form a conspiracy to act when the senior leadership is no longer driving progress toward permanent institutional change.

What really distinguishes this model of collective leadership from others, however, is the notion of using incremental goals to achieve larger goals, including transformation. Data-driven decision making and teamwork are well-established principles in the corporate and, to a lesser extent, nonprofit and governmental sectors. They are only slowly making their way into higher education. But there is now a new impetus that lends unusual momentum to the adoption of these techniques and practices, something beyond retention and graduation rates: the radical idea that higher education should be able to prove that students have not only learned something but learned things that were intended.

Professional degree programs have long since adopted this model with licensure and skills-assessment models, but the expectation is becoming pervasive at the course, program (major), and institutional levels. This is the moment in time that empowers the infrastructure to use its own unique capacities to manage this inevitable institutional change toward the goal of requiring and documenting evidence of student achievement at graduation in preparation for globally competent citizenship. The infrastructure, not the president or provost (no matter how active or committed), controls the process of defining and assessing learning outcomes. A well-intentioned conspiracy of the committed can do something that others cannot to literally transform their institutions.

Riding the Wave of the New Academic Workforce to Enhance Civic Engagement

A tidal wave of change is approaching that is even more likely than learning outcomes to change higher education forever—the radical change in the academic workforce. Data suggest that more than half of all new full-time academic appointments are contingent and already over a third of current total academic appointments are contingent, while fully 40 percent of the academic workforce is part-time. "The professoriate, which has evolved rapidly and dramatically over the past fifty years, is coming undone" (Plater 2008).

Well documented by leading scholars like Gene Rice, Jack Schuster, Martin Finkelstein, Ann Austin, Judith Gappa, Katherine Trower, Richard Chait, and others, the academic workforce will, barring unforeseen changes, increasingly be composed of teachers, researchers, clinicians, and others who are contingent and part time. Under these rapidly changing circumstances, the issues of faculty governance and ownership of academic culture are up for grabs. Parts of the culture may be grabbed in new and unexpected ways. Those grabbing should regard the civic engagement infrastructure, whose own members may already mirror the future academic workforce.

Regardless, there is, again, a unique moment in history when intentional action might secure a more prominent role for collective leadership to guide institutional transformation through the necessity of collaboration and cooperation. When the majority of those responsible for overall institutional performance in all areas of work—teaching, research, and service—are no longer tenured professors, they must rely on others to achieve mission-driven results, even if they retain a privileged or controlling place in institutional management.

By using the opportunity to define learning outcomes in terms of civic engagement and by working effectively among all of the sectors of the workforce, the infrastructure has the opportunity to be more focused, intentional, organized, and persistent than others simply by the fact of their shared goals and longer history of collaboration. Moreover, the infrastructure and its collective leadership can prove most helpful to provosts and presidents in their capacity to act more quickly and effectively than the other components of the new academic workforce, which may not have the advantages of intentional action toward a shared purpose.

Globalization of Learning

For many reasons, globalization is having an impact on the ways institutions think about themselves, including their learning outcomes, the nature of the workforce (consider, for instance, the numbers of foreign-born faculty who dominate some fields of study), the increased emphasis on recruiting students from abroad (even among community colleges), and the rising standards and achievements of other nations in educational performance. One of the key issues facing faculties (and the new academic workforce) is evolving requirements to prepare college graduates to be successful in a much more competitive global environment, and to be globally competent and prepared as a citizen. It is not enough to have knowledge of national history and governmental practices or engagement experiences in a community that is only local or national. If faculty senates are opened to contingent faculty, members of the infrastructure with particular competence in matters of civic engagement have a chance to act directly on campus-level policies and requirements. Even if they are not admitted into governance directly, they will have increased influence out of necessity due to their numbers and roles.

In helping campuses respond to the escalating demands for a more global perspective on learning and the management of institutions, the collective leaders can also play a role in helping craft innovations in practice, such as expanding international service-learning, forming strategic partnerships (i.e., long-term relations based on reciprocity and mutual benefit that do not depend on the personal relations of a few individuals to maintain the interaction) to share resources and experiences, and combining formal with informal learning through the collaboration of student affairs personnel with academic staff.

The interdependencies of financial markets, workforces, climate, health, energy, and food all highlight the degree to which civic engagement must be global. While nations do not yet share a common understanding of democracy and its practices, there is common ground and a belief in the inherent value of many principles. There is enough to build relationships and trust. More importantly, there is a role for academic diplomacy as institutions of higher learning share a common commitment to the pursuit of truth and its dissemination and use across borders both physical and social. In reclaiming the public purpose of higher education, the individuals who make up academic communities have an unprecedented opportunity and responsibility to expand communication, to develop understanding, and to build structures of interaction that remain vital and collegial even when politics, religion, economics, or culture threaten war or isolation. Only faculties and certain professional staff can practice academic diplomacy through their teaching, research, service, and—collectively—their civic engagement. While presidents and provosts may encourage and support academic diplomacy and international civic engagement, only those who are actually engaged substantively with their counterparts (other faculty or staff, perhaps students, occasionally community groups) can make a difference and can create the community of action that transcends borders.

One common denominator among all three of these pathways to collective leadership is their dependence on clear, well-defined goals and the reliance on actual measures of results that allow both internal units and the whole institution to be held accountable for results. Singular leaders such as presidents and provosts are loath to be held personally accountable for results in specific measures, such as retention and graduation rates. In their dependence on multiple infrastructures to achieve institutional goals, the engagement infrastructure can use the concept of benchmarks and measures to solidify their capacity to act and to transform. But first, the members of the collective leadership have to understand what the actual measures of success would be if they were to achieve institutional transformation and to realize second-order change.

BENCHMARKING SECOND-ORDER CHANGE

Once proper and meaningful benchmarks of sustained civic engagement are established by the institution in a process that is recognized as legitimate (which need not necessarily be formal or even explicitly endorsed by the CEO), then the informal collective leadership can work toward meeting the benchmarks as its mandate and as its own form of empowerment. If there are even a few widely accepted benchmarks of engagement for the institution as a whole, these become the anchor or foundation for both persisting and building.

Other chapters in this volume will address more explicitly the benchmarks of sustained and effective engagement. Clearly, each institution must set its own benchmarks in accord with its mission, history, ambition, location, and resources. There are a few general characteristics of performance that tend to be common across institutional types and sizes, however. The most important listing may, in fact, be the criteria used by the Carnegie Foundation in its classification project. Whether or not the Carnegie Foundation persists with its voluntary classification for community engagement, the Foundation has outlined an enduring framework for institutional self-assessment and for benchmarking.

Setting aside CEO (and CAO) involvement, other benchmarks to be considered and the role of collective leadership in defining them include the following (which are not the full Carnegie list of indicators).

Mission. If civic engagement is not already a clearly stated aspect of mission, it can be revised as opportunity permits—if there is intentional persistence, as already discussed. Once engagement is a part of mission, there should be a few quantifiable and measurable ways of demonstrating that mission goals are being met, such as the number of hours of volunteer community engagement activity by faculty, staff, and students; the number of credit hours earned in service-learning and other community-based learning courses; and the percentage of graduates with a transcript notation indicating community engagement. The act of measuring and reporting on engagement in direct support of mission is one of the most effective ways for collective leadership to ensure transformational adoption of the civic engagement movement.

Curriculum. As the domain of faculty, curriculum offers one of the best benchmarks for sustained engagement through service-learning courses and other forms of community-based learning, including clinical education, practicums, internships, field placements, practice teaching, cooperative education, and other forms of experiential learning. But the most important benchmark surely is in the form of documenting that all graduates of the institution have met the mission expectations for engagement: What are the learning goals that implement the ideal of graduating prepared citizens as articulated in missions and other institution-wide value statements, and how is the college or university measuring and assuring success? The Carnegie classification for curricular engagement outlines a number of quantifiable measures that enable the civic engagement infrastructure to act without depending on CEO or CAO approbation. A department, school, committee, office, or even an ad hoc group can collect and publish annual results for a variety of curricular engagements—or request such reports from offices of institutional research or the registrar. If done consistently and persistently, such annual reports generate their own expectations for continued (and, ideally, improving) performance.

Outreach and partnerships. There are many approaches to defining and measuring the institution's actual community engagements, including both the immediate geographical community and other communities of importance to the institution's mission, such as physical communities in other nations or other parts of the state, and communities of association that may have less to do with place than practice. In some form or another, a civic engagement inventory of affiliations, partnerships, and recurring interactions with external organizations that involve generating or using community-based learning becomes a valuable measure of engagement and a means of assessing growth and development. Infrastructure leaders do not need permission to define, document, and report community partnerships (albeit comprehensive data collection may be enhanced with CEO or CAO endorsement). Even when an inventory is unit-specific, as opposed to campus-wide, it is a useful and potentially powerful incentive for continued or improved performance.

The general point to be made—namely, that measurable benchmarks are themselves a powerful means to sustain civic engagement by reporting and making this activity visible to constituents who matter—can take forms suitable to the circumstances to the specific institution, but the overall documentation format for the Carnegie classification is as good a place as any to begin consideration.

Also implicit in the Carnegie approach is a sense of the threshold for sustained civic engagement—what is enough to be classified without necessarily being exemplary. In considering this issue of institutional stagnation, simply maintaining engagement at a satisfactory or threshold level may be enough. Having that threshold validated by external agencies such as regional accrediting bodies or the Carnegie Foundation is surely a necessary and important step to avoid complacency or unwarranted satisfaction by the reputation of engagement earned years earlier.

The managers of the infrastructure can provide the leadership necessary to keep engagement activities above the threshold by their routine and consistent reporting of performance. And they can go beyond local reporting by seeking media coverage for institutional results and by finding ways to forward data to state (e.g., Campus Compact) or national (e.g., the American Democracy Project) organizations.

CONCLUSION

For nearly three decades, presidents and provosts have provided personal leadership for American colleges and universities' increased awareness of their civic responsibilities and their engagement in local communities. Their achievements have been outstanding. But there is nonetheless a sense of stasis, and, for those who have longed for a movement, there is a feeling of stagnation. It is possible, however, that instead of losing executive leadership, civic engagement as an institutional priority has reached a stage of development where the culture is actually changing and the leadership inherent in the infrastructure of the organization is succeeding the more visible individual leaders as the agents of transformed—and sustained—action.

Whether this is a period of stagnation or transition, self-aware and intentional action will have a profound impact on the future performance of a college or university. Whether the president and provost deliberately imbue the infrastructure with the capacity to act as an orderly transfer of authority or the agents of the infrastructure themselves take matters into their own hands as a conspiracy of commitment, the development of collective leadership is a necessary condition of second-order change that ensures sustainability and that is proof of a transformed institution.

The leadership literature is replete with theories, models, and anecdotes, enough to fit any circumstance and to offer a pathway of transformation tailored to each institution. Regardless of the language used to describe such a change or the means of change itself, success depends on the awakening of key members of the infrastructure and their acceptance of roles that make civic engagement an enduring aspect of mission independent of the president or provost. Even when routinized, decentralized, and bureaucratized, civic engagement still requires innovation, assessment, and improvement, which necessitate leadership.

Throughout this volume, much has been made of John Dewey's description of democracy as the very basis of community and, ipso facto, of community as the realization of the ideals and practices of democracy. Through collective leadership—in the forms of face-to-face interactions and the intimacy of shared purpose and place—those individuals who manage the rules, policies, and offices of colleges and universities ensure the vitality of their institutions only when they recognize and accept the legitimate voice and engagement of all members, when—in brief—they act democratically and with an awareness of the consequences of their actions.

The argument set forth in this chapter for the role of collective leadership depends on the awakening and the self-awareness of the infrastructure community, as Dewey conceives community. Once incorporated into the rules, roles, and practices of an institution, civic engagement can become a part of the fabric of the community, interwoven with everything else and invisible as a part of the ongoing background. In this aspect, collective leadership relies on community members as agents and accepts civic engagement as a form of agency, as a means of getting things done. Achieving such a state is no easy feat and is a worthy goal in itself, but it does not fully satisfy the avowed goal of reclaiming or redefining the public purpose of higher education.

With the infrastructure community as the backdrop, this higher calling depends on a form of communal leadership that compels one or more agents to become the catalysts for higher expectations, for action beyond the routine, and for accountability for the whole community. The catalyst is not, emphatically, a surrogate for the president or provost but instead acts solely out of a role as a member of the infrastructure community with an intentionality directed by an awareness of shared goals and assumes a role—perhaps temporarily and for specific purpose—to enhance the effectiveness of the infrastructure itself or to benefit the community. The faculty chair of a committee might seek Carnegie classification as a community-engaged institution; a registrar might offer to list community service on the transcript; a college development officer might solicit an endowment for an annual community service scholarship; the basketball coach might require team members to engage in community service as a condition of play; and a student leader might propose creating a Democracy Plaza. The list of possible actors is extensive, and each acts out of the capacity of the role but with a sense of the larger institutional purpose and with an appreciation for the consequences of the actions.

To awaken, to reclaim, or to compel an institution's enactment of its public purpose, however, requires one or more agents to act beyond the discretion inherent in their roles and to mobilize the infrastructure itself—and thus also the president, provost and larger academic community—as a collective actor. Such catalytic leadership is difficult and time-consuming even as it is ephemeral. Its reward is likely to be only in the cumulative achievement of the institution and in the satisfaction of seeing the college or university act on behalf of the public good. But action motivated by a well-conceived idea or need or opportunity can, like Archimedes' lever, move the world.

And as for a national movement, the time may have come to think globally. It is not without underlying causes that cities—like academic communities—are themselves beginning to see the need for and means to act in a decentralized fashion across national borders. Cities have concerns that are more urgent than nations—transportation, housing, immigration, pollution, equity—and their reasons for empowering each other to act in their own common interest depends on a sense of collective leadership—not that of a prime minister, a president, or even a mayor. In a tragic but nonetheless compelling way, stateless terrorists have also found the means to act in a wholly new way through collective leadership for public horror instead of public good. But these examples of global action should remind us all that we have a duty as well as a means to reclaim and to reassert the role of the university in sustaining civil and democratic societies through engagement and through actions with consequence.

NOTE

1. The APLU was formerly the National Association of State Universities and Land-Grant Colleges (NASULGC).

REFERENCES

American Association of Colleges and Universities. 2010. "Civic Engagement." Available at http://www.aacu.org/resources/civicengagement/index.cfm.

American Association of State Colleges and Universities. 2008. "American Democracy Project." Available at http://www.aascu.org/programs/index.htm.

Association of Public and Land-Grant Universities. 2008. "University Engagement." http://www.aplu.org/NetCommunity/Page.aspx?pid=224.

Campus Compact. 2010. "Civic Engagement Initiatives." Available at http://www.compact.org/initiatives/civic-engagement-initiatives/.

Carnegie Foundation for the Advancement of Teaching. 2010. "The Carnegie Classification of Institutions of Higher Education." Available at http://classifications.carnegiefoundation.org/index.php.

Cuban, L. 1988. "A Fundamental Puzzle of School Reform." *Phi Delta Kappan* 69 (5): 341–344.

Hartley, M., and J. Saltmarsh. 2008. "Author Guidelines." Unpublished prospectus for this volume.

Imagining America. 2008. "The Tenure Team Initiative on Public Scholarship." *Imagining America: Artists and Scholars in Public Life.* Available at http://www.imaginingamerica.org/TTI/TTI.html.

Plater, W. 2008. "The Twenty-First-Century Professoriate." *Academe* 94 (4): 35–40.

Sandmann, L., and W. Plater. 2009. "Leading the Engaged Institution." In *Institutionalizing Community Engagement in Higher Education: The First Wave of Carnegie Classified Institutions*, ed. L. Sandmann, C. Thornton, and A. Jaeger, 13–24. San Francisco: Jossey-Bass.

Senge, P. 1990. *The Fifth Dimension: The Art and Practice of the Learning Organization.* New York: Currency Doubleday.

Tufts University. 2008. "Talloires Network." Available at http://www.tufts.edu/talloiresnetwork/.

ADDITIONAL RESOURCES

American Association of Community Colleges. 2008. "Service Learning." http://www
.aacc.nche.edu/Resources/aaccprograms/horizons/Pages/default.aspx (accessed
December 8, 2010).

Langseth, M., and W. Plater. 2004. *Public Work and the Academy: An Academic
Administrator's Guide to Civic Engagement and Service-Learning*. Bolton, MA:
Anker.

CHAPTER 6

Chief Academic Officers and Community-Engaged Faculty Work

JOHN WOODROW PRESLEY

I was, and now am again, a professor of English. Before becoming a professor of English again, I served as provost or in the Provost's Office at four different universities. Neither of these titles is very useful in continuing conversation at the cocktail receptions so common in academic administrator calendars nowadays. If I say I am a professor of English, the inevitable response is "I hated English in high school. It was my worst subject." If I said, "I am a provost," the comeback was always, "What's that? What does a provost do?"

Well, among other duties, provosts are expected to help foster (and even protect) new directions for colleges and universities, such as the addition of civic and community engagement activities to the curriculum and to the expected roles of faculty. Other institutional officers can, of course, help support these efforts—in fact, the work of department chairs and deans is crucial—but the work of these officers is usually limited to their own units. Until and unless they are already truly committed to community engagement, faculty in one department or college seldom are affected by the opportunities and policies for community engagement in a department or unit other than their own. Indeed, the position of provost or vice president for academic affairs—in other words, the chief academic officer—is designed to make connections across all academic units, to lead deans and department chairs, and to manage strategically to achieve university-wide goals.

Chief academic officers (CAOs) are also expected, in the best of times, to know and understand not only university goals but also individual faculty goals, interests, and even enthusiasms. CAOs are expected to understand faculty culture and the state of the campus at any given time, to know how to turn—sometimes slowly, sometimes quickly—all or as many as possible of the university's assets, both human and financial, toward new goals for the campus curriculum, for support services, and for the campus as an organic culture. CAOs have budgets, large or small, at their disposal for these and other purposes, but a CAO involved in fostering such a new direction must understand where and how to deploy that budget, how to revise rewards and acknowledgement structures, and how to subtly change faculty roles in order to move toward agreed-upon goals—a task difficult enough in relation to existing goals and sometimes nearly insurmountable with new goals.

One might expect a campus president to possess these "soft skills" and also be able to connect them with management skills such as agenda building for governance committees and the like. Of course, many presidents are known for these abilities, but these days, presidents are more often selected—and rewarded—for the complex, if quotidian, skills of fund-raising and building positive relationships between the campus and its external constituencies, especially government offices. Presidents and chancellors seldom, if ever, have time to work with committees, to walk from one faculty or dean's office to another, or to talk up and advocate a new direction like community and civic engagement. Indeed, if many presidents tried to do so, the faculty offices that lay before them in their "walk-through" might suddenly all be empty!

Almost all CAO positions are occupied by individuals who have had successful academic careers, and who understand the demands of academic careers, and it may be this experience that is most relevant and necessary for success in fostering institutional change. Faculty must trust the work of the CAO—if not the CAO himself or herself—and nothing helps engender that trust quite like success in teaching, research, and service. For all these reasons, well-respected and well-informed CAOs are perhaps the most effective advocates for the practice of community engagement activities and for advocating the place of such activity in the campus at large. Certainly few other academic leaders can effect policy revisions and changes as quickly as can a CAO.

It is for all these reasons that CAOs were asked to lead campus efforts to start American Democracy Projects on participating campuses in 2003, when the American Association of State Colleges and Universities (AASCU) combined with the *New York Times* to muster a new commitment to civic engagement from both students and faculty. Over 225 AASCU institutions have joined in this Project, which has grown in scope every year. ADP institutions demonstrate their commitment to the Project goals of increasing student civic engagement in a number of ways. Though ADP has never prescribed particular approaches to civic engagement, annual ADP conferences present "best practices" from around the nation. These practices range from service-learning to voter registration to deliberative democracy to using the introduction of wolves into national parks to teach students about democratic communication and problem solving. Other colleges are participating in a project to support student work on the "Seven Revolutions" that will require international cooperation to solve crises of food, water, population, and demographic changes in world economies. Other universities are participating in the Political Engagement Project, another ADP initiative, aimed at awakening student democratic "conscience" rather than simple civic "consciousness" and at expressing that conscience in the current political arena. Indeed, at the national conferences, it is clear that the ADP schools have responded in an ever-increasing number of ways to student and community needs and to national and community opportunities. In fact, the ADP has been so successful at moving civic engagement toward the center of institutions' priorities that its original three-year timetable was simply overruled, making ADP an ongoing AASCU initiative.

At national meetings, George Mehaffy, vice president of AASCU, has indicated in many speeches and in talks with the CAOs participating in the American Democracy Project that AASCU calculatedly required professional commitment to the goals and practices of civic engagement on the part of CAOs—that is, commitment to attending national conferences and learning as much as possible about the practice, theory, and research involving civic and community engagement. Mehaffy knew from his own experience as a CAO that the public support of the Project by CAOs was critical. Of participating campus presidents and chancellors, AASCU required only a signature on a letter.

So how important, really, have the efforts of chief academic officers been in changing reward structures and policies in these efforts to turn a campus toward achieving the specific goal of increased community engagement activities?

I brought to this task experience in the CAO office at several very different institutions. I had served as an assistant CAO at Augusta State University, then a senior comprehensive university in the university system of Georgia; as assistant CAO, then as interim CAO, then associate CAO at Lafayette College, one of the major national liberal arts colleges; as dean of arts and sciences at a branch campus of the University of Michigan; as CAO at the State University of New York branch at Oswego; and finally as Provost at Illinois State University. None of these is a major research university; each is focused on teaching and on the undergraduate experience, though research is required of all faculty, as at the majority of American universities. Moreover, none of these institutions boasts the full infrastructure to support faculty research, with the possible exception of Illinois State, where certain departments— usually those offering doctoral degrees—do have research funding in place along with the infrastructure to support this research.

So, as provost of Illinois State University, I found myself in 2003 having conversation after conversation with faculty and staff groups to inform and persuade them that civic engagement was a worthy university goal, that our students would be better prepared for their roles as citizens if there were more civic engagement embedded in the Illinois State curriculum. I'd had no real direct experience administering a community-engaged faculty or curriculum. At the University of Michigan–Dearborn, a very substantial program of cooperative education and internships was thriving—the university was founded to give students that experience in Detroit industry and in the surrounding community organizations. Lafayette College has a long history of work with Campus Compact and with student organizations involving themselves with charitable causes. But none of my previous experience was as profoundly focused on civic engagement as preparation for students assuming their roles as citizens, nor had any of my previous experience prepared me for the scope of the American Democracy Project. In fact, I was personally committed to the ADP voter registration activities myself, after my experience in New York, watching voting booths being disassembled in the very student-center ballroom where large television screens had been set up to allow our students, many of whom had family in New York City, to watch the news coverage of the World Trade Center attacks. Few people remember that September 11, 2001, was a primary election day in New York, but I did. I watched the voting booths being taken away, as I was on my cell phone with my back to the huge crowd of grieving and worried and unbelieving students and staff, trying to learn if any of our student interns were in the Towers. The resolve resulting from that moment, and slight experience with coops, internships, and service-learning, was all I brought to Illinois State in direct knowledge of civic engagement, but an informal survey of faculty opinion told me that the campus was prepared to make civic engagement more central to its work.

The very first of my conversations about civic engagement was with some ninety faculty and staff who were already using civic engagement pedagogy and who were engaged in community-based research to some degree. They hardly required convincing. These faculty (mainly from the professional schools and from diverse arts and sciences departments) and student affairs professionals had worked with Campus Compact; they had been "early adopters" of many forms of civic engagement, such as service-learning or even engaged community scholarship and student work, or had worked with registered student organizations in various "service to the community efforts" or in activities like Alternative Spring Break. They understood the benefits such work could bring to the student educational experience and to student development, and they wanted to learn about more complex ways to get students engaged in the community. My second conversation was with a group of faculty and staff who wanted to hear about this new idea, who were open to the possibilities, but who were not currently practicing or using these approaches. I was pleased that there were many smiles and much nodding during my informal talk with them. Then I asked for questions and comments.

Anyone familiar with academic culture will not be surprised that the very first question from this second group was "Will this count?" nor that the room quickly became quiet. This was, and still is, the question to be answered by any CAO who is attempting to promulgate any idea new to faculty, who know that no matter how convinced they become that this new idea is worthwhile, they must invest time in its applications in their classrooms and in their communities. That they will invest even more time in writing about these new pedagogies translates into a faculty performing and reporting research based on student civic engagement. Even if, after a while, they understand that community-based research on questions critical to their communities is a very appropriate application of their professional expertise, they will still ask, "Will all this investment of time and expertise count when we apply for tenure or promotion? Will civic and community-based teaching, research, and service be respected by our colleagues and by administrators in the inevitable reviews and decisions about rank, sabbaticals, salary increases, office space, clerical help, letters of recommendation for fellowships, and on and on?"

I later was surprised to learn that my questioner was not a faculty member. She was an academic professional, a staff member in the student affairs division, who was so committed to the institution's goals and her own goals of professional development that she frequently taught in the evenings. Her concern about "Will it count?" shows how pervasive and important this question is. She would, of course, be evaluated in much the same way as faculty. Contingent faculty—adjuncts and nontenure track—are also evaluated using much the same criteria, at least in regard to their teaching duties.

So faculty culture is very important, permeating the entire campus. And every CAO knows that faculty culture, despite its frequently cited oppositional stance, can be the most effective tool at his or her disposal in trying to turn the institution—or it can be a constant, silent, sullen barrier to the best efforts to bring new ideas to bear on faculty roles and responsibilities.

It is common to complain about faculty culture. And every faculty culture, across divisions and disciplines, is relevant to the CAO because, for example, civic engagement as a university emphasis touches everything from individual courses to requirements for individual majors to student organizations to orientation day planning to computer user guidelines. The CAO and faculty committed to engagement must take into account the facts that the majority of faculty are individuals who are devoted to a single discipline (to the point of frequently ignoring college or university goals); who judge—and are themselves judged—by standards of achievement based on these disciplines to determine their individual "merit"; and whose detached scholarship is designed to qualify them as competitive experts, indeed even as "stars," outside the campus. University faculty frequently identify themselves not in relation to their colleagues in the offices next to them but in relation to national and international figures in the discipline. Turf wars, nationally and locally, competition, and constant ruthless judging are the norms.

Civic and community engagement work is in a particularly weak position in countering this culture because the dominant academic culture

- Knows no systematic definition of civic engagement, public work, or praxis

- Values these activities even less than it values the scholarship of teaching and learning
- Is unaware of any compendium of best practices regarding civic engagement
- Will not notice or value community-based research until and unless it is published in a first-tier, peer-reviewed journal
- Is very likely to view civic engagement as a time-consuming, irrelevant add-on, or as the "initiative du jour"

The lack of knowledge of best practices is something a CAO must help faculty address, with expert speakers, support for conference travel, and assistance with creating learning communities to look for these best practices on campus and around the country. But it may be the final item in the list above that represents the most powerful resistance and inertia. The most senior faculty member, who may be most influential in the culture, and indeed any faculty member who has served a number of years is probably a "change survivor" in the words of Jeanie Daniel Duck (2001, pp. 39–55). Change survivors have lived through many, sometimes unrelated, attempts by CAOs and university presidents to change institutional goals and culture. Sometimes these attempts are successful, but frequently they are not, and the institution moves on, causing faculty to view such efforts as fads (or as evidence that the CAO and president simply don't "get it") and making faculty more and more resistant to the next effort to effect change in the organization. Marguerite Shaffer sums up the problem facing junior faculty interested in community-based work:

> But the university has basically cast "the professional mindset" in stone and, although it might encourage innovative community-based, engaged, or public work, professional guidelines for tenure and promotion relegate that kind of work to service, which counts third, way behind scholarship and teaching, in terms of promotion. (qtd. in Brown 2008a, p. 28)

These features of the dominant culture, though, can be addressed by a thoughtful chief academic officer and his or her faculty "point people." In fact, most faculty have not been passive in describing or constructing faculty roles: They pressure fellow faculty and administrators at the department and college levels; they engage in discussion and revision of tenure and promotion criteria; and, of course, faculty themselves serve on personnel committees and judge the merit of their colleagues. Faculty are constantly—if slowly—exerting force to change culture, especially the culture surrounding faculty roles. But that change moves at a glacial pace—promotion guidelines are revised but certainly not every year—and to move an initiative like civic engagement forward, faculty involvement must be vocal, visible, focused, and led. But in the final analysis, it is faculty who must change faculty culture. And it is most often the CAO who will become the "chief communicator . . . the de facto shaper of change" (Duck 2001, pp. 140–141).

First, a CAO must determine, through a campus audit or other means, what preexisting civic engagement activities are already in place across the campus. Inevitably there will be such work going on, ranging from volunteerism to reflective service-learning to community-based research and consulting (the latter perhaps most likely in business and professional schools). Faculty must be involved in this audit and discovery—this activity alone may help jumpstart a campus conversation. And these existing activities must be recognized on their own terms. Even unreflective volunteer work for local charities, if successful, needs to be embraced. Early on, the excellent and the good must both be embraced; the new ideas "tent" being set up should be as large as possible. While this big tent approach may risk being perceived as the initiative's attempt to be "all things to all people," later attention to best practices and to exemplary work will establish the direction and image of the initiative, and discussions, learning communities, awards, and rewards may even bring some of these outlying early adopters more into line with best practices of community engagement. The CAO, in soliciting a group of faculty to address campus culture, must meet the campus's early practitioners of civic and community engagement on their own ground and build on what is already in place. The CAO himself or herself cannot be seen at the beginning as arbitrarily and personally forcing distinctions—on who knows what grounds?—between the good and the great.

At Illinois State University, for example, I found faculty and staff who were committed to both their national discipline and its views of faculty work, and to the general goals of the university, which include the goal of being the undergraduate "school of choice" for Illinois students. This culture focused on both teaching and research, a tension or balance not uncommon in research-intensive universities. Illinois State faculty are very productive in research and publication, but they are primarily focused on their teaching and on the student experience, and frequently feel—and complain about—the lack of time and support for their research. As CAOs and committed faculty move to change culture, they must understand and respect it; at Illinois State this meant that civic engagement pedagogies might come first, and then engaged scholarship might be presented as balancing teaching and the pressure for research productivity. And, certainly at first, the "found pilots" (Kotter 1996, pp. 51–66) where the hoped-for change is already occurring—faculty and staff whose engaged pedagogy is more effective in interesting ways and whose research and teaching are united by the principles of community engagement—can be celebrated and publicized on websites, in newsletters, and even in community newspapers; they can be discussion leaders and speakers; they can be mentors for junior faculty; and, most importantly, they can serve on faculty personnel and evaluation committees and become very effective advocates for the value of community-engaged pedagogy and research themselves.

What actions do the CAO and this group of advocates undertake? What actions are most likely to successfully address the policies and reward structures that reflect all too strongly the dominant campus culture and its concerns?

The chief academic officer must consistently and constantly deal with the faculty culture head on, and with a number of planned approaches. Inevitably, a CAO will find it necessary to provide funding for increasing engagement activities. When the American Democracy Project was begun, no funding was available from AASCU for its implementation (how could a single organization of AASCU's size fund the work of engagement on more than 200 campuses?), but this did not become a barrier. Campuses found internal funds and reallocated them to ADP, or found external sources in donors and grants. But the questions before each CAO, absent direction from the funding source, were where and how to allocate funding for engagement. Some CAOs centralized funding for all engagement work, creating a competition for resources that was judged by either the CAO or a central Task Force for Civic Engagement. This approach certainly marks civic engagement as a university-wide activity, but I believe that diffusing the funding for engagement throughout the campus is more likely to effect change in culture, policies, and reward structures.

Diffusing funding throughout academic departments and offices will, of course, probably result in more engagement work, but it will also indicate the importance of civic engagement as a university goal, involving many offices and departments. But diffused funding also distributes responsibility for creating and for judging these efforts (after all, funding should go to the most successful efforts; mere funding or mere existence does not equal quality). And competition for the distribution of limited financial resources will probably result in the improvement of existing practices and in new practices that are better planned, executed, and assessed.

Moreover, diffusing funding throughout a number of campus offices respects the existing campus culture, and the chief academic officer must respect the culture that he or she is attempting to modify. For example, the CAO should respect and find ways to make resources available to those community engagement activities that are already in place and to make the usual campus motivating structures and processes available to these early adopters as well as to faculty and staff who wish to begin exploring community engagement. These "motivators" might come in the form of pure cash support, but equally motivating are the more standard "perks" of the successful faculty member in campus culture—for example, time for course revision and experimentation, or travel opportunities that allow learning from other faculty from other campuses. Lunches for faculty discussion groups (it is absolutely astonishing what the promise of a good pizza can accomplish), speakers, and books for beginning learning communities (and, later, communities of practice for engaged teachers and researchers) all have cumulative effect. If a CAO can make these standard signs of support and appreciation available, it sets the stage for the more grand acknowledgements such as annual awards, simple certificates, or, the most grand of all, new honorary titles. Nothing was as effective for increasing Illinois State's participation in the American Democracy Project and one of its allied initiatives, the Political Engagement Project, as the opportunity to award new honorary titles to faculty members leading this work. And rightly so: this extension of the existing processes and products of campus recognition of faculty work was followed by exemplary treatment of award winners and title holders with teaching loads that gave them more time to plan teaching and research agendas and more faculty development funds to support their work. All this served to motivate more participation and more innovation.

Most universities have created a center for faculty development, and these centers coordinate activities that can recognize and foreground research and teaching centered on community engagement. A chief academic officer who makes funding available for the faculty development center in order to create a campus focus on community-engaged teaching or research has made a wise choice: learning communities, communities of practice, speaker series, organized mentoring programs for junior faculty (more dependably goal-oriented than when administered by departments), workshops, and faculty development websites will recognize outstanding work by faculty and will make it easier and simpler to interest more faculty in community engagement. At Illinois State, we made summer support available for outstanding faculty who then created generic web-based modules that now make it easier to add community engagement work for students into existing courses. The following five modules are currently available to all Illinois State faculty:

• What are Civic and Community Engagement?
• Why Incorporate Civic and Community Engagement?
• Innovative Pedagogy for Incorporating Civic and Community Engagement
• Political Engagement: Beyond Politics
• Innovative Partnerships for Student Learning

Other faculty and staff created a website to link interested faculty with experienced mentors to discuss the problems that might forestall such changes in courses and to quickly link these faculty with community and campus resources. The coordination of such activities through the campus faculty-development center can make that center a primary force in fostering community engagement. And a chief academic officer will have used the effort to increase outreach to the community to foreground, acknowledge, and reward those faculty who are exemplars of teaching, research, and service based on this outreach. Such recognition counts when personnel decisions are made by faculty colleagues.

A very powerful way to ensure that community-based research and teaching is valued by colleagues is to interlink the goals of this teaching and research with the campus culture's existing governance structures and protocols. With larger numbers of involved faculty, it can be simple—when the moment arrives for mission statement revision and staffing strategic planning committees—to make civic engagement of faculty, staff, and students a stated goal or strategy of the university. Scores of AASCU provosts have taken this step with strategic plans, academic plans, mission statements, lists of goals, vision statements, hallmarks of graduates, and the like. The campus culture at Illinois State seems unique in my experience in its high regard for the strategic plan, "Educating Illinois," which makes the plan a very effective tool for change; in fact, I have been amazed to hear faculty quoting from the "Educating Illinois" plan and giving the plan credit for changing some campus emphases over the past decade. When the time came for the periodic revision of "Educating Illinois," the effort was to be guided by the Director of Planning and Institutional Research and by a representative from the Provost's Office. We chose an associate provost as our representative, an administrator who was closely involved with the ADP and had in fact served as cochair of the ADP Coordinating Committee for several years. The Educating Illinois Task Force, a group of twenty-one representatives, was appointed by the president of the university, and I am not sure that he knew that a third of the members had experience and commitment to community-engaged work (though including this constituency was not quite a planned act on the part of the Provost's Office). The revision of the strategic plan was, as it should be, an inclusive plan, and it proceeded very smoothly. The Task Force held twenty-five discussion forums to help identify issues pertaining to university strengths, challenges, and opportunities. It was in these meetings that the issue of community engagement arose—which was not surprising, since the ADP had been a presence on campus for three years, with constant attention to faculty and student accomplishment in engagement. While the Task Force developed and discussed an environmental scan of demographic and financial issues, met with specific university offices, and then released a draft to the entire campus community for input, there were no substantive challenges to the proposal that civic engagement become one of the Five Core Values of the plan; rather, specific ways of weaving civic engagement more deeply into the document seemed to be the constant thrust of these discussions. As the two-year process drew to its close, with presentations asking for endorsement by the Academic Senate, the Administrative/Professional Council, the Civil Service Council, the Student Government Association, and finally the Board of Trustees, there was immediate, unanimous approval of the centrality of civic engagement to the university's goals.

When community and civic engagement was approved as a campus value and goal (with strategies to achieve that goal listed) the effect was immediate. The way was clear, for example, to add questions about an academic department's community engagement strategies in curricula and research to the existing program review protocols. As the program review processes were changed in this way, with the dean's urging and support, almost all departments in

Arts and Sciences moved to require civic engagement or reflective service-learning in their capstone courses. This step suddenly made community-based faculty work more valuable and important, and existing resources for program review can now be used for assessment of this faculty work as well as aid in the revision, addition, and support of this work. This one step—holding entire departments accountable for demonstrating community engagement—has valorized research and teaching designed to achieve this goal more than any other effort.

Another example of the power of including the expectation of such work in campus goals and plans is its effect on budget processes and "budget cultures" once this step has been taken. At institutions in which the budget requests of academic units are presented and discussed in any sort of open and transparent process—presentations to a CAO with the Academic Senate present or simply days of "hearings" open to all campus constituencies—it is common for the CAO to ask that such requests address the ways in which funding of new projects or initiatives helps achieve the goals of the campus strategic plan. Some chief academic officers even require that a new budget request first detail how the last year's increments were used to achieve campus goals. When fostering community involvement is a written, specified campus goal, suddenly the professional vocabularies of community-based teaching and research become part of the campus's "shared vocabulary," and these budget hearings generate further campus-wide discussion of engagement. Arguing for funding—surely one of the most common discourses on any campus—involves, at least in part, arguing for more community engagement. Funding for, say, involvement by the College of Nursing in providing free physical examinations to students in a low-income neighborhood school is now more likely to include teaching civic skills and the requirement of reflective service, not just mere volunteerism, on the part of Nursing Students. And the Department of Public Health Services, the College of Education, and even the College of Business are more likely to be interested in joining with the College of Nursing in these efforts of community-based teaching and research. (It has been my experience that professional schools are more accommodating "early homes" for this work and that professional school faculty seem to understand and demonstrate in applications, dossiers, annual reviews, and the like that their work furthers college and university goals.)

This simple step, with its cascading possibilities for altering campus discourse and culture, is an invaluable action for a chief academic officer who wishes to make community-based faculty work count. All these steps may constitute an agenda for the CAO, and they may not be unique to the goal of infusing community engagement throughout a university but may in fact be undertaken and even combined with many other culture- and focus-changing goals such as the creation or revision of First-Year Experiences. In "Institutional Structures and Strategies for Embedding Civic Engagement in the First College Year," Barefoot (2008) provides a list of such strategies that can cut across campus structures, and in a companion piece, "Action Steps to

Move the First-Year Civic Engagement Movement Forward," Gardner (2008) provides a more far-reaching list of steps. Gardner suggests that the CAO consider making civic engagement a focus of the campus's next reaffirmation of regional accreditation—a veritable lever for change on any campus. Both Gardner's and Barefoot's lists should be consulted by CAOs planning a course of action to make campus culture more accommodating to community-based work of all kinds.

Other such culture-shifting actions and activities undertaken by individual AASCU chief academic officers have included:

- Supporting—and thus guiding—the creation of six new academic programs at one campus, all of which, especially a minor in Leadership and an M.S. in Community and Regional Planning, have their curricular and pedagogical foundations in community and civic engagement
- Including student participation in civic engagement and development of civic skills among the goals for a campus's general education programs (which, of course, is likely to have many of the same "cascading possibilities" as does a revised strategic plan, and is particularly effective when the overall number of general education goals is limited; one institution, for example, lists civic engagement as one of five goals for general education in its "Pathway to Intentional Learning")
- Reassigning a Service-Learning Office to the provost and renaming (elevating) it as The Center for Service-Learning
- Providing more reliable, partially internal funding for campus entities such as a Public Policy Institute
- Creating annual Engaged Teaching Awards (which, of course, must be funded at identical levels as other faculty and research awards, to create identical effects on campus cultures)
- Creating new centers and projects specifically designed to provide community engagement, such as Western Carolina's Tsalagi Institute, which offers services to the Cherokee community, and the Digital Heritage Project, which coordinates students from several disciplines who engage with the history and culture of the region
- Modifying existing degree programs into joint interdisciplinary programs, such as an M.L.S. in Political Science and Civic Leadership
- Developing a Leadership Studies Department, and a Center for Civic Leadership that reports to the provost
- Organizing community sharing sessions to improve outreach efforts (there are probably too few such efforts to seek assessment of the effects of our programs in the communities surrounding our campuses)
- Creating Provost's Service-Learning Fellowships, a program to allow engaged faculty reassigned time for work on teaching and

research agendas and providing visibility for such exemplary work
by involving Service-Learning Fellows with provost office initiatives
• Developing an Experiential Learning Scholars (EXL) program,
which formalized and provided structure to several existing experiential learning programs; now students are formally admitted to
the EXL Program, and they must enroll in EXL coursework with
internal and external service-learning components and maintain
e-portfolios of their work

Note that many of these examples of CAO actions involve modification
or creation of interdisciplinary curricula and programs. All of these programs
require academic leadership, or academic advisory committees and teaching
faculty, if not all three. Not only do such programs allow CAOs the opportunity to tailor searches for, and hiring of, new faculty to emphasize the capacities for engaged teaching and research; such curricula can create new and
profoundly important agendas for a Committee on Community Engagement,
investing a community of practice with oversight responsibility similar to
that of a Committee on the First Year Experience or a Committee on General
Education. These are important and visible responsibilities. But I would urge
a CAO to consider giving a Committee on Community Engagement full
responsibility for these interdisciplinary, community-engaged curricula—
for hiring, admission and graduation requirements, and administering
budgets, that is, all the responsibilities one associates with academic departments. A Committee for Community Engagement would then parallel the
governance structures of some of the most prestigious centers and institutes at universities in the United States (which, of course, might also make
such assignment of responsibility simpler for the CAO to achieve). And, if
successful, such investment would address many of the issues of administ-
tering interdisciplinary programs and many of the reward issues facing
engaged faculty.

But, with or without such solutions, many engaged faculty feel that the
central problem of their academic situation is whether or not their activities
count. Many feel that it is a simple enough matter to document many of their
activities, including community-based teaching, and to demonstrate that such
efforts help achieve institutional goals, improve their teaching, or allow for
more complex and interesting student outcomes. Similarly, it is simple enough
to list community service activities as just that—"service to the community"—
and much engagement work can be easily and appropriately characterized
as "service to the institution." We can set aside the category of "service to
the profession," which lies outside this discussion, at least for the moment.
It is the issue of the perceived value of community-based research that more
commonly troubles many engaged faculty, and it is this issue that many leading scholars of community engagement hold primarily responsible—maybe
even solely responsible—for a perceived "stalling" of the national movement
toward more community engagement in higher education.

There are no simple or easy solutions to what is essentially a very local (and in many ways closed) process of faculty evaluation. But there are many actions a chief academic officer can suggest or take, especially once learning communities and communities of practice related to community engagement are in place on the campus.

When promotion and tenure policies are designed to operate at the university level, with departments and colleges simply advising a university-level committee, the revision of these policies can be a simpler task. A CAO can lend his or her authority to a special task force set up, one hopes, in conjunction with the Academic Senate, which can be charged with creating a report to bring promotion and tenure policies at the university level up to date. It is always probably the best tactic to charge this committee in a general way, so that, for example, community-based faculty work can be discussed in the context of other new pedagogies and research directions, such as the Scholarship of Teaching and Learning. This is a step already taken by several AASCU institutions, where CAOs have appointed groups to take into account typologies of research and publication based on local work, like Metropolitan State University's "Circle of Engaged Learning," developed by their Center for Community-Based Learning, or nationally developed typologies like that of Ernest Boyer. (And one assumes the CAOs have ensured that at least some of the members of these groups can advocate for community-based work.) Promotion and tenure policies are, after all, periodically revised, and there is always an expectation that new directions be considered—almost every set of existing promotion and tenure policies in the country has either just been revised or soon will be revised to deal, for instance, with electronically distributed scholarship. Is electronic publishing a step down in status and authority, or is it a step to speed up the publishing process and widen the audience for scholarly work? Does electronic publishing increase the opportunity for student readers to see and discuss the scholarship with the author at virtually the same time as its creation, and if so, is this a positive development? When even poetry is being published by web-based magazines, must departments of English at least consider the status of these outlets? These and other questions about the "new scholarship," including scholarship based on engagement with community organizations and problems, must be discussed in frank terms regarding their effect on promotion and tenure decisions.

A chief academic officer always has the option of personally taking on the revision of merit policies and guidelines, adding personal authority or the authority of the office to the effort. There are obvious problems and limitations when this approach is primary. What will result if the CAO for some reason lacks either the appropriate official or personal authority for this task? The answer is probably a setback for the recognition of community-based work, perhaps for years, or until a new CAO takes office.

When promotion and tenure polices are developed, authorized, and expected to be very specific at the department or discipline level, this personal approach, with the CAO talking and visiting with committees and chairs, is even more likely to be too feeble to create the desired outcomes. Using this strategy, I was, frankly, never able to change the narrow and outmoded description of peer review in one department—so narrow a view that one junior faculty member's research was judged negatively when in fact she had been invited to write articles and guest-edit journal issues without an old-fashioned peer review. In fact, national experts in her discipline recognized, once she had published her dissertation, that she was the only person in the country who had developed particular databases on the treatment of the elderly in public nursing homes. Nor was I able to convince another department—until I had resigned as CAO and resumed my role as a faculty member—that since the university levels of the promotion and tenure process did not view a contracted but unpublished book positively, as did the department, the department's advice to junior faculty to forego work on articles and instead focus on publishing books was dangerous to their careers.

A more successful and quicker approach to personally turning promotion and tenure policies in new directions is available, however. At the State University of New York campus where I served as provost, these policies and guidelines were set, rather generally, at the system offices in Albany where negotiations with the faculty union were situated. As a result, these guidelines were viewed as near holy writ, or certainly as having the effect of law. Nevertheless, the CAO office at each SUNY campus was a near-final decision step in the promotion and tenure process, as it was also in the salary increment process, with the role of the president usually being review and consent with the CAO's decisions. And the CAO's interpretation of the Albany guidelines and definitions was an understandable area of extreme interest, as I learned from talking with faculty. Thus, I was able to write and distribute a complex, ten-page, single-spaced memo (in a small font) that explained how I, as CAO, personally viewed dossiers, reports, and applications in various merit processes. That I carefully explained that I was aware this memo had no statutory standing and that it was simply an explanation of my own personal views of the continuum of meritorious work made it almost immediately acceptable to the Faculty Senate and to the union. In this memo, which is still in effect in a slightly revised version at that campus, I dealt with what were then new pedagogies and new directions of applied research, including Scholarship of Teaching and Learning, along with digitally distributed research and publications. I even added, in my personal explanation, a criterion new to that SUNY campus, collegiality—which was widely accepted because I balanced it with a section on academic freedom and its relation to collegiality. I believe that I could have easily and appropriately introduced the topic of community-based publication and research into the typology that I described in that memo of "Faculty Evaluative Criteria." I also believe that this very powerful method of change is widely available to chairs and deans who wish to make subtle changes in faculty evaluative criteria, even when a single word of the policy itself is not changed.

But the more frequently available and more obvious strategy is still the CAO's assigning to a faculty group the task and authority to revise community-engaged research, or at least to delineate and suggest advice—specific advice aimed at departmental, college, or university-wide personnel committees deciding merit issues, including promotion and tenure. It might, in fact, be an even better idea to aim this advice at administrators—chairs, deans, provosts and presidents—who are involved in merit decisions, and to distribute and promulgate the advice as widely as possible. Many colleges, especially smaller liberal arts colleges, for example, have a process in place to allow the faculty as a whole to Give Advice to an Administrator. The omnipresent capital letters in such policies emphasize the seriousness with which this process of giving advice is invested. And, for obvious reasons, pursuing this route might be a more palatable way of attempting to change promotion and tenure policies.

If a Committee on Community Engagement or a Center for Community Engagement has become a force on campus, perhaps by creating a catalog of best practices, or by creating a typology of such work, or by creating for the campus a description of a developmental sweep of community engagement that might reach from first year seminars to general education to capstone majors courses, and even to graduate education, then such a Committee is better-placed to address directly the value and merit of community-based scholarship. At least one AASCU campus has begun this process, first by sending groups of faculty, at the CAO office's expense, to regional charrettes discussing engaged scholarship, with the expectation that these faculty produce similar charrette discussions on the home campus. After gathering campus reactions, this resulting task force can then in a more empowered fashion effectively offer advice regarding the local value of engaged scholarship (it goes without saying that such advice should always, for rhetorical purposes if no other, take into account whenever possible the student-based outcomes of such scholarship).

There are analogous national action models for the valorizing work of these task forces, such as the steps undertaken by the Conference on College Composition and Communication (CCCC) in creating greater understanding of research done on composition. In 1987, the CCCC distributed "Scholarship in Composition: Guidelines for Faculty, Deans, and Department Chairs" to accompany its "Range of Scholarship in Composition: A Guide for Department Chairs and Deans," also published in 1987, designed to advise faculty members, especially junior faculty whose research agenda was focused on composition theory and teaching. These two statements did much to ease the traditional divide in English departments between composition and literature faculty, a divide in which composition research was frequently ignored or devalued. More recently, in 1998 the CCCC created a similar statement regarding "Promotion and Tenure Guidelines for Work with Technology." Even more relevant to the current subject is the 2009 CCCC report on "Faculty Work in Community-Based Settings." In 2006, the Modern Language Association published its "Report of the MLA Task Force on Evaluating Scholarship for Tenure and Promotion," in which, among other suggestions, departments were advised to create procedures for evaluating "faculty work in new media."

While advice and guidance from the MLA and CCCC are relevant, especially since composition classes were among the first courses to work with service-learning in an academically reflective way, a very successful external model that might be copied for the work of valorizing community-engaged scholarship is the continuing movement to valorize the Scholarship of Teaching and Learning (SOTL). While the Carnegie Foundation has lent its resources and prestige to this effort, campus faculty groups have been responsible for thousands of discussion group meetings and forums to increase the amount of SOTL work done and to increase its prestige so that SOTL is viewed more favorably by faculty and administrators. An International Society for the Scholarship of Teaching and Learning hosts symposia on the issues and posts on its website a list of resources and outlets for publishing SOTL work, and a large literature now surrounds SOTL work, not simply advocating for it but describing—in a mentor-like fashion—the characteristics of the best SOTL work. An example of this approach is the work of Kathleen McKinney (2007) who provides very practical advice on the characteristics of the best SOTL research and advice on presenting SOTL work in merit processes, and even suggests to faculty who publish SOTL a method for obtaining peer review after publication.

Currently, several national disciplinary organizations are working to change the ways community-based scholarship is valued. The most relevant of these, and an interesting model for campuses to consider copying, is that of the Task Force on the Institutionalization of Public Sociology, which at last count had 437 members. This group published its first report in 2005, "Public Sociology and the Roots of American Sociology: Re-Establishing Our Connections to the Public," in which they argue for the primacy of engaged research in the discipline. In August 2006, the group's Task Force on the Institutionalization of Public Sociology submitted to the American Sociology Association their second report, "Standards of Public Sociology: Guidelines for Use by Departments in Personnel Reviews." The members of the Task Force argued that public sociology is literature-based, research-based, and peer-reviewed, but they also argued for an expanded definition of "peer" (to include sociologists working in public policy and other applied areas, and other sociologists working in the community).

Perhaps the most promising national effort, if less well-known at this point, is the work of the group Imagining America: Artists and Scholars in Public Life. This consortium, with eighty institutional members, released a report in June 2008 titled "Scholarship in Public: Knowledge Creation and Tenure Policy in the Engaged University." The report is aimed at department chairs, deans, and directors, and includes interviews with deans, provosts, and national association leaders. The report recommends that "colleges define public work and scholarly work, expand and document what counts toward tenure and promotion, support publicly engaged graduate students and junior faculty members, and broaden the scope of people who can serve as peer reviewers" (Ellison and Eatman 2008, pp. v, 1–4). In at least one way, this report builds on discipline-based efforts such as that of Public Sociology. The leaders of the Imagining America Tenure Team Initiative were Nancy Cantor, Chancellor of Syracuse University, and Steven D. Lavine, President of the California Institute of the Arts, whose working group was composed largely of presidents, deans, provosts, and engaged scholars (Cantor and Lavine 2006).

Junior faculty and faculty new to community-based work need both advice and guidance. Those mentoring these faculty, whether individual mentors or groups, should let them know that Campus Compact has information about "Publishing Outlets for Service-Learning and Community-Based Research" and "Service-Learning in Promotion and Tenure Resources" available on its website, along with a declaration on the civic responsibilities of research universities. These faculty need to know that the Campus Compact website has information available about funding sources, and that foundations like Pew, Carnegie, Bonner, and Kettering, along with federal agencies like the Fund for Improvement of Postsecondary Education (FIPSE) consider civic engagement work in higher education a high priority, and that major organizations such as AASCU and the Association of American Colleges and Universities consider civic engagement of university students a major priority in reclaiming the distinctiveness of American higher education (Meisel 2007; National Leadership Council for Liberal Education and America's Promise 2007). Faculty considering engaged work should know the history of the civic mission of American higher education (Snyder 2008; Peters 2008). In fact, it was the perceptions of the "falling away" of land-grant institutions from their original purpose of preparing students to be citizens that helped spark the thinking behind the American Democracy Project (just as it was the community-engaged vision of one AASCU school, Portland State University, that helped frame the ADP and its approach). They should know about the Kellogg Commission and its efforts to return land-grant institutions to their original purposes. They should know about the Engagement Academy at Virginia Tech; about Jim Votruba, president of Northern Kentucky University, and his engagement work with the Coalition of Urban and Metropolitan Universities; about Lorilee Sandmann and the Higher Education Network for Community Engagement; and about the newest Carnegie Classification System.

Learning about, discussing, using these national models and efforts, and aligning themselves with these organizations' work can certainly inform engaged faculty and staff about best practices, but it seems to me that the most positive effect of knowing about national work is that it convinces engaged faculty that they are not alone, that they are part of a movement, that there is "standing" and status attached to this work across campuses.

These faculty also need to know that many descriptions of the characteristics of effective community-based research are available, sometimes even usefully contrasted with the characteristics of ineffective community-based work (Creighton 2008). These faculty need to know at least some of the criticism surrounding community-based research, even voiced by some of the most highly regarded practitioners. David Brown calls himself a "recovering professional" (2008b, p. 9), reflecting the view that academic culture typically creates a framework in which professionals or experts venture into the community in a condescending fashion to perform research that may be published in first-tier, peer-reviewed journals but that may ultimately be useless to the community and may even deplete or ignore the resources available to the community (Boyte 2008; Brown 2008a; Creighton 2008; Stanley 2008). Perhaps the most concise description of this tension between academic self-interest and effective community-based work is that of Ira Harkavy when he says, "As an aphorism neatly put it, 'Communities have problems, universities have departments'" (Harkavy 2008, p. 52). This tension is spelled out by Marguerite Shaffer in an interview conducted by David Brown, with more emphasis on the negative role of the academy:

I do think that the way in which the university has institutionalized professional standards most definitely works against a broader notion of shared democratic knowledge production and dissemination, and the way it might be defined in American studies. The bureaucratic process of tenure and promotion, and the narrow compartmentalization of teaching, scholarship, and service works against the very interdisciplinary and engaged work that can be done in American studies. (qtd. in Brown 2008a, p. 28)

Shaffer is suggesting, as have many scholars of civic engagement, that community-engaged work is at its best when an academic "expert" does not simply lecture from the standpoint of disciplinary expertise to a segment of a community and then rapidly depart. To truly engage a community, a scholar or student must first listen and consult with the community to determine its priorities for problem solving. Is the first priority of the community the health of children in its local school, or is their first priority a walk-in clinic for everyone? If a faculty member is working with his or her students on discovering the most efficient bus routes for expanding a small city's transit service, do they consult only with the transit director, or with customers, or with citizens who wish desperately that they could ride the bus to work more conveniently from their part of town? And, in either of these cases, what is the outcome or product for the faculty member—an article in a journal of community nursing or nursing education, or an article in a journal of transit studies? I would argue, as would Shaffer and other critics of work that is merely community-sited rather than work that is truly community-engaged, that these articles are a secondary or tertiary product, even if they are a necessary marker for any faculty career. The primary product is the process of problem solving shared with the community, the shared delivery of a solution, and shared communication and testing of that solution.

No chief academic officer can afford to be seen as naïve in any public remarks about these issues that surround engaged work and also complicate its perceived value, nor can the members of a Committee on Community-Engaged Faculty Work, in whose forum discussions of these controversies must occur.

Nor can the CAO or Committee expect to be successful in their advocacy unless they know about universities that have found ways to work through or to compromise between these competing views. One such center of success is the Netter Center, which organizes the work of University of Pennsylvania faculty in West Philadelphia. When asked if "organizations like the Netter Center have to provide 'professional reasons' for faculty to be attentive to civic culture," Netter Center Director Ira Harkavy answered:

> I certainly believe that faculty members in general will do this work if it is a means to do good and do well. Among other things, the Center has to help illustrate that engaged, democratic, locally focused teaching and research can produce first-rate academic work. We do this by being attentive to the need for faculty to present and publish their work and encouraging colleagues. We also assist faculty in acquiring grants that both support their research and teaching and help to advance their careers. (2008, p. 57)

It is, by the way, quite relevant to the success of the Center and to consideration of the chief academic officer's role in advocacy for community-engaged scholarship that it was the Provost's Council on Undergraduate Education at the University of Pennsylvania that "designated academically based community service as a core component of Penn undergraduate education during the next century" (Benson, Harkavy, and Puckett 2007, p. 95).

Importantly, both the CAO and the task force should think about countering the "horror stories" that underlie most informal talk about merit policies on campus. This is a step seldom considered but an action that can be very effective. "Professor W was not promoted," everyone will hear, "because her committee did not understand her research topic, despite her record of good teaching," or "Dr. Z was not awarded tenure simply because his department chair didn't like his teaching approach, even though the rest of his colleagues thought he was on the cutting edge of both teaching and scholarship." In whatever guise, with whatever content, these frequently ill-informed, second- or third-hand horror stories are understandably a subject of fascination on campus, but most of the time they amount to little more than gossip and complaint, and of course the folks who originate these horror stories almost always have an agenda. But the horror stories are so compelling that they frequently are the only source of information about the merit processes except for long, legalistic, difficult-to-read policy manuals that have grown by accretion, sometimes contradicting themselves from page to page. Sometimes such horror stories are even the real, underlying reason for what might seem a scheduled periodic revision of merit policies. And, of course, some of these horror stories will inevitably involve engaged scholarship, and a task force on the value of such work should attempt to counter these negative tales about the merit process.

But how? One method is to create ways to publicize positive stories. A chief academic officer can ask last year's successful applicants for promotion and tenure, especially those who have records of engaged scholarship, to participate in this year's faculty orientation session, on a panel designed to advise new faculty in setting priorities and agendas for their work; the question-and-answer sessions after such panels are always instructive for new faculty in countering horror stories. Or such panels can be part of a mentoring program, matching successful faculty engaged in community-based scholarship with newly hired faculty who have similar scholarly agendas. These mentors need not be from the same discipline; in fact, doubled mentoring from inside and outside the discipline is frequently more effective.

Another approach has definite legal boundaries but is very effective. One senior college, a part of a university system with careful legal counsel, for a while made available to the entire campus all final letters of decision regarding promotion and tenure. This was, for clear reasons, quickly changed to include only those letters that were positive. Another campus, in its publicity surrounding promotion and tenure awards, always included a few sentences explaining the reasons for the decisions—obviously always praise for the successful candidates' achievements. These few sentences almost never were included in external community newspaper announcements, but their presence in the campus publicity helped limit the number of horror stories told on the campus, I'm sure, and when these decisions were based on engaged scholarship and teaching, the positive results were quite specific. The most powerful use of success stories available to CAOs and their task forces and advisory committees is the use, with consent, of dossiers, resumes, and statements of teaching and research philosophies of successful candidates as illustrative examples in policy statements or in memos of advice about dossier preparation for would-be candidates. Today, when many faculty include their resumes on their websites, there is much less concern about disguising their identities as there once might have been. These measures can help counter the horror stories surrounding merit processes, and over time can even help change perceptions of the worth of new directions of research.

Finally, chief academic officers should serve as models of engaged faculty work themselves. If a CAO has found the time to teach a class, it would have enormous impact if his or her colleagues knew that the CAO required service-learning activities. Or if the CAO has found time to continue research, think of the campus model that would result if that research were the result of collaboration with community representatives or community public policy officers. Several AASCU chief academic officers are well known—and highly regarded—for their own personal, local, political service work; serving on local boards and task forces; and even standing for elections. At least one CAO has won community awards for his service in the local community— and for basing his advocacy of the campus American Democracy Project on that service and on the connections he created in the surrounding community. And CAOs themselves must be known for rewarding in the most appropriate ways those faculty members who are engaged in community-based research and teaching. As urged by Colby, Ehrlich, Beaumont, and Stephens (2003), if we are to rid our campuses of "the inhospitable structures and practices . . . still visible at most institutions," chief academic officers must join with the very large numbers of people in the academy and in the community who care about the goals and values of liberal education, and, equally important, with "those who are paying special attention to the moral and civic components of those goals." As these authors observe, "the new developments are gathering strength, but so are the opposing trends of commodification, specialization, and institutional competition, so it is not a time to be complacent" (p. 48). I have focused almost exclusively on the ways CAOs must protect faculty members with a professional interest in community engagement from internal threats and pressures, but there are external pressures as well. These engaged faculty are frequently perceived as having an exclusively left-wing agenda, even when the track record of the entire ADP argues against this view. Careful work with local newspapers and local media can help dispel this notion, as can work with legislative committees and individual legislators—indeed, one must be sure that an equal number of Democrats and Republicans are invited to campus! In fact, even national work with the Political Engagement Project (PEP) recognizes this dilemma. The original framing of PEP included assessment to discover if, after a politically engaged course, student political positions changed radically. Both nationally and locally, we were pleased that the students' political leanings do not change, and we cite this fact constantly on and off campus: We help students learn to participate in the political arena and to give voice to all political positions. One cannot deny that this fact, however pointless its assessment may seem, has given a measure of comfort and harbor to faculty involved in PEP.

But the chief threats and barriers really are internal. As John Tagg noted in a 2008 speech to the provosts of AASCU institutions, there are at least five very strong types of barriers to change in any academic institution—structural barriers, informational barriers, incentive barriers, financial barriers, and of course, cultural barriers. Chief academic officers participating in AASCU's American Democracy Project have successfully addressed each of these barriers on campuses all over America. Chief academic officers have constituted a very strong voice nationally, and a strong and uniquely placed individual voice on each of their campuses, to argue against complacency in the face of these barriers and opposing forces, and to argue successfully for the proper valuing of community-based faculty work.

NOTE

A version of this essay was previously published as "Chief Academic Officers and Change: The Example of Community Engagement" in *Teacher-Scholar* 2, no. 1 (2010): 21–40.

REFERENCES

Barefoot, Betsy. 2008. "Institutional Structures and Strategies for Embedding Civic Engagement in the First College Year." In *First-Year Civic Engagement: Sound Foundations for College, Citizenship and Democracy*, ed. Martha J. LaBare, 23–25. New York: New York Times Knowledge Network.

Benson, Lee, Ira Harkavy, and John Puckett. 2007. *Dewey's Dream: Universities and Democracies in an Age of Education Reform*. Philadelphia: Temple University Press.

Boyte, Harry C. 2008. "Public Work: Civic Populism versus Technocracy in Higher Education." In *Agent of Democracy: Higher Education and the HEX Journey*, ed. David Brown and Deborah Witte, 79–102. Dayton, OH: Kettering Foundation.

Brown, David W. 2008a. "Changing Public Culture: An Interview with Marguerite S. Shaffer." *Higher Education Exchange*: 23–38.

———. 2008b. "The Journey of a Recovering Professional." *Higher Education Exchange*: 5–11.

Cantor, Nancy, and Steven D. Lavine. 2006. "Taking Public Scholarship Seriously." *Chronicle of Higher Education* 52, no. 40 (June 9). Available at http://chronicle.com/article/Taking-Public-Scholarship/22684/.

Colby, Anne, Thomas Ehrlich, Elizabeth Beaumont, and Jason Stephens. 2003. *Educating Citizens*. San Francisco: Jossey-Bass and the Carnegie Foundation for the Advancement of Teaching.

Conference on College Composition and Communication. 1987. "The Range of Scholarship in Composition: Guidelines for Faculty, Deans, and Department Chairs." Available at http://www.ncte.org/cccc/resources/positions/scholarshipincomp.

Conference on College Composition and Communication. 1998. "Promotion and Tenure Guidelines for Work with Technology." Available at http://www.ncte.org/cccc/resources/positions/promotionandtenure.

Conference on College Composition and Communication. 2009. "Faculty Work in Community-Based Settings." Available at http://www.ncte.org/cccc/resources/positions/communitybasedsettings.

Creighton, Sean. 2008. "The Scholarship of Teaching and Learning." *Higher Education Exchange*: 12–22.

Duck, Jeanie Daniel. 2001. "The Change Monster: The Human Forces that Fuel or Foil Corporate Transformation and Change." New York: Crown Business.

Ellison, Julie, and Timothy K. Eatman. 2008. *Scholarship in Public: Knowledge Creation and Tenure Policy in the Arts, Humanities, and Design*. Syracuse, NY: Imagining America.

Gardner, John N. 2008. "Action Steps to Move the First-Year Civic Engagement Movement Forward." In *First-Year Civic Engagement: Sound Foundations for College, Citizenship and Democracy*, ed. Martha J. LaBare, 26–28. New York: New York Times Knowledge Network.

Harkavy, Ira. 2008. "Democratic Partnerships." *Higher Education Exchange*: 47–58.

June, Audrey Williams. 2008. "Colleges Should Change Policies to Encourage Scholarship Devoted to the Public Good, Report Says." *Chronicle of Higher Education* (June 26). Available at http://chronicle.com/article/Colleges-Should-Change/937/.

Kotter, John. 1996. *Leading Change*. Boston: Harvard Business School Press.

McKinney, Kathleen. 2007. *Enhancing Learning through the Scholarship of Teaching and Learning*. San Francisco: Anker.

Meisel, Wayne. 2007. "Connecting Cocurricular Service with Academic Inquiry." *Liberal Education* 92, no. 2 (Spring): 52–57.

Modern Language Association. 2006. "Report of the MLA Task Force on Evaluating Scholarship for Tenure and Promotion." Available at http://www.mla.org/tenure_promotion.

National Leadership Council for Liberal Education and America's Promise. 2007. *College Learning for the New Global Century*. Washington, DC: Association of American Colleges and Universities.

Peters, Scott. 2008. "Reconstructing a Democratic Tradition of Public Service Scholarship in the Land-Grant System." In *Agent of Democracy: Higher Education and the HEX Journey*, ed. David Brown and Deborah Witte, 121–148. Dayton, OH: Kettering Foundation.

Snyder, R. Claire. 2008. "Should Higher Education Have a Civic Mission? Historical Reflections." In *Agent of Democracy: Higher Education and the HEX Journey*, ed. David Brown and Deborah Witte, 53–75. Dayton, OH: Kettering Foundation.

Stanley, Mary. 2008. "The Limits of Public Work." In *Agent of Democracy: Higher Education and the HEX Journey*, ed. David Brown and Deborah Witte, 29–49. Dayton, OH: Kettering Foundation.

Tagg, John. 2008. "Changing Minds in Higher Education: Students Change, So Why Can't Colleges?" Speech delivered at American Association of State Colleges and Universities, Winter Academic Affairs Meeting, Boston, July 24.

Task Force on the Institutionalization of Public Sociology. 2005. "Public Sociology and the Roots of American Sociology: Re-Establishing Our Connections to the Public." Available at http://pubsoc.wisc.edu/tfreport090105.htm.

Task Force on the Institutionalization of Public Sociology. 2006/2007. "Standards of Public Sociology: Guidelines for Use by Academic Departments in Personnel Reviews." Available at http://pubsoc.wisc.edu/pandt.html.

CHAPTER 7

Deliberative Democracy and
Higher Education

Higher Education's Democratic Mission

Nancy Thomas and Peter Levine

American higher education has always had an ambivalent relationship to democracy. On the one hand, colleges and universities have long asserted that a principal purpose of higher education is to prepare young people to be responsible and informed citizens. Thomas Jefferson, for example, advocated for a strong public education system and founded the University of Virginia because "whenever the people are well-informed, they can be trusted with their own government; that whenever things get so far wrong as to attract their notice, they may be relied on to set them to rights" (quoted in Lipscomb and Burgh 1903–1904, p. 253). Perhaps the relationship between democracy and education was best described by Robert M. Hutchins, then Chancellor of the University of Chicago, in 1950:

> In a democratic community every citizen should have as much power of understanding and judgment as he can develop, because every citizen has a voice in the management of the community. The progress, and even the safety, of a democratic community depends in part upon the intelligence of the citizens, and by this we cannot mean the intelligence of some citizens, but the combined intelligence of all. (Hutchins 1950)

At that time, access to college had begun to broaden, with the land-grant system, the GI Bill, the creation of community colleges, and the civic rights movements of the 1950s and 1960s all marking important steps on the path to equality.

On the other hand, American colleges and universities have always selected and served a privileged class and have made choices about whom to admit and what to teach on the basis of values that have not been strictly democratic. The college-attendance rate has stalled since the 1980s at about half of all young adults. About half of those who do attend college fail to graduate, and those who do graduate have very different experiences depending on the institution that enrolls them.

James Fallows of the *Atlantic Monthly* (2001) noted the "insane intensity" of the modern college-admissions process; applicants are sorted into institutions of varying resources and prestige depending on their success in high school, which in turn usually reflects the resources of their parents and neighborhoods. An institution gains the market position to select competitive students because of its reputation, which depends substantially on its endowment and the fame of its faculty. Professors rarely become famous for teaching or modeling democratic citizenship. In 1996, Ernest Boyer, then president of the Carnegie Foundation for the Advancement of Teaching, wrote:

> What I find most disturbing . . . is a growing feeling in this country that higher education is, in fact, part of the problem rather than the solution. Going still further, that it's become a private benefit, not a public good. Increasingly, the campus is being viewed as a place where students get credentialed and faculty get tenured, while the overall work for the academy does not seem particularly relevant to the nation's most pressing civic, social, economic, and moral problems. (Boyer 1996, p. 1)

Students do learn in college. They score higher on tests of knowledge and critical thinking near the end of their undergraduate careers than at the beginning. But what seems to affect their success after college is not the way they were taught (as measured, very roughly, by the mission, size, and type of their institution); rather, it is the degree to which their college or university was selective in its admissions. Pascarella and Terenzini (2005, p. 591) conclude, "These findings could be expected because in the areas of career and economic achievement, the status-allocating aspects of a college and what a degree from that college signals to potential employers about the characteristics of its students may count as much if not more than the education provided."

The previous paragraphs refer to the overall impact of college education. On the specific question of *civic* skills and engagement, college graduates are more involved than community-college graduates, who are more active than non-college graduates (Levine and CIRCLE Staff 2006). For example, in the 2008 presidential primaries, one in four young Americans who had attended college (even for one course) voted. But those young people who had no college experience voted at a rate of only about one in fourteen (Marcelo and Kirby 2008). College graduates are also most active in community service (Marcelo 2007).

We might like to think that the positive relationship between college attendance and civic participation arises because students learn about democracy in college. But studies of civic learning in higher education are disappointing. (The Intercollegiate Studies Institute's 2006 report "The Coming Crisis in Citizenship: Higher Education's Failure to Teach America's History and Institutions" is methodologically imperfect but still presents troubling data.) It is more likely that the correlation between college attendance and civic engagement reflects class inequalities: colleges are serving the empowered and enfranchised but missing the rest of the population. Among colleges, there are huge differences in opportunities for civic learning that mostly reflect differences in institutional endowments and prestige (Kiesa et al. 2007). The disparity seems to be present even before enrollment in college: college-*bound* teenagers and students in successful high schools are already the most likely to experience any interactive and engaging forms of civic education (Kahne and Middaugh 2008).

In short, social stratification is one outcome of higher education. That outcome is antidemocratic and antideliberative insofar as young people of different backgrounds are effectively separated when they are still at a formative developmental age at which they might learn from one another. Despite the increasing racial and cultural diversity of students at some institutions, the system as a whole is highly efficient at segregating young people by future social class. At Harvard, students from families that earn less than $180,000 are considered rare and automatically qualify for financial aid. (In the United States, less than 4 percent of families earn that much.) Only 7 percent of high school sophomores whose families are in the bottom fourth of the income distribution finish four years of college, compared to 60 percent of those from the top quarter of the income distribution (Dynarski and Scott-Clayton 2007).

These facts are compounded by political efforts to reduce higher education's role as a social and economic equalizer. The 1980s were a period in which colleges and universities changed their admissions policies and campus climates in response to the end of legal segregation in the 1960s and lingering de facto discrimination. Campuses overcame legal challenges and considered race (and other "protected classes" such as ethnicity and gender) as one of many admissions criteria. By the 1990s, many colleges and universities offered interdisciplinary programs that considered gender, race, ethnicity, religion, and global issues, and institutions began to view diversity not as a legal mandate but as something integral to academic quality. We are now witnessing backlash against the earlier efforts to provide equity and access to historically underrepresented groups, manifested by assaults on affirmative action and state referendums mandating race-neutrality in college admissions. There appears to be little public understanding of how diversity is an asset and an educational resource in any learning environment, as well as a weakening in public will to correct persistent patterns of racial and class disparity.

Even though colleges and universities do not educate all kinds of young people, they certainly have a responsibility to help their own students

develop civic behaviors and values, including habits of participation, tolerance, and collaboration. In doing so, they must respond to the particular
needs of the time. In the last 30 years, Americans' civic engagement—as
measured by attendance at meetings, membership in groups, working on
community problems, and trust in people and government—has declined
(National Conference on Citizenship 2006). Concurrently, public schools
decreased the number of required civics and current events courses, resulting in a high level of civic illiteracy among Americans, particularly knowledge of Constitutional values, how they evolved, and where they currently
stand (Lane 2008).

To their credit, colleges and universities have responded to these declines
with a flurry of activity aimed mostly at their own undergraduates. They
have rewritten mission statements to emphasize service and citizenship. They
have supported a commendable upsurge in optional student community service and community-based learning. Students now volunteer in record numbers. Faculty members offer courses with service-learning experiences or
community-based research. Many campuses now have offices of community-
university partnerships or centers for civic engagement that facilitate for-
credit and co-curricular student learning experiences in community building
and service.

These efforts, however, have been less than perfect, and there are many
criticisms of civic engagement and education. In particular, three problems
directly impact the overarching goal of educating for democracy. First, a strategy of educating undergraduates for democratic civic engagement is inherently limited since, as noted earlier, about half of young adults do not attend
college, and the vast majority of Americans are past the conventional college
years.

Second, within higher education, there is little connection, and arguably
an inverse relationship, between diversity and civic learning. Responding to
changes in the law and attitudes about civil rights in the 1960s, colleges and
universities started exploring ways to accommodate changing populations
in American society. Initially, campus diversity goals centered upon access
(numbers) and hospitality (a welcoming, equitable climate) for previously
underserved populations. In the early 1990s, diversity advocates worked to
shift those goals, or at least add to them, and focus more on academic programs, scholarship, cultural perspectives on academic content, and the value
of diverse perspectives to a learning community. As civic engagement grew
as a mission, it failed to complement and even took some of the wind out
of the diversity movement. Responding to this disconnection, in 1999, the
late Edgar Beckham, senior scholar at the Association of American Colleges
and Universities and former director of campus diversity initiatives for the
Ford Foundation, challenged proponents of the civic engagement and diversity movements to work together to foster citizen engagement that is attentive
to the needs of a free society, one in which *all* citizens enjoy social, economic,
and political equality.

A third and related problem is that higher education does not consistently or automatically increase students' civic or political knowledge or participation. Colleges and universities provide a range of opportunities that might be expected to achieve those outcomes: courses in political science and other social sciences, service programs, extracurricular organizations such as student newspapers and student governments, foreign travel, and prominent speakers. But evidence that any of this actually works is weak at best. Perhaps the reason is that many of these experiences are not well designed to enhance democratic behaviors or values. One often-used example is that of students who volunteer in a soup kitchen. Their experience rarely includes a broader discussion of the underlying causes of and the need for the soup kitchen in the first place. It cannot be assumed that students who work in a soup kitchen will wonder why hunger persists in one of the world's wealthiest nations or that they will be moved to action to address poverty more broadly.

In the meantime, local, national, and global issues in public life seem even more daunting. One could mention such current global challenges as climate change, terrorism, financial crises, and two wars, but even closer to home for American educational institutions is a high-school dropout rate of almost one in three. More than any time in history, the United States needs a well-informed and engaged citizenry so that Jefferson's vision is realized, that "whenever things get so far wrong as to attract their notice, [citizens] may be relied on to set them to rights." The challenge for colleges and universities is to bring things that are "so far wrong" to the attention of students and to provide them with the skills they will need to "set them to rights." It is a call to provide students with opportunities to practice democracy as a means to realizing the American dream of a free, just, and equitable society.

The task is not simply to educate citizens for democracy but to educate citizens for a democracy envisioned a certain way.

THE DELIBERATIVE DEMOCRACY MOVEMENT IN AMERICAN PUBLIC LIFE

There has always been conflict and division in America, but there is evidence that in the last twenty-five years, polarization worsened; traditions of everyday collaboration weakened; and public leaders provided poor models of civil discussion and problem solving. Since colleges and universities are centrally devoted to discourse, it makes sense for them to take a leading role in improving public discussion.

Discussion is not all there is to democracy. A strong democracy also involves negotiations among interest groups, competitive elections, resistance (in the form of strikes and protests), careers that contribute public goods, and rights that can be defended in courts. Yet public discourse is the element of democracy closest to the purposes and expertise of academia.

The term "deliberative democracy" became popular in the 1990s in response to a debate over the roles of reason and inclusion in public life and governance. In their 2004 book *Why Deliberative Democracy*, Amy Gutmann and Dennis Thompson define the term as

> a form of government in which free and equal citizens (and their representatives), justify decisions in a process in which they give one another reasons that are mutually acceptable and generally accessible, with the aim of reaching conclusions that are binding in the present on all citizens but open to challenge in the future. (p. 7)

According to the ideal of deliberative democracy, citizens should treat each other with respect, even if they disagree. Policy makers and citizens alike must be able to justify their decisions and viewpoints on the basis of mutually acceptable reasons (Gutmann and Thompson 1996, p. 55). They need not be impartial, but citizens and policy makers need to cooperate and find mutually acceptable ways to resolve disagreements (Gutmann and Thompson 1996, p. 2). Most importantly, reasons must be acceptable not to a few but to all citizens equally. Stated another way, "The cultural force behind renewed deliberation is a confluence of multiculturalism and a renewed civic impulse" (Gastil and Keith 2005, p. 14).

Meanwhile, outside academia, a significant group of civic organizations and leaders have emerged as advocates for democracy based on civil discourse that includes diverse citizens. This group includes organizations such as Everyday Democracy, Demos, Public Agenda, America*Speaks*, Public Conversations Project, the Kettering Foundation, and members of the National Coalition for Dialogue and Deliberation (see Additional Resources). These organizations approach democracy building from different perspectives, but most fall into the categories of electoral reform, community development and building, and deliberative democracy (America*Speaks*, Everyday Democracy, Demos, and the Ash Institute 2009).

Advocates of a more deliberative democracy promote democratic dialogue as critical to the health and sustainability of American democracy. Dialogue is more than "just talk" or casual conversation, and it is not a "feel-good" or meaningless exercise. Dialogue is a process of talking and listening with the express purpose of building relationships and fostering mutual understanding. Effective dialogue is a foundation for personal and collective commitment and action; improved intergroup relations; stronger communities; and reasoned and deliberative decision making, action, and sustainable change.

Other theorists and practitioners prefer to use the term *deliberation* to describe this work. *Deliberation* often brings to mind the judicial process and the role of juries: a small group of people charged with the responsibility of listening to evidence, giving that evidence careful consideration, weighing choices, and making decisions. A *public deliberation* operates in much the same way: people come together to study a social or political issue, give careful consideration to the facts, identify possible solutions, weigh the pros and cons of each choice, and them make a decision as to how that issue should be addressed (University of New Hampshire 2007).

While it can be helpful to explore distinctions between dialogue and deliberation, in the end, they may be unnecessary. Well-designed democratic processes involve a number of skills, such as analysis, communication, problem solving, and collaborative decision-making. Democracy is not simply a form of government or a procedural process for policy making. A deliberative democracy is often described in terms of the attitudes, skills, and habits of its citizens. What works has been determined by many years of civic experiments in public participation and discourse. From these experiments, deliberative democracy has come to be described, by the Democracy Imperative (University of New Hampshire 2007), in terms of these key characteristics:

- A reflective and informed citizenry
- Vigorous participation of ordinary citizens in matters of public concern at the local, national, and global levels
- A public process of reasoning and deliberation for decision and policy making
- Political and social inclusion
- An understanding of and appreciation for different cultural or ideological perspectives
- Involvement in decision making by those most likely to be affected by the outcome
- Public officials who are responsive to ideas generated through public discourse and who are accountable to the public for their decisions
- Respect for free expression
- An openness to multiple viewpoints, dissent, and criticism
- An understanding that when disagreements arise, citizens will continue to work to overcome differences to reach more acceptable outcomes

Deliberative democracy is values-driven in two ways. It derives from Constitutional principles of freedom, justice, and equity, *and* it relies on a collective commitment to core principles of inclusion, reason, and respect as guidelines and aims of public discourse.

Inclusion

Public decisions are legitimate only when a broad group of people with diverse perspectives—particularly those most likely to be affected by an outcome—participate in the process. At the very least, the composition of public participants should mirror the social identities, beliefs, and ideologies of those in the community. Dissenting views are welcome. Political scientist Iris Marion Young (2000) explains:

> On a deliberative understanding of democratic practice, democracy is . . . a means of collective problem-solving which depends for its legitimacy and wisdom on the expression and criticism of the diverse opinions of all the members of the society. Inclusive democratic practice is likely to promote the most just results because people aim to persuade one another of the justice and wisdom of their claims, and are open to having their own opinions and understandings of their interests change in the process. (p. 6)

Inclusion calls for an examination of a number of things: Who is "at the table," and who is missing? How can a process be truly inclusive if some constituencies are unable or refuse to participate? Are individual opinions or beliefs appropriate in the public square, or should citizens "check their personal views at the door" and contribute only views that are in the best interest of the community? If a group is represented but they do not have free and equal opportunities to speak (real or perceived), how can the process be managed to ensure equal voice? When community dynamics include a history of inequality, oppression, or subjugation, how can a group establish equal footing for all participants? The challenge is to identify and appropriately manage power inequities.

Reason and Respect

Political theorist John Rawls promoted the idea that the public square should be a place of reason. Responding principally to attempts to introduce religious beliefs into public policy making or efforts to base public principles on religious morals, John Rawls expressed the view that American democracy is based upon secular ideals, a public morality that needs no religious grounding. Democratic ideals of justice and freedom, Rawls contended, are "self-supporting" (qtd. in Macedo 2000, p. 169). He began with the premise that justice is critical to a constitutional democracy (Thomas 2007). Given the diversity of populations and perspectives in the United States, conflict is inevitable. Citizens should seek to introduce only ideas and views that are reasonable and politically acceptable in a just society. In more practical terms, Rawls viewed public reason as almost a ground rule for meaningful and effective democratic dialogue and deliberation.

Reason and inclusion as guiding principles for public engagement can lead to conflict. Reason as a limitation to discourse arguably inhibits free speech and restricts the free exchange of ideas, new perspectives, insights, and innovations. It limits the consideration of multiple viewpoints, often by those "at the margins of the dominant culture" (Macedo 1999, pp. 3–4). It "trivializes" religious perspectives (Carter 1993) and privileges, for example, secularism.

It is much harder and less effective to be "reasonable" if one is oppressed or marginalized rather than satisfied with the status quo and comfortable with the processes and norms that prevail in a community. In many countries, some residents contest the claim that they are even part of the political community; they strive to secede, gain autonomy, or return to an independent status that they or their ancestors held in the past. It can seem particularly egregious to expect them to join a reasonable dialogue or deliberation with the very groups they do not want to be joined to. For all these reasons, many social activists believe that "deliberation" is actually harmful to people who have serious grievances and who contest the standard forums and procedures of any given society (Levine and Nierras 2007).

Part of the response to this view is that deliberation practitioners actually define "reasonableness" much less narrowly and stringently than academic theorists such as Rawls and Gutmann and Thompson do. Moderators of real deliberative forums appreciate expressions of emotion, personal testimony, and storytelling (Mansbridge et al. 2006). They do not expect consensus but are often pleased by increased mutual understanding and social capital. People will not always agree, but they can agree to enter into a discussion with a willingness to be civil and open-minded, to listen to the viewpoints of others, to entertain questions and critique, and to allow for adequate time for not just the expression of all viewpoints but for a reciprocal exchange of ideas. For these reasons, a third critical principle in a deliberative democracy is that of mutual respect.

A Vision for Higher Education

Colleges and universities serve as (1) institutional citizens in local communities and, more broadly, society; and (2) educators of citizens, both enrolled students and the public at large. In both capacities, colleges and universities should participate in this broader movement for deliberative democracy. Planning how to participate requires assessing the strengths and weaknesses of higher education as a sector, compared to other crucial democratic institutions such as K–12 schools, the news media, political parties, and labor unions. The strengths of academia include substantial resources (such as professors and other highly skilled employees, buildings, libraries and other collections, and endowments); nonprofit status; a tradition of political independence; and excellence in research, dialogue, deliberation, and civil discourse. It is also an advantage that colleges and universities exist in thousands of communities in the United States. Because (unlike most corporations) they are unable to relocate, their interests are intertwined with those of their neighbors.

The weaknesses of higher education include a focus on one slice of the population (basically, young adults who were successful in school and who can afford tuition); tight budgets and a dependence on private and state funds; a hyper-competitive market for students, grants, and faculty; pressure to educate students for personal and professional career advancement and not for social responsibility; narrowly tailored disciplinary silos that do not lend themselves to applied, interdisciplinary problem solving; and a limited mission. It would, for instance, be inappropriate for a college to support a political party, yet parties play important roles in almost all democracies. This example underscores the fact that colleges cannot restore democracy on their own.

The broader democratic civic education agenda challenges the academy to make hard choices about who gets an education and what counts as success in student learning and faculty scholarship. Colleges and universities cannot serve every citizen directly, but they should explicitly recognize that their admissions decisions contribute to social stratification. This issue should be openly discussed on campus. Appropriate responses might include adjusting admissions criteria to increase fairness, without jeopardizing excellence; rewarding democratic and civic skills of both students and faculty; inviting the public onto campus for deliberative processes; and producing knowledge, culture, and information collaboratively with outside citizens for public purposes.

Colleges and universities can replace daily newspapers as providers of high-quality information and spaces for discussion on matters of public concern, now that the newspaper industry seems threatened with economic collapse. They can serve as conveners, bringing together members of the campus community, citizens, experts, and policy makers to address local concerns such as health care, poverty, public transportation needs, or public safety. Likewise, colleges and universities can help to strengthen civic education in K–12 schools. And in their business practices, they can model relations between employers and workers and between customers and clients, and take seriously promises of shared governance and democratic decision making.

The full agenda goes far beyond what we can discuss in this chapter. What follows is a sampling of some promising practices in teaching and learning for deliberative democracy. These activities are contributions to the democratic movement, and they would become even more important if higher education began to play a more significant civic role.

INTERGROUP DIALOGUE

Nearly twenty years ago, the University of Michigan–Ann Arbor developed a program in response to several racially charged incidents on campus. As Schoem and Hurtado (2001) explain:

> In a sense, intergroup dialogue is a *diverse* twenty-first-century version of the *homogeneous* nineteenth-century town hall meeting: sleeves rolled up, talking directly, honestly, and sometimes quite harshly about the most difficult and pressing topics of the day, and then moving forward together with solutions to strengthen the community and the nation. (p. 4)

Intergroup dialogue (IGD) is now offered on campuses nationally. How IGD is implemented varies, but most programs share certain characteristics. IGD programs are for credit. They are designed to bring together groups of twelve to eighteen students from diverse backgrounds to engage in in-person, facilitated dialogues over an extended period of time. The express purposes of IGD are to help students "understand their commonalities and differences, examine the nature and impact of social inequalities, and explore ways of working together toward greater equality and justice" (Zuniga et al. 2007).

Like community dialogues, IGD programs are anything but superficial. Students study the difference between dialogue and debate. They practice interactive communication skills such as active listening, clarifying, synthesizing, and paraphrasing. They study terms such as discrimination, racism, prejudice, affirmative action, and oppression. They practice participating in and facilitating difficult dialogues such as conversations about religious beliefs in public life, immigration, structural racism, and white privilege. They develop action plans for meaningful community change. They challenge students to reflect on their own social identity, beliefs, and perspectives.

Comparisons between students in control groups and in IGD programs show consistent positive effects in three categories of desired outcomes: intergroup understanding, intergroup relationships, and intergroup collaboration and engagement. Students in IGD programs gain awareness of inequality and its relationship to structural factors (e.g., economically disadvantaged schools, unequal access to jobs or education, and income disparities), as well as increased empathy and motivation to bridge differences in order to work collaboratively (Biren et al. 2009).

The Difficult Dialogues Initiative

In 2007, the Ford Foundation gave forty-three colleges and universities grants to start "difficult dialogues" on issues of each campus's choice. The goal of the program was to promote academic freedom and religious, cultural, and political pluralism on college and university campuses. The projects addressed a wide range of issues such as religious freedom and public life, racial and ethnic tensions, Arab American conflicts, sexual orientation, and academic freedom (Thomas Jefferson Center 2008). Clark University, for example, organized four months of activities over the course of two semesters, starting with broad issues of American democracy and citizen participation before moving to issues of religious tolerance, race, climate change, and power. The program hosted panel discussions, presentations, and films, all followed by facilitated, small-group dialogues. Faculty developed nine courses ranging from communication and culture to environmental politics. The program is continuing in 2008–2009, long past the grant period (Clark University 2008). As another example, LaGuardia Community College, located in the borough of Queens in New York City, pursued three activities: an ongoing faculty dialogue and development initiative on the role of religion in its classrooms, the collection of digital stories by students, faculty, and staff about their perspectives on faith, and community study circles on the role of religion in public life. For the community study circles, the campus trained over forty facilitators, faculty, staff, and students. The college hosted over fifty small, interfaith dialogues involving most of the 150 faith communities in Queens (LaGuardia Community College 2008) and worked with Everyday Democracy to design the program and create a discussion guide (see Additional Resources).

Sustained Dialogue Campus Network

Sustained dialogue is a change process that brings the same people together repeatedly and often over a long period of time to discuss conflicts. The Sustained Dialogue Campus Network (International Institute for Sustained Dialogue 2008) involves students from dozens of campuses nationally who work to improve race relations and campus climate. Campuses that support sustained dialogue programs include Princeton University, the University of Virginia, Dickenson College, the University of Notre Dame, Vanderbilt University, Colorado College, and the University of Hawaii. These are student-driven, extracurricular initiatives that continue over a long period of time, more than a year. As part of the program, students train to become facilitators and then train others on campus to continue the work. Annually, the Sustained Dialogue Campus Network hosts a national meeting where students can attend workshops, training sessions, and dialogue sessions.

The focus of a sustained dialogue is usually relationship building. Dialogues are facilitated, but because they are relaxed and long-term, there is less pressure to move to action or identify a transformation on the part of the participants. Participants not only discuss an issue. They also study the process of and attitudes about change more broadly. Participants probe the dynamics of group relationships and weigh the consequences (in the same way an issue forum does) for addressing and ignoring those group dynamics.

Centers for, and Programs in, Deliberation

One trend on university campuses is to open centers or start programs in deliberation. Where these are housed varies by institution. Some, like the Center for Public Deliberation at Colorado State University, are linked directly to academic disciplines such as communication. Others, such as the New England Center for Civic Life at Franklin Pierce College, are interdisciplinary.

Some centers focus on civic learning more broadly but include in their student learning agenda opportunities to engage in public deliberation, often in partnership with surrounding communities. The Laboratory for Public Scholarship and Democracy at Pennsylvania State University manages multiple learning experiences. Students work in local communities, organize community dialogues, and conduct community-based research. The center hosts Constitution Day activities and runs a course for the first-year experience.

Some campuses are experimenting with Democracy Lab, a series of courses that teaches students the art of deliberation as they discuss contemporary political issues. Regis University in Denver, Colorado, offers an online Democracy Lab course using National Issues Forums books on health care, ethnic tensions, civic disengagement, and international affairs.

Many of these centers start as hubs for National Issues Forums (NIF) and the work of the Kettering Foundation, which launched and continues to support NIF as a nonpartisan, nationwide network of organizations that sponsor public forums training institutes for public deliberation (Melville, Willingham, and Dedrick 2005). The NIF approach to public deliberation is somewhat like a facilitated town meeting: people come together to examine an issue and carefully weigh the pros and cons of particular policy choices to address that issue. Issues are framed in advance, and forum participants read previously supplied "issue books" or framing materials. While weighing the pros and cons, participants are asked to identify the values that drive their particular viewpoints. Participants complete a survey at the beginning and end of the forum, and, where appropriate, the results of the surveys are forwarded to policy makers.

Centers that serve as hubs for NIF might run forums on previously framed issues, or they might host a Public Policy Institute, a multiday workshop for people interested in learning how to organize and moderate a forum. These centers also host Issue Framing Workshops in which participants study an issue and learn how to frame choices in public policy and write issue books.

PROGRAMS IN CONFLICT RESOLUTION

Universities such as George Mason University and Portland State University support large and well-known programs in conflict resolution. Historically, these programs focused on interpersonal and private disputes from a stakeholder perspective. They offer a variety of concentrations, including

- Theory and practice
- Mediation, negotiation, arbitration, and alternative dispute resolution
- Problem solving and moral reasoning
- Consensus building and other models of decision making
- Community mediation and community building
- Social identity and conflict
- Intercultural learning and communication
- Global and international conflict
- Policy making at the local and national levels
- Peace and social justice, violence prevention, and peacekeeping

Sometimes, programs are combined with other disciplines like social work, philosophy, or the health professions.

Most of these programs provide education and training for people interested in serving as third-party mediators or adjudicators—consultants brought in to analyze, manage, resolve, and occasionally prevent conflict, usually between easily identified stakeholders. The idea is that problems can be solved by individuals or groups who work out their differences face-to-face.

More recently, schools are expanding programs in conflict resolution to apply to public settings. The theory is that the skills, expectations, and approaches to stakeholder conflict management can also apply to communities. The distinction is in purpose: the goal of a public conflict management process is to identify common ground and shared, community values and to facilitate the process so that people can work together to realize those community ideals. With this as a goal, the process does not support the aspirations of an individual or a particular group (Dukes, Piscolish, and Stephens 2000), and the scale is usually larger than most conflict management work. Educating graduates of conflict resolution programs for this kind of work involves courses in the theory and practice of dialogue; models of deliberation; facilitation; and organizing safe, thoughtful forums where people can come together, talk, exchange ideas, and collaboratively seek solutions. Students also study theories of dialogue and how dialogue can enhance more traditional conflict resolution or peace building work.

THE COLLABORATIVE GOVERNANCE MOVEMENT

"Collaborative governance" is a growing effort by governments to work with other government branches (and sometimes with nongovernment organizations, including private corporations and nonprofit organizations) to increase efficiency, make public decisions, and implement changes in public policy. In addition to their typical role providing expertise and data on public issues, some units at colleges and universities facilitate collaborative governance by serving as third-party mediators, organizers, conveners, and facilitators. These centers offer a broad range of outreach services, such as helping public officials address conflict or serving as third-party mediators. Those that are exclusively consultative might be funded by the state. Others run programs and educate students in third-party negotiation and mediation, consensus building and policy making, and conflict management. Most do both.

More and more, these centers are working to advance collaborative governance by providing neutral forums where citizens can engage in dialogue and deliberation on public matters. Many of these centers also provide training in public deliberation, facilitation, and intergroup dialogue.

It is interesting to see where these centers and programs are housed on campus. They can be part of schools of public policy, public administration, law, urban and regional planning, communication, conflict resolution, and environmental sciences. They are sometimes linked to cooperative extension programs. Only a few operate out of offices of civic engagement or undergraduate programs; those are generally part of government departments. Some are freestanding centers, such as the Institute for the Common Good at Regis University or the Fanning Institute at the University of Georgia.

Leadership Education

Images of the ideal leader have evolved significantly, shifting how leadership education is designed. Top-down, hierarchical models of leadership have been replaced with models of participatory and facilitative leadership. At the University of Richmond's Jepson School of Leadership, the nation's first degree-granting student leadership program, students are required to take courses in leadership theory and models, group dynamics, critical thinking, and ethics. The school also offers more advanced courses in conflict resolution, change and policy making, cultural and international contexts, social movements, and political leadership. Central to student learning are the arts of democracy: democratic dialogue, deliberation and reason, conflict management, and collaborative change.

Organizational change and leadership experts such as MIT's Peter Senge and Harvard's Ronald Heifetz advocate for democratic methods to facilitate organizational change. Both point to dialogue as a cornerstone for effective and sustainable organizational change (Senge 1990, pp. 238–257; Heifetz 1994, pp. 113–121). Senge outlines the necessary conditions (analogous to ground rules) for dialogue in organizations—for example, that participants should "suspend" their assumptions and regard each other as equal colleagues, and that the dialogue should be facilitated by a neutral individual (Senge 1990, p. 243). Both Senge and Heifetz point to other elements of effective change initiatives: assessment, careful framing, collaborating, listening, and cultivating a shared vision; involvement of constituents most likely to be affected by the outcomes and seeking diversity of perspective; viewing conflict as an opportunity. Heifetz promotes "orchestrating conflict" through dialogue (Heifetz 1994, pp. 117–121).

Consider the work of two exemplary consulting firms that design and facilitate change initiatives for both corporations and governments: Viewpoint Learning in San Diego and the Interaction Institute for Social Change (IISC) in Cambridge, Massachusetts. Both emphasize dialogue as the foundation for sustainable organizational change. IISC offers public workshops in "facilitative leadership" and "facilitating change," both of which emphasize dialogue and collaboration as central to organizational decision making, strategic planning, and change. Viewpoint Learning suggests a three-stage dialogic approach to "organizational learning" and change. Stage I involves "consciousness raising," the exchange of personal perspectives and facts. Stage II involves "working through" sticky problems. In this stage, organizations identify all viewpoints on an issue and employ a "choice" approach (see the description of National Issues Forums and the work of the Kettering Foundation, above) to weighing the pros and cons of each viewpoint. Stage III involves decision making and action. Both organizations advise clients to establish ground rules for all dialogue stages, such as "listen with empathy" and "look for common ground" (Viewpoint Learning 2010).

Most organizations, governments, and communities know that at some point during a change effort, they will need to do some assessment. They will have to consider, for example, their readiness for and barriers to change, organizational or community culture and understanding of core values, the nature of the problem, and the likelihood that a change initiative will succeed. Assessment can be accomplished through dialogue processes. Consider, for example, evaluating institutional culture. Organizers of a change initiative would want to know how people feel about prior change efforts. Are they cynical? What are their anxieties about change? How much institutional inertia do they need to overcome? Is inertia due to a high level of comfort or a lack of awareness of the need to change, or something else? Consider evaluating institutional values. Organizers of a change initiative might want to ask, what adjectives describe this campus culture? What subcultures exist and what adjectives do they identify as core? What stories do people tell to describe the culture of this campus? In both lines of questioning, these are best answered through qualitative research, through a process of dialogue and inquiry.

DIALOGUE AS PEDAGOGY

Democratic dialogue is not only an important skill to be learned. It is a good *way to learn*. The educational research over the past twenty-five years has led to new conclusions about what and how students learn. The predominant teaching method—lecturing—does not seem to result in lasting learning. What students learn in a lecture is forgotten, by some measures, after a week, and by others, after five years (Finkel 2000). In "experiments involving measures of retention of information after the end of a course, measures of transfer of knowledge to new situations, or measures of problem solving, thinking or attitude change, or motivation for further learning, the results tend to show differences favoring discussion methods over lecture" (McKeachie 1994, p. 54). Students might relearn material to prepare for exams, but in general, by a few months later, they retain barely half of what they have heard through "teaching as telling" (Garvin 1991, p. 4). This view is consistent with the educational philosophy of Paulo Freire, who argued that "banking education"— a form of education that treats students as empty containers into which the teachers "pour" knowledge—fails to stimulate curiosity, creativity, and the production of knowledge (qtd. in Gadotti 1994, pp. 10–13). Quality study is not an act of consuming ideas, but rather one of creating them (Gadotti 1994, p. 12).

Nor does abstract or generalized learning result in the kind of deep, contextualized understanding that educators view as an important learning outcome. Students who learn through passive listening, memorizing, and repeating back what they have memorized do not learn to apply that learning to practical or social contexts. Further, lecturing fails to advance skills in critical thinking, moral reasoning, problem solving, or intercultural sensitivity and competency.

Researchers exploring new teaching methods have found that students learn best when they are actively engaged in the learning process and when they, not the teachers, do the talking. Research shows that when students learn through carefully designed opportunities for collaborative inquiry and discussion, they retain what they learn and have more of an understanding of how to apply what they have learned in life (McKeachie 1994, pp. 32, 279–286).

This model challenges the traditional classroom hierarchy, placing the professor in the roles of facilitator and learner rather than that of the sole classroom authority conveying knowledge. Of course, professors and their students are not equals—the professor identifies the course learning goals, designs the curriculum, and evaluates student performance. In a discussion-based classroom, however, the professor works to overcome assumptions about authority. Discussion-based learning is "predicated on the belief that the most powerful ideas can be produced when people are expressing their ideas on a topic and listening to others to express theirs" (Hess 2009, p. 14). The professor invites students to think, manage their own learning, and contribute to the learning of everyone—including the professor—in the room.

This is not to say, however, that learning environments should be so democratic that the professor is irrelevant or invisible. Quality discussion-based learning experiences require careful planning by teachers who provide information and structure, frame issues, ask thought-provoking questions, and prompt students to pose their own questions. C. Roland Christensen (1991), who developed case-method teaching for Harvard's Business and Medical Schools and, eventually, Harvard University more broadly, described the discussion-based teacher as the "planner, host, moderator, devil's advocate, fellow-student, and judge—a potentially confusing set of roles. Even the most seasoned [discussion] leader must be content with uncertainty, because discussion teaching is the art of managing spontaneity" (16). Indeed, creating effective discussion-based learning environments takes more time and effort. Teachers "must consider not only *what* they will teach, but also *whom* and *how*. And the classroom encounter consumes a great deal of energy; simultaneous attention to the process . . . and content . . . requires emotional as well as intellectual engagement" (Christensen 1991, p. 15). In his Harvard course on discussion leadership, Professor Christensen warned his students that for every hour of a discussion-based class, he typically prepared for three hours.

STUDENT POLITICAL ENGAGEMENT

Political education and engagement are powerful ways to prepare students for their roles as citizens and leaders in a diverse and complex world. In "The

Place of Political Learning in College," author Ann Colby (2008) defines political engagement broadly, inclusive of

> the wide range of ways that people . . . participate in American democracy, without making the definition so broad that it includes all of civic voluntarism. Political engagement, therefore, includes community and civic involvement that has a systemic dimension and various forms of engagement with public policy issues . . . Political activities are driven by systemic-level goals, a desire to affect the shared values, practices, and policies that shape collective life. (p. 4)

The scope of political learning includes education in democratic ideals and practices; social change and public policy making; public dialogue; deliberation; and models of public participation, democratic leadership and organizing skills, and community involvement at the systemic level. These are all critical dimensions to education for deliberative democracy.

Political learning on campus happens through multiple student political education and engagement efforts such as the following:

Voter registration drives
Advocacy work and debates
Summer institutes
Semester-in-Washington programs
Internships with political offices
Residential theme-based learning communities
Invited speakers
Mentoring programs
Deliberation about political issues
Panel discussions
"Political Awareness Day"
Leadership training

Campaign work
Constitution Day activities
Political research and action projects
Structured reflection on political experiences
Courses in democratic values and process
Peer-leadership programs
Informed Voter programs
Political learning outcomes in particular departments
Polling, exit poll studies, research on voting patterns
Voter registration rights initiatives

THE NEXT FORM OF DEMOCRATIC EDUCATION

We began this chapter by expressing our concern that through exclusive decisions about who gets admitted and who has access to institutional resources, colleges and universities fail to remedy—and arguably perpetuate—persistent patterns of social and economic disparity in American society. Responding to concerns in the early 1990s about the "disconnected" academy, a steady decline in citizen engagement in public life, and deepening social and political divides, colleges and universities complemented existing diversity and service programming by adding civic and community-based learning experiences. More recent additions include programs in intergroup dialogue, public deliberation, and political engagement. To circumvent entrenched disciplinary silos in academia, many campuses increasingly support interdisciplinary centers and research institutes. All of these are promising developments—as was the 2008 presidential election. Renewed enthusiasm for political engagement manifested in the months approaching the 2008 election, and the election of the first African American president, were indeed causes for celebration. Perhaps more to the point, President Barack Obama came from a background in deliberative community organizing and spoke consistently on the campaign trail about "active citizenship." As he said in his 2007 "A Call to Serve" speech, "This will not be a call issued in one speech or program; this will be a cause of my presidency" (qtd. in Organizing for America 2007).

Nonetheless, higher education cannot point to additional programs or to the 2008 election as evidence of a civic mission accomplished. Although college students turned out to vote at near-record levels, their same-age peers not attending college remained on the sidelines in the election itself. Those who did vote may easily lapse back into complacent, distant relationships with policy makers, as demonstrated by the low turnout in 2010. Surveys showed low levels of political knowledge: for example, only 46 percent of the public knew, after the 2010 election gave the Republicans control of the House of Representatives, which party would control that body (Pew Research Center, 2010). Civic leaders agree that the task of revitalizing democracy calls for reform. American democracy needs to be more equitable and inclusive, and it should be characterized by active, everyday citizen participation in public discussion, governance and policy making, and community development.

Programs that previously affected a small number of students can be assessed, and those that are effective can be broadened to reach all students. No student should graduate without knowing how a bill becomes a law; what freedoms are protected by the First Amendment; the history of civil rights movements in this country; the role of religion in public life; and the effectiveness of political processes, including community organizing, protest, voting, and public deliberation. Students should develop what Eric Lane (2008) calls a "constitutional conscience," an understanding of the institutions, processes, ideals, and principles of American government and democracy (p. 55). Critical issues and current events should be explored from an interdisciplinary perspective, and students should learn how to solve real public problems, not just theoretical problems, in collaboration with each other and with citizens from outside the campus.

Academic affairs and offices of diversity and civic engagement should unite under one roof or work collaboratively. Campuses need to *get political*. Students need to talk about the things that divide us as a nation: race, gender, ethnicity, class, religion, and ideology. They need to grapple with deeply personal matters of exclusion, injustice, power, structural racism, and privilege. They need to examine free speech and how it can be uncivil, unproductive, and even oppressive. They need to consider rules of discourse such as respect, open-mindedness, and inclusion and how those intersect and perhaps conflict with reason. They need to know how cross-cultural dynamics can stifle the free exchange of ideas, and how those dynamics can be enhanced when managed honestly and openly.

The responsibility for these changes rests with the faculty members who oversee the curriculum and with leaders who help establish institutional priorities. Yet we can envision faculty or academic leaders responding with concerns that deliberative democracy is "just one more thing" in the litany of education reforms. We don't agree. We believe that educating students to be informed about and protective of democracy is not an add-on. Educating for democracy *is* higher education's central purpose—why colleges and universities were established in the first place.

REFERENCES

America*Speaks*, Everyday Democracy, Demos, and the Ash Institute at Harvard University. 2009. "Working Together to Strengthen Our Nation's Democracy: Ten Recommendations." August. Available at http://www.whitehouse.gov/files/documents/ostp/opengov/sond2%20final%20report.pdf.

Beckham, Edgar F. 1999. "Civic Learning and Campus Diversity: Bridging the Language Gap." *Peer Review* 2, no. 1 (Fall): 4–7.

Boyer, Ernest. 1996. "The Scholarship of Engagement." *Journal of Public Service and Outreach* 1: 1–20.

Carter, Stephen. 1993. *The Culture of Disbelief.* New York: Basic Books.

Christensen, C. Roland. 1991. "Premises and Practices of Discussion Teaching." In *Education for Judgment: The Artistry of Discussion Leadership*, by C. Roland Christensen, David A. Garvin, and Ann Sweet, 15–35. Cambridge, MA: Harvard University Press.

Clark University. 2008. "Difficult Dialogues." Available at http://www.clarku.edu/difficultdialogues_2.cfm.

Colby, Anne. 2008. "The Place of Political Learning in College." *Peer Review* 10 (2/3): 4–8.

Dukes, E. Franklin, Marina A. Piscolish, and John B. Stephens. 2000. *Reaching for Higher Ground in Conflict Resolution.* San Francisco: John Wiley and Sons.

Dynarski, Susan M., and Judith Scott-Clayton. 2007. "College Grants on a Postcard: A Proposal for Simple and Predictable Federal Student Aid." Hamilton Project Discussion Paper, the Brookings Institution. Available at http://www.brookings.edu/papers/2007/02education_dynarski.aspx.

Fallows, James. 2001. "The Early-Decision Racket." *Atlantic Monthly*, September.

Finkel, Donald L. 2000. *Teaching with Your Mouth Shut.* Portsmouth, NH: Boynton/Cook.

Gadotti, Moacir. 1994. *Reading Paulo Freire: His Life and Work.* Trans. John Milton. Albany: State University of New York.

Garvin, David A. 1991. "Barriers and Gateways to Learning." In *Education for Judgment: The Artistry of Discussion Leadership*, by C. Roland Christensen, David A. Garvin, and Ann Sweet, 3–13. Camridge, MA: Harvard University Press.

Gastil, John, and William M. Keith. 2005. "A Nation that (Sometimes) Likes to Talk." In *The Deliberative Democracy Handbook*, by John Gastil and Peter Levine, 3–19. San Francisco: John Wiley and Sons.

Gutmann, Amy, and Dennis Thompson. 1996. *Democracy and Disagreement.* Cambridge, MA: Harvard University Press.

———. 2004. *Why Deliberative Democracy?* Princeton: Princeton University Press.

Heifetz, Ronald A. 1994. *Leadership without Easy Answers.* Cambridge, MA: Harvard University Press.

Hess, Diana E. 2009. *Controversy in the Classroom: The Democratic Power of Discussion.* New York: Routledge.

Hutchins, Robert M. 1950. "The Idea of a College." *Measure* 1 (Fall): 363–371. Available at http://www.ditext.com/hutchins/1950.html.

Intercollegiate Studies Institute. 2006. "The Coming Crisis in Citizenship: Higher Education's Failure to Teach America's History and Institutions." Available at http://www.americancivicliteracy.org/2006/summary.html.

International Institute for Sustained Dialogue. 2008. "The Process of Sustained Dialogue." Available at http://www.sustaineddialogue.org/learn_about_sd.htm.

Kahne, Joseph, and Ellen Middaugh. 2008. "Democracy for Some—The Civic Opportunity Gap in High School." CIRCLE Working Paper 59, Center for Information and Research on Civic Learning and Education, Tufts University, Medford, MA. Available at http://www.civicyouth.org/circle-working-paper-59-democracy-for-some-the-civic-opportunity-gap-in-high-school/.

Kiesa, Abby, et al. 2007. "Millennials Talk Politics: A Study of College Student Civic Engagement." Medford, MA: Center for Information and Research on Civic Learning and Education, Tufts University. Available at www.civicyouth.org/college-students-talk-politics.

LaGuardia Community College. 2008. "Issue Guide Exchange." Available at http://www.everyday-democracy.org/Exchange/Guide.29.aspx.

Lane, Eric. 2008. "America 101." *Democracy: A Journal of Ideas*, no. 10 (Fall): 53–63.

Levine, Peter, and CIRCLE Staff. 2006. "Higher Education and Civic Engagement: Summary." CIRCLE. Available at http://www.civicyouth.org/fact-sheet-higher-education-and-civic-engagement-summary/.

Levine, Peter, and Rose Marie Nierras. 2007. "Activists' Views of Deliberation." *Journal of Public Deliberation* 3 (1): article 4.

Lipscomb, Andrew A., and Albert E. Bergh, eds. 1903–1904. *The Writings of Thomas Jefferson, Memorial Edition* 7. Washington, DC.

Macedo, Stephen. 1999. Introd. to *Deliberative Politics: Essays on Democracy and Disagreement*, 1–14. Oxford: Oxford University Press.

———. 2000. *Diversity and Distrust: Civic Education in a Multicultural Democracy.* Cambridge, MA: Harvard University Press.

Mansbridge, Jane, Janette Hartz-Karp, Matthew Amengual, and John Gastil. 2006. "Norms of Deliberation: An Inductive Study." *Journal of Public Deliberation* 2, no. 1 (April): 1–47.

Marcelo, Karlo Barrios. 2007. "Volunteering Among Non-College Youth." CIRCLE fact sheet. Available at http://www.civicyouth.org/PopUps/FactSheets/FS07_Noncollege_Volunteering.pdf.

Marcelo, Karlo Barrios, and Emily Hoban Kirby. 2008. "The Youth Vote in the 2008 Super Tuesday States." CIRCLE fact sheet. Available at http://www.civicyouth.org/PopUps/FactSheets/FS08_supertuesday_exitpolls.pdf.

McKeachie, Wilbert J. 1994. *Teaching Tips: Strategies, Research, and Theory for College and University Teachers.* Lexington, MA: D.C. Heath.

Melville, Keith, Taylor L. Willingham, and John R. Dedrick. 2005. "National Issues Forums: A Network of Communities Promoting Public Deliberation." In *The

Deliberative Democracy Handbook, by John Gastil and Peter Levine, 37–58. San Francisco: John Wiley and Sons.

Nagda, Biren (Ratnesh) A., Patricia Gurin, Nicholas Sorensen, and Ximena Zúñiga. 2009. "Evaluating Intergroup Dialogue: Engaging Diversity for Personal and Social Responsibility." *Diversity & Democracy* 12, no. 1 (January): 4–6.

National Conference on Citizenship. 2006. "America's Civic Health Index: Broken Engagement." Available at http://www.ncoc.net/index.php?tray=content&tid=top5&cid=100.

Organizing for America. 2007. "Obama Issues Call to Serve, Vows to Make National Service Important Cause of His Presidency." Available at http://www.barackobama.com/2007/12/05/obama_issues_call_to_serve_vow.php.

Pascarella, Ernest T., and Patrick T. Terenzini. 2005. *A Third Decade of Research. How College Affects Students 2*. San Francisco: Jossey-Bass.

Pew Research Center. 2010. "Public Knows Basic Facts about Politics, Economics, But Struggles with Specifics." November 18. Available at http://pewresearch.org/pubs/1804/political-news-quiz-iq-deficit-defense-spending-tarp-inflation-boehner.

Schoem, David, and Sylvia Hurtado. 2001. *Intergroup Dialogue: Deliberative Democracy in School, College, Community, and Workplace*. Ann Arbor: University of Michigan Press.

Senge, Peter M. 1990. *The Fifth Discipline: The Art and Practice of the Learning Organization*. New York: Doubleday.

Thomas Jefferson Center for Protection of Free Expression. 2008. *Difficult Dialogues Initiative*. Available at http://www.difficultdialogues.org/.

Thomas, Nancy L. 2007. "Educating for Deliberative Democracy: The Role of Public Reason and Reasoning." *Journal of College and Character* 9, no. 2 (November). Available at http://journals.naspa.org/jcc/vol9/iss2/2/.

University of New Hampshire. 2010. "The Democracy Imperative FAQ." *The Democracy Imperative*. Available at http://www.unh.edu/democracy/faq.html.

Viewpoint Learning. 2010. "Ground Rules of Dialogue." Available at http://www.viewpointlearning.com/about/rules.shtml.

Young, Iris Marion. 2000. *Inclusion and Democracy*. Oxford: Oxford University Press.

Zúñiga, Ximena, Biren (Ratnesh) A. Nagda, Mark Chesler, and Adena Cytron-Walker. 2007. *Intergroup Dialogue in Higher Education: Meaningful Learning About Social Justice*. ASHE Higher Education Report 32, no. 4. San Francisco: Wiley.

ADDITIONAL RESOURCES

Clark University. "Difficult Dialogues." 2008. http://www.clarku.edu/difficultdia logues_2.cfm (accessed October 24, 2008).

Colorado State University. *Center for Public Deliberation*. 2008. http://www.cpd.colostate.edu/ (accessed October 24, 2008).

Everyday Democracy. *Everday Democracy: Ideas and Tools for Community Change*. 2008. http://www.everyday-democracy.org/ (accessed October 24, 2008).

Franklin Pierce University. "New England Center for Civic Life." 2008. http://www.franklinpierce.edu/institutes/neccl/index.htm (accessed October 24, 2008).

Institute for the Common Good, Regis University. Democracy Lab Online Course. 2008. http://www.icgregis.org/index.cfm/id/10/Democracy-Lab/ (accessed November 30, 2010).

Interaction Institute for Social Change. 2008. http://www.interactioninstitute.org/ (accessed November 15, 2008).

International Institute for Sustained Dialogue. "Sustained Dialogue Campus Network." 2008. http://www.sustaineddialogue.org/campus_network.htm (accessed October 24, 2008).

LaGuardia Community College. "Difficult Dialogues." 2008. http://www.lagcc.cuny .edu/difficultdialogues/ (accessed October 24, 2008).

National Coalition for Dialogue and Deliberation. 2008. http://www.thataway.org/ (accessed October 24, 2008).

National Issues Forums. 2008. http://nifi.org/ (accessed November 29, 2008).

Pennsylvania State University. *Laboratory for Public Scholarship and Democracy.* 2010. http://www.berks.psu.edu/Academics/31728.htm (accessed December 9, 2010).

Viewpoint Learning. 2008. http://www.viewpointlearning.com/about/index.shtml (accessed November 15, 2008).

CHAPTER 8

Faculty Civic Engagement

*New Training, Assumptions, and Markets Needed
for the Engaged American Scholar*

KERRYANN O'MEARA

INTRODUCTION

This chapter explores the evolution of the scholarship of engagement and institutional barriers for faculty involvement. In doing so, I discuss three major accomplishments of advocates of the scholarship of engagement in higher education. Next, I consider three barriers to faculty engagement that seem to receive less "air time" in our discussions but that are at the center of faculty professional work and careers. Finally, I examine current and future trends in the appointment types, roles, and rewards of faculty work and where community engagement might find future traction. Throughout the discussion, I draw a distinction between what Cuban (1988) calls "second-order changes"—that is, accomplishments and barriers that touch institutional culture and policy as well as daily practices of faculty, students, and community members—and more surface-level or first-order change.

One of the points made by the editors in framing this book is that the term "engagement" has assumed many meanings in higher education. While some researchers and commentators use the term to refer to student learning and interactions in and out of class, others use "engagement" to refer to theory-to-practice types of learning experiences such as internships, co-ops, or even studies abroad. For the professionals writing in this book, "civic engagement" and "community engagement" comprise a movement defined by teaching, research, and service with public purposes—and this is my intention as well. I am interested in engagement as learning, professional service, community-based research, and applied research that engage professional or academic expertise in partnership and reciprocity with local expertise to address real-world issues (Driscoll and Lynton 1999; Elman and Smock 1985; Lynton 1995; Peters et al. 2005). This definition hinges on the idea that faculty civic engagement takes many forms, requires reciprocal partnership, and involves public work that contributes to our democracy (Sandmann, Saltmarsh, and O'Meara 2008). Ernest Lynton (1995) first distinguished between faculty work that was proprietary in nature—wherein the process and products are essentially purchased as a private commodity—and faculty work wherein the process is intentionally open and inclusive, and the products are shared with community members and organizations that can use them for the public good. The term "scholarship" in "scholarship of engagement" builds on the work of Boyer (1990); Glassick, Huber, and Maeroff (1997); and O'Meara and Rice (2005) to refer to faculty work that draws on expertise and knowledge, is disseminated and shared, and can be assessed for its impact, rigor, and relevance. As Sandmann (2008) points out, civic engagement as scholarship often integrates teaching, research, and outreach roles while inviting reciprocal interactions with partners in knowledge production. Though there have been several evolutions in the construction of the scholarship of engagement (such as from application to reciprocal engagement), changes in traditional scholarship suggest that "the distinction between traditional scholarship and engaged scholarship is becoming less bifurcated" (p. 98).

One final note on definitions of faculty civic engagement: my research on exemplar engaged faculty suggests that while there is relative agreement in the field about good principles of service-learning and community-based research practice, and the importance of reciprocity in partnership work, even those most engaged may not fully understand what it means for faculty work to be tied to public purposes. The very nature of faculty training, appointments, and workload is embedded in a somewhat technocratic understanding of faculty expertise (Boyte 2008). If faculty work were to truly become more public, there would potentially be profound implications for the governance of institutions, and the dominant coin of the realm would not be promotion and tenure but proven relevance and consequentiality.

THE EVOLUTION OF THE SCHOLARSHIP OF ENGAGEMENT

Several effective attempts have been made to record the history of the civic engagement movement overall (Stanton, Giles, and Cruz 1999; Hartley and Hollander 2005; Hollander and Hartley 2000). While historians have traced the beginnings of service missions in higher education back to colonial higher education and to the land-grant era (Peters et al. 2005), Hartley and Hollander (2005) observe that the movement in which most of the authors of this book have been involved is a more recent history beginning with the work of the National Society for Experiential Education in 1978, the International Partnership for Service-Learning and Leadership in 1982, the National Youth

Leadership Council in 1983, the Campus Outreach Opportunity League (COOL) in 1984, and Campus Compact in 1986 (see Table 1.2 in Chapter 1 of this volume). Individual students and groups of students played a key role in the early history of this movement (1978–1991), pushing campuses to establish support for community service and for faculty to integrate service-learning into their courses. The second wave of major events in the movement from the early 1990s to around 2003 seems to have emphasized integration of service-learning into curriculum as a permanent pedagogy and part of institutional mission. Faculty roles and rewards have been a major focus of disciplinary associations and national higher education associations and collaboratives in a third, most recent wave of the movement. These groups tried throughout the late 1990s to the present to make faculty engagement more legitimate and central to faculty socialization, workload, and reward systems. One observation that can be made is that this history has prioritized faculty civic engagement through teaching over other forms of public work. This makes sense because students first pushed for faculty to become involved through coursework—the most central activity of the majority of faculty appointments. Teaching is also perhaps the faculty role around which it is easiest to develop models to export to other campuses, as many similar courses are taught across different institutional types. Indeed, most faculty whom we count today as engaged in public work do so more through their teaching than research, and they have concrete opportunities through institutional grant programs to develop connections between their classes and community partners.

There is, of course, a proud history of community-based research in many disciplines, especially in fields such as anthropology, sociology, social work, education, women's studies, African American studies, and professional schools of law and medicine. While the focus early on may have been on tangible field experiences for students and research opportunities for faculty, the field of community-based research (and faculty involved in such work) has acquired its own set of ethics, values, and skills for public scholarship in communities (Strand et al. 2003).

Likewise, there have long been relationships between university and college professors and public organizations and schools for activities like program development, professional development, technical assistance, and grant writing that serve the public good (Lynton 1995).

Yet only since Boyer's *Scholarship Reconsidered* (1990), published twenty years ago, has the academy begun to consider these three types of faculty work—service-learning, community-based research, and professional service—as potential sources of scholarship for the purposes of faculty evaluation.

Responding to critiques in the late 1980s that higher education, and especially large research universities, were abdicating their responsibilities in the areas of teaching and service in favor of narrow research agendas, Boyer (1990) tried to reframe the conversation in terms of what faculty were contributing and in what ways. In 1990, Boyer advocated in the landmark Carnegie

report *Scholarship Reconsidered* that campuses transform their reward systems to align mission and evaluation in order to acknowledge multiple forms
of scholarship, including discovery, teaching, integration, and application of
knowledge. In subsequent work, "application" was changed to "engagement"
to consider the reciprocal nature of relationships and knowledge flow (Boyer
1990; O'Meara and Rice 2005). This framework, which built directly on
earlier work by Gene Rice, resonated with provosts, deans, and department
chairs struggling with academic cultures that did not seem to be rewarding
teaching and service, much less community engagement. Glassick, Huber, and
Maeroff (1997) followed the initial report with *Scholarship Assessed*, which
provided actual criteria for assessing excellence in the four forms of scholarship. These criteria include clear goals, adequate preparation, appropriate
methods, significant results, effective presentation, and reflective critique.
Hundreds of campuses adopted the Boyer framework and incorporated it
into their promotion and tenure and related reward systems and evaluation
policies (O'Meara and Rice 2005). Yet the framework was adopted by more
baccalaureate and master's campuses than research universities. Likewise, it
was adopted by institutions that might be considered in the middle or toward
the lower end of traditional prestige ladders. For example, very few of the
25 to 30 institutions Bloomgarden (2008) classifies as prestige-oriented liberal arts campuses have formally adopted the framework in faculty evaluation. Additionally, while it has been cited by organizations such as MLA and
Imagining America, the framework and concept of multiple forms of scholarship is more familiar to faculty in education and the social sciences, to provosts and those in academic affairs and faculty development than to faculty
in the hard sciences.

Alongside and contemporaneous with the movement to redefine scholarship came a movement around the idea of the scholarship of engagement—
how to do it, how to document it, and how to assess it for promotion and
tenure (Driscoll and Lynton 1999; Driscoll and Sandmann 2001; Giles
2008; Lynton 1995; O'Meara and Rice 2005; O'Meara 2002; Sandmann
2004, 2006; Sandmann and Weerts 2007; Sandmann 2008; Ward 2003).
For over two decades, the *Journal of Higher Education Outreach and
Engagement*, the *Michigan Journal of Community Service Learning*, and
many disciplinary journals have been publishing articles on helping faculty develop their public work as scholarship and submit it for promotion
and tenure. Likewise, the Outreach Scholarship Conference, the former
American Association for Higher Education Forum on Faculty Roles and
Rewards, the International Association for Research on Service-Learning
and Community Engagement, and many efforts by Campus Compact
have been directed at faculty development toward these same goals. Giles
(2008) observes that as this movement has progressed, many definitions of
"scholarship of engagement" have been used. These definitions emphasize
different aspects of the work such as institutional mission, public or civic
dimensions, ties to scholarly expertise, or integration of teaching, research,

and service (Giles 2008). Regardless, Giles concludes, and I agree, that this work has in fact "arrived" and is present in many different disciplines and institutional types. We do not want to "impose academic imperialism" on what is still an emerging field of theory and practice (Giles 2008, p. 98) but instead want to learn from the accomplishments of the movement and from the nuances in how faculty and administrators are defining the work and acting in practice and rhetoric, and how the work is being integrated into academic cultures.

The next section of this chapter describes three particular accomplishments of faculty, administrators, and policy makers who have been working to move faculty engagement from a peripheral activity (first-order) to a core faculty activity (second-order).

Accomplishments of the Movement to Advance the Scholarship of Engagement

Accomplishment 1

There is more of it. As we consider what might be thought of as the top three accomplishments of the recent civic engagement movement, I think the first one, most plainly, is the increase over the last twenty-five years in the number of institutions that have made a commitment to this work, the number of faculty reporting that they are engaged in service-learning and community engagement research, and the number of opportunities campuses now have available for students to become involved in engagement with their communities.

Many argue, and I agree, that there was much "service-learning" and "action research" occurring before the movement adopted and began promoting these terms—particularly in professional schools in education, social work, public policy, legal and medical clinics, as well as through campus ministries and fraternities and sororities. Over the last twenty-five years, as this movement has spawned new offices of community service, new careers as directors of service-learning (O'Meara 1995), new faculty development opportunities in service-learning, new funding sources, and new partnerships with community service, there is, simply put, just much more going on now. Indeed, Zelda Gamson's 1995 tag line that "service-learning has hit higher education big time" could read today "faculty and student engagement is here, there is a lot of it, and it isn't going away soon" (p. 4). The continued support of the Corporation of National Service and its AmeriCorps and Learn and Serve America Programs, the expansion of Campus Compact to over 1,100 institutions, and the continued interest among students in service-learning in their courses all suggest that, like the use of technology in classrooms, the increased use of post-tenure review in reward systems, or the increasing diversification of the student body and faculty, service-learning is now a part of the permanent landscape of higher education. It is important to distinguish between research-based and teaching-based public work because, while an argument will be made later that more disciplinary associations have advocated public-oriented research and there are new organizations popping up every day to connect faculty research to public purposes, such research-based work seems much less prevalent than faculty connections with teaching and community organizations.

Although it is important to recognize that most research universities and elite liberal arts colleges have not embraced faculty engagement in their reward systems, we must also acknowledge that there is no institutional type—public, private, liberal arts, or comprehensive—untouched by the service-learning and engagement movement. And while perhaps not embraced, many reward systems accommodate civically oriented service-learning and community-based research quite well. In 1986, there were 113 institutions in Campus Compact; today there are over 1,100, with all institutional types represented. Four-year institutions are better represented in Campus Compact than two-year institutions, yet the American Association of Community Colleges observes that over 60 percent of its campuses are engaged in service-learning, which is significant considering that almost half of all undergraduates begin their degrees at community colleges.

After establishing that the engagement movement has been successful in extending the number of students, faculty, and institutions involved, we must ask, "But involved in what?" As noted above, faculty and institutions define engagement differently according to discipline, faculty member, and institution. Thus, while we know we have more of "this" going on, we do not know exactly what "this" is. Many campuses are engaged in what Keith Morton (1995) refers to as "thin," as opposed to "thick," engagement, wherein there is minimal time committed, little integration of engagement with learning, and only nominal reflection or attention to reciprocal university or college partnerships (p. 21).

Most importantly, researchers and practitioners have no idea how much of the current engagement movement is actually enhancing student civic agency, making institutions more democratic places, and enhancing the civic capacity of community partners and citizens.

Accomplishment 2

Faculty civic engagement has reached disciplinary associations and developed a research base, well-established networks, discourse communities, and invisible colleges. Over the last twenty years, the movement to advocate for the scholarship of engagement has produced new journals, national associations, and invisible colleges and networks, as well as a research base. In the last five years, for instance, many disciplinary and interdisciplinary associations have advocated for the scholarship of engagement through national conferences or by adopting written policies supporting assessment of engagement for promotion and tenure. By no means comprising an exhaustive list, the following associations, reports, and journals are illustrative of the amount and quality of disciplinary activity happening around the scholarship of engagement:

- The American Historical Association's "Public History, Public Historians, and the American Historical Association: Report of the Task Force on Public History" (www.historians.org/governance/tfph/TFPHreport.htm)
- Public Anthropology (www.publicanthropology.org)
- The American Sociological Association (www.asanet.org)
- Queen's University's *International Journal for Service Learning in Engineering* (http://library.queensu.ca/ojs/index.php/ijsle/index)
- The Modern Language Association's "Report of the MLA Task Force on Evaluating Scholarship for Tenure and Promotion" (http://www.mla.org/tenure_promotion)
- Community-Campus Partnerships for Health (http://www.depts.washington.edu/ccph)
- Imagining America's Tenure Team Initiative on Public Scholarship (http://www.imaginingamerica.org/TTI/TTI.html)

The Modern Language Association's 2007 "Report of the MLA Task Force on Evaluating Scholarship for Tenure and Promotion" concludes that institutions and departments affiliated with the MLA need to do a better job of connecting institutional mission and reward systems, and amending reward systems to acknowledge broader forms of and new venues (e.g., media) for scholarship. The report acknowledges the importance of the "applied work of citizenship," wherein faculty members partner with public organizations, and recommends that this work be better included in reward systems.

Likewise, in 2007 the American Sociological Association (ASA) recognized the longstanding contributions of sociologists to the public's understanding of, and ability to act on, the social issues of our time by convening a task force to develop guidelines for the evaluation of public sociology for promotion and tenure. The report, titled "Standards of Public Sociology: Guidelines for Use by Academic Departments in Personnel Reviews," was submitted by the Task Force on the Institutionalization of Public Sociology and suggests guidelines for defining and assessing what public sociology is and contains. Specifically, the report notes that public sociology builds on previous literature, is research-based, upholds rigorous methodological standards, is subject to peer review, includes or should include an expanded definition of "peer," and demonstrates how portfolios can be used to display and evaluate public sociology.

The Community-Campus Partnerships for Health Collaborative (CPHC), under the auspices of Cathy Jordan (2007), developed the Community Engaged Scholarship Toolkit, which, while applicable to faculty in many disciplines, provides very concrete tools for faculty in the health fields to define their community engagement for promotion and tenure and develop a portfolio that demonstrates rigor in both teaching and research aspects of community engagement.

Last but certainly not least is Imagining America's 2008 Tenure Team Initiative report, "Scholarship in Public: Knowledge Creation and Tenure Policy in the Engaged University: A Resource on Promotion and Tenure in the Arts, Humanities, and Design," created by Julie Ellison and Timothy Eatman. This report advocates for the recognition and assessment of a "continuum of scholarship" (iv), which includes work created with specific publics and communities outside academe and thereby embraces multiple products and expanded notions of peer review. The report also gives concrete examples of public engagement in the arts, humanities, and design. These are only a few examples of a sea shift of attention by disciplinary associations to issues of faculty public work.

It is important to note that as the currency of service-learning has risen and become more mainstream within higher education, it has done so alongside a greater legitimacy for action research and an increasing acknowledgement of how the ways in which we discover and disseminate knowledge are changing (Holland and Hollander 2006). That the disciplines have begun advocating in very concrete ways for engagement bodes well for its integration into the core of these different fields. What needs to be interrogated, however, is whether the approach will be largely instrumental and technocratic or democratic. That is, do these efforts argue for engagement as a way to change the world or to show the world why the discipline is still relevant—that is, how important it is? Do recent efforts by disciplinary associations to integrate engagement into promotion and tenure allow for epistemological shifts in what those disciplines consider rigorous contributions to knowledge, or are disciplines being encouraged to integrate engagement into existing belief and value systems around promotion and tenure?

Accomplishment 3

There has been significant attention to structures and processes for supporting faculty, students, and institutions in this work. The service-learning and civic engagement movements have come a long way since the early 1980s, when most administrators were directing community service while serving concomitantly as (for example) director of campus ministry, student activities, or honors programs; fraternity or sorority director; or faculty advisor to student groups (O'Meara 1995). There has been a steady growth in centers of service-learning, with an attendant increase in the number of directors of service-learning. In 2010, 86 percent of Campus Compact institutions had community service or service-learning offices to coordinate campus-based service work (Campus Compact 2010). In addition to budget allocations for full-time positions (the most valuable resource in organizations whose budget is 60 to 80 percent personnel), most of these centers or offices have permanent operating budget allocations, though small in most cases, to facilitate student and faculty involvement in community engagement.

Within the last ten years alone, many prestigious liberal arts colleges have had centers for service-learning endowed by large gifts from alumni (e.g., Tufts, Amherst, DePaul, and Duke). Similarly, many colleges and universities have moved engagement into the provost's or faculty development office, symbolizing the centrality of engagement to faculty roles and growth (O'Meara 2008d).

Thousands of directors of service-learning and individual faculty have likewise participated in Campus Compact and discipline-specific professional development workshops held by higher education associations (such as AASCU, CIC, AAC&U, and APLU) that provide strategies for institutionalizing engagement on campus and developing reciprocal university-community partnerships off campus. Such efforts range from integrating service-learning into general education, getting engagement to "count" within reward systems, and semester-long service-learning communities for faculty.

Of course, a valid critique of such efforts is that differences in academic cultures and historic relationships between universities and communities make one-size-fits-all approaches less helpful. Yet there is certainly more scaffolding in place than before to support engagement with communities, in terms of bridge personnel, coordination, and even transportation.

However, a critical question that we must ask is, does increased service-learning or community-based research necessarily mean enhanced student, faculty, or community civic agency? Are all of the resources supporting faculty and student civic engagement also enhancing community capacity for participation in a democracy? Are there aspects of the structures and processes we have set up to facilitate student learning that are either improving or limiting the potential of the public partners to fully invest in and benefit from the work?

In summary, the engagement movement has made at least three first-order changes that have the potential to become second-order if advocates are more reflective and intentional about goals and purposes related to civic engagement. We have more engagement, and it has invaded disciplinary associations and found a foothold in terms of structures and processes to support it. With this traction, the movement now needs to focus more intently on how the disciplines and structures supporting engagement work can be re-envisioned to enhance democracy.

Barriers to Community Engagement

With the above accomplishments in mind, this next section addresses three barriers to advancing faculty engagement. Each of these barriers, if addressed, would contribute to second-order change and connect higher education with public purposes.

The process, products, and socialization of doctoral education, which emphasizes competitive individualism, without attention to the consequentiality of research for public purposes. There is a long and insightful literature on graduate education and its importance to future faculty professional identity and graduate student development as teachers and scholars, as well as more recent attention to these subjects (Austin 2002; Colbeck, O'Meara, and Austin 2008; Golde 2008; Weidman, Twale, and Stein 2001). For example, Weidman, Twale, and Stein (2001) apply socialization theory to the understanding of preparation for the professoriate. They find, as others have, that if graduate students do not have an apprenticeship of sorts in engagement, (Golde 2008) and if they do not develop professional identity as engaged scholars (Colbeck 2008), they will not develop the knowledge, skills, and professional orientation (Austin and McDaniels 2006) to truly become engaged scholars (O'Meara 2008c). What is needed are specific opportunities or "critical experiences" in masters and doctoral programs for graduate students to develop the knowledge, skills, and orientation most relevant to their future engaged work (O'Meara 2008c; O'Meara and Jaeger 2007).

As such, the problem for the future of faculty community engagement regarding graduate education is twofold. First, as mentioned above, graduate students who do not have opportunities to practice engaged scholarship, either in their teaching or research, are unlikely to feel prepared to do so later as faculty. Second, students who do not experience engagement in graduate education are less likely to gravitate toward it later as a core part of their work. There are simply too many competing demands. For example, Sweitzer (2008) and Colbeck (2008) have used professional identity theory (Stryker 1968) to understand how future faculty balance their teaching interests with an environment that strongly emphasizes research. According to Stryker (1968), individuals organize their identities in a hierarchy that affects the likelihood that one identity will be more salient than others. Salience is determined by commitment to each identity. Students will develop a commitment to a specific identity (e.g., teacher, researcher, engaged scholar) based in large part on the work they do in graduate school, the network they develop, their chosen commitments, and the degree to which the environment around them confirms or rejects these commitments (Colbeck 2008).

I have written elsewhere about the many exciting movements of community engagement within graduate education (O'Meara 2008c, 2007a; O'Meara and Jaeger 2007). Of particular note are efforts initiated and led by graduate students within disciplines and the critical work of disciplinary associations and major conferences (such as the International Association for Research on Service-Learning and Community Engagement, the Imagining America graduate networks, and the Outreach Scholarship Conferences) to create concrete and formative experiences for graduate students in community engagement (O'Meara 2007a).

It is impossible, however, to ignore that most faculty are educated in research and doctoral-granting universities that remain more focused on research as traditionally defined than engaged teaching and engaged scholarship. The bottom line of research universities is that they continually strive for prestige in *U.S. News and World Report* rankings, for external grant funding, and for faculty to be ranked in the top group of researchers (as more narrowly defined) by their disciplines (O'Meara 2007a). As strategic planning and goal setting trickles down to actual graduate program and department planning, there is pressure for faculty and doctoral students to focus less on teaching and development of community partnerships and more on quantifiable indicators of success. For research university faculty this means numbers of articles and books written for top-tier journals and presses: for doctoral students, it means placement after graduating in top postdoctoral and junior faculty positions. As such, the central work of doctoral students—the dissertation—is focused on individual, as opposed to collaborative, work that is more likely to be read by other academics—that is, more private than public in its focus. While many natural sciences engage graduate students in collaborative lab work for dissertations, there is still hierarchy in terms of where names appear on papers. As in other fields, the process often does not connect faculty with public purposes.

The dissertation process itself seems to be at odds with the very values of public, engaged scholarship as collaborative, jointly owned, and interested from its start in impact (O'Meara 2008c). Engaged scholarship engages community partners and publics on what research will be done, involving partners when possible in projects and getting results into the hands of those who can use them immediately and with high priority. The current process of dissertation writing, however, does not have this set of priorities. Rather, most dissertation writing is done alone with the supervision of a dissertation chair, with the purpose of adding to academic knowledge, and most dissertation findings remain with academic audiences.

In sum, while many graduate students are creating new service-learning classes and beginning engaged scholarship as doctoral students, engaged scholarship has not systematically spread throughout graduate education and across disciplines. This is a second-order problem and, if addressed, would move higher education toward more and higher quality public work.

The foundation of faculty work as private in nature. Moving from graduate socialization into the structures and cultures of higher education institutions, one finds another pervading barrier to faculty engagement: though differing by institutional type, the pedestal or foundation upon which faculty do much of their work is considered by most to be innately private (O'Meara qtd. in Barker and Brown 2009). While many have written about the prized and valued autonomy of faculty members in pursuing their work, there are structural disadvantages to the way in which engagement fits into many faculty appointments and careers.

For the sake of illustration, imagine an umbrella—the handle and long stick at the center, with spokes branching out and supporting the top material. The central stick and spokes in this metaphor represent the foundation of a faculty career, such as one's appointment in a discipline or unit of a college or university. This appointment is made with an understanding of accountability to an essentially private interest—the effective running of that department or unit, and, in a broader way, the college (O'Meara qtd. in Barker and Brown 2009). The more research-oriented the unit, the more it will call upon disciplinary peers outside the institution to make sure that person's work is accountable to the unit's interest—that that person is cutting-edge in their research in the field. The more teaching-oriented, the more that unit will hold the faculty member accountable to teaching evaluations from "private, paying students" and advising and service work to the unit. In any case, though, the unit holds the faculty member accountable to its own interests through reappointment to contracts, tenure, and promotion. It then becomes in that faculty member's self-interest to be reappointed and promoted by serving the interests of that unit. This encourages the spokes that emanate from the central stick—that is, the teaching, research, and service—to be more private activities, in that they are accountable only to the interests of their units (O'Meara qtd. in Barker and Brown 2009).

Thus, even when faculty engage in excellent public work, it is in many ways also private work. That is, the faculty members decided to do this work and may have public partners in it, but they are not accountable for it at the core of their appointment. Rather, it is considered something "nice" that they do as social entrepreneurs (of sorts) on top of or in addition to their appointments (O'Meara qtd. in Barker and Brown 2009). In such instances, public work is not considered central to their appointments.

As a result of this structure, the public comes to think of 90 percent of what faculty do as private work (O'Meara qtd. in Barker and Brown 2009): "Faculty educate someone else's children, or mine only, because I am paying them as I would a financial adviser for a service." Research is considered something faculty do to get tenure, not an activity that relates to real problems with the economy, war, or global warming.

Clearly, an argument can be made that as nonprofit institutions, the interests of departments, especially those in public state institutions, are not just private; they are also the interests of the state and region. Do citizens of the state not want a leading research university or top-ranked program? Teaching influences the preparedness of the workforce; however, for most citizens who live near a college or university, it does not seem that faculty are available to serve public purposes. Many doors and windows to faculty work are closed. Most colleges and universities do not have vehicles to disseminate research to local community partners, either in person or electronically. Very few academic programs invite alumni or local citizens onto advisory boards to comment on curriculum and relevancy to current issues. Rarely do faculty try to instill civic agency by opening their classrooms so community partners can see what is happening. Public discourse sheds much more light on faculty unions attempting to accrue better benefits and salaries, and on problems with tenure, than on what faculty are learning about and contributing to public issues.

In sum, the governance of most institutions does not hold faculty accountable to public interests or open up their work for viewing or participation from local partners.

I say this realizing that much of the creativity and inspiration found in excellent faculty engagement work stems from the autonomy the faculty member had to envision and construct the project without interference or oversight from university administrators or even peers (O'Meara qtd. in Barker and Brown 2009). Indeed, the autonomy many faculty have in their public work does provide excellent fertilizer for social entrepreneurship. But the fact that even public faculty work can have an essentially private foundation (i.e., the faculty member could just decide not to do this work anymore and there would be no public accounting for that), does seem to be at the crux of the issue of why more faculty are not involved in public work. It is a bigger and more complex issue than the often-mentioned complaint that "it doesn't count" for promotion, tenure, contract renewal, or merit pay. The issue is more about how the structures and cultures in our institutions have shaped us to view the purposes of our work and what makes it meaningful.

Different markets and assumptions for faculty civic engagement versus more traditional scholarship. Shaffer (2008) observes that the "metaphor of the market" has become the organizing concept of our time. This is to say that most arguments for higher education today, as well as for other major aspects of our society (e.g., health care and public safety), pose higher education as a solution to a private interest—the capacity to get a good job and join or stay in the middle or upper classes.

Positioning higher education as a private good simultaneously poses faculty work as private, as noted above. Likewise, as organizational theorists have pointed out, each of the institutions in which faculty work have their own political and cultural economy. This is particularly relevant when considering how institutional type influences faculty roles and rewards. For example, while Boyer's framework was used by many at research and doctoral universities to advocate for greater attention to teaching, in many baccalaureate institutions it became a way to encourage faculty participation in any form of scholarship, though most often teaching scholarship (O'Meara 2005). As such, while the chief barriers to greater civic engagement in research universities might be inhospitable reward systems and pressures for publications and grants, in more teaching-oriented institutions high teaching and advising loads may be the major barrier (O'Meara 2005). Yet there are also issues that cut across institutional type to influence academic cultures and their acceptance of faculty public work. Beyond the purely technical issues of needing bridge personnel to help cultivate relationships with community, supports like vans to transport students, and curricular structures and centers to house these experiences, there is a marketplace in every institution of higher education. Within this marketplace, some activities are more valued commodities than others, depending on institutional goals, institutional leadership, faculty goals and leadership, workload, and past practice. When faculty bring certain aspects of their work to this marketplace (such as external grant funding, a book published with a competitive press, or a research award) they are rewarded with both tangible and intangible currency. This currency may take the tangible form of tenure or promotion and merit pay or the intangible form of greater respect by colleagues or persuasive power in shared governance. Similar rewards might accrue to the winner of a college-wide teaching award in a very teaching-focused college.

The problem that faculty who are involved in public work face is that it is harder to gain distinction for this work within institutional marketplaces, for at least three reasons. First, very few institutions have marketplaces where engagement is considered a prized commodity. Even in institutions that have made civic engagement a commitment, civic engagement in and of itself is not considered as valuable, even in its best forms, as other potential currencies. Second, it is harder to distinguish oneself or demonstrate excellence within the institutional marketplace for engagement. In part, this is because the values and priorities of engagement are in conflict with the values and priorities of more traditional research, and thus excellence looks different. Because of the diversity of civic engagement projects across institutions, there are few norms that can be easily established for quality or quantity of work for faculty to clearly rise above.

Third, establishing legitimacy and excellence involves witness of the work within a specific context or community. In the case of the institutional marketplace, faculty have their research witnessed through their disciplinary associations, university presses, and top-tier journals, and they bring their assessments back to the institutional community. Those judging the research are considered "of the university," and their recognition brings prestige back to the institution. While there are national teaching awards and programs, most teaching excellence is witnessed "in-house" by students, colleagues, and alumni, and therefore it is legitimized there. It is given currency for its immediate value to institutional goals and recognized through internal measures of teaching evaluations and rewards. Institutional marketplaces are, of course, influenced by the national higher education system, which uses the acquisition of prestige—by increasing selectivity or research productivity and improving *U.S. News and World Report* rankings—to try to acquire greater resources to support their activities (O'Meara 2007b).

Engagement unfortunately faces a triple threat in the academic and institutional marketplace. While the other two major forms of faculty work—traditional research and teaching—are providing the marketplace tangible outcomes that add to either the prestige or direct betterment of its members (students, faculty, institutional goals, and reputation), civic work often has as its goal the improvement of conditions for citizens not associated with the university. Likewise, at least some of the "witnesses" that count most to civically engaged scholars are community partners who are often not formally organized in ways that allow them to evaluate excellence or in any way distinguish the work for the institutional marketplace. Finally, the greatest impact of the work is often not a contribution to theory or even to student learning (though both may be present), but the amelioration of a social, political, educational, or economic problem. While an institution may praise faculty in their efforts to end global warming or impact local economic development, we can also see why the work itself may not add much to faculty currency in the institutional marketplace.

Table 8.1 extends this concept of the barrier of markets to something deeper—the assumptions that guide the markets. A foundation for this idea of assumptions was Gene Rice's (1996) pivotal work "Making a Place for the New American Scholar," which described how, after World War II, an "assumptive world of the academic professional" that prioritizes certain types of faculty work over others emerged. While Rice recognized these priorities will vary by institutional type and across disciplines, he noted that they tend to establish a set of expectations at the top of the prestige hierarchy, which has reverberations throughout the system. This assumptive world of the academic professional guides many reward systems in American higher education and prioritizes empirical research and dissemination of peer-reviewed research to academic audiences. In my own research (O'Meara 2002) on the evaluation of community engagement as a form of scholarship for promotion and tenure, I also found such traditional values, beliefs, and assumptions of the academic professional working against the positive valuation to engagement. A few notes about Table 8.1:

- For effect, I have intentionally contrasted two sets of assumptions (one based on the academic professional Rice [1996] wrote about— the more traditional research university model vs. the engaged American Scholar) as if they were polar opposites. I do not personally know any faculty member engaged in public work who doesn't maintain a foothold in at least some aspects of both sets of assumptions simultaneously.
- Likewise, a faculty member may have a very traditional set of assumptions about teaching and a seemingly opposite set regarding public work. While we know that many faculty members integrate their personal and professional work and different work roles, we also know that many compartmentalize for different reasons.
- I have added the term "American" to the phrase "engaged scholar" in the same tradition of Rice's "new American scholar." Rice points out that in the vision of the engaged American scholar, "theoretical reflection and practice are mutually reinforcing, each enriching the other" (1996, p. 16). While pragmatism and utility are by no means solely American virtues, it does seem to me that the visions we have of democracy and civic work of faculty are influenced by our national context. As in Rice's earlier work, the point is not to be nationalistic but to acknowledge that the call for greater faculty civic work in the United States is influenced by contexts that are local and woven into traditions in American higher education. In the best possible sense, the engaged American scholar employs the

TABLE 8.1   THE ASSUMPTIVE WORLD OF THE ACADEMIC PROFESSIONAL AND ENGAGED AMERICAN SCHOLAR

Assumptions about Goals and Purposes of One's Work as a Professional

Post-WWII Academic Professional	*Engaged American Scholar*
Research is the central professional endeavor and the focus of academic life (Rice 1996).	Impact, whether found in classrooms, with community partners, in policy making, or in dissemination of research, is a central professional endeavor and focus of academic life.
Knowledge is pursued for its own sake (Rice 1996).	Knowledge is pursued to improve the world.
The distinctive task of the academic professional is the pursuit of cognitive truth (Rice 1996).	The distinctive task of the academic professional is the pursuit of learning that has consequence.

Assumptions about Approaches to the Pursuit of Knowledge

Post-WWII Academic Professional	*Engaged American Scholar*
The pursuit of knowledge is best organized according to disciplines and departments (Rice 1996).	The pursuit of knowledge is best organized according to problems, understood in local context.
Scholarship is completed apart from practitioners, and often for them (O'Meara 2002).	Scholarship is completed with those who will use it, in collaborative knowledge construction. (O'Meara 2002).
The methods used to create knowledge should be as scientific, reliable, objective, and devoid of error and bias as possible.	The process used to make knowledge should be as transformative, democratic, and inclusive as possible; engaged scholars are attentive to their own locations in higher education institutions, and the social capital and resources therein, and have a heightened sensitivity to cultural literacy and relevancy (O'Meara 2008a).

Assumptions about How to Judge the Quality of One's Work and about Rigor

Post-WWII Academic Professional	*Engaged American Scholar*
Reputations are established through national and international professional associations (Rice 1996).	Reputations are established through relationships and through creation of knowledge with consequence.
Quality in the profession is maintained by peer review and professional autonomy (Rice 1996).	Quality is maintained by peer review by academic and nonacademic peers and is also found in impact.
Writing is scholarly because of where it is, not what it is (O'Meara 2002).	Scholarship is a process as well as a product, one best informed by expertise as well as local context. It has many potential products and outcomes that are disseminated and shared widely.
Scholarship is empirical research disseminated to the academic community (O'Meara 2002).	

TABLE 8.1   THE ASSUMPTIVE WORLD OF THE ACADEMIC PROFESSIONAL AND ENGAGED AMERICAN SCHOLAR (*Continued*)

Assumptions about the Products of Scholarship

Post-WWII Academic Professional	Engaged American Scholar
Scholarship should be published in places that reach other academic professionals in a field or discipline (peer-reviewed journal articles and academic presses).	Engaged scholars value disseminating the products of their work in the places where it will have the most impact (O'Meara 2008a).

Assumptions about Partners in Knowledge Production

Post-WWII Academic Professional	Engaged American Scholar
Partners need to be informed; they lack expertise and knowledge.	Partners have critical knowledge and can solve the problems of their own community.
	Engaged scholars give credit to community partners for collaborative work (O'Meara 2008a).

Assumptions about Reward Systems

Post-WWII Academic Professional	Engaged American Scholar
Professional rewards and mobility accrue to those who persistently accentuate their specialization (Rice 1996).	Professional rewards, but more importantly meaning, purpose, and a sense of consequence accrue to individuals that emphasize relationships and capacity building in solving problems.

Assumptions about the Most Important Contributions of Faculty to Society

Post-WWII Academic Professional	Engaged American Scholar
Scholars' most important contribution to society is the application of expertise to the discovery and dissemination of knowledge.	Scholars' most important contribution to society is their ability to bring values and skills of academic professionals as well as expertise to partnerships with students, community partners, and knowledge circles to solve problems.

This table takes statements from Rice (1996) and O'Meara (2002, 2008a) and was furthermore influenced by ideas in Strand et al. (2003) and Saltmarsh, Hartley, and Clayton (2009).

best of the German research university model and the best of the extension land-grant and community college models of higher education, wherein theory and practice are both relevant and in conversation with each other as opposed to polar opposites.

In the assumptive world of the academic professional described by Rice and that we all know as more standard practice, we see an epistemology that gives greater currency to work that is done alone, is more theoretical and separated from practice, and whose end result is a brick on a disciplinary wall of knowledge, as opposed to a change in practice. By contrast, in the example of the American engaged scholar we see an epistemology that gives greater currency to work that matters to society, is more comfortable merging theory and practice, and whose end result is actionable knowledge. Another way to look at assumptions in regard to markets is that while traditional scholarship assumes an audience in the academic community and therefore does not have to develop one, engaged scholarship actively works to develop, as Peters and colleagues (2005) have observed, "publics" for its work.

Higher education marketplaces clearly pose a barrier for engaged scholars because the higher education system as a whole does not typically share the same assumptions and values about their work and scholarship. Faculty take many different approaches to this problem. Bloomgarden's (2008) research in a set of prestigious liberal arts colleges illustrates that some faculty compartmentalize their civic work into a service category and do not try to have it evaluated as scholarship, essentially accommodating the assumptions of traditional work and bringing that to bear when looking for institutional rewards. Some faculty make the best case possible, using many of the models mentioned earlier by think tanks and disciplinary associations. Still others use hybrid approaches, not engaging in the work until after tenure, integrating it into their teaching but not their scholarship, and making the case for the work in some arenas but not others. Many of these faculty are successful regardless of their chosen path, as they often bring with them other "currency" (e.g., being highly rated teachers, external grants) to reward systems that interact for positive affect.

In summary, doctoral education, the structural foundation of faculty appointments as private, and the different sets of market assumptions of civic engagement and more traditional faculty work act as significant barriers to the movement to expand and improve faculty civic engagement efforts. Though a lengthy discussion is not possible here, I do also think we could do a better job providing role models and descriptions of civic work with real consequence in different disciplines. This would provide faculty with more visible examples of cases of faculty civic work that is political and democratic *and* rigorous and engaged. I also believe we need to emphasize the skills and competencies faculty employ as academic professionals that are not based on expertise (see O'Meara 2008b).

One piece of positive news related to these barriers is that most studies with exemplary engaged faculty (Boyte 2004; O'Meara 2008c) suggest that faculty are motivated to be involved in civic engagement for intrinsic reasons. This provides a buffer to the lack of graduate socialization (as it can be adopted later in career), to the structure of the academic career as private, and against market interests (as intrinsic motivation can occur outside of and in direct conflict with reward systems). Engagement seems to pull faculty toward students, their colleagues, and the public, whetting their appetites for engaged work. In addition to its intrinsic good in terms of providing a sense that the work matters, engagement offers an alternative to "lone ranger," isolated departments and ways of being (Boyte 2004; O'Meara 2008c; Peters et al. 2005; Rice 1996).

LOOKING AHEAD

Looking ahead, those interested in supporting and extending the civic work of faculty need to find ways to make the distinctly political and democratic components of the work and its impact more visible. Likewise, we need to look at how the sea change in faculty appointments might be harming faculty capacity to become involved in civic work. For example, Schuster and Finkelstein (2006) have shown that the greatest number of new positions are now emphasizing teaching—and are less likely to have well-financed, structured opportunities for faculty growth—such as sabbaticals, professional development programs, and learning communities (O'Meara, Terosky, and Neumann 2009). The new frontier for faculty engagement with democratic purposes will surely mean both making campuses more democratic and fair for nontenure-track and tenure-track faculty and creating hospitable environments for these faculty to link their work with public purposes. This will be particularly difficult in appointments without any research focus. At the same time, Generation X and Y faculty are joining faculty positions looking for opportunities to have impacts in their communities and for balance and meaning in their work lives. Whether in tenure-track or nontenure-track appointments, these will be exceptionally well-educated and prepared scholars who are able to find just what they are looking for in civic work. Faculty development aimed at developing civic agency (O'Meara 2008b) and new reward systems that include this work for nontenure-track appointments will be key to these efforts.

REFERENCES

Austin, A. E. 2002. "Creating a Bridge to the Future: Preparing New Faculty to Face Changing Expectations in a Shifting Context." *Review of Higher Education* 26 (2): 119–144.

Austin, A. E., and M. McDaniels. 2006. "Using Doctoral Education to Prepare Faculty to Work within Boyer's Four Domains of Scholarship." In *Delving Further into Boyer's Perspectives on Scholarship*, ed. J. M. Braxton, 51–65. New Directions for Institutional Research 129 (Spring). San Francisco: Jossey-Bass.

Barker, W. M., and D. W. Brown, eds. 2009. *A Different Kind of Politics: Readings on Democracy and Higher Education.* Dayton, OH: Kettering Foundation.

Bloomgarden, A. 2008. "Prestige Culture and Community-Based Faculty Work." PhD diss., University of Massachusetts–Amherst.

Boyer, E. 1990. *Scholarship Reconsidered.* Princeton: Carnegie Foundation for the Advancement of Teaching.

Boyte, H. C. 2004. *Going Public: Academics and Public Life.* Dayton, OH: Kettering Foundation.

———. 2008. "Against the Current: Developing the Civic Agency of Students." *Change* 40 (3): 8–15.

Campus Compact. 2010. "2010 Annual Member Survey." Available at http://www.compact.org/about/statistics.

Colbeck, C. L. 2008. "Professional Identity Development Theory and Doctoral Education." In *Educating Integrated Professionals: Theory and Practice on*

Preparation for the Professoriate, New Directions for Teaching and Learning 113, ed. C. L. Colbeck, K. O'Meara, and A. Austin, 9–13. San Francisco: Wiley.

Colbeck, C. L., K. O'Meara, and A. Austin, eds. 2008. *Educating Integrated Professionals: Theory and Practice on Preparation for the Professoriate*. New Directions for Teaching and Learning 113. San Francisco: Wiley.

Cuban, L. 1988. "A Fundamental Puzzle of School Reform." *Phi Delta Kappan* 69 (5): 341–342.

Driscoll, A., and E. Lynton, eds. 1999. *Making Outreach Visible: A Workbook on Documenting Professional Service and Outreach*. Washington, DC: American Association for Higher Education.

Driscoll, A., and L. R. Sandmann. 2001. "From Maverick to Mainstream: The Scholarship of Engagement." *Journal of Higher Education Outreach and Engagement* 6 (2): 9–19.

Ellison, J., and T. Eatman. 2008. *Scholarship in Public: Knowledge Creation and Tenure Policy in the Engaged University: A Resource on Promotion and Tenure in the Arts, Humanities, and Design*. Imagining America. Available at http://www.community-wealth.org/_pdfs/articles-publications/universities/paper-ellison-eastman.pdf.

Elman, S. E., and S. M. Smock. 1985. *Professional Service and Faculty Rewards: Toward an Integrated Structure*. Washington, DC: National Association of State Universities and Land-Grant Colleges.

Gamson, Z. 1995. "Faculty and Service." *Change* 27, no. 1 (January/February): 4.

Giles, D. E. 2008. "Understanding an Emerging Field of Scholarship: Toward a Research Agenda for Engaged, Public Scholarship." *Journal of Higher Education Outreach and Engagement* 12 (2): 97–108.

Glassick, C. E., M. T. Huber, and G. I. Maeroff. 1997. *Scholarship Assessed: Evaluation of the Professoriate*. San Francisco: Jossey-Bass.

Golde, C. M. 2008. "Applying Lessons from Professional Education to the Preparation of the Professoriate. In *Educating Integrated Professionals: Theory and Practice on Preparation for the Professoriate*, New Directions for Teaching and Learning 113, ed. C. L. Colbeck, K. O'Meara, and A. Austin, 17–26. San Francisco: Wiley.

Hartley, M., and E. Hollander. 2005. "The Elusive Ideal: Civic Learning and Higher Education." In *Institutions of Democracy: The Public Schools*, ed. S. Fuhrman and M. Lazerson, 252–276. Oxford: Oxford University Press.

Holland, B. A., and E. Hollander. 2006. "Campus Compact's 20/20 Vision: Celebrating Our First Twenty Years and Planning for the Next Two Decades." Campus Compact. Available at http://www.compact.org/wp-content/uploads/2009/04/framing_essay.pdf.

Hollander, E., and M. Hartley. 2000. "Civic Renewal in Higher Education: The State of the Movement and the Need for a Natural Network." In *Higher Education and Civic Responsibility*, ed. T. Ehrlich, 345–366. Phoenix: Oryx Press.

Jordan, C., ed. 2007. "Community-Engaged Scholarship Toolkit." Community-Campus Partnerships for Health. Available at http://depts.washington.edu/ccph/toolkit.html.

Lynton, E. 1995. *Making the Case for Professional Service*. Washington, DC: American Association for Higher Education.

Morton, K. 1995. "The Irony of Service: Charity, Project and Social Change in Service-Learning." *Michigan Journal of Community Service Learning* 2: 19–32.

O'Meara, K. 1995. "Community Service Professionals: An Emerging Profession." Masters thesis, Ohio State University.

———. 2002. "Uncovering the Values in Faculty Evaluation of Service as Scholarship." *Review of Higher Education* 26 (1): 57–80.

———. 2005. "Effects of Encouraging Multiple Forms of Scholarship Nationwide and Across Institutional Types." In *Faculty Priorities Reconsidered: Encouraging Multiple Forms of Scholarship*, ed. K. A. O'Meara and R. E. Rice, 255–289. San Francisco: Jossey-Bass.

———. 2007a. "Graduate Education and Civic Engagement." NERCHE Working Brief 20, New England Resource Center for Higher Education, Boston.

———. 2007b. "Striving for What? Exploring the Pursuit of Prestige." In *Higher Education: Handbook of Theory and Research* 22, ed. J. C. Smart, 121–179. Dordrecht, The Netherlands: Springer.

———. 2008a. "Graduate Education and Community Engagement." In *Educating Integrated Professionals: Theory and Practice on Preparation for the Professoriate*, New Directions for Teaching and Learning 113, ed. C. L. Colbeck, K. O'Meara, and A. Austin, 27–42. San Francisco: Wiley.

———. 2008b. "Making the Case for the New American Scholar." Campus Compact Toolkit on Engaged Scholarship. Available at http://www.compact.org/wp-content/uploads/2009/04/omeara-final.pdf.

———. 2008c. "Motivation for Public Scholarship and Engagement: Listening to Exemplars." *Journal of Higher Education Outreach and Engagement* 12 (1): 7–29.

———. 2008d. "Taking Public Work Seriously: Enhancing Civic Agency Through Faculty Development." Paper presented at the Annual Conference of the Association for the Study of Higher Education, Jacksonville, FL.

O'Meara, K., and A. Jaeger. 2007. "Preparing Future Faculty for Community Engagement: History, Barriers, Facilitators, Models, and Recommendations. *Journal of Higher Education Outreach and Engagement* 11 (4): 3–26.

O'Meara, K. A., and R. E. Rice, eds. 2005. *Faculty Priorities Reconsidered: Encouraging Multiple Forms of Scholarship*. San Francisco: Jossey-Bass.

O'Meara, K., A. Terosky, and A. Neumann. 2009. *Faculty Careers and Work-Lives: A Professional Growth Perspective*. ASHE Higher Education Report vol. 34, no. 3. San Francisco: Jossey-Bass.

Peters, S. J., N. R. Jordan, M. Adamek, and T. Alter, eds. 2005. *Engaging Campus and Community: The Practice of Public Scholarship in the State and Land-Grant University System*. Dayton, OH: Kettering Foundation.

Rice, R. E. 1996. "Making a Place for the New American Scholar." Working Paper Series 1. American Association for Higher Education Forum on Faculty Roles and Rewards.

Saltmarsh, J., M. Hartley, and P. H. Clayton. 2009. "Democratic Engagement White Paper." Boston: New England Resource Center for Higher Education.

Sandmann, L., J. Saltmarsh, and K. O'Meara. 2008. "Creating Academic Homes: An Integrated Model for Advancing the Scholarship of Engagement." *Journal of Higher Education Outreach and Engagement* 12 (1): 47–63.

Sandmann, L. R. 2004. "Scholarship of Engagement: An Oxymoron?" In *Adult Education for Democracy, Social Justice, and a Culture of Peace: Proceedings for the Joint International Conference of the Adult Education Research Conference and Canadian Association for the Study of Adult Education*, ed. D. Clover, 580–582. Victoria: University of Victoria.

———. 2006. "Scholarship as Architecture: Framing and Enhancing Community Engagement." *Journal of Physical Therapy Education* 20 (3): 80–84.

———. 2008. "Conceptualization of the Scholarship of Engagement in Higher Education: A Strategic Review, 1996–2006." *Journal of Higher Education Outreach and Engagement* 12 (1): 91–106.

Sandmann, L. R., and D. J. Weerts. 2007. "Reshaping Institutional Boundaries to Accommodate an Engagement Agenda." Presentation at Annual Meeting of the American Education Research Association, Chicago.

Schuster, J. H., and M. J. Finkelstein. 2006. *The American Faculty: The Restructuring of Academic Work and Careers.* Baltimore: Johns Hopkins University Press.

Shaffer, M. 2008. *Public Culture: Diversity, Democracy, and Community in the United States.* Philadelphia: University of Pennsylvania Press.

Stanton, T., D. E. Giles, and N. Cruz. 1999. *Service-Learning: A Movement's Pioneers Reflect on Its Origins, Practice, and Future.* San Francisco: Jossey-Bass.

Strand, K., S. Marullo, N. Cutforth, R. Stoecker, and P. Donohue. 2003. *Community-Based Research and Higher Education: Principles and Practices.* San Francisco: Jossey-Bass.

Stryker, S. 1968. "Identity Salience and Role Performance." *Journal of Marriage and the Family* 4: 558–564.

Sweitzer, V. L. 2008. "Networking to Develop a Professional Identity: A Look at the First Semester Experience of Doctoral Students in Business." In *Educating Integrated Professionals: Theory and Practice on Preparation for the Professoriate,* New Directions for Teaching and Learning 113, ed. C. L. Colbeck, K. O'Meara, and A. Austin, 43–56. San Francisco: Wiley.

Ward, K. 2003. *Faculty Service Roles and the Scholarship of Engagement.* ASHE-ERIC Higher Education Report, vol. 29, no. 5. San Francisco: Jossey-Bass.

Weidman, J. C., D. J. Twale, and E. L. Stein. 2001. *Socialization of Graduate and Professional Students in Higher Education—A Perilous Passage?* ASHE-ERIC Higher Education Report, vol. 28, no. 3. Washington, DC: George Washington University.

CHAPTER 9

Putting Students at the Center
of Civic Engagement

RICHARD M. BATTISTONI AND NICHOLAS V. LONGO

There has been much progress toward institutionalizing civic engagement in higher education, as the Democracy and Higher Education colloquium at the Kettering Foundation and chapters in this book illustrate. Over the past decade, a laser-like focus on faculty and staff development has produced notable gains in the capacity of higher education to accomplish civic engagement outcomes, for students as well as the campus as a whole. Yet we agree with the central premise set forth by the editors of this volume, who are concerned that the civic engagement movement has "struggled to find conceptual and operational coherence." As the editors note in the first chapter of this volume, a narrow approach to civic engagement "that accommodate[s] the status quo" does not challenge the "dominant institutional culture." Thus, for higher education to realize its full civic potential, it must focus on transformational, rather than strategic, advances.

In this chapter, we argue that in order for civic engagement to successfully address second-order changes, practitioners must reframe the way they think about and collaborate with their students in community-based work. This involves not only including students in conversations about the engaged academy but also changing the way civic engagement is conceptualized, taught, and practiced on campus. In short, democratic-minded practitioners who care deeply about the civic engagement agenda in higher education must now focus on putting students at the center of their efforts.

INSTITUTIONALIZING ENGAGEMENT

Ironically, the most recent surge in the movement for increased civic engagement in higher education began with students in a central role. In writing about the dramatic founding of the Campus Outreach Opportunities League (COOL) in 1984 and other student-led efforts on campuses during that time, Goodwin Liu (1996) notes tellingly that "*students* catalyzed the contemporary service movement in higher education" (p. 6; original emphasis). Yet in the late 1980s, Liu argues, faculty and administrators began taking over the leadership of the movement in the interests of consistency and sustainability. This focus on institutionalization has only deepened in the more than ten years since his writing.

The success of community engagement's institutionalization is exemplified in the growth of Campus Compact, an organization dedicated to promoting the civic purposes of higher education. In a little over twenty years, Campus Compact's membership has grown to nearly 1,200 campuses served by thirty-four state offices. Moreover, there are centers of service-learning and civic engagement at perhaps as many as three quarters of colleges and universities, along with majors, minors, and a new career track for directors of community engagement in higher education, and a rubric has been created that allows campuses to judge their own progress toward the institutionalization of service-learning (Furco 2002). There is also significant financial support for community engagement, including federal funding through the Corporation for National and Community Service; a growing number of refereed journals dedicated to service-learning and community engagement; the impressive twenty volumes in the American Association for Higher Education's series on service-learning in the academic disciplines, edited by Edward Zlotkowski (1997–2004); an international research association that recently held its eighth annual conference; and countless conferences, books, and new initiatives by national and international associations in higher education.

In terms of the development of *civic* engagement efforts, more specifically, institutionalization has been equally impressive. By the late 1990s, concern about citizen disengagement from public life (Galston 2001; Keeter et al. 2002; Putnam 2000) and an ever-deepening feeling that our educational institutions were leaving students unprepared for a life of engaged, democratic citizenship had reached their apex. The effort to change higher education, to make it more civically responsible, began with the development of conceptual understandings of civic engagement in higher education, ones that could then be translated across the curriculum (Battistoni 2002), across academic departments and programs (Kecskes 2006), and into indicators of institutional engagement (Hollander, Saltmarsh, and Zlotkowski 2002). Out of this initial conceptual framework came the work of scholars, most notably John Saltmarsh (2005), who defined a set of civic learning outcomes for students based on three elements: civic knowledge, civic skills, and civic values.

With a concrete articulation of specific sets of knowledge, skills, and values, campuses have been able to develop courses and curriculums, while "engaged department" initiatives have moved entire disciplines and interdisciplinary programs on campuses to restructure their courses and faculty roles with student civic engagement outcomes in mind. This has created significant first-order changes in many colleges and universities.

But while institutionalization at the curricular or departmental level is essential to sustaining civic engagement, these kinds of changes have not had a particularly positive effect on student leadership and voice. What Liu (1996) argues about service-learning more generally can be applied to civic engagement: "Institutionalization gradually shifts control and resources away from students to people who have formal power and bureaucratic authority on campus" (p. 18, note 19). While students continued to lead on the margins, mainstream academia denied them a major role in defining civic engagement or determining how it would be implemented on campuses. With a few exceptions to be discussed later—the Wingspread Conference that produced "The New Student Politics," and Campus Compact's Raise Your Voice and Students as Colleagues initiatives—students have been largely left out of leadership roles in institutional civic engagement. Liu questions "whether or not institutionalization has dampened student leadership on individual campuses" (p. 18), to which one respondent replied rather bluntly, "This is surely not progress" (Bastress and Beilenson 1996).

A look at the literature on the engaged academy reveals a significant tilt toward faculty development and a lack of thinking about how to strategically include students in the implementation and development of civic engagement initiatives. Consider, for instance, the Institutional Assessment Model, developed by Sherril Gelmon and her colleagues (2005), which provides a useful and detailed twelve-page rubric of characteristics of what the engaged academy looks like. The model's rubrics are largely focused on the role of faculty and chief academic officers (with brief mention of community partners). Students are included primarily as recipients of community-engaged initiatives; their potential role as agents in the engaged campus is largely omitted (Fretz and Longo 2010). The same can be said of the self-assessment rubric developed by Andrew Furco for institutionalizing service-learning in higher education. One of the rubric's five dimensions does include students, but it mainly measures student support for and awareness of opportunities for involvement in service-learning courses and activities. Even the "student leadership" portion of the rubric is thin on voice and decision making, merely measuring students' roles in "advancing service-learning" on the campus (Furco 2002). This is also true of the self-assessment rubric developed by Kevin Kecskes for Community-Engaged Departments (which builds on Furco's), in which the student dimension is titled "Student Support for Community Engagement," and only one component examines student leadership (Kecskes 2006). The only real exceptions to this rule of neglecting students as agents in the civic engagement of higher education can be found in the 2008 framework for the Carnegie Foundation's Elective Classification for Community Engagement, which requires campuses to show how students have a leadership role in community engagement, and in the Campus Compact Indicators of Engagement initiative, which values "student voice" as a distinctive component (albeit the final one) of measuring campus engagement, and whereby campuses are judged on how much students participate in campus decision making and have opportunities "to discuss and act upon issues important to them" (Hollander, Saltmarsh, and Zlotkowski 2002).

Reframing Civic Engagement: Voice, Practice, and Motivation

The language of campus institutionalization, as exemplified in the rubrics above, casts students primarily as passive agents of community engagement. Measuring students' awareness of community engagement is most often a matter of "informing" students about community engagement opportunities as faculty or staff "lead" community-engaged initiatives. Institutionalization efforts rarely judge themselves on the level of student participation in the development and implementation of community-engaged projects and courses. They stop short of asking institutions to imagine their students as "colleagues" or "coproducers" in the process of civic engagement.

So while civic engagement efforts have enabled faculty, staff, and administrators to create new programs and courses across the curriculum, and then to assess a wide range of institutional indicators of civic engagement, they have not done much to transform traditional notions of epistemology or pedagogy. Ninety years after John Dewey referred to a "static, cold-storage ideal of knowledge" (1916/1993, p. 158), fifty years after Margaret Mead spoke about a "vertical cultural transmission model" (1958, p. 24), and almost forty years after Paulo Freire criticized the "banking model of education" (1970, p. 72), hierarchical methods of conceiving and conveying civic knowledge still dominate. We have created centers for community and/or civic engagement on most of our campuses, but we have not *put students at the center* and given them opportunities to cocreate in real democratic spaces within the academy.

This issue goes at the very core of the engagement agenda in higher education: we can choose to reinforce the dominant way of knowing in higher education, which tends to ignore the capacities and experiences of the very people we most want to engage—in this case, our students (and community partners)—or we can take student empowerment seriously as part of the larger civic mission of higher education. When this happens, the goal of engagement becomes second-order transformation.

Arguably, the mainstream civic engagement framework—using the tripartite definition of "civic learning" as knowledge, skills, and, to a lesser extent, values—is itself part of the problem. The idea of *imparting* knowledge, *developing* skills, and *instilling* values is completely consistent with traditional pedagogies that treat students as passive receptacles rather than civic agents. Missing from the theory and definition of civic learning articulated in the literature and in campus practices are elements necessary for a fuller understanding of democratic civic engagement and for transforming institutional structures with student leadership in mind. To create space for student leadership in civic engagement efforts on campus, practitioners need to begin by adding what we argue are three key missing elements to the conceptual framework: voice, practice, and motivation.

Student Voice

Researchers have long documented the positive impact of student voice— understood primarily as a student's choice of the kind of community service placement he or she takes on in connection with a course—on service-learning outcomes (Billig, Root, and Jesse 2005). But in thinking about voice as an essential component of democratic civic engagement, we consider two elements as central: (1) allowing students to define civic and political engagement for themselves, and (2) allowing students to contribute to campus decision making on the issues that impact and matter to them.

In a 1993 report for the Kettering Foundation titled "College Students Talk Politics," David Mathews makes a statement about the complicit role of higher education institutions in actually depressing student political engagement: "Sometimes [students] learn what politics is in class. Most of the time they learn politics from the way it is practiced on campus" (qtd. in Creighton and Harwood 1993, p. xi.). Mathews goes on to say that

> higher education runs the danger of perpetuating a narrow and constricting understanding of the political, of modeling, rather than challenging, the conventional wisdom. And it appears to leave students without concepts or language to explore what is political about their lives. (qtd. in Creighton and Harwood 1993, p. xii)

The corrective for this tendency among higher education institutions to constrict student understandings of civic engagement is to allow students to define politics and civic engagement for themselves. This was a major conclusion we reached in an earlier essay examining the lessons learned from the Raise Your Voice initiative and a course that was part of the Carnegie Foundation's Political Engagement Project (Longo, Drury, and Battistoni 2006). In our interviews with students, the notion of "voice" emerged quite strongly as a key dimension of a "new politics" on campus.

The Wingspread Conference that resulted in "The New Student Politics" is a good example of what happens when students are allowed to give full voice to their ideas about civic engagement. In 2001, thirty-three college students met at the Wingspread Conference Center in Racine, Wisconsin, to discuss their "civic experiences" in higher education. This conversation led to the student-written report "The New Student Politics" (Long 2002), which forcefully argues that student work in communities is not an alternative to politics but rather an "alternative politics." This new politics enables students to blend the personal and the political and address public issues through community-based work. While many of the students at Wingspread expressed frustration with politics-as-usual, they were not apathetic or disengaged. To the contrary, they pointed out that what many perceive as disengagement may actually be a conscious choice; they argued that, in fact, many students are deeply involved in nontraditional forms of engagement. These students saw their "service politics" as the bridge between community service and conventional politics, combining public power with community and relationships.

This new student politics attempts to connect individual acts of service to a broader framework of systemic social change. The students at Wingspread further noted that they see democracy as richly participatory, that negotiating differences is a key element of politics, that their service in communities was done in the context of systemic change, and that higher education needs to do more to promote civic education.

Empowering student voice also means that administrators and faculty need to be ready to be challenged. There is another dimension to Mathews' notion that students learn about politics from the way it is practiced on campus: when students become engaged, the campus is often where they turn their attention. For instance, in addressing civil rights, apartheid in South Africa, sweatshop labor practices, and the working poor, students have organized politically in ways that might have threatened some administrators.

Former Duke president Nannerl Keohane experienced this when she was confronted by one of the nation's first antisweatshop campaigns. She speculates that the protests at Duke—asking that university apparel manufacturers provide a living wage and independent monitoring of their workers—grew out of the students' sensible and relational approach, along with their interest in seeing the impact of their efforts, which often gets credited for the rise in community service. "This generation is one where there's a strong sense of personal responsibility to make a difference for immediate, real people you can see and touch," Keohane said, adding, "My own hunch, as a political theorist, is this sweatshop movement is a direct outgrowth of this practical mindset" (qtd. in Greenhouse 1999, A14).

In the 2007 follow-up study to the Kettering Foundation's original focus groups, students reported that they sought a civic landscape that allowed them authentic opportunities to voice their ideas and deliberate about what should be done to improve campuses, communities, and the larger world (Kiesa et al. 2007). One student contended that because of manipulation and polarization in most public debate, "people don't feel like their voice matters because rarely do we see discussions or something where you feel non-threatened and able to voice your opinions" (qtd. in Kiesa et al. 2007, p. 27). Our conclusion is that student voice, which includes an understanding of what Langston Hughes (1968) once called "listening eloquently," needs to be included in any definition of civic engagement in higher education.

Practice: Opportunities for Direct Participation

Theorists going from Aristotle to John Stuart Mill and John Dewey have argued that education for engagement in a democracy requires practice, and opportunities for direct participation are essential to civic engagement. More recently, Malcolm Gladwell (2008) has advanced the "10,000-Hour Rule," suggesting that success in any field requires 10,000 hours of practice. Civic engagement, like athletics, music, and many other endeavors, is best learned through practice. Thus, civic educators must find ways to allow students to practice politics through public work.

By claiming that politics is learned through practice, we mean to challenge the approach that seems to dominate contemporary American politics, whereby politics is a "spectator sport" played by the experts and passively watched by ordinary citizens. Our study of the Raise Your Voice initiative revealed that students want to be active producers of political change. In the process of such change, students develop a diverse set of democratic skills—working in teams, speaking in public, and thinking strategically. In particular, democratic practices seem to lead, as the study suggests, to the establishment of horizontal relationships and accountability between students, which in turn produces positive political learning outcomes (Longo, Drury, and Battistoni 2006).

The recent *Educating for Democracy* (Colby et al. 2007) details findings from the Carnegie Foundation Political Engagement Project (PEP), which examined twenty-one college and university courses and co-curricular programs that address preparation for democratic participation. The study found that (1) participation in PEP courses resulted in greater political understanding, skills, motivation, and expected future political action; (2) contrary to claims that education for political development will indoctrinate students, increased political learning did not change student party identification or political ideology; and (3) students with little initial interest in political issues made especially substantial learning gains. The authors of *Educating for Democracy* contend that high-quality education for political development increases students' political understanding, skill, motivation and involvement while contributing to many aspects of general academic learning.

As students become cocreators, as opposed to customers or clients, they develop "the broader set of capacities and skills required to take confident, skillful, imaginative, collective action in fluid and open environments where there is no script" (Boyte 2008a)—or what Harry Boyte has referred to as developing "civic agency." Involving students as coproducers in civic engagement initiatives, then, means that we will need to go beyond offering them opportunities to participate in focus groups and surveys or even inviting them to sit on boards and task forces. When we talk about building student civic agency through the practice of democracy, it means including students in the planning, development, and implementation of civic engagement opportunities. Education, like politics, is not a spectator sport, and seeing students as coproducers is about including them in the central effort of higher education—the pursuit and dissemination of knowledge.

In one powerful example of practice, Colgate University organized a multiyear campaign led by the then dean of students, Adam Weinberg, to rebuild campus life around a rich conception of civic learning, including using residence halls as "sites for democracy" (Weinberg 2005, 2008). Colgate redefined the role of residence advisers from rule enforcers to coaches who catalyze teams of students; in addition, student leaders in the residence halls are trained as community organizers, fostering a mentorship, rather than programming, model. In trying to move from a culture of student entitlement to a culture of student responsibility, they also created community councils that function as neighborhood associations within residential units. "This required a lot of faith in our students, a keen and specific sense for what we are trying to accomplish, and an eternal vigilance to educate for democracy across the campus," concludes Weinberg (2005, p. 44).

Like Weinberg's work at Colgate, our work with students at Miami University in Ohio and Providence College also provides insights into the challenges and possibilities for practice and is detailed elsewhere (Battistoni 1998; Fretz and Longo 2010; Longo and Shaffer 2009).

Motivation: Finding "Civic Calling"

By concentrating too much on civic knowledge and skills, faculty and administrators have neglected the important impetus of civic motivation. A person can have all the knowledge and skills in the world, but if he or she isn't motivated or "called" to participate in public life, these capacities will take that person nowhere. Beginning in the 1990s, when civic engagement efforts grew in response to the seeming lack of engagement among traditional college-aged youth, young people's seeming disengagement and lack of care about public life was often blamed on civic apathy and ignorance—that is, a lack of motivation. Some attributed this lack of motivation to a failure of politics and the public realm to connect with students' interests, passions, or values, but many chose to blame or write off young people themselves (see Bauerlein 2008). But since then, a number of studies clearly suggest that motivation to participate comes from opportunities to participate and to be engaged in the first place. Motivation, it seems, may be the *result* of engagement rather than the cause (see Colby et al. 2007; Kiesa et al. 2007; Youniss and Yates 1997). This is another reason why opportunities to participate on students' terms are so important.

But there is evidence to suggest that motivation to participate in public life also comes from a deep and profound sense of "civic calling" or "vocation." Ninety years ago Max Weber (1918) gave an address titled "Politics as a Vocation," in many ways playing on the notion of vocation, which normally has religious connotations, to describe those who are politically engaged. But stripped of the sectarian religious undertones, there is something in the language associated with spiritual vocation that can be translated into the civic sphere. When students say they want to "make a difference" in the world, they are, in effect, saying that they feel "called" to "respond" to a problem or injustice they perceive in the world. As a recent study of youth civic engagement put it, "To be called to 'make the world better,' to 'make a difference' in the public sphere, is to be and to do citizen" (Roholt, Hildreth, and Baizerman 2008).

Jim Wallis discusses this understanding of vocation in his 2004 Stanford Baccalaureate Address, in which he encourages students "to think about your vocation more than just your career. . . . Consider your calling, more than just the many opportunities presented to [you], connecting your best talents and skills to your best and deepest values." This response to the world's call, as each of us hears it, is powerful: We clearly saw it evoked in college-age youth in the United States during the civil rights movement, the Vietnam War, and, in more recent years, the response to Hurricane Katrina and its after-math. This notion of civic calling or vocation also comes through in *Habits of the Heart*, a now classic exploration of civic engagement (Bellah, Madsen, Sullivan, Swidler, and Tipton 1985), and more recently in CIRCLE's report "Millennials Talk Politics" (Kiesa et al. 2007).

The notion that "one can be called to live life in particular ways best suited to oneself . . . in response to a call or to the world's address" (Roholt, Hildreth, and Baizerman 2008) also comes through in studies based on interviews with graduating students and alumni from longer-term engagement programs, such as Providence College's Public and Community Service Studies major, Miami University's Acting Locally, and the Jane Addams School for Democracy, which is now housed at Augsburg College in St. Paul, Minnesota.

One study of Providence College's unique interdisciplinary Public and Community Service Studies major, for example, concluded that the program, "centered on the clarification of personal values and greater understanding of who [students] are as people. Often these ideas were framed in terms of how one will make a difference in the world" (Grove 2006). Students involved in Acting Locally at Miami University, a two-year curriculum in American Studies focusing on civic engagement, likewise talked about the ways in which this intensive program gave them a profound shift in their sense of vocation and the type of professionals they plan to be in the future. One student, who went on to participate in Teach for America after graduation, explained:

> Before Acting Locally I had never even heard the words "community organizing"—I didn't know what any of that kind of thing was. I just planned on using foreign affairs to make the world a better place and go into the state department. But I really found out a lot more about change from the bottom up. And so that changed my interests and what I studied and the classes I took, and it's leading to me doing Teach for America on the Mexican border, which I never thought to do. (interview, 2008)

As seen in this student's reflection, to be called to involvement in public life is often the result of opportunities for civic practice in which students' voices are valued.

The notion of democratic practice leading to a sense of civic calling is also central to the efforts of the Jane Addams School for Democracy in St. Paul, Minnesota, one of the most innovative campus-community collaborations. Founded in 1996, the Jane Addams School involves immigrant families, college students from multiple institutions in the Twin Cities area, and faculty in reciprocal learning and public work projects. A guiding tenet of the school's method of collaborative learning is that citizenship is not a fixed idea; it is a "life's work." At the school, diverse people come together to "craft a common purpose, transform their lives, and make a difference in the world" (Kari and Skelton 2007, p. 14). In reflecting on her many years as a participant in the Jane Addams School—first as an undergraduate student and later as a graduate student in education at Columbia University doing research during summers—Terri Wilson reflected on how engagement in this project shaped her work. Wilson writes that the space "was where I found my way into capacities I wasn't quite sure I had, where I tried out ideas, tested my voice, became a better listener, [and] learned to ask questions." In the essay, aptly entitled, "A Call to Vocation," Wilson concludes, "I learned, above all else, that asking questions implies a commitment to respond" (2007, p. 92).

Advancing Civic Engagement: Concrete Implications

We have argued that civic transformation for students requires practitioners to adjust conceptual frameworks of democratic citizenship education to include voice, democratic practice, and motivation (or civic calling). But there are also concrete implications for how faculty and administrators do things on an everyday basis on their campuses. The remainder of this chapter will point to lessons learned from models of promising practices we have located in our own work and experiences.

Before addressing these practical implications, however, we need to issue two important warnings to those seeking to harness increased student voice and leadership. The first has to do with the potentially stifling effects of institutionalizing student leadership. In a multi-institution study examining institutionalization efforts on campuses, Matthew Hartley, Ira Harkavy, and Lee Benson (2005) heard the caution that "our students can do remarkable things all on their own" and that more formal initiatives might, in the words of one administrator, put a "pin [on] the butterfly" (p. 218). Thus, in bringing students into the center of efforts to institutionalize civic engagement, there is rightly the concern that this might suffocate the unpredictable and creative work students are already undertaking on their own, often outside of the classroom and on the margins of the campus.

This concern was evident in past student movements, as well. For example, during the civil rights movement, the Student Nonviolent Coordinating

Committee (SNCC) was careful not to simply become a "student wing" of the Southern Christian Leadership Conference (SCLC), the organization headed by Martin Luther King Jr. Ella Baker, an early adviser and mentor for the students advocating for civil rights while she was working for SCLC, warned that becoming part of SCLC would suppress the creativity of the students. Baker played an important coaching role "guarding the student movement" against those who would push them in an undemocratic direction, but student autonomy was an essential component to the founding of SNCC (Ransby 2003, p. 243). This same approach is often seen in efforts to preserve student autonomy for student groups, learning communities, and residence halls on college campuses. It is also apparent in an innovative "professorless classroom" at the University of Massachusetts–Amherst, where students lead a course and several alternative break trips as part of the UMass Amherst Alliance for Community Transformation (UACT) (Addes and Keene 2006).

Another concern involves the too often elusive goal of addressing community-identified needs. Empowering students in campus-community partnerships means giving ownership of civic engagement efforts to the most transient and least experienced people involved in the partnerships. In his essay "Michelle's Quandary," Richard Cone (1996) raises this issue in a response to Goodwin Liu's essay on the history of the service-learning movement. The ethical dilemma for "Michelle," which Cone shares, is the uncertainty about "how to engage students in a way that they [acquire] a sense of humility and a respect for those they 'serve.'" Cone questions the privilege associated with many students in institutions of higher education, who, he fears, "would use their service experiences to acquire skills and knowledge they could use to further disenfranchise those already disenfranchised" (p. 21). In giving students more responsibility for civic engagement, do we run the risk of exasperating the privileges of students and at the same time shifting control of the learning even further away from the community?

With these concerns in mind, we conclude by considering three key areas necessary to advance new models for civic engagement that put students at the center: (1) empowering students to name their work on civic issues, (2) creating opportunities for longer-term engagement, and (3) reconstituting faculty roles to develop "students as colleagues."

Empowering Students to Define Civic Issues and Public Work

Tapping the talents and energies of students will necessarily involve empowering students, especially in the area of defining their civic work. This is also an essential component for connecting voice, practice, and motivation. If we want students to "respond" to their call in the world, we need to give them the opportunity to figure out what that might entail.

If we are able to create more open-ended spaces between campuses and communities where students and community members are involved in the cocreation of knowledge, there are sure to be dramatic shifts in the very way we understand such ideas as "democracy," "politics," "service," "public," and "leadership." Famously, John Dewey (1916/1993) stated that "democracy must be reborn in every generation" (p. 122). This can occur rather naturally if we give the next generation opportunities to wrestle with and then rewrite democracy's very meaning.

This can happen if we create multiple opportunities for various forms of dialogue and deliberation, especially in connection with service and community engagement. In this process, space must also be created for ongoing reflection and evaluation, along with real public products. And student voice needs to go beyond giving students space; students should be given opportunities to define politics and civic engagement for themselves.

Civic educators must use their roles and authority to create space for students to authentically voice discussions of the issues that impact them. This also requires being strategic: educators must find the places where student voice will be most effective in colleges and universities, community institutions, and government agencies. In courses, this can mean finding ways for students to partner in creating the curriculum, developing the grading criteria, and leading class discussions.

Beyond the pedagogical processes in the classroom, faculty can create substantive content in courses that encourages students to work on issues that matter to them. A great example here is the model for curricular innovation around community organizing begun by Marshall Ganz at Harvard and now replicated on a number of campuses (see Ganz 2010 for further details). Outside of classes, on campuses, this can mean that students have a voice on college policy issues, service-learning programs, and community issues. It also means immersing students in the communities that surround campus so that they can learn to "listen eloquently" themselves (again, a key component of voice) and bring the voices of the community to campus, as they themselves deliberate on key community issues.

Creating Opportunities for Longer-Term Engagement

There have been increases in youth participation in public life, most especially through volunteering in communities (Longo and Meyer 2006). And colleges and universities offer implicit and explicit incentives to be involved in community service—not least of which are the criteria for admissions. Indeed, a recent study from CIRCLE finds that "resume padding" is a major reason why young people volunteer. One of the authors of the study, Lew Friedland, writes, "Much of the reported volunteerism was shaped by the perception that voluntary and civic activity is necessary to get into any college; and the better the college (or, more precisely, the higher the perception of the college in the status system) the more volunteerism students believed was necessary" (Friedland and Morimoto 2005).

It is now time to build upon this interest in volunteering by developing new kinds of programs that invite long-term participation in civic engagement projects. The evidence seems to illustrate that developing programs that invite long-term relationships are more likely to lead to the kind of transformation we are hoping to accomplish. This has been the experience with students and community partners in the Public and Community Service Studies major at Providence College, and the work of Dan Butin suggests that, nationally, academic service-learning programs that allow students to major or minor enhance rigor, critical reflection, and the ability to shape for themselves an understanding about what constitutes community engagement (Butin 2008). The priority of faculty and administrators should be to create long-term developmental programs, with both curricular and co-curricular components, that allow students to develop deep relationships and establish more integrated public work projects. These types of approaches to the engaged academy help civic engagement transform, rather than simply accommodate, higher education.

Not every college or university may be able to create academic majors or minors as a vehicle to advance longer-term civic engagement. But every campus should be able to create scholarship programs for students who have a passion for service and civic engagement connected to sustained community work or leadership roles on campus. Models for these kinds of scholarship programs exist at campuses like DePaul, Bentley, Providence College, and Indiana University–Purdue University Indianapolis, and at other campuses through the Bonner Scholars Program. Students also need more opportunities to get credit, funding, and pay for providing leadership in service-learning courses on campus, such as acting as teaching assistants leading reflection in the classroom or community assistants serving as liaisons for their peers in the community. Campuses should also rethink undergraduate research funding and expectations; specifically, this entails asking that the substantial research funding that colleges and universities provide to undergraduate students *always* include a public dimension. Finally, in light of increasing levels of student debt, colleges and universities need to provide more post-graduate opportunities that enable students to continue to act as social entrepreneurs, while getting debt relief and/or money for graduate school in the process.

Reconstituting Faculty Roles: Faculty Members as Coaches; "Students as Colleagues"

Our final and most important area for advancing civic engagement—around reconstituting faculty roles—may seem unlikely for an essay about reframing students' roles. But student voice, practice, and motivation are integrally linked to the practice of faculty. We are framing this final insight around faculty roles because we believe that faculty members and administrators who are interested in engaging students as coproducers in civic engagement initiatives will need to find new models for involving students in their community-based teaching and research practices. An earlier study of three educational interventions designed to create political engagement outcomes showed that the metaphor of "faculty as coach" or "maestro" may be the best model for working with students in the area of civic engagement (Longo, Drury, Battistoni 2006). The knowledge and skills necessary for political engagement are more akin to what is learned through athletics or music performance than the traditional academic model, so the role of the educator needs to adjust to this reality.

As in athletics and music, the main lesson of democratic citizenship is learned through practicing democracy; the "teacher" is one who sets up the practice routine and is there to guide the student through tasks and in reflecting upon the performance afterward. This doesn't diminish the role of educators at all; in fact, it enhances their place in setting the ultimate goals and context for practicing politics, and in providing tools and opportunities for reflection on student practice.

This argument is rooted in the new professional practices associated with the scholarship of engagement as developed by Ernest Boyer (1990, 1997), William Sullivan's emphasis on "civic professionalism" (1995), and Harry Boyte's (2004, 2008a, 2008b) notion of "public work." Boyte (2008b), specifically, argues that for our institutions of higher education to become "agents and architects" of democracy, a radical shift is required in the way scholars see themselves and their work. Scholars cannot simply be dispassionate researchers, critics, service providers, or educators of future leaders; rather, they must also be "engaged public figures" who "stimulate conversations to expand the sense of the possible, and to activate broader civic and political energies" (p. 79). Engaged scholarship should also include the energies and talents of our students as we include them as partners in this effort.

Some of the best programmatic, research, and course-related models for including students as "colleagues" in academic service-learning and civic engagement programs are presented in *Students as Colleagues* (Zlotkowski, Longo, and Williams 2006), an edited collection that includes nineteen chapters (most of which are coauthored by students) and numerous vignettes that document examples of student collaboration with faculty, staff, and community partners. Among the growing practices highlighted in the volume is the way students at campuses like Marquette University and Providence College are given responsibilities as staff members in service-learning centers and as community liaisons to community partners in service-learning courses. Chapters by students and staff from the University of Pennsylvania and Duke University reveal the possibilities of student-generated, community-based research. Finally, the chapter from University of Massachusetts–Amherst, mentioned earlier, describes "the professorless classroom," part of an innovative program in which students teach courses with embedded alternative spring-break service trips that are supported by training and mentoring from a distinguished faculty member.

The civic engagement movement has grown out of the desire to connect learning with real-world problem solving. It has also aspired to transform the very nature of higher education. This requires a radical restructuring in the dominant ways of knowing and learning. And while there have been substantial changes in the academy that offer opportunities for engagement to students, faculty, and staff, these efforts are not nearly sufficient. Change will not occur by asking the same people to keep doing the same thing. As Peter Senge and his colleagues (2008) explain in *The Necessary Revolution*, "All real change is grounded in new ways of thinking and perceiving" (p. 10). If the civic engagement movement is to meet its greatest aspirations, colleges and universities will need to reconstitute the roles of faculty and community partners, and practitioners will need to recognize the assets their students bring to this effort. At the same time, we believe this only can happen if the notion of "civic learning" is expanded, giving students opportunities to use their voices, practice democracy, and ultimately, find their civic callings.

REFERENCES

Addes, D., and A. Keene. 2006. "Grassroots Community Development at UMass Amherst. In *Students as Colleagues: Expanding the Circle of Service-Learning Leadership*, ed. E. Zlotkowski, N. Longo, and J. Williams. Providence: Campus Compact.

Bastress, J., and J. Beilenson. 1996. "Response." In *Community Service in Higher Education: A Decade of Development*, 19–20. Providence: Providence College.

Battistoni, R. 1998. "Making a Major Commitment." In *Successful Service-Learning Programs: New Models of Excellence in Higher Education*, ed. E. Zlotkowski, 169–188. Bolton, MA: Anker.

———. 2002. *Civic Engagement Across the Curriculum: A Resource Book for Faculty in All Disciplines*. Providence: Campus Compact.

Bauerlein, M. 2008. *The Dumbest Generation: How the Digital Age Stupefies Young Americans and Jeopardizes Our Future; or, Don't Trust Anyone Under 30*. New York: Penguin.

Bellah, R., R. Madsen, W. Sullivan, A. Swidler, and S. Tipton. 1985. *Habits of the Heart: Individualism and Commitment in American Life*. Los Angeles: University of California Press.

Billig, S., S. Root, and D. Jesse. 2005. "The Impact of Participation in Service-Learning on High School Students' Civic Engagement." CIRCLE Working Paper 33, Center for Information and Research on Civic Learning and Engagement, University of Maryland, College Park.

Boyer, E. 1990. *Scholarship Reconsidered: Priorities of the Professoriate*. New York: The Carnegie Foundation for the Advancement of Teaching.

———. 1997. *Selected Speeches 1979–1995*. Princeton: The Carnegie Foundation for the Advancement of Teaching.

Boyte, H. 2004. *Everyday Politics: Reconnecting Citizens and Public Life*. Philadelphia: University of Pennsylvania Press.

———. 2008a. "Against the Current: Developing the Civic Agency of Students." *Change* 40 (3). Available at http://www.changemag.org/Archives/Back%20Issues/May-June%202008/full-against-the-current.html.

———. 2008b. "Public Work: Civic Populism Versus Technocracy in Higher Education." In *Agent of Democracy*, ed. D. W. Brown and D. Witte, 79–102. Dayton, OH: Kettering Foundation.

Butin, D. 2008. *Rethinking Service Learning: Embracing the Scholarship of Engagement within Higher Education*. Sterling, VA: Stylus Publishing.

Colby, A., E. Beaumont, T. Ehrlich, and J. Corngold. 2007. *Educating for Democracy: Preparing Undergraduates for Responsible Political Engagement*. Stanford, CA: Carnegie Foundation for the Advancement of Teaching.

Cone, R. 1996. "Michelle's Quandary." In *Community Service in Higher Education: A Decade of Development*, ed. R. Battistoni and K. Morton, 21–22. Providence: Providence College.

Creighton, J., and R. Harwood. 1993. *College Students Talk Politics*. Dayton, OH: Kettering Foundation.

Dewey, J. 1916/1993. *Democracy and Education*. New York: Free Press.

Freire, P. 1970. *The Pedagogy of the Oppressed*. New York: Continuum Publishing.

Fretz, E. and N. Longo. 2010. "Students Co-Creating an Engaged Academy," In *Handbook of Engaged Scholarship: Contemporary Landscapes, Future Directions*, ed. H. Fitzgerald, C. Burack, and S. Seifer, 313–329. East Lansing: Michigan State University Press.

Friedland, L., and S. Morimoto. 2005. "The Changing Lifeworld of Young People: Risk, Resume Padding, and Civic Engagement." CIRCLE Working Paper 40, Center for Information and Research on Civic Learning and Engagement, University of Maryland, College Park.

Furco, A. 2002. *Self-Assessment Rubric for the Institutionalization of Service-Learning in Higher Education*. Campus Compact. Available at http://www.tufts.edu/talloiresnetwork/downloads/Self-AssessmentRubricfortheInstitutionalizationof Service-LearninginHigherEducation.pdf.

Galston, W. 2001. "Political Knowledge, Political Engagement, and Civic Education." *Annual Review of Political Science* 4: 217–234.

Ganz, M. 2010. "Practicing Democracy Network." Available at http://www.hks.harvard.edu/organizing/Courses/courses.shtml.

Gelmon, S., S. Seifer, J. Kauper-Brown, and M. Mikkelsen. 2005. "Building Capacity for Community Engagement: Institutional Self-Assessment." Seattle: Community-Campus Partnerships for Health.

Gladwell, M. 2008. *Outliers: The Story of Success*. New York: Little, Brown.

Greenhouse, S. 1999. "Activism Surges at Campuses Nationwide, and Labor Is at Issue." *New York Times*, March 29: A14.

Grove, M. 2006. "Conversations with Public and Community Service Studies Majors and Alumni: The Articulation of Values in Education, Life, and Work." Unpublished Internal Report to Feinstein Institute, Providence College.

Hartley, M., I. Harkavy, and L. Benson. 2005. "Putting Down Roots in the Groves of Academe: The Challenges of Institutionalizing Service-Learning." In *Looking In, Teaching Out: Critical Issues and Directions in Service-Learning*, ed. D. Butin, 205–222. New York: Palgrave/St. Martin's Press.

Hollander, E., J. Saltmarsh, and E. Zlotkowski. 2002. "Indicators of Engagement." In *Learning to Serve: Promoting Civil Society through Service-Learning*, ed. L. A. Simon, M. Kenny, K. Brabeck, and R. M. Lerner, 31–50. Norwell, MA: Kluwer Academic Publishers.

Hughes, L. 1968. *The Best of Simple*. New York: Hill and Wang.

Kari, N., and N. Skelton. 2007. *Voices of Hope: The Story of the Jane Addams School for Democracy*. Dayton, OH: Kettering Foundation.

Kecskes, K., ed. 2006. *Engaging Departments: Moving Faculty Culture from Private to Public, Individual to Collective Focus for the Common Good*. Boston: Anker.

Keeter, S., C. Zukin, M. Andolina, and K. Jenkins. 2002. *The Civic and Political Health of the Nation: A Generational Portrait*. College Park, MD: Center for Information and Research on Civic Learning and Engagement.

Kiesa, A., A. Orlowski, P. Levine, D. Both, E. Kirby, M. Lopez, and K. Marcelo. 2007. *Millennials Talk Politics*. College Park, MD: Center for Information and Research on Civic Learning and Engagement.

Liu, G. 1996. "Origins, Evolution, and Progress: Reflections on the Community Service Movement in Higher Education 1985–1995." In *Community Service in Higher Education: A Decade of Development*. Providence: Providence College.

Long, S. 2002. "The New Student Politics: The Wingspread Statement on Student Civic Engagement." Providence: Campus Compact.

Longo, N., C. Drury, and R. Battistoni. 2006. "Catalyzing Political Engagement: Lessons for Civic Educators from the Voices of Students." *Journal of Political Science Education* 2 (3): 313–329.

Longo, N., and R. Meyer. 2006. "College Students and Politics: a Literature Review." Circle Working Paper 46, Center for Information and Research on Civic Learning and Engagement, University of Maryland, College Park.

Longo, N., and M. Shaffer. 2009. "Leadership Education and the Revitalization of Public Life." In *Civic Engagement in Higher Education*, ed. B. Jacoby, 154–173. San Francisco: Jossey-Bass.

Mead, M. 1958. "Thinking Ahead: Why is Education Obsolete?" *Harvard Business Review* (November/December): 23–30.

Putnam, R. 2000. *Bowling Alone: The Collapse and Revival of American Community*. New York: Simon and Schuster.

Ransby, B. 2003. *Ella Baker and the Black Freedom Movement*. Chapel Hill: University of North Carolina Press.

Roholt, R., R. W. Hildreth, and M. Baizerman. 2008. *Becoming Citizens: Deepening the Craft of Youth Civic Engagement*. Binghamton, New York: Haworth Press,.

Saltmarsh, J. 2005. "The Civic Promise of Service Learning." *Liberal Education*. Available at http://www.iun.edu/~cetl/servicelearning/S-L-Articles/The%20 Civic%20Promise%20of%20Service%20Learning.pdf.

Senge, P., B. Smith, N. Kruschwitz, J. Laur, and S. Schley. 2008. *The Necessary Revolution: How Individuals and Organizations are Working Together to Create a Sustainable World*. New York: Doubleday.

Sullivan, W. 1995. *Work and Integrity: The Crisis and Promise of Professionalism in America*. New York: Harper Collins.

Wallis, J. 2004. "Building Global Justice: We Are the Ones We Have Been Waiting For." Stanford Baccalaureate Address, June 12, 2004. Available at http://www.sojo.net/index.cfm?action=news.display_archives&mode=current_opinion&article=CO_040616_wallis.

Weber, M. 1918. *Politics as a Vocation*. Lecture given to students at Munich University, January 1919. Available at http://www.ne.jp/asahi/moriyuki/abukuma/weber/lecture/politics_vocation.html.

Weinberg, A. 2005. "Residential Education for Democracy." In *Learning for Democracy* 1 (2). Available at http://www.bowdoin.edu/mckeen-center/pdf/weinberg-civic-education.pdf.

Weinberg, A. 2008. "Public Work at Colgate: An Interview." In *Agent of Democracy: Higher Education and HEX Journey*, ed. D. W. Browne and D. Witte, 102–120. Dayton, OH: Kettering Foundation.

Wilson, T. 2007. "A Call to Vocation." In *Voices of Hope: The Story of the Jane Addams School for Democracy*, ed. N. Kari and N. Skelton. Dayton, OH: Kettering Foundation.

Youniss, J., and M. Yates. 1997. *Community Service and Social Responsibility in Youth.* Chicago: University of Chicago Press.

Zlotkowski, E. 1997–2004. *Service-Learning in the Disciplines.* Series of 20 monographs. Washington, DC: American Association of Higher Education.

Zlotkowski, E., N. Longo, and J. Williams. 2006. *Students as Colleagues: Expanding the Circle of Service-Learning Leadership.* Providence: Campus Compact.

CHAPTER 10

Civic Engagement on the Ropes?

EDWARD ZLOTKOWSKI

as the civic engagement movement "stalled," as some, including the editors of this volume (p. 4), have claimed? Does service-learning need to be "disciplined" in order to survive (Butin 2006)? Mark Twain once famously quipped: "The reports of my death have been greatly exaggerated." Can the same—*mutatis mutandi*—be said about the recent alarm being voiced in some corners of the engagement camp?

Certainly, few would deny that in a relatively short amount of time—approximately two decades—the civic engagement movement has made some impressive gains. In a 2005 essay entitled "The Disciplines and the Public Good," I outlined some of the ways in which the academic disciplines have embraced a civic agenda, and a year later, Nicholas Longo, James Williams, and I introduced our edited volume *Students as Colleagues: Expanding the Circle of Service-Learning Leadership* (2006) with the following paragraph:

By many measures, the adoption of service-learning as a legitimate teaching-learning strategy in American higher education has been a remarkable success story. Over the course of the 1990s, we saw the founding and flourishing of the Corporation for National Service as well as the Community Outreach Partnerships Centers (COPC) program coming out of the Department of Housing and Urban Development. We have seen the phenomenal growth of Campus Compact from a few hundred members to over 1,000 institutions, and the founding of affiliated state compacts in almost two-thirds of the states. We have seen the publication of 21 volumes in the former American Association for Higher Education's (AAHE) series on service and the academic disciplines (Zlotkowski, 1997–2006)—a series that helped prepare the way for many other discipline-specific publications and initiatives. Indeed, we have seen the disciplinary associations themselves begin to take on the work of engagement, from major initiatives at the National Communication Association to more limited but nonetheless significant developments in the sciences and the humanities. . . . Associations organized by institutional type— associations such as the American Association of Community Colleges, the Council of Independent Colleges, the National Association of State Universities and Land-Grant Colleges, the private Historically Black Colleges and Universities (HBCUs) working through the United Negro College Fund—have launched significant engagement efforts designed to redefine higher education in a post–Cold War world. So extensive has the service-learning literature become that it is now too large for any single individual to master. (p. 1)

To be sure, *Students as Colleagues* goes on to suggest that new strategies will be needed before service-learning is "able to exert a truly transformative influence on academic programming." In other words, it recognizes that much more needs to be done if this "teaching-learning" dimension of the scholarship of engagement is, at last, to fulfill its potential in helping effect civic renewal. Such a recognition, however, was less a cry of alarm than a call to embrace new opportunities. Furthermore, this call was married to a decidedly concrete set of recommendations, namely, strategies that would empower students to assume new positions of responsibility in the service-learning, if not the overall civic engagement, movement. The remainder of this chapter argues that both these positions—that is, a reframing that stresses opportunity more than alarm, and a reframing that stresses concrete strategies and relevant constituencies—offer our best hope for the future of civic engagement in higher education.

PRAGMATIST PRINCIPLES

In November 1994, the College Board convened an invitational seminar on the future of liberal education in the United States. Bruce Kimball, author of *Orators and Philosophers: A History of the Idea of Liberal Education* (1995a), was invited to give the keynote address, and shortly thereafter, the work on which he based his address, "Toward Pragmatic Liberal Education" (1995b), was published as the central essay in *The Condition of American Liberal Education: Pragmatism and a Changing Tradition* (1995). Robert Orrill, the executive editor of that volume, sums up Kimball's argument as follows:

Closely examining recent reform proposals, he makes a carefully wrought argument that a new and distinctly American version of liberal education *is* emerging in the closing years of the twentieth century. This reform "consensus" can best be grasped, he believes, if we understand how its core elements or themes . . . fit with and are "deeply rooted in the resurgent intellectual tradition of pragmatism." (p. xvi; original emphasis)

These core elements or themes include (1) multiculturalism, (2) values and service, (3) community and citizenship, (4) general education, (5) commonality and cooperation between college and the other levels of the education system, (6) teaching interpreted as learning and inquiry, and (7) assessment (Kimball 1995b, p. 97).

Of the approximately two dozen individuals invited to respond to Kimball's essay, Orrill (1995) goes on to note, "Almost none [found] the case that [he] makes to be without a substantial basis in fact or lacking in descriptive power," though few, if any, could be said to have been "entirely persuaded" by his argument (p. xvi–xvii). In a follow-up essay, "Naming Pragmatic Liberal Education" (1997), Kimball himself notes that the

response to the consensus theory . . . seems to vary with the perspective and context of the observer. Most of the original respondents who were doubtful of the consensus thesis work at institutions in the "top" 10 percent of the more than 3,000 postsecondary institutions in the country. Those tending to be persuaded by the consensus thesis come from the other 90 percent or from national associations or programs whose membership includes many from this sector. The correlation is not perfect, but still significant. (p. 60)

We will return to this interesting "correlation" later in this chapter.

Kimball's work focuses on liberal education in general, not on civic engagement, but it provides a broad intellectual context for a far more specific connection—that between John Dewey and the civic engagement movement. Well before Kimball's essay, this connection had already been foregrounded in various essays and articles, some of which found their way into Jane Kendall's pioneering three-volume set, *Combining Service and Learning: A Resource Book for Community and Public Service*, published in 1990 by what was then the National Society for Internships and Experiential Education (NSIEE). One of NSIEE's intellectual leaders was Dwight Giles Jr., so it is not altogether surprising that when the *Michigan Journal of Community Service Learning*, the country's first peer-reviewed service-learning journal, appeared in 1994, Giles and his colleague Janet Eyler contributed an essay titled "The Theoretical Roots of Service-Learning in John Dewey: Toward a Theory of Service-Learning." Since then the connection between Dewey and the civic engagement movement has only grown stronger, with

Lee Benson, Ira Harkavy, and John Puckett's *Dewey's Dream: Universities and Democracies in an Age of Education Reform* (2007) representing only one the important recent testimonies to Dewey's central place in the hearts and minds of engaged scholars.

I have taken the time to sketch the civic engagement-pragmatism connection not because I have something to add to our understanding of it or because I wish to challenge its validity. I have introduced it solely to establish a jumping-off point for the question: What, if anything, can a pragmatist orientation contribute to our thinking about the development of the contemporary civic education movement? Indeed, to be more specific, I am especially concerned with what such an orientation can contribute to our thinking about service-learning—the teaching-learning dimension of that movement—and I think such an emphasis is justified both by the prominence of service-learning within that movement and the fact that, as a teaching-learning strategy, service-learning necessarily includes students.

In their essay "The Theoretical Roots of Service-Learning in John Dewey: Toward a Theory of Service-Learning" (1994), Giles and Eyler note that "theory is necessary, first and foremost, for developing and refining a solid research agenda for service-learning" (p. 77). They also speculate that "perhaps the foremost reason" for service-learning's tardiness in "developing a clearly defined and commonly shared body of knowledge" is that "the practitioners of service-learning are more oriented to action than to scholarly pursuits, and thus their writings have tended to be focused more on processes and program descriptions" (p. 77). They then go on to speculate that "there is a general resistance to theorizing in service-learning" and illustrate this by citing a recent article in which the author wrote, "Progress will be made through a series of successful and unsuccessful programs, and it will be this extensive work in the field . . . that will validate or invalidate Dewey's ideas" (p. 77). This view they label "a kind of anti-intellectualism" (p. 77).

Whether or not Giles and Eyler are correct in their speculations, it is especially interesting to note the way in which this passage contrasts "scholarly pursuits" with "actions" and assigns the documentation of processes and program descriptions to the latter, not the former. This is more than a little puzzling in light of Boyer's expanded concept of scholarship, but it also reminds me of an observation Richard Rorty made about Dewey himself:

> Dewey's conservative critics denounced him for fuzziness, for not giving us a criterion of growth [when he claimed that to "protect, sustain, and direct growth is the chief *ideal* of education" (original emphasis)]. But Dewey rightly saw that any such criterion would cut the future down to the size of the present. . . . Instead of criteria, Deweyans offer inspiring narratives and fuzzy utopias. Dewey had stories to tell about our progress from Plato to Bacon to Mills, from religion to rationalism to experimentalism, from tyranny to feudalism to democracy. (1999, p. 120)

As a contemporary pragmatist, Rorty is emphatic about the impossibility of drawing a clear distinction between theory and practice. In the introduction to *Philosophy and Social Hope* (1999), he explains that

> for pragmatists there is no sharp break between natural science and social science, nor between social science and politics, nor between politics, philosophy and literature. . . . There is no deep split between theory and practice, because on a pragmatist view all so-called "theory" which is not wordplay is always already practice. (p. xxv)

He later offers what can almost be read as a gloss on this assertion when he writes: "Contexts provided by theories are tools for effecting change. The theories which provide new contexts are to be evaluated by their efficiency in effecting changes" (p. 221).

As Giles and Eyler would themselves be the first to admit, pragmatism values a wide range of intellectual activities, but one of its key criteria is utility: What will be the actual return on a given intellectual investment? A good illustration of this line of questioning can be found in Robert Tucker's "Biting the Pragmatist Bullet: Why Service-Learning Can Do without Epistemology" (1999), also published in the *Michigan Journal of Community Service Learning*.

In this article, Tucker takes issue with two earlier pieces published in the same journal: Goodwin Liu's "Knowledge, Foundations, and Discourse: Philosophical Support for Service-learning" (1995) and Kenneth Richman's "Epistemology, Community and Experts: A Response to Goodwin Liu" (1996), both of which attempt to sketch an appropriate epistemology for service-learning. For Tucker, viewing this exchange from within the pragmatist camp can lead to only one conclusion: "Service-learning does not need a discrete and well-articulated epistemology. Such an epistemology could accomplish little more than the construction of a procrustean bed in which our practice must painfully lie" (p. 5).

In exploring and defending this position, Tucker hardly exhibits "anti-intellectualism." His critique is sharp, specific, and demonstrates extensive familiarity with the pragmatist tradition. For example, with regard to Liu's attempt to build theoretical support for his own position, Tucker (1999) points out that Liu

> primarily relies on the work of West and Rorty. This is problematic because both Rorty and West take extensive pains to distance themselves from the notion of pragmatism as replacement epistemology. In West's case, a central theme of his position is that pragmatism represents an *evasion* of epistemology-centered philosophy. (pp. 7–8; original emphasis)

A few paragraphs later Tucker concedes that "to be fair to Liu, much of his difficulty comes from citing only the earliest of Rorty's works," for it was only later in Rorty's career that the full impact of his anti-epistemological stance began to make itself felt (p. 8).

My point in referencing this debate is twofold. First, it should be clear that proponents of engagement, especially with regard to service-learning, need not view theory as the key to academic legitimacy—certainly not within the framework of Boyer's expanded understanding of scholarship. Nor is this to denigrate the importance of theory. Theory is certainly one path engaged scholars may take in their work. Research and theorizing, however, represent only one of several paths that can help the civic engagement movement advance. We may do well to recall again Kimball's observations regarding the institutional perspectives of his respondents, namely, that the ten percent who questioned his contention that a pragmatist consensus is emerging around a new, distinctly American understanding of liberal education work at institutions in the "top" 10 percent of the more than 3,000 postsecondary institutions in the country. In other words, the academy's *traditional* bias in favor of research and theorizing should not be allowed to influence unduly our sense of what civic engagement needs in order to move to its next phase.

Second, in all the efforts the movement makes to enhance its effectiveness and scope, the pragmatist stress on demonstrable results, on *practical* efficacy, should never be left out of sight. As Tucker (1999) puts it, a "crucial aspect of pragmatist thought"

> is its emphasis on the practical consequences of certain ways of thinking, speaking, and acting. Richard Rorty claims that the "Pragmatist thinks that if something makes no difference in practice, it should make no difference to philosophy." Charles Sanders Pierce offered a similar notion when he wrote "[T]he whole function of thought is to produce habits of action. . . . To develop its meaning, we have, therefore, simply to determine what habits it produces . . . ." (p. 9)

Again, this is not to denigrate the importance of theory. Kurt Lewin's remark that "There is nothing more practical than a good theory" (1951, p. 169) is more than a clever *bon mot*. Yet questioning the strategic utility of pursuing certain theoretical interests—especially if these occur at the expense of other possibly more useful strategies—should be part of the agenda-setting process. Replacing an interest in getting things "right" with a desire to make things happen—especially in the nearer future—may be counter-intuitive for many academics, especially academics who work at research-centered universities. But that does not mean one cannot or should not take such a move seriously.

Not One Size

In a piece entitled "The Struggle Against Positivism" (2000), Harry Boyte points to the way in which the legacy of positivism acts as a powerful brake on our attempt to develop a more civically engaged academy. Positivism, he notes, "structures our research, our disciplines, our teaching, and our institutions, even though it has long been discredited intellectually" (p. 48). The same can be said for many other intellectual habits; while we consciously distance ourselves from them, we nonetheless continue to draw upon perspectives and practices they have planted in us. A prioritizing of formal definitional clarity may be one such holdover. Another may be a prioritizing of universal over regional considerations.

In an appendix to his essay "Toward Pragmatic Liberal Education" (1995b), Kimball links his thesis of an emerging pragmatic consensus to the work of Stephen Toulmin, specifically to Toulmin's book *Cosmopolis: The Hidden Agenda of Modernity* (1990). According to Kimball,

> Toulmin's central claim is that "the contributions of the Renaissance to Modernity" have been neglected. . . . Thus Toulmin joins the neo-pragmatists in "dismantling the last timbers of the intellectual scaffolding" of modern philosophy, and his historiographical tactic is "to reappropriate the wisdom of . . . Renaissance Humanism" in order to balance "the abstract rigor and exactitude of the seventeenth century 'new philosophy'" that became characteristic of modern philosophy. (p. 101)

What this "reappropriation" entails is a newfound respect for "four different kinds of practical knowledge: the oral, the particular, the local, and the timely" (Toulmin 1990, pp. 30, 186), and in a world ever more appreciative of such practical knowledge, a key virtue is *adaptability* (pp. 184ff.).

By and large, the civic engagement movement of the last two decades has shown itself to be impressively adaptive. Ever since the mid-1990s, it has recognized the importance of developing strategies appropriate to specific disciplinary and interdisciplinary contexts (Zlotkowski 2005). Shortly thereafter, it entered into fruitful dialogues with associations representing different types of academic institutions, and in some cases, such as the American Democracy Project of the American Association of State Colleges and Universities or the Broadening Horizons project of the American Association of Community Colleges, the results have been impressive. Still, the strategy of building on particular values, interests, and needs has not been carried as far as it could be.

Take, for example, the embedding of civic engagement in the academic curriculum. At most higher education institutions, service-learning has been the primary vehicle used to accomplish this task. Campus Compact captured the logic behind this strategy in a document titled "Educating the Next Generation of Active Citizens: A Strategy for Deepening Civic Engagement in American Higher Education" (2002):

> Service-learning is the most widespread, well-known **practice** of the civic education aimed at preparing students with the knowledge and

the skills needed for democratic citizenship. It has proved itself as a vehicle for exposing students to "the other America," deepening multicultural understanding and tolerance, increasing student ability to understand community dynamics and to relate theory to practice. Service-learning has engaged students, faculty, administrators, departments, discipline associations, and community partners in addressing the civic mission of higher education. (p. 3; original emphasis)

Students themselves have agreed. In "The New Student Politics: The Wingspread Statement on Student Civic Engagement" (Long 2002), the student authors note that "Through service-learning, [we] have had the opportunity to share and relate [our] experiences with others and to explore the broad context of [our] service activity" (p. 3). And in their recent review of youth involvement in civic and political engagement over the past few decades, Cliff Zukin and colleagues (2006) reach a similar conclusion—namely, that "what happens in schools matters," evidenced by the fact that "increases in voluntary activity among young adults [are] directly attributable to the greater attention paid to this form of public involvement in schools, largely through the service learning movement" (p. 205).

Still, service-learning has hardly been a panacea for civic engagement, and at institutions that stress research—both as the premier form of faculty scholarship and as the focus of student academic achievement—service-learning must yield pride of place to other expressions of the scholarship of engagement and/or itself assume a more research-intensive form, such as participatory action research. Furthermore, even where service-learning is institutionally stressed, it often falls short of delivering the full range of concepts, skills, and attitudes one might reasonably expect to be developed in a citizen, either American or global. This has led some (e.g., Boyte 2004) to call for its replacement and others (e.g., Butin 2006) to call for its reconceptualization.

Such suggestions, however, would not seem to represent a judicious investment of time, energy, and resources—no more so than attempts to pin down its governing epistemology. The fact is that "service-learning" has become the "koine," the common dialect, of the civic engagement movement in its teaching-learning form, and in doing so has shown itself capable of considerable adaptability. Institutions have not hesitated to mold its nomenclature, emphasis, and practice to meet their individual needs while still recognizing in it a set of broadly shared principles, values, and goals. Thus, as a phenomenon, service-learning would seem to embody precisely that respect for "the oral [in this case, read "personal"], the particular, the local, and the timely" that Toulmin (1990) sees as lying at the heart of a reformed, humanized modernism (p. 180).

To be sure, not all the variations that pass for service-learning deserve either our academic or our civic respect. Indeed, too much of what passes for service-learning could more accurately be labeled "academically sponsored community service." Furthermore, for those who include a more or less explicitly political dimension in their understanding of civic engagement, service-learning often fails to deliver. Toulmin's focus on "adaptability," however, suggests several practical ways to move forward.

In an attempt to better understand the extent to which contemporary Americans, especially young Americans, are and are not publicly engaged, Zukin and colleagues (2006) systematically analyzed data from a wide variety of sources. In their words, the "research had two principal goals: (1) to develop a reliable but concise set of indicators of civic and political engagement, with a special focus on youth aged fifteen to twenty-five; and (2) to assess the civic and political health of the nation" (p. 211). They distinguish political from civic engagement in the following way:

> Political engagement is activity aimed at influencing government policy or affecting the selection of government officials. For most Americans most of the time, this means participating in the electoral process, usually by voting. Civic engagement on the other hand, refers to participation aimed at achieving a public good, but usually through direct hands-on work in cooperation with others. Civic engagement normally occurs within nongovernmental organizations and rarely touches upon electoral politics. (p. 51)

It is their contention that neither form of engagement by itself is sufficient to maintain a healthy democracy. Yet it is also their contention that the line between these two kinds of engagement is less distinct than it might at first appear. Indeed, this is the thrust of their first two conclusions:

> First, the line between civic and political engagement is blurry at best, with as many as half of those engaged in civic activities seeing or treating their actions as political. Second, this line is also a porous one, with many of the citizens we have characterized as civic specialists also expressing their public voice in other arguably political, if not always or obviously electoral or government-focused ways. (p. 199)

The authors are at pains to stress that this does not mean there is no problem with public disengagement, particularly with political disengagement among the young. They carefully call attention to the debate that exists among scholars about whether civic activities "such as volunteering for nonprofit service organizations or supporting charitable causes" might not only be politically irrelevant but also "even serve as substitutes for . . . political activity, displacing the essential work citizens need to do to keep a democracy healthy" (p. 198). Still, it seems safe to say their research findings lead them to shy away from drawing exclusively negative conclusions. As they put it,

> For the vast majority of citizens, civic engagement is neither a pathway to nor substitute for political engagement, because they either

do not participate regularly in the former or because they do not see or act on a connection in the latter. In the end this suggests that the connections between civic and political engagement that we do find are more instructive in pointing to the *potential* for forging such links than their actual existence among citizens today. (p. 192; original emphasis)

As qualified as this "endorsement" is, it actually offers considerable hope to the civic engagement movement as the latter seeks to move to a new level of efficacy, especially in the political realm. There are two reasons for such optimism. First, in "The New Student Politics: The Wingspread Statement on Student Civic Engagement" (Long 2002), thirty-three students committed to civic engagement make it quite clear that *they* at least do see a political dimension in their community work:

Many of us at Wingspread perceive service as alternative politics, as a method of pursuing change in a democratic society. We want to address immediate problems in our communities as a way to begin. Building relationships with others through service is often preparatory to building a movement, as we learn skills that can help us take on the roles of community organizers. (p. 2)

Hence, they identify this "alternative politics" as "service politics" and explicitly differentiate it from "an alternative to politics" (p. 18). Such a concept accords well with Toulmin's (1990) description of a "humanized modernity" in which "the oral, the particular, the local, and the timely" play an important and respected role. To be sure, the students themselves recognize the limits of "service politics" and have no qualms about acknowledging that there is more to "political engagement" than the civic work in which they are currently engaged (p. 1). Nonetheless, they clearly recognize what Zukin and colleagues (2006) call the "potential" for linking the civic and the political and even go so far as to suggest that "while many have argued that this generation is neither politically active nor civically engaged, we at Wingspread think time may prove that ours is one of the most politically active generations in recent history" (p. 18). This is precisely the possibility Robert Putnam suggested in an op-ed piece written in the midst of the 2008 presidential primary season:

Last month the UCLA researchers reported that "For today's freshmen, discussing politics is more prevalent now than at any point in the past 41 years." This and other evidence led us and other observers to speak hopefully of a 9/11 generation, perhaps even a "new Greatest Generation."

Second, while Zukin and colleagues (2006) may be cautious in suggesting a "necessary" link between the civic and the political, they do not hesitate to identify the many—relatively economical—ways in which specifically "political" engagement can be enhanced. Indeed, they point to the success of the service-learning movement in fostering *civic* engagement as an example of what might be accomplished in the *political* sphere, were a comparable effort to be made there (p. 205). The key to such a possibility would seem to be curricular "scaffolding," for nothing except home environment seems to be more productive of youth engagement than what happens in school (pp. 142ff.).

Although Zukin and colleagues (2006) do not themselves use this term and do not organize their findings into a coherent educational strategy, it is not hard to draw practical, concrete lessons from their work. For the purposes of this chapter, those lessons can be grouped into two complementary strands. First, they found that structured reflection plays perhaps *the* critical role in helping to develop a commitment to engagement:

> Student volunteers who are encouraged to talk about their volunteer work in class are much more likely to stick with it. Fully 63 percent of high school and 58 percent of college students who volunteered within the last year had an opportunity to talk about their service work in the classroom. The members of this group are twice as likely to volunteer regularly as those who don't get a chance to talk about their experiences (64 percent versus 30 percent, respectively). They are also much more likely than those without such discussions to work on a community problem (47 percent versus 32 percent) or to influence someone's vote (50 percent versus 34 percent). (p. 145)

This is closely related to one of the key points the Wingspread students (Long 2002) make about the potential importance of service-learning: "Service-learning, with its rich integrations of readings, reflection, and class discussion, offers feedback and recognition and makes us realize that collectively we are a powerful force for social change" (p. 7).

Of course, this is not exactly news. Civic engagement scholars and practitioners have known for years that quality reflection is of critical importance to the full service-learning experience. Still, it is disturbing to see that *only* 58 percent of "college students who volunteered" had an opportunity to process their experiences in class, a figure that suggests that, despite what we know about reflection, we have not been putting that knowledge sufficiently into practice. This, in turn, suggests that, before we invest enormous time and energy in trying to replace or reconceptualize service-learning, we should test the far easier path of developing a new set of reflection resources, inclusive with regard to goals (e.g., critical thinking, mental models, policy implications) as well as disciplines and interdisciplinary areas. It was precisely this kind of deliberate investment in needed academic resources that led in the 1990s to the proliferation of discipline-specific course and program models, and that helped service-learning find greater acceptance not only in a wider range of academic departments but also in a wider range of academic publications. Our premise should be that if we want more faculty to help their students move beyond discrete community experiences in order to understand better the social and political systems in which those experiences are embedded, we should try to help them do so. Most faculty *need* help in teaching their students to think like citizens.

Yet we need not rely on quality service-learning alone to take faculty and student engagement to the next level. In addition to those activities that Zukin and colleagues (2006) see as constituting political and civic engagement, they identify activities in two other areas:

> One is *public voice*, the ways citizens give expression to their views on public issues. Included here are activities such as signing petitions, engaging in e-mail campaigns, starting or contributing to political blogs, or writing letters to the editor. Contacting public officials . . . may be the most direct type of expression of public voice. . . .
>
> The fourth type of activity is *cognitive engagement*, that is, paying attention to politics and public affairs. Cognitive engagement includes such activities as following the news in newspapers, talking about politics with friends and family, or simply being interested in public affairs. (p. 54)

Activities such as these, which establish a connection between the classroom and public concerns but do not require students to leave the campus or work with a community partner, could serve as a valuable complement to service-learning projects and would provide many more faculty with an opportunity to promote some form of public engagement. Zukin and colleagues (2006) conclude that schools have an especially powerful impact on student engagement "when they require students to develop specific civic skills," such as letter writing and debating, and that students who have developed these skills "are much more likely to be involved in a range of participatory acts inside and outside the school environment" (pp. 143–144).

Furthermore, since the development of such skills does not require faculty to stretch their understanding of relevant course work to the extent that many service-learning projects do, and since these skills can be readily adapted to almost any disciplinary context, failure to promote them actively and to make them an explicit part of an institution's overall public engagement strategy makes no sense. To be sure, breaking through faculty insecurities and faculty inertia—providing faculty with both the training and the intellectual resources they need to move forward with confidence—will require planning and persistence, but there already exist many models for how this can be accomplished. (See, for example, the resources available through the National Coalition for Dialogue and Deliberation [http://www.thataway.org/], the Kettering Foundation's Deliberative Democracy Exchange and Workshops [http://www.kettering.org/index.aspx], and The Democracy Imperative [http://www.unh.edu/democracy/index.html].)

MAPPING OPPORTUNITIES

Approximately ten years ago, I proposed in an essay called "Pedagogy and Engagement" (1999) that service-learning—in the fullest sense of the term—could be usefully understood as a form of teaching and learning that took place where two axes or creative tensions intersected, with

> a horizontal axis spanning academic expertise and a concern for the common good, and a vertical axis that links the traditional domain of the student—i.e., classroom activities—with that of those who teach and mentor him/her [in the community—i.e., community-based activities]. (p. 100)

I further proposed that one could visualize this arrangement as a conceptual matrix:

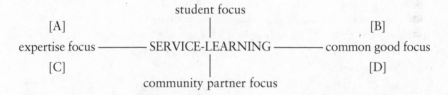

Most of the details of this matrix need not concern us here except to clarify that "expertise focus" referred to the academic content of the sponsoring course while "common good focus" pointed to extra-academic social and political factors that defined the larger significance of that course content. In the case of the vertical axis, "student focus" signified traditional classroom- and campus-based learning mechanisms, while "community partner focus" pointed to the experiential learning that occurred in and through community-based activities. Furthermore, the place where these two axes intersected was not fixed. As I wrote then, "Although the point where the two axes intersect will necessarily differ from one service-learning situation to the next, as either academic or civic learning, classroom or community experience is more or less emphasized, all four poles are always to some degree represented" (p. 101).

Over the past decade this matrix has proven itself to be quite serviceable in helping faculty identify both key components of and design options in service-learning courses. I believe, however, that it can also help map a range of civic engagement activities over and beyond service-learning, and in this way can help both institutions and individuals more easily and appropriately prepare their students for citizenship in a diverse democracy.

In this reinterpretation, the areas above and below the horizontal axis basically retain their original values in that this axis serves to demarcate teaching-learning activities of a more traditional kind from teaching-learning activities that require the participation of a community partner and are also designed to meet that partner's needs. The former would include lectures, class discussion, reports, debates, and other classroom-based activities—all, of course, having some kind of civic content or focus. The latter would include all direct service arrangements as well as documents and other deliverables framed in collaboration with a community partner and intended to increase that partner's capacity and enhance that partner's effectiveness.

The areas left and right of the vertical axis also retain much of their original significance. Activities that fall to the left of this axis demonstrate an immediate connection to academic knowledge and academic competencies while those to the right emphasize more generic knowledge and skills. Examples from the left side would include discipline-specific case studies taken from the public and nonprofit sectors, problem-based and problem-focused disciplinary courses, and the utilization of technical expertise to address a community or general public issue. Examples from the right side would consist largely of those generic civic skills Zukin and colleagues (2006) identify as so important to the development of a sense of civic and political efficacy, namely, developing a public voice through communication with public officials and the general public, awareness of public issues, and the ability to explain and debate them in nonexpert forums. This side would also include community-based experiences whose primary student benefit is to develop an awareness of public issues and community needs.

Each of the four quadrants (labeled A, B, C, and D) created by these intersecting axes can already boast a wealth of both theoretical and practical models. For example, most of the courses included in the Science Education for New Civic Engagements and Responsibilities (SENCER) digital library of the National Center for Science and Civic Education (2010) model traditional pedagogical strategies focused on public issues, public policy, and public problem solving in the sciences. Such discipline-specific, classroom-based work is the province of the A quadrant. On the other hand, the deliberative democracy initiatives identified in the last section of this chapter provide resources for the kinds of traditional classroom-based work signified by the B quadrant. Here the emphasis is less on mastery of disciplinary content or the acquisition of discipline-specific expertise than on the development of transferable civic skills, habits of mind, and ways of communicating that underlie the democratic process itself (though, of course, discipline-specific knowledge and competencies may also be involved).

Below the horizontal axis, community-based learning becomes a key part of the work at hand, and in C, the lower left quadrant—where disciplinary relevance is at a premium—many traditional service-learning projects could be located. For present purposes, however, perhaps it would be more useful to see this quadrant as the quadrant of "democratic professionalism." Dzur (2008) explains this concept when he notes that professionalism necessarily "has a civic dimension," and, "rightly understood, democratic professionals are some of the best candidates today for bolstering the deliberative democracy urged by contemporary commentators" (p. 10). For such professionals, dialogue and collaboration are built into the very definition of what it means to acquire and use expert knowledge. Demands for "reciprocity" and "community partnering"—which, in their service-learning formulation may strike some as external impositions on professional expertise—become in this way a dimension of professional identity through which civic roles actually "strengthen the legitimacy of professional authority" (p. 10). Van de Ven's *Engaged Scholarship* (2007) lends additional support to this argument by demonstrating how only active collaboration among all stakeholders can yield even the kind of technical effectiveness professionals claim to be able to deliver.

Finally, in D, the lower right quadrant, we come to community-based learning that does not depend on disciplinary or professional specialization. Many service-learning projects could be placed here, too, since not all such projects require technical expertise. Unfortunately, the fact that the activities associated with this quadrant often lack a strong element of academic specialization as well as a clear focus on policy issues can lead them to be seen as weak links in the chain of civic engagement opportunities. (Colby et al. [2003] explicitly single out "some kinds of direct service volunteer work, such as tutoring in after-school programs" as a form of civic involvement that does not "count as political" [p. 19].) Such mistrust is justified in that much of what one would locate here is—when lacking a developed reflection component—often little more than community service sponsored by a course. The potential of this quadrant, however, is enormous since it is, perhaps, precisely in this kind of engaged work that students have their best chance of outgrowing parochial cultural and socioeconomic attitudes. According to research undertaken by Daloz and colleagues (1996), "The single most important pattern . . . in the lives of people committed to the common good is . . . *a constructive, enlarging engagement with the other*" (p. 63; original emphasis). Again, the challenge in bringing about such engagement is primarily practical, not conceptual.

Taken together, these four modes of civic engagement or civic learning provide natural opportunities for faculty in every discipline and students at every stage of development to participate *naturally* in activities that promote democratic values and competencies. While the modes often overlap and may not be comprehensive, my point in introducing them in this manner is not to lay claim to an exact classification system, let alone to advance any new theory. The English poet Percy Bysshe Shelley (1975) once lamented, "There is no want of knowledge respecting what is wisest and best in morals, government, and political economy, or at least, what is wiser and better than what men now practice and endure. But we let '*I dare not* . . .' wait upon '*I would* . . .'" (p. 609; original emphasis). With all the civic engagement resources we have developed over the past fifteen years, we can hardly claim a "want of knowledge" respecting what can and should be done. Yet our efforts have evinced little larger sense of coherence, and we have not always planned strategically. We have, moreover, failed to mobilize one of our most important resources: students themselves.

Students as Colleagues

In the introduction to *Students as Colleagues: Expanding the Circle of Service-Learning Leadership* (2006), I and my coeditors, Nicholas Longo and James Williams (himself a student at the time), wrote, "In organizing and editing this book, we contend that service-learning's academic and social impact will, in fact, not be achieved until the circle of service-learning leadership is further extended to include students themselves" (p. 2). We based this statement on several arguments. First, we noted that students had played an important role in launching the current civic engagement movement in the 1980s, and they bring to civic engagement a distinctive kind of energy and vision. Second, the operational complexity of service-learning, especially when widely utilized at a university or college, places a practical burden on all involved. Bringing qualified students into leadership positions where they can work alongside faculty, professional staff, and community partners not only facilitates quality engaged work; it also gives these students a unique personal and professional development opportunity. Third, service-learning's very *raison d'être* demands student leadership. Referring to the 2001 Wingspread conference, we pointed out that "a major theme of the . . . gathering was creating platforms for student voice. Students . . . were critically aware that they are often treated like 'fine china' brought out to impress trustees and honored guests" (p. 6).

Our final rationale spoke directly to the potential of the current generation of students and briefly explored the unique circumstances and interests that help set them apart from their predecessors. Much of what we wrote has since been corroborated by others. Zukin and colleagues (2006) not only confirm the current generation's strong interest in community involvement but also note that in many of its social and political attitudes that interest points to new possibilities. For example, as a generational cohort, young people today are

> *less* cynical than older cohorts, including members of Generation X. And despite their lower level of involvement in traditional politics, both GenXers and, especially, DotNets [i.e., the current generation] are more likely than older Americans to believe that government should do more to solve problems, that government regulation of business is necessary, and even (for DotNets) that government generally does a better job than it gets credit for. (p. 190; original emphasis)

Such a relatively positive attitude toward government is especially worth noting because it complements an interest articulated by the Wingspread students, namely, an interest in having a greater say in the workings of their own educational institutions and their own educations. In the Wingspread document's (2002) section on student voice, the students note:

> We feel that the leaders of colleges and universities often consider the voices of trustees and donors to be more important than that of their

students, creating an academic atmosphere that is not necessarily conducive to civic engagement. . . .

In addition, students are generally unaware of how to participate
in the college community. They know little about the administrative
functions of higher education and are organizationally illiterate about
the particular universities they attend. Many of us who do try to navigate the bureaucracy often lack access to the institutional system. . . .
It is conceivable that colleges and universities do not educate students
about their bureaucratic pathways just so that students will not try to
"reform" the system. (pp. 11–12)

Not surprisingly, the Wingspread students are also very aware of what their
instructors do or do not do to facilitate quality community-based learning.
More often than not, their observations dovetail with critiques of the teaching-learning process made by scholars who have studied the contemporary
academy.

Thus, from a substantive standpoint, it is difficult to understand why students typically play so minor a role in the civic engagement movement—why
they are not regularly invited, for instance, to address professional conferences, collaborate on publications, or participate in think tanks. Indeed, it is
ironic that a movement so centrally concerned with democracy should be so
unconcerned about the pervasive absence of what is probably the single largest constituency affected by its work. Although faculty are and will remain the
ultimate arbiters of the curriculum, they are often open to serious student suggestions, and many of the students who have become deeply involved in civic
engagement are precisely the kind of students in whom faculty and institutions take pride. As Williams, the student coeditor of *Students as Colleagues*
(2006) frequently reminded his coeditors: "the current generation of
students . . . represents an ideal group with which faculty, staff, and administrators can renew both service-learning and the structures of the academy"
(p. 10). No less committed to the common good than activist students of the
past, they also demonstrate a degree of thoughtfulness and maturity many in
their parents' generation did not possess.

CONCLUSION

Given the amount of interest and activity the civic engagement movement
continues to generate, it does not seem to have plateaued, let alone "hit a
wall." It may, indeed, be developing as quickly as can be expected given the
academy's famous reluctance to change. Nevertheless, as this chapter has
tried to point out, the movement may not be taking maximum advantage
of the opportunities available to it. A preoccupation with more abstract, more
theoretical issues often seems to hold the attention of its leaders, and while
such issues are indeed intellectually rich, they may not yield the kind of "facts
on the ground" that could accelerate national momentum. In this regard,

I am reminded of the split that has long characterized disciplinary communities, whereby the national association, headquartered in Washington, D.C., and dominated by scholars from research-intensive universities, routinely sets an agenda that faculty at teaching institutions find irrelevant to their circumstances and concerns. While this may not currently be the case with civic engagement, one would certainly want to forestall such a development.

For the fact is that most faculty members at America's colleges and universities are teachers who do some research, not researchers who sometimes teach. Furthermore, what impacts that majority in deciding how and what to teach is often closely related to specific local circumstances, such as teaching load, sense of competence and preparedness, and availability of resources. I suspect very few faculty take theoretical or epistemological considerations into account when planning their semesters—even if such considerations implicitly inform their work. Hence, if the civic engagement movement wants to win a larger percentage of the nation's faculty to its side, it will need to meet them where they are: on the level of concrete opportunity. How many science faculty, for example, are aware that the SENCER project makes available over three dozen course models designed "to improve undergraduate STEM (science, technology, engineering and mathematics) education by connecting learning to critical civic questions"? (National Center for Science and Civic Education n.d.). And of those that are aware, how many receive institutional help in adapting those models to the needs of their departments and students? Helping hundreds, perhaps even thousands, of additional faculty appreciate the *discipline-specific* value of SENCER resources is only one of dozens of low-cost, potentially high-yield strategies of which the civic engagement movement could avail itself.

Implementing such a strategy would, of course, require leadership. Over the last few years, the American Association of Colleges and Universities (AAC&U) has begun playing a major role in putting civic engagement on the nation's higher education agenda. Campus Compact's network of state affiliates could also make a major contribution to any such undertaking. But in the end, as Toulmin's (1990) historical analysis and the overall thrust of this chapter suggests, the key change agents will probably have to be more local, namely, the individual community and civic engagement centers that have sprung up on so many campuses around the country. (For a partial list of such centers see "The Service and Service-Learning Center Guide to Endowed Funding" [2003] published by Campus Compact.)

Most centers, as currently constituted, would need to reorient themselves and assume a more deliberately academic focus. Partnering would still be an important concern, but familiarity with a wide range of civic course models and resources—whether or not off-campus work was involved—would now be essential. On most campuses this would probably require a closer working relationship between the community or civic engagement center and the faculty development office or program. This arrangement was, in fact, a key component of Portland State University's pioneering effort to make substantive civic and community engagement central to its institutional identity (Driscoll 1998). But even without such a formal arrangement, faculty development offices on many campuses have already played a key role in promoting both civic and community engagement as one path to teaching excellence. (See, for example, the service-learning resources available through the Center for Teaching at the University of Iowa [2007].)

I have already stressed the necessity of extending the circle of service-learning leadership to include qualified students. Moving to a more comprehensive approach to academic civic engagement only reinforces the importance of reaching out to students in new ways. In an essay entitled "Citizenship-Oriented Approaches to the American Government Course" (Bernstein 2010), Jeffrey Bernstein describes how he redesigned his American government course to help students acquire not just factual knowledge about American government but an entire "tool belt" (p. 27) of citizenship skills. Bernstein's class is large—approximately 100 students—and incorporating into it an effective experiential component would hardly have been possible had he not hit upon the idea of utilizing undergraduate student assistants. These were "honors students concurrently enrolled in an honors seminar on Cultivating Civic Competence" and their work in his government class counted as "the 'laboratory' part of their seminar" (p. 21). In the end, they became the "linchpins" in making his course design work.

The potential for and of such arrangements is vast, and dovetails very well with students' own inclination to be active at the local level. As "The New Student Politics" (Long 2002) explicitly points out, democracy is, to an extent, "place-based": "Students exercise their responsibility foremost at the local level where they can make direct connections and experience feedback that reassures them that their actions have a meaningful impact" (p. 5). For an initiative that so frequently stresses the importance of the political, the civic engagement movement has shown itself surprisingly uninterested in the kind of on-the-ground "political" organizing that could help empower more students as change agents in their own education. For that matter, the movement has shown little interest in reaching out to a whole host of potentially valuable allies, including socially aware businesses, service organizations like Rotary International, and local government.

Especially in his later years, Rorty never tired of pointing out to academics interested in a more just society, a more genuinely democratic America that social change does not come about as a result of finely tuned philosophical distinctions. In *Achieving Our Country* (1998), he suggested that in America at the end of the twentieth century a "cultural Left" had largely replaced a Left able to engage effectively in national politics and that concerned academics would have to learn to transition from the former to the latter. To make this transition, he thought these academics would have to "put a moratorium on theory" (p. 91). In *Cosmopolis* (1990), Toulmin makes an analogous distinction when he argues that the model of achieving a "'theoretical grasp'" is everywhere "giving way to a substantive ability to discover the local temporary relations" (p. 91) embodied in specific phenomena. I am not suggesting that the civic engagement movement needs to "put a moratorium on theory" or should abandon all attempts to achieve larger orders of intellectual clarity. I am suggesting that the weight of cultural history and the needs of the present moment encourage us, as members of that movement, to invest more in creating concrete tools and academic resources that our colleagues—inside and outside the academy—can use to make a difference.

REFERENCES

Benson, L., I. Harkavy, and J. Puckett. 2007. *Dewey's Dream: Universities and Democracies in an Age of Education Reform.* Philadelphia: Temple University Press.

Bernstein, J. L. 2010. "Citizenship-Oriented Approaches to the American Government Course." In *Citizenship Across the Curriculum,* ed. M. B. Smith, R. S. Nowacek, and J. L. Bernstein, 13–35. Bloomington: Indiana University Press.

Boyte, H. C. 2000. "The Struggle Against Positivism." *Academe* 86 (4). Available at http://www.aaup.org/AAUP/pubsres/academe/2000/JA/Feat/Boyt.htm.

———. 2004. "The Necessity of Politics." *The Journal of Public Affairs* 7 (1): 75–85.

Butin, D. W. 2006. "Disciplining Service Learning: Institutionalization and the Case for Community Studies." *International Journal of Teaching and Learning in Higher Education* 8 (1): 57–64.

Campus Compact. 2002. "Educating the Next Generation of Active Citizens: A Strategy for Deepening Civic Engagement in American Higher Education." Unpublished position paper.

Campus Compact. 2003. "The Service and Service-Learning Center Guide to Endowed Funding." Providence: Campus Compact.

Colby, A., T. Ehrlich, E. Beaumont, and J. Stephens. 2003. *Educating Citizens: Preparing America's Undergraduates for Lives of Moral and Civic Responsibility.* San Francisco: Jossey-Bass.

Daloz, L.A.P., C. H. Keen, J. P. Keen, and S. D. Parks. 1996. *Common Fire: Leading Lives of Commitment in a Complex World.* Boston: Beacon Press.

Driscoll, A. 1998. "Comprehensive Design of Community Service: New Understanding, Options, and Vitality in Student Learning at Portland State University." In *Successful Service-Learning Programs: New Models of Excellence in Higher Education,* ed. E. Zlotkowski, 150–168. Bolton, MA: Anker.

Dzur, A. W. 2008. *Democratic Professionalism: Citizen Participation and the Reconstruction of Professional Ethics, Identity, and Practice.* University Park: Pennsylvania State University Press.

Giles, D. E. Jr., and J. Eyler. 1994. "The Theoretical Roots of Service-Learning in John Dewey: Toward A Theory of Service-Learning." *Michigan Journal of Community Service Learning* 1 (1): 77–85.

Kendall, J. C., ed. 1990. *Combining Service and Learning: A Resource Book for Community and Public Service* 1–3. Raleigh, NC: National Society for Internships and Experiential Education.

Kimball, B. A. 1995a. *Orators and Philosophers: A History of the Idea of Liberal Education.* New York: College Board.

———. 1995b. "Toward Pragmatic Liberal Education." In *The Condition of American Liberal Education: Pragmatism and a Changing Tradition,* ed. R. Orrill, 3–122. New York: College Board.

———. 1997. "Naming Pragmatic Liberal Education." In *Education and Democracy: Re-imagining Liberal Learning in America*, ed. R. Orrill, 45–67. New York: College Board.

Lewin, K. 1951. *Field Theory in Social Science: Selected Theoretical Papers*. Ed. D. Cartwright. New York: Harper and Row.

Liu, G. 1995. "Knowledge, Foundations, and Discourse: Philosophical Support for Service-Learning." *Michigan Journal of Community Service Learning* 2: 5–18.

Long, S. 2002. "The New Student Politics: The Wingspread Statement on Student Civic Engagement." Providence: Campus Compact.

National Center for Science and Civic Education. n.d. "About SENCER: Overview." Available at http://www.sencer.net/About/projectoverview.cfm.

National Center for Science and Civic Education. 2010. "Resources: Model Courses." SENCER. Available at http://www.sencer.net/Resources/models.cfm.

Orrill, R. 1995. "An End to Mourning: Liberal Education in Contemporary America." In *The Condition of American Liberal Education: Pragmatism and a Changing Tradition*, ed. R. Orrill, ix–xx. New York: College Board.

Putnam, R. D. 2008. "The Rebirth of American Civic Life." *Boston Globe*, March 2. Available at http://www.boston.com/bostonglobe/editorial_opinion/oped/articles/2008/03/02/the_rebirth_of_american_civic_life/.

Richman, K. A. 1996. "Epistemology, Community and Experts: A Response to Goodwin Liu." *Michigan Journal of Community Service Learning* 3: 5–12.

Rorty, R. 1998. *Achieving Our Country: Leftist Thought in Twentieth-Century America*. Cambridge, MA: Harvard University Press.

———. 1999. *Philosophy and Social Hope*. London: Penguin.

Shelley, P. B. 1975. *The Poetical Works of Percy Bysshe Shelley*, ed. N. F. Ford. Boston: Houghton Mifflin.

Toulmin, S. 1990. *Cosmopolis: The Hidden Agenda of Modernity*. New York: Free Press.

Tucker, R. E. 1999. "Biting the Pragmatist Bullet: Why Service-Learning Can Do without Epistemology." *Michigan Journal of Community Service Learning* 6: 5–14.

University of Iowa. 2007. "What Is Service Learning?" *Center for Teaching*. Available at http://centeach.uiowa.edu/programs/servicelearning.shtml.

Van de Ven, A. H. 2007. *Engaged Scholarship: A Guide for Organizational and Social Research*. Oxford: Oxford University Press.

Zlotkowski, E., ed. 1997–2006. *Service-Learning in the Academic Disciplines*. 21 vols. Washington, DC: American Association for Higher Education.

———. 1999. "Pedagogy and Engagement." In *Universities as Citizens*, ed. R. Bringle, R. Games, and E. Malloy, 96–120. Boston: Allyn and Bacon.

———. 2005. "The Disciplines and the Public Good." In *Higher Education for the Public Good: Emerging Voices from a National Movement*, ed. T. Chambers, A. Kezar, and J. Burkhardt, 166–186. San Francisco: Jossey-Bass.

Zlotkowski, E., N. V. Longo, and J. R. Williams, eds. 2006. *Students as Colleagues: Expanding the Circle of Service-Learning Leadership*. Providence: Campus Compact.

Zukin, C., S. Keeter, M. Andolina, K. Jenkins, and M. X. Delli Carpini. 2006. *A New Engagement? Political Participation, Civic Life, and the Changing American Citizen*. London: Oxford University Press.

CHAPTER 11

Remapping Education for Social Responsibility

Civic, Global, and U.S. Diversity

CARYN MCTIGHE MUSIL

Very few commentators have made explicit the vital connection between the civic learning movement and its close cousin, the movement to support *campus diversity* and *diversity education*. However, as our colleges and universities, workplaces and cities, and public institutions become ever more enriched by cultural, ethnic, linguistic, and religious varieties of experience, mustn't we rethink the very definition of civic learning? Mustn't we prepare our students not merely for democratic life but for life in a *diverse* democracy?

—Rafael Heller (1999; original emphasis)

Higher education plays a key role in training leaders who are responsible for enacting a vision of a multi-racial democracy that is equitable, inclusive, and thrives as a healthy exchange of perspectives.

—Sylvia Hurtado (2006)

Global learning . . . must challenge students to gain deep knowledge about the world's people and problems, explore the legacies that have created the dynamics and tensions that shape the world, and struggle with their own place in that world. . . . Global questions require students to connect, integrate, and act.

—Kevin Hovland (2005)

INTRODUCTION: GOOD INTENTIONS UNREALIZED

In the fall of 1999, the Association of American Colleges and Universities (AAC&U) published a special issue of its quarterly journal, *Peer Review*, titled "Civic Learning in a Diverse Democracy," from which the above quotation from Rafael Heller is derived. The issue captured the dynamics between two powerful but self-contained education movements, each of which was cresting. One was connected to U.S. diversity; the other, to service in the community. In the first, there was frantic but fruitful attentiveness to an investigation of diversity, which was the harvest of the slow move from exclusionary to inclusionary campuses that gathered momentum in the last quarter of the twentieth century. In the second, campuses abandoned the isolation of their bounded property and became newly engaged in their local and regional communities. The latter movement was driven first by students' volunteerism and presidential leadership and later by faculty tying civic engagement to students' academic learning.

The 1999 special issue of *Peer Review* was spurred by a conference earlier that year held at the Johnson Foundation Wingspread Conference Center in Racine, Wisconsin, that brought academic and community leaders together to discuss the renewal of the civic mission of research universities. What should have been a coupling of two similar educational reform movements with shared goals became instead a conference that revealed the gulf separating them. The splintering has ultimately contributed to the inability of either movement to continue to make sufficient deep institutional change in higher education. This chapter argues that it is time to capitalize on the intellectual, pedagogical, and social power of both movements if higher education is to be equipped to educate students for responsible choices in the multicultural, interdependent, but deeply riven world they share.

AAC&U was invited to the Wingspread conference because of its national leadership in what by then was a seven-year signature initiative, American Commitments: Diversity, Democracy, and Liberal Education, of which I was associate director.[1] American Commitments had been working broadly within the academy through multiple strategies: direct faculty and curriculum development work with over 400 colleges and universities; focused work on reframing institutional leadership, policies, and practices; amassing research on the educational benefits of diversity; a library of new diversity books; establishment of a new quarterly publication on campus practice called *Diversity Digest* (renamed *Diversity & Democracy* in 2007); and the creation of a national website, DiversityWeb.org. The initiative's guiding inquiry examined both the deeply entwined drama of diversity and democracy throughout U.S. history as well as higher education's historic and contemporary responsibility to prepare students for life and work in the diverse democracy that the United States has always been.

In his reflection a decade ago about the Wingspread conference, Edgar F. Beckham, who had been a principal funder of AAC&U's American Commitments while he served as a program officer at the Ford Foundation, sought to understand what kept these two movements operating in parallel universes, despite the avowed desires by many leaders in both spheres to conjoin them. "Although civic education and campus diversity have each become an important and lively focus of academic reforms," Beckham wrote in *Peer Review*, "the recent Wingspread meetings illuminated how difficult it may be to bring these efforts together" (1999, p. 5). He attributed the rifts to three causes: differing representations of democracy's past, the language each group used to describe itself, and shallow notions of each other's work.

Ten years later, the three conundrums—and the rifts—persist. The focus of this chapter is to understand why and to suggest ways out of the self-imprisoning mazes they create. Much is at stake if these disabling disconnections continue. Rafael Heller has captured the distinction well. It is not enough to prepare students for democracy; rather, they must be prepared for *diverse* democracies. Without a clear understanding of the difference that the adjective makes, civic engagement—or even the new focus recommended by this volume's editors, democratic engagement—will be partial, hindered by underdeveloped concepts that will limit civic scholarship, teaching, and practice and thus its power to transform higher education.

The bifurcation of the civic engagement movement and the diversity movement—along with its kin, the global learning movement—continues to suppress the intellectually dynamic and educationally transformative power of all three educational reform movements. Each needs to embrace the fundamental insight: democracy is threatened or can be stifled entirely when stark inequalities persist. Diversity and global education movements have kept such historic and contemporary analyses of power and inequality at the intellectual forefront of their work. The civic engagement movement, on the other hand, has established a wide range of hands-on practices that engage students and higher education institutions directly in addressing pressing unmet social needs. It is time to braid these divided movements into one strand. Students deserve an education that prepares them to become responsible citizens deliberately working to repair dangerously stratified societies. Faculty and staff energies suffer from fragmentation when these individual educational reform efforts operate as if they lived in parallel universes rather than in a common one. Troublingly, community-based programs at the center of so much of the current civic engagement research and practice today falter, sometimes disastrously, when students and faculty are sent into neighborhoods and partnerships, here or abroad, with profound ignorance of the history, politics, culture, economics, or other factors that explain social inequalities and tensions.

While there has been progress, there has not been enough. On the vast majority of campuses and in professional associations organized to address the issues of civic, global, and U.S. diversity education, each too often operates as if the other two simply do not exist. When they do recognize one another, it is often in the context of tensions over resources, turf, and respect. Predictably, frustrations then arise about why higher education itself has not changed more quickly and why each enterprise has such difficulty moving to second-order change. Ironically, each has one foot firmly planted in the academy through scholarship, teaching, and campus life, and the other squarely anchored in the daunting challenges, both local and global, that threaten our shared futures. What the movements have thus far not succeeded in adequately doing is putting their remaining limbs around each other in understood solidarity of common, larger purposes. Nonetheless, I believe that it is possible to integrate civic, diversity, and global education, but I also recognize that it will not be easy.

Rather than waiting, however, until all three muster the intelligence, will, and skill to remedy the current conundrums, I have organized this chapter to address what the civic engagement leaders, scholars, and practitioners *themselves* might actually do from their positions of power to begin to address this debilitating dilemma. Within the limits of a single chapter and in the context of a volume written specifically for a civic engagement audience, such a strategy seemed the most efficacious. While I could make recommendations to diversity and global practitioners about what they might also do, I have focused on civic practitioners. As people who are invested in making democracy flourish at all levels, we civic practitioners should be especially well versed in how to bring disparate people together for common public purposes. It is time to practice what we preach, not outside the academy, but within it: not with external partners as much as with our own colleagues from other campus units or down the hall from our own offices. This chapter, then, will singly address what is in the power of civic educators themselves to enact.

GETTING THE CIVIC ENGAGEMENT MOVEMENT UNSTUCK

This section offers four recommendations that can be implemented whether higher education as a whole changes or not. That is, no one needs to wait for something to happen first, somewhere else, or through someone else before adopting the recommendations below. By incorporating them into how civic engagement is practiced on and off campuses, the civic learning movement will have a far more powerful effect in transforming higher education. Adapting these strategies will also dramatically improve the educational power of civic engagement itself, whatever its final nomenclature. Here, then, are the four immediate recommendations that could be started, but certainly not completed, tomorrow:

1. **Describing democracy:** Recognize the differing descriptions of democracy's past and define diversity back into the narrative.
2. **Deepening knowledge about diversity and global work:** Actively seek to learn more about the research, teaching, and civic work within the diversity and global educational areas of practice.
3. **Abandoning exclusionary habits:** Recognize and then actively disrupt old habits of exclusion in the civic engagement movement.
4. **Inventing integrative structures and patterns of collaboration:** Defy current structural impediments and build alliances with colleagues leading diversity and global campus initiatives.

Describing Democracy

Recognize the differing descriptions of democracy's past, and define diversity back into the narrative. There is little hope that the civic engagement reform movement can integrate diversity frameworks as part of its own

purposes if it does not first understand how such acts defy centuries of defining diversity *out* of democracy. That process has been a collective exorcism
for centuries. Too many academic civic practitioners perpetuate that exorcism, often unwittingly, but with similar consequences. Only in the last five
decades has diversity across multiple differences been partially restored as
part of the drama of democracy in the *national* narrative, despite the fact
that some of the most powerful civic movements in U.S. history have their
origins in populations excluded from full access to the promises of democracy: from struggles against religious discrimination to the abolitionist and
civil rights movement, the nineteenth- and twentieth-century labor and wom-
en's movements, and the contemporary disability rights and gay and lesbian
rights movements, to name only a few. Unfortunately, it is typically educators
identified as diversity practitioners who are making the most sustained cases
for analyzing diversity's contribution to democracy's progress. It is time for
civic educators as well to do their part in educating students about the historic
links between diversity and democracy to set the dominant narrative straight.
In fact, such education should be a centerpiece of civic engagement's scholarship and practice.

From the inception of U.S. democracy, the multicultural reality of its pop-
ulace and of the world was essentially excised out. Glossing over that history
has been a crippling conceptual fallacy within the civic engagement movement. So apparent was the multicultural nature of the young republic that the
government had to legislate exclusion through the Constitution itself, which
defined enslaved African Americans as chattel and white women as too insig-
nificant to be named as citizens. In that same period, the Naturalization Act
of 1790 wrote out another diverse group, extending citizenship to immigrants
only if they were white and male. A century later the 1882 Chinese Exclusion
Act made Chinese immigrants ineligible for citizenship, followed in 1924 with
the Asian Exclusion Act, which dramatically restricted Asian immigrants'
permanent residence, a bill that remained a law until 1965.

In Toni Morrison's provocative book *Playing in the Dark: Whiteness and
the Literary Imagination* (1993), she reminds readers both of the habit of pre-
tending an entire population has had no influence as well as the intellectual
absurdity of such a feint. She applies her critique in this instance to how such
efforts have played out in literary criticism. Morrison exposes how incongru-
ous it is to assume that "traditional, canonical American literature is free of,
uninformed and unshaped by the four-hundred-year-old presence of, first
Africans and then African-Americans in the United States" (pp. 4–5). Such a
delusion, Morrison continues, "assumes that this presence—which shaped the
body politic, the Constitution, and the entire history of the culture—has had
no significant place or consequence in the origin and development of that culture's literature" (p. 5). The same type of delusion is at work when diversity is
excluded from the concept and practice of democracy.

But these faulty assumptions have governed the dominant democratic
narrative, and the academy helped reinforce those inaccurate, exclusionary

notions. AAC&U's American Commitments initiative was launched to begin to correct the record and open up clogged intellectual arteries. The existing scholarship on which such misinformation rested was largely unchallenged for so long because higher education itself served a narrow slice of citizens for its first two hundred fifty years, despite its origins as a resource to strengthen the young colony and then the young democratic republic. Few who might have challenged such a diminished understanding of what democracy was or should be about were allowed entrance to the ivied halls for centuries.

Imitating restrictions on who can be a citizen, colleges regulated who could be students, faculty, and administrators. Until the middle of the twentieth century, clear restrictions denied women access to most colleges and universities or required that they be far more qualified than their male peers. Quotas were imposed on Jews and Catholics. African Americans and Latinas and Latinos were excluded either by law or effectively by practice until the 1960s, except in an apartheid higher education system that in the nineteenth century had accommodated historically black colleges, women's colleges, and, in some cases, religiously affiliated colleges. In the face of centuries of such deeply embedded habits, efforts to transform conscious or unwitting exclusionary structures into inclusionary ones pose formidable challenges, echoing similar contentious struggles within American society at large for full equality.

While civic educators have impressively involved students in unprecedented numbers working hand in hand with community partners, too often the historical context of the present work is under-theorized, under-studied, and unacknowledged. The scholarship, however, is readily available, the courses typically right there in the curriculum, and local community-based knowledge of the long legacy of exclusion a palpable reality of historical and lived experiences. Struggles for democratic inclusion are not only a matter of history but also an all too familiar part of many people's everyday contemporary lives. Even though charitable responses to people's unmet needs can be a positive motivation for civic engagement, these responses can sometimes leave the existing power structures unexamined, which contributes to social disparities in the first place. Campus-based civic work is diminished when stripped of deeper understandings about how such inequalities and human suffering came to be. To counteract that possibility, the Bonner Foundation's civic curricular model insists on a required gateway course focused on an analysis of poverty (Hoy and Meisel 2008, pp. 37–39). The foundation argues that the course is a necessary foundational piece for students' democratic engagement. Ultimately, the goal is to move from only civic altruism, that is, action by some for others, to civic prosperity, action by all for everyone's benefit (Musil 2003, pp. 4–8).

Deepening Knowledge about Diversity and Global Work

Actively seek to learn more about the research, teaching, and civic work within the diversity and global educational areas of practice. A recognition of both the historic and the contemporary struggles for full inclusion in democracy's promise is critical for civic educators to integrate throughout courses, in student preparations before going into local and global communities, and in the language civic educators use to describe civic engagement. Developing new expertise in this expansive scholarship, accrued especially within the past four decades, is crucial for both the practice and the future scholarship of civic work. Civic educators could begin by reading a handful of prominent texts, whose titles they can solicit from colleagues who teach in these areas or by doing private research scans. Here are three that offer a possible starting place: James Joseph's *The Remaking of America* (1995) describes how examining the historic legacies of communities of color offer rich lessons about democratic engagement, cultivating strong communities, and contributing to the public good. Similarly, the late Ron Takaki's *A Different Mirror: A History of Multicultural America* (1993/2008) chronicles the struggles for justice and democracy of Jewish Americans, communities of color, Irish Americans, and Afghanistan Muslims, among others, while Sara Evans's *Born for Liberty: A History of American Women* (1989) tells the dramatic story of women organizing, not without tensions and failures, across colors and classes for women's full inclusion in and improvement of the democratic experiment in the United States.

Immersing oneself in civic scholarship rooted in U.S. diversity and global learning should be regarded as an expected practice and an invigorating opportunity. Like all academic learning, it takes time and commitment, and it is most effective when done in conversation with others. AAC&U's curriculum and faculty development project within American Commitments understood this kind of intellectual investment as absolutely essential. It therefore organized three intensive, weeklong summer institutes between 1994 and 2000 called Boundaries and Borderlands: The Search for Recognition and Community in America, which were attended by hundreds of faculty, academic administrators, and student affairs professionals from 130 colleges and universities. Everyone realized we were charting new territory by suggesting there *was* a link between the scholarship of democracy and the scholarship of diversity that had not yet been well articulated. Our institutes included a series of eight topically arranged three-hour seminars that included more than 1,000 pages and several books focused on those two scholarly arenas by authors from wide-ranging disciplines, perspectives, and identities. Participants who served as cocreators of an emerging integration of these two disparate bodies of scholarship were subsequently tasked with the responsibility of appropriately weaving their new learning into the curriculum, pedagogies, and institutional practices at their home institutions.

While these institutes were externally funded, it is possible to initiate virtually thousands of smaller scale efforts that can deepen the knowledge of civic educators about both U.S. diversity and global learning without relying on outside funding. All colleges and universities have mechanisms for professional development. Civic educators could take the initiative to approach colleagues in diversity and global initiatives to confer about different ways of enhancing civic practitioners' knowledge about diversity. Teaching and learning centers frequently organize such opportunities, faculty retreats often give space for focused examination of new scholarship and teaching, and typically there are funding pots, even if they are small, for faculty and staff grants. Civic engagement programs could also take the initiative themselves and organize faculty development opportunities with their own resources, soliciting the expertise of local colleagues in diversity and global education.

At the University of Nebraska at Omaha, for example, the Service-Learning Academy organized a weeklong seminar to deepen faculty knowledge about the Latina and Latino history in preparation for initiating new service-learning opportunities in South Omaha. In addition to giving faculty themselves an immersion experience in service-learning at agencies under the leadership of local community leaders, the Office of Latino and Latin American Studies introduced scholarship about "Latino immigration to Nebraska, the history of South Omaha, the role of Latinos in regional and national politics, and the issues of identity and acculturation" (Sather and Bacon 2005, p. 9). From community leaders, faculty learned about important local factors affecting the lives in the Latina and Latino community such as local housing issues, the pace of work at the local meatpacking plant, and health issues.

Civic educators could also audit diversity and global courses or team-teach courses to delve deeply into unfamiliar scholarship and different framings. Like AAC&U summer institutes, the team-taught courses would themselves cocreate new frameworks across disciplines and scholarly areas of expertise and practice. On a smaller scale, civic educators could organize brown-bag lunch sessions to discuss articles or books, or they could use travel funds to attend conferences specifically with a U.S. diversity or global focus, where they could meet new colleagues, listen to what subjects dominate conversations, and become more familiar with differing cultural milieus.

In the process of deepening knowledge about global and diversity scholarship, civic educators could also familiarize themselves with the research, especially well developed within U.S. diversity, about the impact of diversity experiences on student learning, and, specifically for civic educators, about the impact of diversity on democracy outcomes. Sylvia Hurtado has been a leading researcher in this area along with Patricia Gurin, Jeff Milem, Mitchell Chang, Eric L. Dey, Anthony Antonio, and Daryl G. Smith, to name only a few. Hurtado organized a multiyear research project called Preparing College Students for A Diverse Democracy that explored the "links between diversity experiences, learning or cognitive development, and potential skills for civic engagement in a diverse society" (Hurtado 2006, p. 250). Her findings indicate that when students are exposed in constructive ways to different ideas through interaction with diverse peers in courses, campus, and community experiences, such disruptions of students' unquestioned world views, stereotypes, and internal scripts can trigger cognitive and democracy outcomes. Her discoveries have enormous implications for how civic practitioners design their programs. As she explains, "While the college curriculum may provide the theory and concepts necessary for understanding a multi-racial and multi-ethnic society, students' experience with others of diverse backgrounds (inside and outside the classroom) provides an opportunity to practice living in a pluralist democracy among 'equal status' peers" (Hurtado 2006, p. 265).

Abandoning Exclusionary Habits

Recognize and then actively disrupt old habits of exclusion in the civic engagement movement. The long, slow drama of diversity and democracy was matched by the excruciatingly long journey from practices of exclusion in the academy to those of inclusion. While the nineteenth century saw some progress, it was the twentieth century, especially the last half, that witnessed the democratization of higher education, a process that is not yet complete. At the beginning of the twentieth century, only 3 percent of Americans even went to college. By the end of the century, 75 percent of those who graduated from high school had access to a year or more of a college education. In terms of gender and race representation, in 2005 women made up 41 percent of full-time faculty at degree-granting institutions (Touchton, Musil, and Campbell 2008) and 16.5 percent of all faculty were of color (Snyder, Dillow, and Hoffman 2008); in terms of institutional leadership, in 2006, 23 percent of college and university presidents were women (Touchton, Musil, and Campbell 2008) and 14 percent of presidents were people of color (American Council on Education 2007). The period also led to expanding the canons of academic disciplines and transforming the designs of general education. With initiatives in admissions and in hiring, campuses around the country are more representative and inclusive than ever before.

But old habits are hard to break, even when so much has changed in the demographic profiles on campus, in who is authoring civic transformations in the curriculum and co-curriculum, and in the production of scholarship itself. Even though it is largely inadvertent, the civic engagement movement persists in recreating pockets of exclusion for its work. It need not do so. But in current everyday practice, the leaders and scholars who are most frequently held up as civic engagement spokespeople, even at this late date, are consistently white and male, whether speaking from a podium, authoring articles, or cited as references. Go to the footnotes in many of civic engagement's most frequently cited articles, and you will also typically see sparse references to the scholarship of people of color, white women, or voices from beyond the U.S. border.

However, civic scholars with authority over journals and book publications have the power to decide whom to invite as authors, reviewers, and editorial board members; what directives to give their authors about what to consider in articles; and how to organize topically across a wider spectrum of subject areas. As civic scholars, we could review citations in our own scholarly work to be sure we have named diverse scholars across many different perspectives. We could, in effect, practice a scholarship of inclusion in our civic work and, in doing so, expand and improve it.

Similarly, if one attends a civic engagement or democracy conference, typically its speakers, participants, and sessions lack diversity across race, ethnicity, class, religion, and other kinds of differences, all of which must be traversed successfully in serious, significant civic work in a country and globe as diverse as the one we share. To go against the grain of exclusionary practices typically requires one to actively and consciously become *inclusionary advocates*. Civic educators can assume that role. It would require civic leaders to always be sure someone who comes from a different kind of background, offering a different voice and set of experiences, is on the podium with them—or even instead of them. Civic conferences, publications, events, and programs could routinely be organized from their inceptions by a diverse group of people deliberately sought to bring the broadest range of participants and feature the fullest arc of civic work, a good deal of which occurs under the umbrella of diversity and global work. These are small gestures, but they can be implemented tomorrow and can have powerful long-term intellectual, civic, and political consequences.

In addition to leaders and scholarship, there are the exclusionary habits of language to break. What irritated many of the participants of color in particular at the Wingspread conference in 1999, for example, was the constant use by many white civic scholars of the term "reclaiming," "reviving," or "restoring" a previous civic legacy that had been allowed to wither. For contemporary racial minorities who understood that their forebearers were never permitted to be citizens, vote, or run for office, they looked back and didn't see practices they sought to restore. By contrast they identified with their own community's historic and contemporary struggle to *achieve* democracy's promise *in spite of* the "civic" culture of the day. They looked instead to their own community's practices that imbued them with values and skills in how to organize to take care of each other's needs in the shadows of larger, reputedly democratic civic structures that excluded them from participating and denied them equal access to the chance to succeed educationally, economically, and politically. It is exactly that divergent view on what "civic" means that needs to be at the heart of the civic engagement inquiries, whether in scholarship, campus programs, or community practice.

The language most closely identified with civic engagement includes "community service," "service-learning," "voting," "common good," "public good," "the individual," "civic knowledge and skills," "political participation" in elections, and "democratic" structures and practices. The words most often used in self-descriptions of diversity education are "social change," "social justice," "social movements," "identity," "intercultural knowledge and skills," "achieving equality," "power," "rights," and "recognition." As the language indicates, the civic has become the domain largely of those who have typically been able to exercise it; they assume agency. Diversity has become the domain largely of those who have had to struggle for civic rights or what is more popularly known as civil rights. They have had to exercise agency to obtain the right to be part of the civitas. It is no surprise that the lexicons of the two educational and social movements are different, but the origins and meanings of those differences are crucial to explore—*across* the two domains *with one another* so each can understand how the deep meanings of the language might enrich each other's work, correct historic misrepresentations, and change what democratic engagement means when it is inclusive.

When global language is added to the mix, the canvas both opens up and narrows. Global vocabulary frequently includes "cross-cultural," "transnational," "interdependency," "bilingual" or "multilingual," "experiencing the other," "globalization," and "global citizen." Inequalities evident in a U.S. context are magnified in a global context, but most study-abroad programs, one of the most visible manifestations of global education, overwhelmingly occur in first world, not developing countries where inequalities are less starkly apparent. Without the lens of diversity and the language of social justice, global education like charitable civic work can merely perpetuate structures that produce dangerous economic disparities. A faculty member in one of AAC&U's global curricular projects voiced with anxiety, "Are we simply producing the next and best educated generation of new American imperialists?" (pers. comm.).

Whatever language is employed is highly contentious both within and across all three movements. At a 2009 civic conference, Shawn Ginwright of San Francisco State University cautioned that pathways to traditional civic life are more available in schools where they are least needed and explained that often some of the most powerful civic expressions emerge in poor communities in the form of protesting current civic norms (pers. comm.). At that same conference, David Scobey of Bates College said, "The nature of the public realm for public work inevitably means you are crossing boundaries with others where you have common beliefs and values but not common experiences and identities" (pers. comm.). However, in the process of interrogating language use, essential insights about means ascribed, differential group histories, and perspectives driven by geographic vantage points can be fruitfully explored. Engaging in sustained, self-revealing, and self-reflective dialogues emerge, then, as a necessary component if we are to move to greater integration and complementarity across civic, diversity, and global learning.

Inventing Integrative Structures and Patterns of Collaboration

Defy current structural impediments and build alliances with colleagues leading diversity and global campus initiatives. When I visit campuses trying to map the interrelationships of the three reform movements, I typically have to visit at least three different centers—a multicultural center, a civic engagement center, and an international center. Most often there is nary an intellectual, personnel, or activity footbridge between them. The structures, focus of attention, budgets, and personnel for what is actually common work have been parsed into splintered pursuits. Each of the three centers is also asked to do a great deal of activity on a very modest budget. Students stream through each center, but in most cases they, too, are differently segmented student groups who don't realize how much in common they share. As Hurtado (2007) concurs, "The diversity initiatives and civic initiatives inhabit distinct physical, social, and administrative space" (p. 185).

Although this situation is changing on some campuses, most often each of those centers is run by someone located in student affairs, typically without a doctorate. That can, but should not, make those centers themselves divided from their academic counterparts in the faculty or academic administration, which only compounds the fracturing across the different centers. There is often further splintering within each of the three areas. There might be a volunteer community-service center, an urban center, and a service-learning center that may or may not coordinate with one another. There might be a women's center that has little contact with an academic women's studies program. The challenge to create more inclusive, coherent, and collaborative partnerships is a daunting one, even *within* global, diversity, and civic structures, let alone *across* them.

But cross these divides we must if we hope to transform our respective work and higher education as a whole. It is time for civic educators to do what is in their power to do so this critical work can commence. In some cases that means inventing new positions and new structures. Increasingly, colleges and universities have tried to create high-profile positions that integrate multiple units under one administrative home that promises to address the current fragmentation and lack of coordination. This trend of linking responsibilities for civic and diversity initiatives was apparent in recent applications by institutions seeking the Carnegie classification for a unit of community-engaged campuses. Such a trend was echoed in the eighty institutional profiles submitted for an AAC&U global forum in 2009. In the latter case, the links were often made across civic, global, and diversity work.

The University of Minnesota also repositioned its Office for Equity and Diversity under Vice President and Vice Provost Dr. Nancy "Rusty" Barceló, who is now president of Northern New Mexico College, and brought together previously dispersed multicultural units under a single administrative unit, which, in turn, has allied itself with civic work by decisively redefining itself within the university's public mission. Campus-wide involvement produced a cutting-edge document in 2009, *Reimagining Equity and Diversity: A Framework for Transforming the University of Minnesota*, whose title etches lines on a new institutional map. Equity and diversity work are cast as integral to Minnesota's civic mission, and together they promise deep transformation of how the institution organizes itself and defines its priorities. The document uses language that braids multiple units and asserts that they share fates. It refers to "integrative vision," "shared responsibility," "linking expertise and resources," "aligning across units," and making "university transformation a collective enterprise." In a radical reconception, the document inverts the pyramid by locating its narrow point squarely in the public mission. The university both serves and partners with diverse communities from which everything else derives. The document also posits that future collective work should be driven by seven core values that combine crosscutting values: social justice, excellence, system-wide collaborations, community engagement, accountability, sustainability, and transformation (Office for Equity and Diversity 2009, p. ii).

To move toward similar reimaginings of a collective larger purpose, campuses could do a variation of women's commissions, those campus-wide structures designed to bring all the concerns of women under one umbrella. Diversity practitioners imitated the same structure for comprehensive diversity work. To jumpstart progress in braiding what are now separate strands, it is time for an administrative structure or convening to bring together those working in civic, U.S. diversity, and global arenas. It could name itself the Commission on Our Shared Futures. Initially, such a convening can be authorized from the top or not, since grassroots organizing often begins from the bottom up before it is recognized institutionally. Eventually, it should secure official sanctions. Such a convening could map out where the three are doing work, where such work could be strengthened through partnering, how they might join forces to increase and share resources, and what locations promise fruitful collaborations, such as new interdisciplinary general education arenas, resident life and learning centers, or new investments in community-based partnerships both here and abroad. The group might devote time to discussing, agreeing upon, and then working as allies within their institution to implement ongoing structures that integrate, accelerate, and facilitate their joint work, which will in turn transform their institutions.

Think of how such a conversation might blast apart what "counts" as civic work in the curriculum for just one example. In this volume's introduction, the authors use the number of service-learning courses as one of the key means of measuring progress in interjecting civic learning into the curriculum. What might the numbers look like if people around the Commission on Our Shared Futures began to identify courses that also addressed issues of power, privilege, social stratification, and struggles for justice? And how might those numbers expand if diversity courses with a social-change focus were included that spanned such departments as ethnic studies, women's studies, labor studies, and disciplinary-based diversity courses within majors?

By remapping what civic means and does, what "counts" as civic could expand dramatically by also acknowledging kinship with innovative general education requirements for U.S. diversity and global studies. The University of Buffalo, for example, requires a freshmen-level course, World Civilizations, and a sophomore course, American Pluralism and the Search for Equality. St. Edward's University in Austin, Texas, offers sequential general education requirements that begin with the American Experience and American

Dilemmas in sophomore year, the Identity of the West and Contemporary World Issues in junior year, and culminate in a senior year capstone course analyzing a controversial issue and proposing a resolution. Wouldn't those "civic" numbers also grow if the newly convened group counted global courses organized around social change and social responsibility, questions about human rights, post-colonial struggles, United Nations Millennium Development Goals, sustainability, poverty, peace, or emerging democratic experiments? In the fall of 2009, Worcester Polytechnic Institute launched innovative, team-taught, interdisciplinary, problem-based freshmen seminars organized around global themes. Among the series are Feeding the World, Fueling the World, and Healing the World. How might other conversations with the Commission on Our Shared Futures lead to other programmatic connections, themed clustering of courses, new concentrations within majors, new majors, new joint research projects, or new team teaching? Collectively, such a remapping offers a more accurate sense of the full force of what democratic engagement across difference and geared toward social responsibility might actually look like.

Under the current divide-and-weaken status quo, global studies is expected to keep its focus on the world beyond the U.S. border, while diversity educators plant their intellectual and civic feet resolutely within U.S. boundaries. Those presumably clear lines have, however, become more complex as communities of color in the U.S. today represent such a rich, varied, and high proportion of new immigrants from around the globe, and the United States is, after all, part of the globe, not a separate planet unto itself. Similarly, civic educators serve and partner with local communities for the most part, but as they increasingly do their work in global contexts and serve new immigrant communities, they find themselves straddling both local and international territories, providing again another very fertile location for cross-pollination among the three spheres of educational reform. Some global studies programs like Arcadia University or Pacific Lutheran University, for example, link their study-abroad experience to a follow-up course that explores the concept of global justice within a disenfranchised local community at home.

Ana Maria Garcia, a professor at Arcadia, initially was suspicious that the exotic attraction by many to global education would erase discussion of the inequalities so central to U.S. multiculturalism. However, her global colleagues continued to reach out to her as they both listened to her concerns and shared their AAC&U global institute reading of Paul Farmer's *Pathologies of Power*. The combination provided Garcia with a way to embrace global learning without sacrificing her deepest intellectual and personal commitments: "I now realize that . . . global diversity and U.S. multiculturalism are closely intertwined by threads of power and privilege. Across the globe social realities operate within the contexts of inequality, of 'birthright' poverty, and of racism. . . . My work is now informed by the recognition that the local is the global, and that powers work inside and across borders" (2007, p. 5).

Convening a group or a commission could start with a small step, tomorrow. It would be radical and potentially transformative if civic educators on campuses across the country invited their counterparts in global and/or diversity studies out to lunch one day to plan how begin to meet regularly to explore common commitments, complementary areas of expertise, and possible collaborations. Such proactive outreach to diversity and global peers on campus, in effect, initiates multicultural alliance-building right inside the campus itself. It might also be the first step toward convening that Commission on Our Shared Futures. At a minimum, it might be the first step in planning common programming across centers and across student and academic affairs. It might result in sharing economic and in-kind resources to support one another and ultimately have greater impact within and beyond the campus. It might lead to a collaborative research project or even some paired hiring. And those changes might all be initiated by deliberate inclusive actions—extending a simple invitation to lunch.

RECONFIGURING CIVIC ENGAGEMENT ON CAMPUS: WHAT ARE THE LEVERS FOR CHANGE?

There are several levers that campuses are turning to in order to accelerate their ability to reconfigure the focus of the civic work and build alliances with diversity and global practitioners. Three levers have proven especially productive: adopting more unifying concepts to shape the work, recognizing similar pedagogical practices, and rallying around common educational commitments that are necessary in this global century.

Concepts

A concept like "citizenship," for instance, offers an intellectual footbridge across the three spheres of inquiry. It has long been a centerpiece of civic work, long sought as a right within diversity work, and used to capture cross-national responsibilities in global work. Examining the contested nature of each term in all three locations and the differing and similar usages of the term in the separate fields of inquiry and practice is yielding new levels of integration and cross-collaborations. In AAC&U's global research project that examined college mission statements, both preparing for citizenship and global citizenship were newly asserted as institutional goals.

Similarly, the term "democracy" offers common space for scholarship, teaching, and practice. AAC&U, for instance, is a member of a steering committee for the International Consortium for Higher Education, Civic Responsibility, and Democracy (IC) headquartered at the University of Pennsylvania. Since its initial collaboration began in 2000, the IC's partnership with the Council of Europe (CoE) has involved hundreds of colleges and universities, primarily in Europe and the United States, in joint forums, research projects, and publications. The IC and CoE steering committee also cocreated a draft of a declaration of principles to guide transnational efforts to educate for democratic engagement that was approved in principle by participants during the first global forum in 2006 (International Consortium 2006). Institutions and governmental bodies indicated their approval by joining a global network of member institutions and associations, and members have contributed examples of practice, available on the IC website. Again, the contested nature of the term and its forever incomplete practice provide rich intellectual space for cooperative and integrative inquiry and practice.

Flowing from democracy are the twin terms "social responsibility" and "social justice," which are emergent crosscutting terms that suggest both agency and public policy action. Both concepts also help move civic engagement from purely service to also advocacy, and from a cautiously apolitical stance to an unabashedly political but not doctrinaire one. There is evidence that more civic engagement programs are using the term "justice" or "social justice" in their mission statements and learning goals. The concept is absolutely central to U.S. diversity work across its multifaceted academic areas. While the term seems less common in global work, the concept is implicit in efforts to generate global commitments to remedy the world's deep inequalities, which are visible in efforts like the United Nations Millennium Development Goals, increasing cooperation about sustainability, and ongoing cross-national movements about human rights. When AAC&U launched its Core Commitments initiative in 2006 to promote personal and social responsibility as an essential rather than an optional learning goal for undergraduates, its first open symposium attracted 450 people from 265 different institutions. More than 300 presidents have also pledged to champion these outcomes, and many campuses find the term offers an expansive umbrella for civic, global, and diversity work.

A triumvirate of interlocking concepts holds promising intellectual and practice space for integration and collaboration: identity, recognition, and community. Identity and recognition are absolutely central to the intellectual framing of U.S. diversity work and directly tied to social movements by marginalized groups seeking recognition of their full worth and dignity, which has been typically linked to acquiring full rights as citizens. Post-colonial struggles documented in global scholarship are often organized around these same struggles. These concepts are used, for example, in the influential book *Multiculturalism: Examining the Politics of Recognition* (Taylor et al. 1994), and Arab writer Amin Maalouf, now living in France, explored a different context in his book *In the Name of Identity: Violence and the Need to Belong* (2003).

Three recent pieces argue powerfully for giving more prominence to identity and recognition as a defining dimension of civic work, with the understanding of how identity formation is inextricably tied to one's inherited and self-chosen communities. In 2003, a civic engagement working group organized through AAC&U's Greater Expectations[2] described its theoretical model of the civic-learning spiral as being composed of three parts. The first component is self, understood to be an identity embedded in relationships, in a social location, and within a specific historic context, that then, in dynamic interplay, influences and is influenced by the other components of the civic spiral that includes communities, values, skills, knowledge, and public practice (Musil 2009, pp. 59–63). L. Lee Knefelkamp authored the groundbreaking lead article, "Civic Identity: Localizing Self in Community," for *Diversity & Democracy* (2008), which argues that civic identity is "an identity status in its own right," and should be "one of the outcomes of a liberal education." She proceeds to articulate its essential characteristics, including "deliberately chosen and repeatedly enacted aspects of the self" (pp. 1–2). She lays out the multiple ways the academy can contribute, paramount among them, "students need to witness the academy's ongoing commitments to creating a more just society" (p. 3).

Similarly, Anne Colby, an advisory board member of AAC&U's Core Commitments and noted scholar on civic and moral development whom Knefelkamp draws upon as an authority, coauthored "Strengthening the Foundations of Students' Excellence, Integrity, and Social Contribution" with William M. Sullivan (2009), in which they, too, make links between identity, recognition, and community. They argue that higher education needs to "pay attention to questions of meaning, purpose, and personal identity in the classroom" (p. 29) because of "the critical role that moral and civic identity play in making espoused values real in one's own behavior" and because of higher education's power to "contribute to . . . that evolving sense of self positive ideals, concern for the common good, and a strong sense of responsibility" (p. 24). They go on to articulate the connection between identity, the desire to learn, developing motivation and purpose, and experiential knowledge-in-action practice. The two scholars name one other key developmental factor: repeated experience in taking seriously the perspectives of others. "Engaging diverse perspectives on issues that are important to them," Colby and Sullivan assert, "leads students to rethink their identities, their moral values, and other unquestioned assumptions toward the achievement of a more mature and thoughtfully examined identity" (p. 28). The ground is thus already laid for ways in which civic educators have a fertile space for future work with their diversity and global counterparts by linking identity, recognition, and community.

Pedagogical Practices

This is the low-hanging fruit of collaboration and integration across civic, diversity, and global work. Prominent in all three is the pedagogical practice of *dialogue*. In civic work it is typically called "deliberative dialogue"; in U.S. diversity work, "intergroup dialogue"; and in global, it is known as "intercultural dialogue." In all three, the practices are well honed, the scholarship well defined, and the research on its impact on learning well documented. What is missing is the recognition across the three of their shared practice, what can be learned from each other, and how to use this shared practice as a common organizing strategy for shared work, whether in classroom pedagogy, community based dialogues, or global interactions. In many of the campus-based civic engagement program examples included in the next section, the importance of dialogue across differences is more frequently explicitly stated as a necessary aspect of civic learning. There is extensive research across all three areas of its power to accelerate complex learning, share personal stories, listen more effectively, recognize differing points of view, and hone collaborative problem-solving skills.

Another area in which all three already work in similar pedagogical domains is *community-based learning*. When black studies, women's studies, and other U.S. diversity academic programs were initiated, the practitioners of each program had a sense of themselves as the academic arms of existing social movements. These origins affected their scholarship, course subject design, pedagogies, and engagements with communities beyond the walls of the academy. Learning from, with, and for the benefit of the community is threaded through these academic programs, which, in their co-curricular formulations, typically also have strong ties with community concerns and a history of community partnerships. Activist students flock to these courses and programs in disproportionate numbers. Civic-engagement work through voluntary service programs, academic service-learning, community-based research projects, and entrepreneurial economic development partnerships with community leaders and organizations has the most developed and integrated infrastructures for organizing the work on a larger scale. Global education is just beginning to do more of the community-based learning and research in its courses, with institutions like Worcester Polytechnic Institute taking the national lead. The school's Global Perspectives Program involves 50 percent of all WPI students in semester-long academic projects in their junior year to address pressing community issues defined by governments, nonprofit organizations, and local citizens. These include everything from health and human services in Bangkok to transforming squatters' villages into ecovillages in Cape Town, green building design in Worcester, and water and sanitation in Windhoek, Namibia.

The last shared practice to highlight straddles both pedagogy and scholarship: the emerging and newly recognized field of *public scholarship*. It has developed sufficiently to now have its own literature of debate about what public scholarship means or should mean, but it captures efforts, as one set of authors describes it, to bring academic scholars and students "into public space and public relationships in order to facilitate knowledge discovery, learning, and action relevant to civic issues and problems" (Peters et al. 2003, p. 73). Research institutions, where scholarship is the coin of the realm and necessary for tenure, have begun to define guidelines for public scholarship so it is counted, rewarded, and recognized in tenure and promotion decisions. Institutions like the University of Minnesota, Pennsylvania State University, Cornell University, University of Michigan, Stanford University, and Syracuse

University have taken the lead on establishing, defining, and valuing public scholarship in professional faculty advancement.

Public scholarship has obvious relevance to civic engagement work, but it has already been the purview of scholarship in U.S. diversity scholarship, which, like civic work, often roots its research within the community and community contexts, and which understands its scholarship as being profoundly about advancing social justice movements. Well-known African American and feminist scholars like bell hooks and Cornell West have long carved out a different kind of scholarship as public intellectuals both trying to engage with a broader nonacademic public through their scholarship and through traditional scholarship that is the result of deep engagement with publics. The Institute on Ethnicity, Culture, and the Modern Experience at Rutgers University–Newark organizes itself to integrate scholarship, teaching, and mutual engagement in civic life using public scholarship as a means for doing that and Newark as the source of investigation and partnership. As described at a 2005 AAC&U meeting in New Jersey, in a presentation by the institute's director, Clement Price, the institute has fostered fascinating local and global scholarship, like Kimberly DaCosta Holton's investigation of the traditional white Portuguese American population in Newark as it intersects with more recent immigrants, most of whom are of color, from Brazil. Holton has continued to publish widely on this topic in scholarly journals and her two books, *Performing Folklore: Ranchos Folclóricos from Lisbon to Newark* (2005) and *Building Ethnic Communities: Portuguese Immigration to the Northeastern United States* (forthcoming). The two ethnic communities share language and some cultural customs, but the Brazilian immigrants' own experience as a former colony of Portugal generates a complex relationship between the colonized and the historic colonizer, as does the differently racialized responses to their presence in the United States.

Educational Commitments

Finally, one of the levers that should create common ground on which civic, diversity, and global educational reform movements can foster greater integration and collaboration is their *shared educational commitments*. The three actually helped invent and promote what are emerging, even if they are not yet always practiced, as consensus educational goals that define what students need for the diverse, interdependent world where they will live and work. AAC&U describes these as Principles of Excellence in "College Learning for the New Global Century":

- Teach the arts of inquiry and innovation
- Engage the Big Questions
- Connect knowledge to choices and action
- Foster civic, intercultural, and ethical learning
- Assess students' ability to apply learning to complex problems

The academy is coming to recognize that students learn best when they are applying what they know to real-world problems, when they see the relevance of knowledge inquiry to pressing issues in their home communities, when they view themselves as creators of knowledge, and when they engage in learning through dialogue and deliberation with others. These principles help the academy enact the larger purposes that this volume is calling for, and these principles are driving overall higher education reform today. This all makes it an ideal moment for civic, diversity, and global programs to join forces through their scholarship, pedagogy, and community-based work to illustrate effective ways these principles have been put into practice.

The final overriding educational commitment that all three share is the practice of asking faculty, staff, and students to walk the walk as well as talk the talk. Civic learning takes practice, as does learning about diversity and global knowledge. All three educational spheres have a history of fostering communities of practice. By remapping their relationships to one another, they can more comprehensively offer students the moral and civic rehearsals that will help them become socially responsible and morally anchored in democratic engagements for justice in life's big, messy, urgent questions.

CAUSING PARALLEL LINES TO TOUCH:
ENACTING THE VISION

Reconfiguring the intellectual contours, structural embodiment, and everyday behaviors on and off campus is a formidable undertaking. While there are flashes of new architecture emerging from the shadows of the old academy, I could find no institution that had integrated civic, global, and U.S. diversity components in a pervasive way. Most were just beginning to figure out how to weave together even two strands, and those were usually evident only in singular programs or initiatives. The challenging but invigorating work is before us. No guidebook yet exists for this territory; no blueprint can be unfolded for us to follow. Instead, this next decade will need to be one of invention, experimentation, and exploration.

The challenge will require colleges and universities to redefine how, where, and under what conditions they will engage with local, national, and global communities. Those partnerships will need to be driven by ethical questions about what promotes more just, humane, and equitable societies. Without abandoning their central mission to advance knowledge, they will need to ask new questions about how knowledge is applied, who is benefiting from it, and how it addresses enduring questions and urgent social problems that affect our shared futures and the planet's sustainability. A remapping will redraw the boundaries between disciplines and inevitably demand more interdisciplinarity. Structurally, the academy desperately needs new architectural drawings that can untangle the fragmented, stratified compartments that interfere with holistic education and democratic engagement. Finally, the academy needs to vigorously continue its long march toward providing full access to higher education, whether as students, faculty, staff, or its senior leaders.

While no institution can be held up as an exemplary model of having braided the three disparate educational reform movements and thus transforming higher education, the still largely inchoate shape has begun to have visible map lines within some institutions and programs. Below are some examples of partial integrative conceptual and practice models that give hope of what may emerge more fully. In her book *Civic Engagement in Higher Education: Concepts and Practices*, Barbara Jacoby (2009) describes how the Coalition for Civic Engagement and Leadership at the University of Maryland in College Park defines civic engagement. The use of the word "coalition" in its name and the reconciling, more political language quoted below suggests that the university has convened some version of the Commission on Our Shared Futures. Vestiges of global, civic, and U.S. diversity values comingle throughout. Maryland's coalition explains that to be civically engaged is to act "upon a heightened sense of responsibility to other communities . . . and [encompass] the notions of global citizenship and interdependence" (Jacoby 2009, p. 9). The coalition's definition braids together through its language inviting, inclusive phrases and concepts when it claims that civic engagement involves, among other things, learning from others, self, and environment to develop informed perspectives on social issues; valuing diversity and building bridges across difference; behaving, and working through controversy with civility; developing empathy, ethics, values, and a sense of social responsibility; and promoting social justice locally and globally.

The University of Southern California's Center for Diversity and Democracy, affiliated with the Department of American and Ethnic Studies, which is already an unusual integration of two academic disciplines, chose its name carefully because, as their director George J. Sanchez (n.d.) argues, "We do not believe one effort can seriously advance without the other." Encouragingly, newer centers like the Center for Civic Engagement at Drew University, though still modest in scope, has embraced strong, inclusive language in its mission statement: "We believe that well-informed civic participation and the active pursuit of a just and humane society are crucial to a strong democracy and the vibrant communities that make up its fabric" (Drew University, n.d.). The center includes international arenas for their civic work as well as local ones.

The California State University system of twenty-three different campuses offers a model of how an enabling larger infrastructure, in this case called the Center for Community Engagement, can expand civic vision and practice, thus making the parallel worlds of civic, global, and U.S. diversity actually touch. In 2006, the center offered mini-grants to eleven campuses, several of which are integrating diversity themes across their service programs and using service as a platform for a far more ambitious set of educational and societal social-change goals (California State University 2008). The Monterey Bay campus, already a nationally exemplary program because it had integrated diversity as one its core defining dimensions of civic engagement, chose to work on first year seminars required of all students. The goals of the seminars are to have students show an understanding of diverse personal, cultural, and global perspectives; build an academic learning community that fosters cross-cultural communication; enable students to engage in difficult dialogues with others who are different from themselves; find their voice and know it matters; and develop a passion for the common good. The Chico campus allocated its grant to explore the civic-learning outcomes of interpersonal participation skills, especially across difference; knowledge of community and civic issues; knowledge of community values; and responsibility for the common good. For its part, California Polytechnic was seeking to establish a set of progressive civic-learning outcomes across courses that moved progressively from values and attitudes to civic knowledge, then to global responsibility, and finally to personal commitment.

Another mode of using a consortium to integrate diversity issues, spur interdisciplinary and cross disciplinary collaborations, and create more just democracies by focusing on a common topic, in this case health care, is represented by the Community-Campus Partnerships for Health (CCPH) under the able leadership of Sarena Seifer. The organization's subtitle, Transforming Communities and Higher Education, makes explicit its larger, unapologetic political goals. Housed at the University of Washington, the coalition of over 2,000 communities and campuses embraces the three typical organizing principles in higher education—research, teaching, and service—but locates community engagement, as the University of Minnesota's document did, at the center of these, as shown in a Venn diagram on their website. The partnership explains that its ultimate goal is to apply "institutional resources to address and solve challenges facing communities through collaboration with these communities" (Community-Campus Partnerships for Health 2010). Engagement has replaced outreach, yet CCPH does not shy away from the importance of research. In fact, it helpfully distinguishes between the three terms, defines what makes some community-based work research, and has developed extremely useful guidelines for how to create persuasive tenure and promotion portfolios. CCPH's milestone report, "Linking Scholarship and Communities" (2005) could apply as a template for other disciplines. The report underscores the connections among diversity, global, and civic work when it asserts, "Recruiting and retaining diverse community-engaged faculty members are essential to developing and sustaining the community partnerships that form the foundation for community-based teaching, research, and service." Importantly, the authors also argue that "community engagement can enhance the rigor and facilitate study of issues and research questions not effectively studied apart from communities, such as health disparities" (Commission 2005, p. 6).

Syracuse University has assumed aggressive and visionary leadership in central New York under its chancellor, Nancy Cantor, who has seeded and nourished democratic engagement throughout her professional career and consistently advocated integrating the lessons of diversity as touchstones to educating for democracy. The scope, ambition, and commitment to remapping education for social responsibility at Syracuse offers one of the clearest road maps to what deep institutional transformation might look like when a civic vision is informed by social justice values and a keen sense of the differential experiences of democracy across multiple groups. The university has launched a region-wide massive collective enterprise with many partners engaged in economic and social development throughout the city of Syracuse. Building upon a distinguished legacy within the faculty, the university launched an initiative under the rubric of Scholarship in Action, which describes its methods as "draw[ing] upon [the] institution's traditional and emerging strengths [and] connecting our academic excellence to ideas, problems, and professions in the world as we engage pressing issues of our time" (Office of Publications n.d., p. 2). Scholarship in Action thus underscores that academic expertise is not at odds with promoting the public good but can be a means to that end. The university's senate has unanimously passed a new version of the Faculty Manual, establishing guidelines for integrating consideration of public scholarship into tenure and promotion decisions. Internally, the Chancellor's Leadership Projects fund scholarly collectives to bring faculty, students, and community experts together to address thorny problems.

Through external funding and internal realignment of resources and rewards, Scholarship in Action has unleashed a dizzying series of well crafted, locally based, connected enterprises that link students and faculty and staff on campus with a wide range of partners off campus. With major funding of nearly $14 million from Syracuse University and New York state, they seeded a thriving collaborative network of members, organizations, institutions, and firms working closely in all cases with community members functioning within a new 501(c)(3) to coordinate the flood of newly generated projects within and beyond the university. Students and faculty engagement occurs at every conceivable level. One of those new efforts is the West Side Initiative, which involves "multiple projects aimed at rebuilding the residential and commercial vibrancy of the neighborhood," a historic, working-class industrial section of the city that is one of its most racially diverse and economically depressed. The collaborative of organizations involved in the West Side Initiative is redeveloping warehouses into mixed use facilities designed to incubate green technologies, house culinary centers, and provide living and working space for artists. Similarly, it is revitalizing residential properties by increasing owner occupancy and working with current residents rather than driving them out as the neighborhood gentrifies. In contrast, the South Side Initiative, a public memory project in a largely African American community, was spurred by neighborhood requests to preserve family and cultural heritages through a virtual museum library. It thus recognizes and adds back to the narrative of democracy the history and heritage of the African American community in Syracuse from the abolitionist period to the present.

CODA

The final plenary of the January 2009 annual meeting of the Association of American Colleges and Universities, which occurred just days after the inauguration of Barack Obama, featured two national scholars. Melissa Harris Lacewell is a noted African American Princeton political scientist, author of *Bibles, Beauty Shops, and BET: The Development of Black Political Thought,* and a professor who designs community-based courses. Eric Liu, a Yale graduate and news commentator, is author of *The Accidental Asian* and in the midst of a campaign to reframe patriotism to spur greater democratic engagement across differing, often sparring groups. Harris explained that while watching Obama accept the nomination as the democratic candidate for president, she felt like an American for the first time. For her, it was a transformative moment in which Du Bois's double consciousness was erased. She confessed to the audience that before that moment she had not really cared whether she felt fully American or not, but once she felt it, she realized it mattered enormously. Immediately before his remarks, Eric Liu passed out his little red book called *The Patriot,* in which he and his coauthor have organized a national campaign for a reengagement in public life through a reimmersion into the founding documents of our democracy and a commitment to a progressive vision of social responsibility, both locally and globally.

The civic engagement movement could be poised to help people in and out of the academy become even more socially responsible participants in public life if it fully committed itself to being as inclusive in its concepts, practices, and programs as the ideals of democracy it seeks to honor. To do so will require the very things that are at the heart of the best civic engagement work, and therefore within our power. Those capacities include a deep knowledge of and honest self-reflection about our civic movement and its practice; an understanding of the webbed relationships with others and recognition of how some members within that larger body are striated by fearful asymmetries; intercultural dialogue that requires skills of deliberation in the face of being misunderstood and of misunderstanding; a sense of ethical responsibility to and for each other that rests at the core of civic responsibility; and finally, negotiated practice and action with each other to achieve what will ultimately lead to the common good.

Clearly some civic engagement educators have begun to be inclusionary advocates and have made those commitments and alterations, but most have not yet made it a priority. We dare not wait any longer to enact the most fundamental democratic aspirations within civic engagement programs in alliances with our diversity and global counterparts. As Sylvia Hurtado importunes, "In the same way that we propose not to leave learning to chance in higher education, we cannot leave the acquisition of critical skills for citizenship to chance that may help enact a vision of a more equitable and inclusive society" (2006, pp. 265–266).

NOTES

1. For more information on the multiproject initiative, see http://www.aacu.org/american_commitments/index.cfm.

2. For a full report on the initiative's goals and recommendations, see Greater Expectations National Panel 2002. For a more recent iteration of these goals, see National Leadership Council for Liberal Education and America's Promise 2007.

REFERENCES

American Council on Education. 2007. *The American College President* (2007 ed.). Washington, DC: American Council on Education.

Beckham, E. F. 1999. "Civic Learning and Campus Diversity: Bridging the Language Gap," *Peer Review* 2, no. 1 (Fall): 4–6.

California State University. 2008. "CCE at the CSU—Historic Milestones." Center for Community Engagement. Available at http://www.calstate.edu/cce/about_us/milestones.

Colby, A., and W. M. Sullivan. 2009. "Strengthening the Foundations of Students' Excellence, Integrity, and Social Contribution." *Liberal Education* 95 (1): 22–29.

Commission on Community-Engaged Scholarship in Health Professions. 2005. *Linking Scholarship and Communities: Report of the Commission on Community-Engaged Scholarship in Health Professions.* Seattle: Community-Campus Partnerships for Health. Available at http://depts.washington.edu/ccph/pdf_files/Commission%20Report%20FINAL.pdf.

Community-Campus Partnerships for Health. 2010. "Community-Engaged Scholarship." Available at http://depts.washington.edu/ccph/scholarship.html.

Drew University. n.d. "About the Center." Center for Civic Engagement. Available at http://www.drew.edu/depts/depts.aspx?id=58058.

Evans, S. 1989. *Born for Liberty: A History of American Women.* New York: Free Press.

Garcia, A. M. 2007. "Expanding the Definition of Multiculturalism: A Personal Reflection." *Diversity & Democracy* 10 (3): 6. Available at http://www.diversityweb.org/DiversityDemocracy/vol10no3/shultz.cfm.

Greater Expectations National Panel. 2002. *Greater Expectations: A New Vision for Learning as a Nation Goes to College.* Washington, DC: Association of American Colleges and Universities.

Heller, R. 1999. "From the Editor." *Peer Review* 2, no. 1 (Fall): 3.

Holton, K. D. 2005. *Performing Folklore: Ranchos Folclóricos from Lisbon to Newark.* Bloomington: Indiana University Press.

———. Forthcoming. *Building Ethnic Communities: Portuguese Immigration to the Northeastern United States.* Dartmouth: University of Massachusetts.

Hovland, K. 2005. "Shared Futures: Global Learning and Social Responsibility." *Diversity Digest* 8 (3): 1, 16–17.

Hoy, A., and W. Meisel. 2008. "Civic Engagement at the Center: Building Democracy through Integrating Cocurricular and Curricular Experiences." Washington, DC: Association of American Colleges and Universities.

Hurtado, S. 2006. "Diversity and Learning for a Pluralist Democracy." In *Higher Education in a Global Society: Achieving Diversity, Equity, and Excellence,* ed.

W. R. Allen, M. Bonous-Hammarth, and R. T. Teraniski, 249–268. St. Louis: Elsevier.

———. 2007. "Linking Diversity with the Educational and Civic Mission of Higher Education." *Review of Higher Education* 30, no. 2 (Winter): 185–196.

International Consortium on Higher Education, Civic Responsibility, and Democracy Steering Committee and Representatives from the Council of Europe. 2006. "The Declaration on the Responsibility of Higher Education for a Democratic Culture, Citizenship, Human Rights and Sustainability." Strasbourg, France. Available at www.internationalconsortium.org/declaration.html.

Jacoby, B. 2009. "Civic Engagement in Today's Higher Education: An Overview." In *Civic Engagement in Higher Education: Concepts and Practices*, 5–30. San Francisco: Jossey-Bass.

Joseph, J. A. 1995. *Remaking America: How the Benevolent Traditions of Many Cultures Are Transforming Life.* San Francisco: Jossey-Bass.

Knefelkamp, L. L. 2008. "Civic Identity: Locating Self in Community." *Diversity & Democracy* 11 (3):1–3.

Maalouf, A. 2003. *In the Name of Identity: Violence and the Need to Belong.* New York: Penguin.

Morrison, T. 1993. *Playing in the Dark: Whiteness and the Literary Imagination.* New York: Vintage.

Musil, C. M. 2003. "Educating for Citizenship." *Peer Review* 5, no. 3 (Spring): 4–8. Available at http://www.aacu.org/peerreview/pr-sp03/pr-sp03feature1.cfm.

———. 2009. "Educating Students for Personal and Social Responsibility: The Civic Learning Spiral." In *Civic Engagement in Higher Education: Concepts and Practices*, ed. B. Jacoby, 49–68. San Francisco: Jossey-Bass.

National Leadership Council for Liberal Education and America's Promise. 2007. *College Learning for the New Global Century.* Washington, DC: Association of American Colleges and Universities. Available at http://www.aacu.org/leap/documents/GlobalCentury_final.pdf.

Office for Equity and Diversity. 2009. "Reimagining Equity and Diversity: A Framework for Transforming the University of Minnesota." Minneapolis/St. Paul: University of Minnesota. Available at http:www.academic.umn.edu/equity/pdf/reimagining.pdf.

Office of Publications. n.d. *Chancellor's Leadership Projects.* Syracuse: Syracuse University. Available at http://sunews.syr.edu/CLPbrochure-web.pdf.

Peters, S. J., N. R. Jordan, T. R. Alter, and J. C. Bridger. 2003. "The Craft of Public Scholarship in Land-Grant Education." *Journal of Higher Education Outreach and Engagement* 8 (1): 75–86.

Sanchez, G. J. n.d. "Message from the Director." Center for Diversity and Democracy, University of Southern California. Available at http://college.usc.edu/cdd/about/message.cfm.

Sather, P., and N. Bacon. 2005. "There Is No Substitute for Experience." *Diversity Digest* 9 (1): 9. Available at http://www.diversityweb.org/Digest/vol9no1/sather.cfm.

Snyder, T. D., S. A. Dillow, and C. M. Hoffman. 2008. *Digest of Education Statistics 2007.* Washington, DC: National Center for Education Statistics, U.S. Department of Education. Available at nces.ed.gov/pubs2008/2008022.pdf.

Takaki, R. 1993/2008. *A Different Mirror: A History of Multicultural America.* Boston: Little, Brown.

Taylor, C., A. Gutman, K. A. Appiah, J. Habermas, S. C. Rockefeller, M. Walzer, and S. Wolf. 1994. *Multiculturalism: Examining the Politics of Recognition*. Princeton: Princeton University Press.

Touchton, J., C. M. Musil, and K. P. Campbell. 2008. *A Measure of Equity: Women's Progress in Higher Education*. Washington, DC: Association of American Colleges and Universities.

CHAPTER 12

Sustained City-Campus Engagement

Developing an Epistemology for Our Time

LORLENE HOYT

It seems to me that for the first time in nearly half a century, institutions
of higher learning are not collectively caught up in some urgent national
endeavor. Still, our outstanding universities and colleges remain, in my
opinion, among the greatest sources of hope for intellectual and civic
progress in this country. I'm convinced that for this hope to be fulfilled,
the academy must become a more vigorous partner in the search for
answers to our most pressing social, civic, economic, and moral problems.

—Ernest Boyer (1996, p. 11)

INTRODUCTION

We, as Americans, are sharing a pivotal moment in history. We have
elected an African American President to lead our union. Half a
dozen states have enacted legislation affirming marriage as a civil
right. A Latina has been confirmed to the U.S. Supreme Court. At the same
time, hundreds of banks—large and small—have failed, corporations are fil-
ing for bankruptcy, people are losing their jobs and their pensions, families
are losing their homes to foreclosure, and every twenty-nine seconds a student
drops out of high school. This historic moment of social transformation and
economic upheaval demands that we rethink and reconfigure the relationship
between institutions of higher education and society.

Since 1999, hundreds of Massachusetts Institute of Technology (MIT)
students have unknowingly advanced Ernest Boyer's call by connecting the
rich resources of one of the world's most powerful universities with the small
and impoverished city of Lawrence, Massachusetts, located thirty miles
north of campus. In this chapter, I share what I have learned while observing
and participating in the partnership known as MIT@Lawrence, and "challenge the epistemology built into the modern research university" (Schön
1995, p. 27).

This chapter, like my own intellectual journey, begins with a story of practice. The data in the first part of the chapter, which I collected over a period of

more than eight years, comes from a variety of sources, including course syllabi and assignments, student theses and dissertations, meeting notes and transcripts, organizational reports, funding proposals, books, newspapers, journal articles, and personal interviews, as well as my own personal reflections;[1] and draws on participant voices[2] focused on thoughts and feelings about the partnership's history, evolution, and aspirations. In the second part I present an engagement theory, and in the third part I present strategies for practicing engagement. Each of the second and third parts relies primarily on data gathered during the 2008–2009 academic year through the more than forty reflective interviews students conducted with MIT@Lawrence participants, past and present, as well as data from a series of reflection exercises completed by student participants.[3] The emphasis on reflective practice contributes to what the late Donald Schön, MIT professor of urban studies and education from 1968 to 1997, called the "battle of snails," in which participant voices represent small but vital movements toward "the new scholarship":

> All of us who live in research universities are bound up in technical rationality regardless of our personal attitudes toward it, because it is built into the institutional arrangements—the formal and informal rules and norms—that govern such processes as the screening of candidates for tenure and promotion. Even liberal arts colleges, community colleges, and other institutions of higher education appear to be subject to the influence of technical rationality by a kind of echo effect or by imitation. Hence, introducing the new scholarship into institutions of higher education means becoming involved in an epistemological battle. It is a battle of snails, proceeding so slowly that you have to look very carefully in order to see it is going on. But it is happening nonetheless. (1995, p. 32)

In short, this chapter tells a story of practice, but also a story of theory, and how each informs and transforms the other through a two-way flow of people and knowledge from the city to the campus and back again. It also makes the case for a new epistemology—reciprocal knowledge—of knowledge development and real learning on both sides, achieved through a diverse, dynamic, and complex network of human relationships.

OUR STORY OF PRACTICE

What we have to learn to do, we learn by doing.

—Aristotle

The first part of this chapter is organized into five chronological episodes, each ranging from one to four years, and in it I introduce some of the faculty, students, staff, civic leaders, and residents who comprised the partnership between MIT and the city of Lawrence. Over the course of a decade, these partners collaborated to analyze complex problems, implement new ideas, and, in so doing, began to develop a new epistemology. The details of this story of practice represent a foundation for the theory and strategies to follow.

Following Families, Following Alumnae (2002–2003)

In January 2002, during my first week as a tenure-track assistant professor in the Department of Urban Studies and Planning, I attended a talk given by Kristen Harol, who had been invited to campus to share the work underway by Lawrence CommunityWorks, a community development corporation that she and two other MIT alumnae—Jessica Andors and Tamar Kotelchuck—had recently reinvigorated. These alumnae had engaged with the people of Lawrence, a former mill town on the Merrimack River, during an economic development course they had taken together (J. Andors, K. Harol, and T. Kotelchuck 2006, pers. comm.). By June 1999, with master's of city planning degrees in hand, Harol, Andors, and Kotelchuck were working in Lawrence. Though they had planned to immediately apply the economic and community development theories they had studied at MIT, they discovered—by going house-to-house, knocking on doors, and talking with families—that parents in Lawrence wanted a summer program for their children. So they began to lead trips to the zoo and other activities with the children in the North Common neighborhood—an impoverished Latino neighborhood adjacent to the mill district. By following the parents' advice, Harol, Andors, and Kotelchuck earned the trust and respect of the neighborhood families; these relationships gave them the credibility they later needed to develop large-scale projects for the city.

During her talk, Harol described Lawrence as the last and grandest textile city built by the Essex Company, one of America's first corporations. Once a planned utopia and the American solution to England's own neglected textile cities, the core of Lawrence, made up of dams, canals, boardinghouses, and several textile mills, was built in three busy years, from 1845 to 1848. For nearly seven decades, Lawrence, "the immigrant city," employed successive waves of newcomers in the mills (Cole 1963). Harol, whose grandfather had sold shoes on Essex Street, told the audience how presently there was a vibrant population of newcomers, mostly Latino, transforming the city by creating a thriving commercial corridor with new bodegas and clubs in the once store- and theater-lined downtown. She also noted that Lawrence was one of the poorest cities in the nation, with home ownership rates less than half the national average, unemployment rates two times higher than the state average, a legacy of environmental contamination, and an average high school graduation rate of about 44 percent (Hoyt 2005b). "We should work together to return the investment," she concluded, explaining that the Essex Company that had designed and built Lawrence had invested its massive profits not in Lawrence but in prominent rooted institutions that are the lifeblood of New

England today, including the Boston Public Library, the Boston Athenaeum, Massachusetts General Hospital, and MIT.

At the time, I was actively seeking a client for a seven-week course aimed at teaching undergraduate and graduate students of urban planning how to analyze data from the U.S. Census Bureau using a geographic information system. Inspired by Harol's talk, the innovative planning and community development practice she described, and her vision for connecting city and campus, I met her in the hallway after her talk and agreed, by a handshake, to form a relationship with Lawrence CommunityWorks. By the end of the following semester, in November 2002, Lang Keyes, longtime MIT professor and former community organizer in Boston's South End, encouraged me to formalize the partnership within the university by expanding the seven-week workshop to a full-semester, required service-learning practicum that we would coteach. This would take time, I learned (Hoyt 2005a). Meanwhile, the workshop was offered again in spring 2003 when we had two clients—Lawrence CommunityWorks (a resident-led organization dedicated to equitable development and economic justice) and Groundwork Lawrence (a nonprofit organization focusing on improving the physical environment then run by another MIT alumna, Maggie Super Church). The MIT alumnae, now a team of four, asked students to help them create a zoning overlay for the mill district. I worked with students to set up a web-based neighborhood information system rich with data from both the U.S. Census Bureau and the City of Lawrence, while Harol asked students to work with Lawrence teenagers to collect data about, and on, the actual streets. In November 2003, the Lawrence City Council—after a crowd of civic leaders, parents, and children filled City Hall—voted unanimously to approve the zoning overlay to permit housing in the historic mills. This early victory not only emboldened partnership participants, but also unleashed the redevelopment potential of the historic heart of Lawrence.

Increasing Community Voice (2004–2005)

By January 2004, the workshop had become a required service-learning practicum in the Masters of City Planning curriculum at MIT.[4] When Keyes and I invited Andre Leroux, a neighborhood planner at Lawrence CommunityWorks, to campus to approve our syllabus, the blueprint for advancing *our* five-year plan to build an expert-driven mapping system for Lawrence, Leroux demanded that we work hand-in-hand with residents to collect data on the ground in addition to acquiring and analyzing administrative data sets for civic leaders. Wanting Leroux and the alumnae to know that we respected their way of working in the community, Keyes and I agreed. Practicum students serendipitously helped with the transition from a top-down to a bottom-up approach to data collection and relationship building. A practicum student from Peru who had worked in New Delhi's slums led a series of participatory meetings with Latina mothers and children, teaching faculty and classmates the necessity of talking, listening, and singing to gather useful information. Other students taught us the importance of bringing the city to the campus by showing teenagers how to create maps of vacant properties in their neighborhood on campus computers. The partnership began to expand. As word spread at MIT about the partnership, a graduate student in the Center for Real Estate with an interest in mill redevelopment asked me how to meet mill owners in Lawrence. She studied successful redevelopment projects in other cities, and the Lawrence mill owners invited her to share her ideas with civic leaders, business owners, artists, parents, and teenagers (Clark 2004).

Keyes encouraged me to make research out of the Lawrence work. Consistent with my doctoral training, I started with hard data, analyzing nearly 1,900 cities to create a typology for cities like Lawrence, and identified 151 small, impoverished American post-industrial cities. I invited people from forty-one of these "forgotten"[5] cities (from eight states) to campus to teach us. Each week, throughout the fall 2004 and spring 2005 semesters, an array of city councilors, mayors, private developers, community activists, consultants, professors, and leaders of think tanks and foundations taught us that such cities can move forward by investing in people, especially new immigrants and youth disconnected from political structures who should be in the decision-making mainstream. Revitalizing these cities is especially difficult because they often suffer from inadequate governing capacity, a lack of civic engagement, and a chronically negative mind-set. But, together, we learned how it can be done. Whether guided by residents, business leaders, government, or nonprofit organizations, revitalization can be achieved by harnessing the resources of rooted institutions to improve communication across long-standing racial and class divisions, shift expectations, and articulate an inclusive and positive vision of the future (Hoyt and Leroux 2007).

The academic calendar was a formidable foe; outside the university, people's lives are not lived in semesters. When a group of us, including my MIT faculty collaborator, two MIT alumnae working in Lawrence, Andre Leroux, and myself met at a restaurant in Cambridge to discuss the future of the partnership, Leroux insisted that faculty find funding to ensure continuous engagement in Lawrence. Speaking on behalf of our primary partner, Lawrence CommunityWorks, he gave us an ultimatum: either engage with the people of Lawrence year-round or disengage entirely. In my view, the latter was not a viable option, as we had recently learned about the devastating impact that foreclosures would have on Latino families and neighborhoods. It was urgent now to secure funding to support uninterrupted work with people in Lawrence. In response to Leroux's ultimatum, a group of faculty applied for resources available through the U.S. Department of Housing and Urban Development's (HUD) Community Outreach Partnerships Centers (COPC) program. This funding would not only support continuous engagement but also help to "uncover and expose the practices of sub-prime lenders by finding, recording, and sharing resident stories" (Hoyt 2005b). I felt that university faculty, staff, and students needed to learn more about and take action to mitigate the predatory lending and imminent foreclosure crisis in Lawrence.

While our funding proposal was under review, alumnae working in Lawrence pushed Keyes and me to expand the partnership by connecting the fall 2005 practicum students with other rooted institutions in the city: Bread and Roses Housing, Inc., the Merrimack Valley Habitat for Humanity, and the City of Lawrence Office of Planning and Development. Together, faculty, students, civic leaders, and residents studied vacant property acquisition processes in Lawrence and other forgotten cities. By now, the people in Lawrence were no longer clients; they were friends. On a Saturday morning, I drove to Lawrence to deliver good news to one of the MIT alumnae at her home. When she opened the door to find me standing on her porch with a bouquet of roses, Jessica Andors exclaimed, "Does this mean we got the HUD grant?"

Encountering and Coping with Crises (2006)

With funding from HUD, more MIT students, faculty, and staff joined the partnership—now dubbed MIT@Lawrence—along with a cadre of civic leaders representing rooted institutions in Lawrence. By January 2006, though we had detailed project plans and skilled students eager to act, we found ourselves at a stage of stabilizing and trying to cope with the mishaps that serious human relationships inevitably create. A series of creative failures ensued. Through no fault of its own, one group of graduate students in the MIT Sloan School of Management disappointed the Lawrence Higher Education Resource Center, a new partner in Lawrence. A doctoral student in the MIT Media Lab who spent his afternoons with teenagers from Movement City, a nonprofit organization for youth in Lawrence, ran into "security and privacy" issues as he launched a neighborhood news system they had helped him design (Burd 2007). One student had to learn to be patient with civic leaders too busy with pressing problems to meet with her or return her e-mail and phone messages. Another student, who had worked with shelter-bound survivors of domestic violence, was met with resistance from residents when she proposed to "give a voice" to those who had become victims of predatory lending. And another student, who had conducted action-research as an undergraduate at Cornell University, made numerous trips to Lawrence, but failed to find a committed partner (Schwieger 2008).

Students taking the 2006 practicum experienced adversity as well. Even a graduate student with a background in engineering and a knack for computerized mapping, who had done an extended internship with residents, struggled to maintain stable relationships with people in Lawrence. When he led a group of practicum students in informing the Lawrence city council's president and a state senator at a public meeting that the vacant property disposition process in Lawrence violated state law, MIT's burgeoning relationship with the City's Office of Planning and Development was damaged.

Gradually, however, what appeared to be failure began transforming into success. Though the semester was officially over, the Lawrence city council's president asked the class to present their recommendations to the City of Lawrence Housing Committee. Soon after the student presentation, the Lawrence city council voted to eliminate the Real Property Task Force—an important victory for Lawrence's nonprofit housing developers, who wanted a more streamlined and transparent vacant property disposition process.

Following Civic Leaders, Following Students (2007)

By January 2007, relationships began to stabilize, and collaboration between the people inside and outside the university resulted in production of useful knowledge. For example, a student introduced Damon Rich, an architect-in-residence in MIT's Center for Advanced Visual Studies, to victims of fore-closure in Lawrence, and together they produced a widely disseminated film, *Predatory Tales*, in which people in Lawrence manipulated puppets to demonstrate, in English and Spanish, how to avoid becoming victims of predatory lenders and losing their homes to foreclosure (Hoyt et al. 2007).

Students began initiating their own projects: An MIT student repaired a tattered relationship by connecting the Lawrence Higher Education Resource Center with the student-led MIT Educational Studies Program, resulting in sixty-three teenagers from Lawrence High School riding the bus to campus every Sunday for free SAT tutoring. Another student, after taking the 2006 practicum, convened an educators' summit in Lawrence during the summer; there she met the principal of the Lawrence Family Development Charter School and introduced her to Eric Klopfer, professor and head of MIT's Teacher Education Program. Professor Klopfer's team acquired new computers and new software for eighth-grade students to test in Lawrence, while the charter school transported fifty-five eighth-graders to campus monthly to conduct experiments with faculty, staff, and students at the MIT Museum, the Edgerton Center, and the Toy Lab. As this initiative grew, it became known as Lawrence@MIT.

Students found multiple points of entry into the partnership. For example, a student who had built homes for Habitat for Humanity won a fellowship to work in Lawrence studying mortgage delinquency patterns for the Merrimack Valley Habitat for Humanity; he also took the fall 2007 practicum, where he emerged as a leader. An MIT undergraduate first taught Lawrence teenagers on Sundays and later took the 2007 practicum to help families facing recurring floods and foreclosures in the Arlington neighborhood. Another student, now in her second year as the practicum teaching assistant, worked during the winter break to finalize and deposit the practicum report, written in both English and Spanish, in the Lawrence Public Library.

The city-campus partnership became part of a larger learning network in which ideas and practice interacted and were enhanced to produce local and statewide policy outcomes. In 2007, the city councilors, mayors, private developers, community activists, consultants, professors, and leaders of think tanks and foundations who had taught us in 2004 and 2005 about revitalizing forgotten cities gathered on MIT's campus. With a new cohort of students, we brainstormed a state-level action agenda. Subsequent to the coproduction of two complementary national policy reports highlighting the need to invest public dollars in "forgotten" cities, Tina Brooks, Massachusetts' Housing Undersecretary and MIT alumna, attended our last convening on campus, where she announced the availability of new planning grants for revitalizing small cities throughout the state.

Broadening the Partnership (2008–2009)

January 2008 marked a turning point for MIT@Lawrence as students organized and ran the partnership's first retreat, where we elected three students to function as managers. We had begun moving toward a next stage in which conversations between people inside and outside the university are continuous, fluid, and maintained by the potency of enduring human relationships. For example, under the leadership of another student, who had worked as a seventh- and eighth-grade science teacher in Camden, New Jersey, Lawrence@MIT expanded as participants won scholarships to participate in MIT's Science, Technology, Engineering, and Mathematics (STEM) summer program. The partnership began reaching into every corner of MIT as student volunteers, staff, and faculty from the chemistry, physics, biology, and civil engineering departments as well as the Solar Electric Vehicle Team, GAMBIT Lab, and Spanish House worked on projects with eighth-graders from the charter school.

By 2009, we were beginning to complete a full circle with our practice. We had unleashed the mill district's redevelopment potential with the passage of a zoning overlay in 2003 and, as an alliance of civic leaders, residents, students, and faculty, we were now working to convert the mill complex, known as Union Crossing, into a green neighborhood of apartments, stores, childcare facilities, parks, and playgrounds. When my faculty colleague Lang Keyes retired, Ezra Glenn, former director of the City of Lawrence Community Development Department, cotaught the 2009 practicum with me. Also, a former community organizer from Lawrence enrolled at MIT and introduced fellow students to our friends in Lawrence.

It became increasingly difficult to negotiate all that was happening without some kind of coordinating structure. To create a space for students, staff, and faculty participating in MIT@Lawrence to meet regularly to build camaraderie, share information and strategies, and develop a relevant theory of practice, I implemented a course called Theories From, and For, Practice. Enrolled students and I cocrafted the syllabus. We rotated agenda-setting, facilitation, note-taking, and time-keeping responsibilities. Students organized and ran advisory committee meetings in Lawrence, giving civic leaders and residents opportunities to evaluate current and planned future collaborations.

We also used the course to reflect, both individually and collectively, on our practice in Lawrence. I worked with several students to cocreate the story of the partnership, in the form of a documentary, by helping past and present MIT@Lawrence participants reflect on their involvement (Hoyt et al. 2009). Together, we began to formulate an engagement theory and also identified strategies from, and for, the practice of engagement.

An Engagement Theory

> We should think about practice as a setting not only for the application of knowledge but for its generation. We should ask not only how practitioners can better apply the results of academic research, but what kinds of knowing are already embedded in competent practice.
>
> —Donald Schön (1995, p. 29)

This second part of the chapter introduces a nascent theory of engagement. Codeveloped through systematic reflection on a decade of practice by an array of MIT@Lawrence participants, this theory seeks to integrate thought and action through a continuum of five stages. For each stage, ranging from pseudo- to sustained engagement, I identify institutional opportunities that allowed the stage to emerge while highlighting associated implications for the practice of democratic engagement. The stages below present engagement as a progression from a technocratic to a democratic way of knowing. In practice, learning occurred in each stage, and people—depending on their prior experience and motivations—entered, navigated, and exited the respective stages on their own terms. Therefore, none of the stages should be understood as superior to another. Rather, each is vital to our understanding of why people choose to participate in city-campus partnerships and how people and partnerships, as a result, evolve.

Stage 1: Pseudo-Engagement

In the pseudo-engagement stage of engagement—where I myself began—people inside a university perceive cities as laboratories for learning. In 2002 and 2003, I collected hard data in Lawrence—clean, measurable facts, to analyze and teach in an academic approach that Ernest Lynton (1994, p. 87) described as "the persistent misconception of a uni-directional flow of knowledge, from the locus of research to the place of application." I imagined a one-way street whereby the faculty, staff, and students at MIT gave expert advice to clients needing our expertise. During this stage, I had no expectation of sustained involvement, but I did intend to help solve real-world problems by objectively studying the people living and working in Lawrence.

There were two institutional conditions allowing this stage of engagement to emerge: a group of faculty, many of whom had worked with Donald Schön, continued to question MIT's prevailing epistemology, and faculty were given considerable latitude in shaping their teaching agendas. The combination of these two unique conditions not only made it possible for the MIT alumnae to work with the people of Lawrence while studying at MIT but also allowed me to design a workshop connecting the alumnae in Lawrence to the next cohort of students advancing through the Department of Urban Studies and Planning. Schön's new epistemology, whereby practitioner knowledge is valued in the academy, also explains why faculty had maintained strong personal relationships with the alumnae. Many faculty valued the ability of our alumnae to solve complex problems outside the academy and frequently invited them to campus to reflect on their practice with students. In turn, the practice of democratic engagement was advanced because the alumnae, who were motivated to continue a relationship with MIT in order to bring resources to Lawrence, possessed a firsthand understanding of how and under what conditions students could contribute to the city's renewal. They also knew that launching a common enterprise of learning in the practice of doing would require ongoing faculty involvement and that I, as a new faculty member, would benefit from the support they could give in planning and coordinating the workshop I needed to teach. Their working knowledge of both sides, the civic and academic cultures, allowed partnership participants to achieve victories early on, enhancing solidarity and contributing to our mutual interest in continuing the partnership.

For me—and my professional experience as a scholar is not unique—an institutional barrier to moving beyond pseudo-engagement loomed large. As a tenure-track assistant professor in a research university, no harm was done to my career by teaching a workshop in partnership with the people of Lawrence. However, colleagues, both near and far, urged me to resist integrating these relationships into my research. I took their advice and kept my research apart from my teaching and service. Sacrificing the reward of tenure was not a risk I was willing to take in this early stage of engagement.

Stage 2: Tentative Engagement

Next, I moved from pseudo- to tentative engagement as knowledge began to flow in nontraditional directions, from outside to inside the university. By teaching the Lawrence practicum and inviting people from forgotten cities to campus to teach us in 2004 and 2005, I slowly began to integrate my teaching and research. Before I launched my research on forgotten cities, my understanding of such cities was limited to what I was learning by teaching the Lawrence practicum. My research on forgotten cities helped me to understand Lawrence as belonging to a class of cities. I began to teach practicum students that Lawrence belongs to a class of small, post-industrial cities characterized by particular challenges and strengths. This led me to giving talks in class comparing and contrasting Lawrence's history with the history of other "forgotten cities" such as Reading, Pennsylvania, and Youngstown, Ohio. Also, through the practicum as well as student theses, we began interviewing civic leaders and residents in other cities (namely Flint, Michigan, and Oakland, California) to deepen our understanding (of vacant property disposition and asset building by way of individual development accounts) in Lawrence. That is, we began studying strategies used in cities outside Lawrence and applying them in Lawrence.

In this stage, linking city and campus also involved expanding the partnership in the city and across the campus. I no longer kept the people of Lawrence at arm's length; we were now working and learning hand in hand.

Institutionally, several opportunities permitted this stage of engagement. First, the department's core curriculum was revamped and now included, among the many changes, the addition of several practicums. The Lawrence practicum, which materialized during this time, deeply embedded the relationship between people inside and outside the university in practice by creating a continuous point of entry for faculty, staff, and students into the city as well as residents and civic leaders into the classroom. Additionally, the department supported the burgeoning partnership with its own financial resources. The department head at that time, for example, assigned $25,000 in funding to bring engaged scholars to campus to share their knowledge of forgotten cities; he also supported our funding application to HUD by promising more than $300,000 in matching funds (Vale 2005). The executive leadership, too, "whole-heartedly endorsed" the partnership. In a letter supporting our application to HUD, MIT's chancellor, Phillip Clay, explained, "We are happy to provide financial and human resources, work to make the program activities part of MIT's on-going mission, and cultivate a climate that rewards faculty work in neighborhoods by including it in decisions affecting rank, tenure, and promotion" (Clay 2005). These shifts in curriculum and resource allocation enhanced the practice of democratic engagement by creating additional opportunities for dialogue among people inside and outside the university. For example, through the practicum, we learned to integrate academic and community knowledge on such subjects as collective asset building through matched savings programs (Alexander et al. 2004). By bringing engaged scholars to campus, we developed a conceptual framework for understanding the history, unique challenges, and untapped potential of forgotten cities like Lawrence (Hoyt and Leroux 2007).

Yet institutional barriers to engagement persisted. The flow of people between the city and campus was not continuous; faculty, staff and students at MIT were, in effect, engaged in Lawrence at their own convenience. Our empowered friends demanded more, which put me—as a young scholar seeking tenure—in a particularly difficult position. Scholars who face such crossroads, however, have options. For example, many decide to conform to traditional academic standards for the purpose of achieving tenure, postponing, in effect, their calling as engaged scholars. I chose to frame the challenge as a dilemma: career or calling? Should I subscribe to the dominant epistemology at MIT by conducting the type of research commonly rewarded or explore Schön's epistemology by joining the people of Lawrence in learning to solve pressing economic and social problems and risk my career at MIT?

Stage 3: Stable Engagement

Stable engagement is characterized by tension between creativity and failure. In 2006, as the partnership continued to expand, I had to make hard choices about how to spend my time. Though the HUD grant increased the perceived legitimacy of the partnership to some, a number of colleagues in the department viewed my engagement with the people of Lawrence as a form of service—an activity at odds with and diverting my attention from research. During this stage, however, I was learning to arrange my research, teaching, and service to overlap. I began to see these traditionally walled-off domains as inextricably linked and mutually reinforcing modes of inquiry. But, still, I struggled to find ways to connect and balance my time among them.

This stage was possible because MIT has a culture that encourages faculty, staff, and students to collaborate, explore, and innovate. New relationships formed as a steady flow of people from different departments, laboratories, and centers from MIT began interacting with business owners, public officials, and community activists in Lawrence. Some relationships were unproductive, while others immediately resulted in useful ideas and products. We learned in this stage that many relationships had to fail before they began to flourish. As participants took risks, some relationships were damaged and achievements were delayed. But, learning resulted nevertheless, especially when participants reflected on their actions. In this stage, we came to appreciate firsthand John Dewey's assertion that "failure is not mere failure. It is instructive" (Dewey 1933/2008, p. 206).

Moving gradually from tentative to stable engagement was also possible because MIT students are motivated to realize the institute's motto, *Mens et Manus* (Mind and Hand). In this stage, they began discovering and teaching me how to establish continuous engagement with people outside the university by creatively sequencing such curricular artifacts as courses, fellowships, internships, and theses; together, we learned the importance of an exchange of people, resources, and ideas over time between the city and the campus. What we now call "a commitment to continuity" means that people inside the university are dedicated to the practice of democratic engagement insofar as they are willing to adapt the academic culture to respond to the demands of civic culture. The risks and compromises that occur in this stage require trust among participants; such relationships are built one day at a time.

By the end of this stage, I had decided to follow Schön's call for a new epistemology. As the director of a rapidly growing partnership, I found it necessary to work closely with dozens of participants on both sides. The daily management of MIT@Lawrence was daunting and consumed much of my attention and energy. Colleagues who understood the scope and depth of our work began warning me against spending too much time with the people of

Lawrence, but the partnership had come to life in this stage and I was in the center of it. My promotion to associate professor without tenure was fast approaching, and traditional research publications, I sensed, might be viewed more favorably than the scholarship we were producing through our engagement. An abrupt departure from the partnership, however, was not a reasonable option for me at this stage. I felt responsible for holding the collaboration together.

Stage 4: Authentic Engagement

In the fourth stage, authentic engagement, practice and ideas flowed, were fed back, and improved within a complex and dynamic system of relationships. Here, a city was no longer simply a lab under a microscope (a viewpoint characteristic of pseudo-engagement), but a living partnership between a university and a city for the purpose of reciprocal knowledge. A "commitment to continuity" had been achieved, and people were creating lasting relationships and building knowledge together over time. In this stage, my research, teaching, and professional service were integrated and interacting in new ways. For example, I incorporated my research on matched savings programs as an economic revitalization strategy into the practicum and supervised student theses aimed at improving and expanding such programs in Lawrence.

Authentic engagement emerged, in part, due to several institutional conditions. MIT recognizes and rewards faculty professional service and gives students substantial latitude in shaping their own intellectual agendas. By the start of this stage, I had received MIT's Martin Luther King Jr. Leadership Award for directing the MIT@Lawrence Partnership and MIT—for its service to the people of Lawrence—had been named to the President's Higher Education Community Service Honor Roll by the President's Council on Service and Civic Participation. These and other forms of acknowledgment encouraged participants, especially students, to think more boldly and creatively about their work. Now, students had mastered the art of engaging with the people of Lawrence by using different curricular artifacts to connect their work and were regularly contributing to existing bodies of knowledge. For example, Cindy Wu used her master's thesis to engage with the people of Lawrence in 2006 and 2007 to build on Lawrence CommunityWorks' idea of neighborhood revitalization through resident-led matched savings programs. As Cindy entered the partnership, she benefited from the investigations and relationships that other students previously had forged. For example, the six students taking the 2004 practicum researched the use and potential use of matched savings programs for increasing home ownership opportunities in the North Common neighborhood. In 2005, an MIT student used her thesis to investigate matched savings programs in other cities, building on the work done by practicum students. This collaborative intellectual process spanned a period of more than three years and involved faculty, staff, and students at MIT and Washington University in St. Louis, as well as civic leaders and residents in Lawrence, Massachusetts; Chicago; and Oakland, California (Alexander et al. 2004; Boddie et al. 2004; Rice 2005; Wu 2007).

By the end of this stage, tenured colleagues in my department had voted unanimously to support my case for promotion to associate professor without tenure. With my tenure review on the horizon, I decided to reconfigure the career-or-calling dilemma by asking, How can I restructure the partnership such that it will be sustained if key participants, including myself, exit? Because students, both present and former, were the driving force behind MIT@Lawrence, and many faculty colleagues were busy with sustained partnerships of their own—from New Orleans to Beijing—I kept returning to the idea of shifting the partnership from a faculty-led to a student-led enterprise. A fundamental operational change of this sort would require me to lead an extensive and collaborative decision-making process. This experiment had promise in that it seemed to offer a responsible solution to an unrelenting problem.

Stage 5: Sustained Engagement

The climactic stage of sustained engagement is reached when the partnership gains power through the mutual accrual of knowledge, influencing local and regional policies and city-campus relationships toward real social change. In 2008, people began entering the partnership through different portals, some created for them and others created by themselves. Individual levels of participation intensified, waned, and intensified again, according to the problems at hand as well as the ability and desire of individuals to cocraft solutions. Students now led the partnership. Programs did not just survive; they thrived as participants on both sides entered and even exited the partnership. Individuals and groups frequently reflected on their practice and recalibrated their actions accordingly. A new theory of engagement was codeveloped.

In sustained engagement, people inside and outside the university engage in an evolutionary continuum between the ever-present themes of practice and knowledge; they seek to overcome, rather than reinforce, the false dichotomy between the two. Here, perhaps only in small ways at first, the university's view of knowledge begins to shift away from the dominant epistemology, illustrated in the following quote by Schön related to the dilemma of rigor or relevance, and toward a new epistemology of reciprocal knowledge.

> In the varied topography of professional practice, there is a high, hard ground overlooking a swamp. On the high ground, manageable problems lend themselves to solution through the use of research-based theory and technique. In the swampy lowlands, problems are messy and confusing and incapable of technical solution. The irony of this situation is that the problems of the high ground tend to be relatively unimportant to individuals or to society at large, however great their technical interest may be, while in the swamp lie the problems of

greatest human concern. The practitioner is confronted with a choice. Shall he remain on the high ground where he can solve relatively unimportant problems according to his standards of rigor, or shall he descend to the swamp of important problems where he cannot be rigorous in any way he knows how to describe? (1995, p. 28)

In sustained engagement, Schön's practitioner need not choose the "high ground" or the "swamp of important problems" because a new epistemology, with new standards of rigor, begins to emerge as people inside the university recognize the need to develop participatory methods of knowledge production on questions of economic, social, physical, and cultural revival. The once-distinct boundary between people in the city and people on campus is blurred and easily penetrated. Solving problems and generating ideas are no longer separate tasks taken on by two separate sides.

This stage was achieved because MIT grants each department tremendous freedom with regard to resource allocation and faculty oversight. The department head at the time exceeded his earlier financial commitment by awarding student participants with aid, in the form of tuition and stipends, which motivated students to begin managing and guiding the partnership. He also allowed me to create a new year-round course to foster reflective practice among participants and hired the City of Lawrence Community Development director to assist with teaching the Lawrence practicum. This stage reflects coleadership amongst faculty, administrators, and students for guiding the university's commitment of resources and infrastructure to support the partnership.

Student-led city-campus engagement has profound implications for the practice of democracy, especially as linkages to such rooted institutions as public schools are established. Jeff Beam, a graduate student from Louisville, Kentucky, who was continuously engaged with the people of Lawrence while studying at MIT, insightfully reflected,

> MIT's long-term engagement can give Lawrence residents, especially the youth, an understanding of the institute as more than a place for cutting-edge science. They experience MIT's dedication to *Mens et Manus* firsthand, the practical application of education, or what we call reflective practice. Lawrence youth begin to understand MIT not just as a place that could possibly contribute to their well-being, but also as a place to which they can contribute through participation and even matriculation. (pers. comm., November 19, 2008)

Tenured faculty, embedded in institutional cultures dominated by technical rationality, hold the exclusive power to incrementally enlarge the customary paradigm of knowledge generation in higher education by using reward systems such as tenure to assign value to new forms of scholarship. A group of tenured colleagues at MIT recently voted on whether to solicit external letters to evaluate the scholarship I have produced since 2002. A majority of these colleagues decided not to choose to perceive my tenure case as an opportunity to reignite a productive conversation, among faculty both inside and outside our department, about the promises and consequences of introducing the new scholarship into institutions of higher education. I continue to believe that the battle of snails is worth fighting. Every scholar can make a difference.

STRATEGIES FROM, AND FOR, ENGAGEMENT

> It's obvious that the problems of urban life are enormously complex; there are no simple solutions. I'm almost embarrassed to mention it as a problem because it is so enormously complex, but we live in cities. They determine the future of this country. And I find it ironic that universities which focused with such energy on rural America a century ago have never focused with equal urgency on our cities.
>
> —Boyer (1996, p. 19)

This portion of the chapter presents two strategies from, and for, the practice of engagement that evolved during MIT's partnership with the City of Lawrence. Creative, cogenerated strategies are necessary to overcome the cultural and structural barriers within the academy that actively detach scholars from society. Said another way, a theory of engagement needs corresponding strategies that can be shared with and used by people who want to learn how to create lasting city-campus partnerships that bring together civic leaders, residents, faculty, and students in transforming a city. I call these strategies "investing in human relationships" and "using instruments-for-action."

Investing in Human Relationships

People are central to the idea of engagement; therefore, human actions and interactions, in the form of stories, have provided the scaffolding for this chapter. In developing mutually beneficial human relationships between city and campus, we encountered a number of impediments. To begin, MIT's academic culture promotes a hierarchical system of relationships, while the civic leaders and residents in Lawrence are experimenting with the idea of "network organizing"—a horizontal system of relationships whereby collective action is valued above individual achievement. In moving from pseudo- to sustained engagement, we learned from the director of Lawrence CommunityWorks and other Lawrence civic leaders how to connect people to each other and to opportunities "to step into public life—from the neighborhood group to the City Council—in a way that feels safe, fun, and productive" (Traynor 2008; Traynor and Andors 2005). Our work, over time, began to mirror their work in revitalizing Lawrence, once a forgotten city, as we learned that healthy communities are the aggregate of reciprocally advantageous human relationships.

In pseudo-engagement, we learned that human relationships matter. For nearly two decades, MIT faculty and students studied Lawrence from a distance; their involvement with the people of Lawrence was fundamentally one-sided (Hoyt 2005a). The relationship between people on both sides, however, shifted dramatically when the alumnae decided to work in Lawrence after graduation. MIT@Lawrence was not a chance event. Kristen, an MIT alumna, had a familial relationship with the city, and she convinced her friends to work and live there; and their personal ties to MIT helped to sustain the city-campus partnership. People inside and outside a university with an interest in engagement should look for meaningful relationships among people. Are there university alumni working or living in the city? Were university faculty, staff, or students born or raised in the city?

The importance of trust emerged as a central tenet during tentative engagement. In practice, faculty followed civic leaders and students who were following residents. We trusted that civic leaders and residents had a deep understanding of the city—its history, politics, and vision for revival; we trusted that students had acquired relevant knowledge and experience from working in other contexts that allowed them to apply their knowledge and skill in Lawrence. Engaged faculty can lead city-campus partnerships by example by taking the risk of placing their trust in others. Students, civic leaders, and residents are eager to engage and have much to teach.

In achieving stable engagement, we learned the necessity of a "commitment to continuity," which is dependent on establishing and maintaining human relationships. For university faculty, staff, and students to genuinely participate in the burgeoning civic life of such cities as Lawrence, people inside the university cannot disappear during breaks or on weekends because conversations must continuously flow among participants. For people outside the university, this means making time to join classroom discussions, inviting people inside the university to public meetings and events, and keeping university faculty, staff, and students informed in real time as problems arise, decisions are made, and opportunities unfurl. Trusting relationships are built day by day, by showing up, again and again, talking with people, and getting to know their histories, fears, and aspirations.

In authentic engagement an unencumbered flow of people, as well as ideas and practices, are moving back-and-forth, and in multiple directions. Here, faculty, staff, and students challenge the conventional epistemology of universities by cultivating connectivity with people in cities as participants. With each small action, they readily connect to, work with, and influence one another regardless of institutional rank or political power. As Eric Mackres (2009), a graduate student at MIT, pointed out, such connectivity is laborious: "It is essential that the community sees us get our hands dirty down in the trenches. There is no better way to build trust and break down barriers of class in a partnership than working side by side for the same thing." Faculty, staff, and students must meet civic leaders and residents where they are by contributing to the civic life of the city in a variety of ways. Some students might engage for a single semester by providing much-needed technical assistance to a small nonprofit organization. Other students might engage for several years forming deep personal relationships with civic leaders and residents and affecting decisions at multiple levels of government. A range of interactions is vital, and none is too small.

For several years, I had taken the lead on designing and teaching courses, writing grant applications, and negotiating new projects with civic leaders and residents. As the partnership expanded throughout the city and campus, however, this top-down management structure floundered. To improve linkages between the hierarchical structure of the university and the increasingly horizontal structure of the growing civic network in Lawrence, I decided to apply the idea of "network organizing" in the academy. Students were resistant, at first, because they expected faculty to lead the partnership. Students who had worked as community organizers and valued engagement one by one assumed leadership positions within the partnership and recruited new participants, and relationships among people on both sides became more fluid, responsive, and resilient. Jeff Beam (2009), a graduate student, observed, "The horizontal, student-run model is the right management idea for a loose-knit network such as ours, and it lessens the reliance on any one faculty member as the focal point." Yet, a horizontal, democratic structure also requires a new role for faculty, who provide an anchor of permanence commensurate with the students' transient journey of study. The new role for faculty of facilitating the democratic value of sharing leadership for public problem solving with students (and community partners) also needs to be valued and supported by the university (Dzur 2008). Investing in human relationships is a strategy that runs counter to the technocratic culture of many research universities. Simultaneously, human relationships, particularly those that are resilient and capable of thriving through adversity, are the most critical element for achieving sustained engagement.

Using Instruments-for-Action

The academic calendar is organized into semesters and breaks that disrupt continuous engagement with the outside world. Despite the problematic way in which academic structures partition engagement into periods of time incongruent with the incessant demands of practice, we gradually learned to view curricular artifacts as instruments for—rather than barriers to—action. By shifting our perspective, we explored and discovered new avenues for democratic engagement. In moving from pseudo- to tentative engagement, for example, an elective workshop became a required practicum that created a regular connection by which people outside the university came to count on a group of students joining them "on the ground" for fifteen weeks every year. Before a commitment to continuity is achieved, faculty might consider using required courses to develop working relationships with people outside the university. If both sides agree to engage over a period of three to five years, such courses may be used to accumulate knowledge about a particular problem, such as property rights (i.e., vacant property acquisition and disposition processes), over time. People outside the university may reciprocate by applying their own instruments-for-action to their relationships with faculty, staff, and students. For example, civic leaders may invite faculty to serve on related community boards or task forces. In principle, all participants may seek ways to build on previous work and knowledge, thus attaining higher goals for themselves as well as the conditions they aim to improve. After a commitment to continuity is achieved, people on both sides might look for instruments-for-action to structure or support engagement activities in the absence or scarcity of outside funding. For example, a student who wants to work with civic leaders or residents on a particular problem could consider using a course of independent study to bring interested parties together. Courses of independent study give faculty, students, and civic leaders the flexibility necessary to shape a shared agenda for learning from action while ensuring that students receive the rewards they need (i.e., course credits, mentorship, and so on). Additionally, many universities and colleges have internship and fellowship programs that may be used to maintain city-campus relations. These instruments are especially useful during summer and winter breaks when community-based organizations and local governments are short-staffed and students seek monetary compensation in exchange for their time.

Once engaged, students can seek opportunities to integrate their outside relationships with faculty inside the academy. Increasingly, students engaged in MIT@Lawrence integrated academic knowledge and civic knowledge by selecting Lawrence as the focal point for writing assignments in a variety of courses (including Urban Labor Markets and Employment, Enabling an Energy Efficient Society, and Media in Cultural Context) taught by instructors who have no relationship with the city or the people of Lawrence. By initiating improbable interactions among faculty and civic leaders, students, in effect, expanded the partnership and uncovered a new instrument-for-action. For instance, civic leaders in Lawrence directly incorporated content from student writing assignments into federal stimulus funding applications (Leavy-Sperounis, Mackres, and Marshall 2009). In this case, civic leaders in Lawrence recognized the benefits of engagement and took action through instruments of their own, identifying MIT as a partner and creating a budget line item for MIT students in the funding application. As engagement is sustained, participants playfully investigate improbable instruments-for-action. For example, a number of universities and colleges require students to write a thesis or dissertation. These are particularly powerful instruments because, as a capstone project, they require a substantial amount of student time and energy; student work on these projects typically spans at least one semester, often two or more. Students with an interest in action-research might use the thesis or dissertation as a means for working closely with engaged faculty and civic leaders to identify, define, and solve pressing problems for which resources are limited. Such theses and dissertations may, in turn, facilitate new city-campus relationships while enriching students' learning experiences. Moreover, theses and dissertations are published and archived in university libraries and are therefore available to the public. Engaged students, through their theses and dissertations, not only can work in collaboration with engaged faculty and civic leaders to make relevant contributions to society but also can aim to capsize conventional wisdom by offering new paradigms for advancing such ideals as equity, prosperity, and justice.

Department chairs are in a position to grant engaged faculty the freedom to use courses to create a space for city-campus participants to reflect on their practice. As we have seen in practice, engaged students may find multiple portals into a community by combining an array of instruments. Opportunities for students to work in partnership with civic leaders and residents, at home and abroad, may be plentiful, but there are fewer prospects within the walls of the academy for students to critically evaluate, document, and disseminate what they have learned from such experiences.

The full potential of such instruments has yet to be realized. While this chapter illuminates how curricular artifacts can be understood as instruments-for-action, it also suggests that we begin rethinking the purpose of other academic artifacts. Can journal articles and other publications function as instruments-for-action? What about promotion and tenure guidelines? Should scholarship be more widely defined? Does the documentary created to complement this chapter, *Sustained City-Campus Engagement: Reflections on Our Practice*, represent a form of scholarship?

AN EPISTEMOLOGY FOR OUR TIME

Knowledge does not move from the locus of research to the place of application, from scholar to practitioner, teacher to student, expert to client. It is everywhere fed back, constantly enhanced. We need to think of knowledge in an ecological fashion, recognizing the complex, multifaceted and multiply-connected system by means of which discovery, aggregation, synthesis, dissemination, and application are interconnected and interacting in a wide variety of ways.

—Ernest Lynton (1994, pp. 88–89)

Reciprocal knowledge is an idea whose time has come. Universities and colleges still functioning as ivory towers have a responsibility to respond to pressing needs of real people outside, not only for the people's sake but also for their own. Without practice, no theory can be tested; without theory, practice can be aimless and wasteful. Theories of practice that materialize from practice are more likely to be relevant and, therefore, capable of impacting, through their application, the crises affecting people's daily lives. Such theories should be tested, quickly, and improved through an ongoing dialogue among a diverse network of people inside and outside the academy.

An epistemology of reciprocal knowledge, realized through a two-way network of human relationships, allows faculty, students, civic leaders, and residents to experiment as they learn the norms and develop the values of democracy through sustained city-campus partnerships. For students, this means that writing assignments for courses as well as the theses and dissertations they complete to meet graduation requirements do not simply fill recycling bins or sit on library shelves. It means they earn specialized degrees, which help them to get jobs, while practicing good citizenship, mentoring, and being mentored by peers, faculty, and civic leaders. For people living and working in cities, it means that new and meaningful linkages develop between public schools and institutions of higher education for combating the dropout crisis in ways that improve the quality of life for individuals, families, neighborhoods, and society. It also means investing in civic life by participating in public meetings and community events. For faculty it means integrating research, teaching, and service in ways that not only are rewarded by promotion or tenure but also lead to new discoveries and personal fulfillment. It also means learning to solve problems in the outside world as they arise, thus forging a "closer relationship between knowledge and social transformation" (Edwards 2006). For higher education, it means conceiving of knowledge differently, rethinking how professionals are prepared in the academy and how knowledge generated by citizens is valued in the university; it also means adopting broader and more humanistic modes of scholarship and evolving into more nimble and responsive civic institutions. In response to an earlier iteration of this chapter, Maggie Super Church (2009), an MIT alumna living and working in Lawrence, reflected:

> The scholarly work produced by MIT@Lawrence students has consistently been among the most rigorous and empirically sound I've seen—with the added benefit that it is connected to real people and community needs. I would argue that the existence of these network relationships creates a unique space for students and faculty to conduct crisp, tightly focused research that is responsive to specific, on-the-ground problems happening in real time—something that is often missing from traditional planning practice. Particularly as the pace of change in cities continues to accelerate, there is a compelling argument to be made for research that is firmly grounded in current realities and incorporates new media tools to keep pace with a dynamic, rapidly evolving, and often volatile urban environment. (pers. comm.)

Now is not the time for protecting the status quo. We need an epistemology for our time. Will we begin "creating a special climate in which the academic and civic cultures communicate more continuously and more creatively with one another" (Boyer 1996, p. 251) and, in the process, reconfigure the relationship between institutions of higher education and society? In a speech at Notre Dame's 2009 commencement ceremony, President Barack Obama conveyed the necessity of working together and learning from one another by inviting graduates to make democratic engagement "a way of life." He explained:

> It doesn't just improve your community, it makes you a part of your community. It breaks down walls. It fosters cooperation. And when that happens—when people set aside their differences, even for a moment, to work in common effort toward a common goal, when they struggle together, and sacrifice together, and learn from one another—then all things are possible.

NOTES

1. I first combed through these data sources to construct our story of practice in the form of a detailed timeline.

2. Through a series of meetings, I shared the timeline with a small group of students who later designed, conducted, and recorded face-to-face interviews with partnership participants, both in the city and on campus, to validate the facts that I provided and to contribute their own information and perspectives to the story. Simultaneously, I presented the idea of sustained engagement to students and other city-campus partnership participants who helped to develop it through a course entitled Theories From, and For, Practice I and II. Last, I distributed earlier drafts of this chapter to all of the participants referenced herein; most responded with keen insights, many of which I incorporated into the final version.

3. See the fifteen-minute documentary *Sustained City-Campus Engagement: Reflections on Our Practice* (Hoyt, Dougherty, Leavy-Sperounis, Martin, Mills, and Sisk 2009), which vividly portrays participants' voices; available at www.MITatLawrence .net.

4. The Department of Urban Studies and Planning is somewhat unique in its approach to service-learning, as evidenced by the criteria established for core practicums that were added to the core curriculum in 2004. For more, see Hoyt 2005a.

5. Forgotten cities are defined by the following three criteria: old—cities with an industrial history, meaning they had a population of more than 5,000 inhabitants by 1880; small—cities with between 15,000 and 20,000 residents according to the 2000 U.S. Census; and poor—cities with a median household income of less than $35,000 according to the 2000 Census. There are 151 cities in the country that satisfy these criteria, representing a total of 7.4 million people. For more, see Hoyt and Leroux 2007a.

REFERENCES

Alexander, J., C. Canepa, E. Pauls, S. Rice, A. Port, and M. Weisner. 2004. "People and Place: Individual Development Accounts, Technology, and Community Revitalization in Lawrence, Massachusetts." Unpublished paper, Massachusetts Institute of Technology.

Beam, J. 2009. Reflection exercise. Coursework for Theories From, and For, Practice II, Massachusetts Institute of Technology.

Boddie, S. C., Michael Sherradan, L. Hoyt, P. Thirupathy, T. Shanks, S. Rice, and Margaret Sherradan. 2004. "Family Saving and Community Assets: Designing and Implementing Family-Centered, Place-Based Individual Development Account Programs." Center for Social Development Report, Washington University, St. Louis.

Boyer, E. L. 1996. "The Scholarship of Engagement." *Journal of Public Service and Outreach* 1 (1): 11–20.

Burd, L. 2007. "Technological Initiatives for Social Empowerment: Design Experiments in Technology-Supported Youth Participation and Local Civic Engagements." PhD diss., Massachusetts Institute of Technology.

Clark, H. 2004. "Redeveloping Lawrence, Massachusetts' Historic Mill District: Insights into Adaptive Reuse in Untested Residential Markets." Master's thesis, Massachusetts Institute of Technology.

Clay, P. 2005. Letter to Sherone Ivey, Acting Associate Deputy Assistant Secretary for University Partnerships, U.S. Department of Housing and Urban Development, Office of University Partnerships. June. Cambridge, MA: Office of the Chancellor, Professor of City Planning, Massachusetts Institute of Technology.

Cole, D. B. 1963. *Immigrant City: Lawrence, Massachusetts, 1845–1921*. Chapel Hill: University of North Carolina Press.

Dewey, J. 1933/2008. *Volume 8: Essays and How We Think*. The Later Works of John Dewey, 1925–1953, ed. J. A. Boydston. Carbondale, IL: Southern Illinois University Press.

Dzur, A. W. 2008. *Democratic Professionalism: Citizen Participation and the Reconstruction of Professional Ethics, Identity, and Practice*. University Park: Pennsylvania State University Press.

Edwards, M. 2006. "Looking Back from 2046: Thoughts on the 80th Anniversary of the Institute for Revolutionary Social Science." Keynote Address presented at the Anniversary of the Institute for Development Studies, University of Sussex, Brighton, UK, September 22.

Hoyt, L. 2005a. "A Core Commitment to Service-Learning: Bridging Planning Theory and Practice." In *From the Studio to the Streets: Service-Learning in Planning and Architecture*, ed. M. C. Hardin, 17–31. Washington, DC: American Association for Higher Education.

———. 2005b. Funding Proposal: MIT@Lawrence Community Outreach Partnership Center. June 22. U.S. Department of Housing and Urban Development, Community Outreach Partnerships Centers Program.

Hoyt, L., C. Balderas-Guzman, J. Bonilla, A. Bopp Stark, L. Caraballo, C. Espinoza-Toro, et al. 2007. *Predatory Tales*. Cambridge, MA: MIT@Lawrence, U.S. Department of Housing and Urban Development. DVD.

Hoyt, L., A. Dougherty, M. Leavy-Sperounis, D. Martin, A. Mills, and E. Sisk. 2009. *Sustained City-Campus Engagement: Reflections on Our Practice*. Cambridge, MA: MIT@Lawrence, U.S. Department of Housing and Urban Development. DVD.

Hoyt, L., and A. Leroux. 2007. *Voices from Forgotten Cities: Innovative Revitalization Coalitions in America's Older Small Cities*. New York: PolicyLink.

Leavy-Sperounis, M., E. Mackres, and S. Marshall. 2009. "Green Jobs in Lawrence." Unpublished paper. Cambridge: Massachusetts Institute of Technology.

Lynton, E. 1994. "Knowledge and Scholarship." *Metropolitan Universities: An International Forum* 5 (1): 9–17.

Obama, B. 2009. Commencement speech. South Bend, IN: University of Notre Dame.

Rice, S. 2005. "From Individual Development Accounts to Community Asset Building: An Exploration in Bridging People- and Place-Based Strategies." CSD Research Report, Center for Social Development, Washington University, St. Louis.

Schön, D. A. 1995. "Knowing-in-Action: The New Scholarship Requires a New Epistemology." *Change* 2 (6): 26–34.

Schwieger, A. 2008. *In Pursuit of Continuity: Engaged Scholarship for Personal and Institutional Transformation*. Master's thesis, Massachusetts Institute of Technology.

Traynor, W. 2008. "Building Community in Place: Limitations and Promise." In *The Community Development Reader*, ed. J. DeFilippis and S. Saegert, 214–224. New York: Routledge.

Traynor, W. J., and J. Andors. 2005. "Network Organizing: A Strategy for Building Community Engagement." *Shelterforce Online* 140 (March/April). National Housing Institute. Available at http://www.nhi.org/online/issues/140/LCW.html.

Vale, L. 2005. Letter to Sherone Ivey, Acting Associate Deputy Assistant Secretary for University Partnerships, U.S. Department of Housing and Urban Development, Office of University Partnerships, Washington, DC, from Chair, Department of Urban Studies and Planning, Massachusetts Institute of Technology, June 15.

Wu, C. 2007. "Building Community Assets through Individual Development Accounts: Growing a Strategic Network in Lawrence, Massachusetts." Master's thesis, Massachusetts Institute of Technology.

CHAPTER 13

Conclusion

Creating the Democratically Engaged University—
Possibilities for Constructive Action

MATTHEW HARTLEY AND JOHN SALTMARSH

Every generation needs a new revolution.

—Thomas Jefferson

Three crucial traditions fuel deep democratic energies. The first is
the Greek creation of the Socratic commitment to questioning—
questioning of ourselves, of authority, of dogma, of parochialism, and
of fundamentalism.

—Cornel West, *Democracy Matters* (2004)

We have learned to say that the good must be extended to all of society
before it can be held secure by any one person or any one class. But we
have not yet learned to add to that statement, that unless all [people] and
all classes contribute to a good, we cannot even be sure that it is worth
having.

—Jane Addams

The impetus for this book emerged from our observations of civic and
community engagement efforts at American colleges and universities and our resulting conviction that the civic engagement movement
had not yet fulfilled its great promise. There is no question that the past
two decades have seen a dramatic increase in civic activities, such as service-
learning and engaged scholarship. Also, diversity initiatives have sought to
promote greater racial, ethnic, gender, and cultural understanding and equity.
Deliberative democracy efforts on many campuses have spurred dialogues
and debate about difficult societal issues. The breadth and scope of these
activities constitute a firm foundation for building an academy dedicated to
serving society. But they are insufficient if our intention is to strengthen our
democracy.

The broader movement to create a vibrant, diverse democracy faces two pressing challenges. First, the various strands of the movement are comprised of discrete efforts wholly disconnected from one another on campus—service-learning offices, diversity initiatives, global citizenship programs, difficult dialogue forums and so forth. The right hand of the movement does not know what the left is doing. Individual projects, regardless of the number, will never produce transformative change.

Of equal concern is that what has emerged is a rather conventional, even timid, civic engagement—one that rests easily within the status quo and rarely challenges it. Rather than openly questioning the prevailing norms, customs, and structures of the academy, civic engagement efforts have instead adapted in order to ensure their acceptance and legitimacy within it. All too often, service-learning courses are indistinguishable from internships or clinical placements: their chief aim is disciplinary learning or improved clinical practice. Democratic outcomes—encouraging students to understand and question the social and political factors that cause social problems and to challenge and change them—at best remain hoped-for by-products. What seems evident to us is that the systems and structures of higher education are changing civic engagement work far more than the civic engagement work is changing higher education.

These observations led us to explore a series of questions about democratic practice: What are the responsibilities of a college or university in our democracy? How do we foster civic awareness, interest, and agency in the core activities of students, staff, and faculty? What assumptions should guide faculty work: Are we cocreators of knowledge, or do we operate out of a division between authoritative experts who produce knowledge and consumers who are passive consumers—technocrats and clients? Should research agendas of academics be sanctioned by disciplinary interests or the needs of society? Should the aims of the academy be directed toward cultivating a wider public culture of democracy on campus and off? Should faculty members strive for dispassionate neutrality or wade into the essential but messy work of public problem solving? Such questions guided our inquiry toward grappling with the core purposes of higher education, the epistemological underpinnings of academic culture, and the existing warrants for what constitutes legitimate knowledge. It led us to attempt to respond to more questions: What *are* the implications of the current state of affairs for our democracy, and how *should* academic culture be constructed? Exploring these questions led us to attempt the development of a fresh conceptual frame that would enliven and sharpen our thinking about our work going forward. We drew a distinction between "civic engagement" efforts focused on activities and place and compliant with the status quo and a "democratic civic engagement" attentive to process and purpose (specifically democratic purposes) that fundamentally compels transformational change.

In a sense, the heart of the issue is one of purpose. What larger purpose are we trying to achieve? The lack of clarity causes all kinds of mischief. It leads to the fragmentation described above, as individual programs seek their own narrow ends rather than looking beyond these confines to a larger purpose that might unite their efforts. It leads to an impoverishment of imagination. At some institutions service-learning or engaged scholarship are held up as proxies for civic engagement as if they were equivalent, while other efforts, such as diversity initiatives, as Caryn Musil notes in Chapter 11, languish in the shadows. "Civic engagement" becomes merely an accretion of various projects and programs on a campus than are pointed to as badges of honor rather than a way of life—a rethinking and restructuring of the core work of the university.

A reconceptualization is needed. It is imperative to reclaim as the central project of the movement the shaping of a creative, vibrant, and inclusive democratic future. As Paul Hawken (2007) writes in his most recent book, "To be sanguine about the future, however, requires a plausible basis for constructive action: you cannot describe possibilities for the future unless the present problem is accurately defined" (p. 1). By conceptually clarifying "democratic engagement," we have attempted to accurately define the present problem, which we see as the need to reconceptualize democratic practice in order to spur institutional change.

No purpose, however important, can inspire if it remains ethereal. We have therefore tried to describe democratic engagement in this volume as a dynamic process rather than a static and rigid dogma or fixed set of activities. At the center of the process is creating the broader purpose for higher education that Boyer talked about. The metaphor of the Ivory Tower has often been evoked to emphasize the aloofness of the university—its inclination to dwell in the rarified air of the esoteric and arcane. There is no doubt that many academics have garnered success describing the challenges facing society ("problematizing" is the oft-evoked word), without offering a single suggestion for how to address them. It's a small wonder the phrase "it's academic" has a very different resonance on Main Street than within academy. Some have made invidious comparisons between the Ivory Tower and the engaged university—one that is responsive to the needs of society. In our view, such critiques somewhat miss the mark. Historically, the university has at times had to purposefully shield itself from meddling by external forces and the state (or, more recently, corporate interests). Independence of thought is the cornerstone of academic freedom. Also, there are valuable purposes of the university—its role as the conservator of knowledge, history, culture, and the pursuit of knowledge for its own sake—that serve a vitally important public purpose in a democracy where rich discourse requires deep contextual understanding. It is the reason the first things to be destroyed in a totalitarian regime are the books and the arts. The project to create a democratically engaged university, as we see it, requires preserving the intellectual independence of the university while also spurring within its ranks a desire to make a difference in our democracy.

The solution to advancing civic engagement thus far has been cultivating new initiatives within the existing structures and cultures of academy—expanding the number of service-learning courses on campuses, establishing

new and better partnerships with the community, developing new courses in
the undergraduate general education curriculum that asks students to carefully examine societal challenges. But as H. L. Mencken caustically remarked,
"There is always a well-known solution to every human problem—neat,
plausible, and wrong" (1920, p. 158). Although hundreds of colleges and
universities are undertaking all of the activities just mentioned, no accretion
of programs will produce the democratically engaged university. What is
required is a rethinking of the entire enterprise.

The contributors to this volume have provided both a deeper examination
of the implications of democratic civic engagement for higher education and
recommended models for practice and for institutional action though concrete
work "on the ground" in shaping democratic forms of civic engagement in
colleges and universities. Their chapters connect the conceptual work around
democratic engagement with actual campus and community-based practice
that is intentionally connected to strategies for institutional change, addressing the question we raised in the Introduction: "What, then, is required to
spur the deep change in institutional priorities and values needed to create the
conditions for sustained civic engagement?"

What we offer up here are examples of the kinds of efforts that would
move beyond first-order change toward such a transformation, what we see
as a set of propositions that offer possibilities for constructive action. We are
keenly aware that there is no "one-size-fits-all" strategy; indeed our premise
is that each institution will have to undertake this work in light of its own
historic mission, understanding of its students, and attentiveness to the local
social and political context within which it operates. Our intent, rather, is to
imagine the kinds of change that might lead to a more democratically responsive university, and we do this by offering up several propositions.

PROPOSITION 1

Transformation change requires a broad-based consensus about purpose.
Change at colleges and universities (unless it is driven by crisis and therefore
reactive, or the unthinking slow drift produced by the vagaries of internal
and external pressures) is built on dialogue and debate. This truism is evident if we consider the governance processes on campuses or examine conventional strategies for change, such as strategic planning. Discourse produces
a shared understanding of what the group hopes to achieve. The literature on
organizational change is replete with evidence of the importance of a shared
mission (Collins and Porras 1994; Hartley 2002; Tierney 1988). Building
the democratically engaged university requires building a consensus (at least
among a substantial proportion of the academic community) that the college
or university *has* in fact some responsibility to our democracy. Some institutions may cast this conversation in another way, emphasizing the public
purpose of the institution. The particular terminology is unimportant as long
as the underlying substance is aimed at creating an institution committed to

strengthening our communities and our democracy. The historic missions of most colleges and universities have deep civic and democratic roots. Many institutional leaders have found it fruitful to discuss how (or whether) these purposes are relevant today. In many cases these roots have been forgotten. Accreditation, periodic strategic planning efforts, and the entrance of a new president all offer occasions for institutions revisit their core mission. Finally, it is also helpful for institutions to simply begin to notice and recognize existing examples where the democratic mission is already being realized in the curriculum, co-curriculum, and research. In fact, the vast majority of colleges and universities have civic outcomes described in their mission statements (e.g., developing civic leaders, service to society).

It is important to note, however, that even if a shared purpose is articulated and becomes codified in an eloquent mission statement, it has a half-life. To keep that purpose alive, people across the institution have to understand and embrace the ideal and alter their activities (or, at a minimum, alter how they talk about and think about their work) in a way consonant with the democratic purpose. The sort of institutional dialogue required to produce transformational change has to occur on several levels (institutional, school, and departmental). It also has to be sustained. Over time, people enter and leave the university. New members of the community must be introduced to the idea (or, in some cases, selected because their qualifications indicate they can contribute to it). In sum, a democratically engaged mission is not a lofty inspirational credo; it is alive and rooted in the messy day-to-day work of the institution.

PROPOSITION 2

The democratically engaged university entails cocreating a different kind of educational experience with its students. Fostering an educational environment that promotes democratic practices and values entails purposefully shaping the experiences of students. This requires grappling with a number of key issues. For example, to what degree are the undergraduate curriculums of various programs and departments purposefully designed to build a greater awareness of how our democracy works, of the central challenges of our common life, of how we live together despite difference, and of how the interests of our nation relate or conflict with the interests of other ideologies and systems? It is important to recognize that there will be elements of the curriculum that contribute to the democratic end indirectly. Faculty members in the sciences who teach students to carefully scrutinize evidence and think critically or colleagues in the humanities who ask students to grapple with the complexities of human life can be equal partners in this effort alongside those who teach political science or choose to incorporate service-learning into a course. Intent and the overall meta-design of the curriculum are what matters.

We must scrutinize our pedagogical approaches—do they reflect democratic ideals? Lecturing has its place, but a curriculum dominated by it is unlikely to build competency in deliberation and civic discourse. To what extent do current courses allow students to develop their own opinions about various issues and then learn and practice the precepts of public deliberation to refine them? How much agency do students experience in the context of service-learning or problem-based learning courses? Is service-learning an add-on or an integral element of the course? By the end of the semester, do students have a better understanding of the sociopolitical factors that cause a situation than they do at the beginning? Are students offered the opportunity to see the results of their efforts (perhaps as only a part of a series of classes that will grapple with a particular issue)?

Many academic programs purport to prepare students for particular roles or jobs, especially in professional education programs. Do these programs invite students to develop what Albert Dzur (2008) calls a sense of "democratic professionalism"? Is the conception of the professional identity narrowly conceived, or does it invite students to find ways to creatively imagine professional roles in which they can make a difference to society (an impetus that draws many into professional fields in the first place)?

A great deal of learning occurs outside the classroom as well. On many campuses student affairs professionals support students' efforts to shape campus life through student activities, residence life, clubs, and student government. There are excellent examples of institutions that have asked students to assume significant responsibility in running their residence life programs—establishing norms of conduct, establishing forums such as community meetings to discuss issues that emerge, and mediating problems. This is an area ripe for further development. Another question is whether the voice of the student body is evident in discussions of important institutional issues. What committees are students asked to serve on (and on what important committees are they notably absent)? Is student government invited to participate in important campus work or relegated to party planning?

An important characteristic of all of the activities we have mentioned is that they rely on a reciprocal relationship between faculty and student. In curricular matters, the sort of experience we advocate stands in contrast to Freire's noted critique of the "banking model" of education (where experts deposit facts in students' heads). The co-curriculum is also a key place for students to practice the skills of collective decision making with one another and, at times, with staff or faculty who also have an interest in the issue at hand. In all these instances the foundation for democratic civic engagement involves cocreating the overall educational environment.

PROPOSITION 3

Leadership should model democratic values. Students learn all the time, both with us and despite us. Often what we model—individually or institutionally—is inconsistent with what we formally teach our students. Active and collaborative forms of teaching, learning, and scholarship should be reinforced by and model active and collaborative forms of leadership. Leadership for democratic engagement should be modeling the value of collaboration and participation across the institution. This means breaking down hierarchies and opening up dialogue. Multiple voices and perspectives need to be included in institutional decision making in inclusive and authentic ways. It means including community partners on committees and advisory boards and involving students as full participants on university-wide committees—with voting power. Having students serve as full participants with voice and power in campus policies and practices is another opportunity to develop their civic capacity though involvement in their campus community.

Those in leadership positions also should be vigilant about adhering to both the academic and civic missions of the institution. Academic leaders should resist the insidious prestige culture of striving that permeates higher education and is defined by narrow views of research and scholarship that undermine engaged knowledge generation and derail civic engagement efforts. The problem is not that of striving itself; every institution should aspire to better its work and have a vision for an ideal. The problem is what institutions strive to be. Many colleges and universities have resisted the temptation to aspire to become top-tier research universities and have instead realistically assessed their missions and set their sights on striving to be institutions that are, in the framing of the American Association of State Colleges and Universities, "stewards of place." An institution as a "steward of place" means that even as "the demands of the economy and society have forced institutions to be nationally and globally aware," colleges and universities "are inextricably linked with the communities and regions in which they are located"(2002, p. 9). Community responsibility through stewardship of place establishes a new model of excellence in higher education where the standard become one of improving the lives of local residents by addressing issues of health, the economy, housing, jobs, and education and helping to build the capacity of all citizens for democratic agency and participation. Community responsibility is reflected in a set of institutional indicators that allow for assessing excellence through a different lens (see the Carnegie Foundation for the Advancement of Teaching Elective Community Engagement Classification, available at http://classifications .carnegiefoundation.org/descriptions/community_engagement.php).

One area of community responsibility and stewardship that has emerged on campuses across the country is higher education's involvement with local K–12 schools. Amy Gutmann, president of the University of Pennsylvania, in her book *Democratic Education* wrote that "higher education cannot succeed unless lower education does"(1987, p. 172). A number of authors in this volume have reinforced the perspective that the academic success of youth into and through higher education is (1) achievable only if the schools are viewed within a larger community perspective that includes issues of housing, jobs, health, and crime, as well as education, and (2) essential for the success of vibrant and thriving democracy. Thus, if higher education is to take seriously democratic civic engagement, leadership should take seriously higher education's relationship to local schools and the success of traditionally underserved students. This calls for deliberate and organized efforts to partner with schools and with community-based organizations to address educational issues at all levels.

For the campus, this can mean things like college students tutoring school-aged youth. It can mean college students working with high school youth around a number of college readiness issues including navigating admissions and financial aid, supporting the balancing of jobs and academic study, and other challenges. It can mean shifts in the curriculum so that the campus offers a minor in urban education to involve college students in service-learning opportunities that benefit the schools. In can mean interdisciplinary collaborations to work with community partners around issues in the community that support student success. And—in making a commitment to education across the P–16 continuum—it can mean an institutional commitment on the part of the campus to realign its efforts to create a culture of retention and success for underserved students (low-income students, first-generation students, culturally diverse students, and students of color) so that academic success and not access alone becomes the goal. Ultimately, this means that faculty should enact pedagogical practices that reflect active and collaborative forms of teaching and learning and that draw upon and value the knowledge and experience that all students bring to the classroom as assets in the education process.

Proposition 4

Graduate education must be realigned to promote a larger public purpose. Top-tier research universities, while relatively few in number, disproportionately influence higher education in part because they are the training ground for the faculty who teach at all types of higher education institutions, and especially at the institutions that educate a majority of students. The training they offer, particularly at the doctoral level, tends to be disproportionately oriented toward the development of research skills and disciplinary knowledge. Many graduate students, however, often those from diverse cultural backgrounds, have deep interests in developing research agendas tied to pressing societal and community issues. Many graduate students have been involved in community-based projects since high school and can envision how they will bring their social commitments into their roles as future faculty. Many are specifically looking for opportunities in their studies to develop professional capacities around democratic, engaged practice. These future faculty are also assessing their professional commitments and are looking to shape faculty lives in which their roles around teaching, scholarship, and service are integrated and whole.

They are looking for academic homes to both do their graduate work and settle in as faculty as they establish their careers. They are attentive to the role of the academy in providing a supportive environment for new ways of generating knowledge. Many young scholars whose work originates in a rich and complex intersection of feminist, postmodern, postcolonial, and critical race theories are raising questions of power, privilege, and voice not only in their research but in an examination of academic privilege and standards—including what kind of "knowledge" is being valued, what research methods are legitimized, and what kinds of research are validated. Graduate students are looking for programs that provide training in rigorous research methods that underscore community production of knowledge, research in which people who are the subjects of the research play a central role, not as "informants" or "data sources," but as knowledgeable participants in the entire research process. They are drawn to research in which the scholar works "in dialogue, collaboration, and alliance with people who are struggling to better their lives" and the scholarship produced "embodies a responsibility for the results" as they affect those in the community who collaborate in the research in a way that they "can recognize as their own, value in their own terms, and use as they see fit" (Hale 2008, p. 4).

Graduate programs have an opportunity to prepare students with knowledge and skills that will serve them well as democratically engaged faculty by providing development in active and collaborative forms of teaching and learning; in community engaged teaching, learning, and scholarship; and in leadership as change agents in their professional practice. Some institutions have underscored this commitment by the development of particular programs. For example, Michigan State University offers both a graduate certificate in college teaching as well as a graduate certificate in civic engagement. Certificate programs in postsecondary teaching and learning are also offered at the University of Kentucky, the University of Missouri–Kansas City, the University of Southern Florida, George Mason University, and the University of Iowa, to name a few. More attention should be given to establishing programs that prepare future faculty as engaged teachers and scholars, and as agents of democratic action on campus and in local communities.

PROPOSITION 5

Evolving perspectives on knowledge generation must be validated. At many institutions of higher education, particularly those whose identities are shaped by characteristics of research universities, the long-term sustainability of reciprocal partnership work is determined by faculty roles and rewards—and in a research culture, sustainability is fundamentally determined by the norms and values of scholarship that are validated in the promotion and tenure process. This will remain true for research universities even as the trends for higher education broadly continue to shift toward the dominance of contingent faculty who will not be held to account for high scholarly productivity.

The point here is that what is at issue is not whether promotion and tenure guidelines and criteria need to change to accommodate community-engaged scholarship (although this is beginning to happen at more and more campuses), nor is it a question of the kind of scholarship that should be legitimized and supported, but, rather, underlying the questions of criteria and varieties of scholarship is the broader question of how knowledge is generated and disseminated. When knowledge generation, either through scholarship or through teaching and learning, is a process of cocreation (with students and with community partners), then democratic forms of civic engagement are more likely to emerge and become institutionalized. As a number of authors in this volume emphasize, reciprocal knowledge generation provides the foundations for repositioning the role of students because their knowledge and experience is essential to the generation of new knowledge—and their participation draws upon and builds their capacity for civic agency and democratic action.

Proposition 6

Institutions must provide resources for faculty professional development for democratic civic engagement. A theme running through a number of chapters in this volume emphasizes the need to prepare students with the skills they need for democratic participation in an inclusive and just democracy. If this kind of skill building and intellectual development is to take place as part of students' education—particularly as curricular-based activities as the authors suggest—then faculty should be skilled in the practice of democracy as translated into educational practice.

This means that democratic skills and the political dimensions of democracy work should be acknowledged and incorporated into core faculty work. Professional development should provide faculty with opportunities to develop the skills of democratic practice if faculty are going to be competent and confident in making that practice a part of the teaching and learning process. Institutional resources should be directed to professional development that allows faculty to bring dialogue and deliberation into the classroom and to approach the curriculum through a lens that asks, "What is the public relevance of the discipline?" This means that faculty should not only frame disciplinary contents in terms of the public dimension of the discipline but also provide opportunities for students to practice the skills of democracy through the course.

Providing opportunities for faculty to develop and incorporate democratic frameworks and skills into their courses allows those faculty members to model the democratic values that they want students to learn. Their practice can be consistent with the civic learning outcomes they hope to achieve. As faculty facilitate reciprocal knowledge generation and learning, they will enact collaboration with students and with community partners. Developing capacity among faculty allows for building democratic engagement from the bottom up as a complement to other strategies of achieving institutional change for democratic civic engagement.

CONCLUSION

The possibilities for constructive action discussed by the authors in this volume and the six propositions outlined in this concluding chapter do not constitute a set program of action. They are, however, an invitation for those who care deeply about this work to lift up their heads from their various independent activities in order to see that there are many smaller tributaries that, together, could feed a movement capable of reshaping the landscape of American higher education. The history of social movements suggests that their success is not tied to the use of particular strategies. Rather, movements succeeded because they were animated by a powerful and compelling sense of purpose that produced committed action by countless people. The movement has sought to encourage community involvement. What we need to do now is focus our attention on building a strong, participatory democracy. Such a purpose reveals new possibilities and new synergies. A new and exciting set of activities suddenly become central to the work when its aim is cultivating democratic practice and pursuing real change in our communities. We begin to see a host of new partners who are deeply invested in building a more just, more equitable, and more inclusive society. But this sort of change can only occur when we move beyond the pursuit of legitimacy (as it is currently defined in the academy) and begin to confront and counter those aspects of the status quo that produce persistent inequality and deaden efforts to recognize and confront it. Then we may be able to look back at some future point in time and see that the civic engagement movement was not stalled but merely poised to reshape American higher education and our society.

REFERENCES

American Association of State Colleges and Universities. 2002. "Stepping Forward as Stewards of Place." Washington, DC. Available at www.aascu.org/pdf/stewardsof place_02.pdf.

Collins, J. C., and J. I. Porras. 1994. *Built to Last: Successful Habits of Visionary Companies.* New York: HarperCollins.

Dzur, A. 2008. *Democratic Professionalism: Citizen Participation and the Reconstruction of Professional Ethics, Identity, and Practice.* University Park: Pennsylvania State University Press.

Gutmann, A. 1987. *Democratic Education.* Princeton: Princeton University Press.

Hale, C. R., ed. 2008. *Engaging Contradictions: Theory, Politics, and Methods of Activist Scholarship.* Berkeley: University of California Press.

Hartley, M. 2002. *A Call To Purpose: Mission-Centered Change at Three Liberal Arts Colleges.* New York: RoutledgeFalmer.

Hawken, P. 2007. *Blessed Unrest: How the Largest Movement in the World Came Into Being and Why No One Saw it Coming.* New York: Penguin.

Mencken, H. L. 1920. *Prejudices: Second Series.* New York: Alfred A. Knopf.

Tierney, W. G. 1988. "Organizational Culture in Higher Education." *Journal of Higher Education* 59 (1): 2–21.

CONTRIBUTORS

Richard Battistoni is professor of political science and public and community service studies at Providence College, where he recently served as chair of the Political Science Department. Formerly the director of the Feinstein Institute for Public Service at Providence College, Rick also developed and directed civic engagement efforts at Rutgers and Baylor University. He served from 2001 to 2004 as director of Project 540, a national high school civic engagement initiative funded by a grant from the Pew Charitable Trusts, and has published scholarly articles based on data from that project. A scholar in the field of political theory with a principal interest in the role of education in a democratic society, he is author of several publications, including *Civic Engagement across the Curriculum: A Resource Book for Service-Learning Faculty in All Disciplines. Education for Democracy: Citizenship, Community, Service*, which he coedited with Benjamin R. Barber, is a principal textbook used in service-learning classes taught around the country.

Lee Benson is professor emeritus of history and a Distinguished Senior Fellow of the Netter Center for Community Partnerships at the University of Pennsylvania. Dr. Benson's pioneering work, *The Concept of Jacksonian Democracy*, introduced the application of social science theory and methodology to the discipline of history. He has authored numerous books, chapters, and articles in the discipline. He is cofounder of the university-assisted community school program that, since its inception in 1985, has been seen as a national model of university civic engagement. Benson is co–executive editor of *Universities and Community Schools* and is the author or coauthor of dozens of articles on university civic engagement and the role of higher education in educating students for democratic citizenship. In 2007, *Dewey's Dream: Universities and Democracies in an Age of Education Reform*, which Benson coauthored with Ira Harkavy and John Puckett, was published by Temple University Press.

Harry Boyte is founder of Public Achievement, the international youth civic and political education initiative; director of the Center for Democracy and Citizenship, now at Augsburg College; and a senior fellow at the Humphrey School of Public Affairs. His most recent books include *The Citizen Solution: How You Can Make a Difference* and *Everyday Politics: Reconnecting Citizens and Public Life*.

Eric Fretz is assistant professor of peace and justice studies at Regis University in Denver, Colorado.

Ira Harkavy is associate vice president and director of the Netter Center for Community Partnerships at the University of Pennsylvania, where he has helped to develop university-community-school partnerships as well as academically based community service courses and participatory action research projects that involve faculty and students from across the university. His recent publications include *Dewey's Dream: Universities and Democracies in an Age of Education Reform*, which he coauthored with Lee Benson and John Puckett, and *The Obesity Culture: Strategies for Change: Public Health and University-Community Partnerships*, which he coauthored with Francis E. Johnston.

Matthew Hartley is associate professor and chair of the Higher Education Division at the University of Pennsylvania's Graduate School of Education. His research and writing focuses on academic governance and organizational change at colleges and universities. He is especially interested in exploring how academic communities define their educational purposes. His most recent research has centered on a particular academic purpose—civic engagement. Dr. Hartley received a National Academy of Education postdoctoral fellowship for 2006–2007 to examine the civic engagement movement in American higher education. He recently completed a project with the Council of Europe in Strasbourg, France, that explored partnerships between universities, schools, and civil society organizations to promote the council's Education for Democratic Citizenship program. Dr. Hartley has published articles in a wide variety of journals and currently serves on the editorial boards of the *Review of Higher Education* and the *Journal of Higher Education Outreach and Engagement*. He earned an Ed.M. and Ed.D. from Harvard University's Graduate School of Education and served as cochair of the editorial board for the *Harvard Educational Review*.

Lorlene Hoyt is an associate professor of urban planning and director of the MIT@ Lawrence Partnership at the Massachusetts Institute of Technology. With an educational background and professional experience in landscape architecture and city planning, Hoyt's core interests include community economic development, city-campus partnerships, and urban planning pedagogy. Her research has been published in the *Journal of Planning Education and Research*, the *Journal of Urban Technology*, and the *Michigan Journal of Community Service Learning*. She received the Ernest A. Lynton Award for the Scholarship of Engagement in 2007 and is cofounder of Urban Revitalizers, LLC, a minority-owned real estate development and planning firm in Boston.

Peter Levine is director of the Center for Information and Research on Civic Learning and Engagement (CIRCLE) at the Jonathan M. Tisch College of Citizenship and Public Service at Tufts University. His books include *The Future of Democracy*, *Engaging Young People in Civic Life*, and *Reforming the Humanities*.

Nicholas V. Longo is director of global studies and associate professor of public and community service studies at Providence College. He is the author of *Why Community Matters: Connecting Education with Civic Life* and coeditor of *From Command to Community: A New Approach to Leadership Education in Colleges and Universities*.

David Mathews is president of the Charles F. Kettering Foundation. He served as secretary of the Department of Health, Education, and Welfare in the administration of President Gerald Ford. Between 1969 and 1980, he was president of the University of Alabama. He has written extensively on education, political theory, Southern history, public policy, and international problem solving. His books include *Why Public Schools? Whose Public Schools?*, *For Communities to Work*, and a revised second edition of *Politics for People*. His newest book, *Reclaiming Public Education by Reclaiming Our Democracy*, focuses on the relationship between the public and public education. He serves on the board of a variety of organizations, including the Gerald R. Ford Foundation, the National Issues Forums Institute, and Public Agenda.

Caryn McTighe Musil is senior vice president of the Association of American Colleges and Universities and oversees the office of Diversity, Equity, and Global Initiatives, where she has directed nearly twenty national projects. Before moving into national-level administrative work in higher education, she was a faculty member for eighteen years. She has special expertise in curriculum and faculty development, civic engagement, diversity and global learning, and women's issues. She currently is directing a multiproject initiative, Core Commitments: Educating Students for Personal and Social Responsibility, and is a partner in a Department of Education project called Civic Learning and Democratic Engagement. For the past ten years, Dr. Musil has also served on the steering committee of the International Consortium for Higher Education, Civic Responsibility, and Democracy in partnership with the Council of Europe.

KerryAnn O'Meara is an associate professor of higher education at the University of Maryland. Her research and practice focus on community and civic engagement, the academic profession, and academic reward systems. She is particularly interested in how reform in academic reward systems and in opportunities for professional growth can advance faculty civic work and institutional missions. She received the Early Career Research Award from the Internation Association for Research on Service-learing and Community Engagement (IARSLCE) and serves as the associate editor for research articles for the *Journal of Higher Education Outreach and Engagement*.

William M. Plater is Chancellor's Professor Emeritus of public affairs, philanthropic studies, and English at Indiana University–Purdue University Indianapolis (IUPUI), where he served as chief academic officer from 1987 to 2006, a period during which the campus made community engagement a defining characteristic of its mission. Author of numerous articles and chapters on community engagement and leadership, Plater is coeditor with Mark Langseth of *Public Work and the Academy: An Academic Administrator's Guide to Civic Engagement and Service-Learning*. Plater is currently senior consultant for higher education strategies at Epsilen, a learning technology company focused on student engagement.

John Woodrow Presley is professor of English at Illinois State University, teaches in ISU's doctoral programs in higher education administration, and serves as editor of *Planning and Changing* at the Center for the Study of Education Policy. He was provost at ISU from 2003 to 2008 and previously served as chief academic officer or dean at four other institutions, including Lafayette College and the University of Michigan–Dearborn. Presley coedited *The Future of Higher Education: Perspectives* *from America's Academic Leaders* for Paradigm Press and *Educating Students for Political Engagement*, published by the AASCU. Presley serves on the National Implementation Committee for the American Democracy Project.

John Puckett is professor of education and chair of the Policy, Measurement, and Evaluation Division of the University of Pennsylvania Graduate School of Education. He has been involved in the development of academically based community service seminars in West Philadelphia schools for twenty years and has a long-standing affiliation with Penn's Netter Center for Community Partnerships. He is a former National Academy of Education/Spencer Foundation postdoctoral fellow and Fulbright Scholar to Germany. His recent books are *Leonard Covello and the Making of Benjamin Franklin High School: Education as If Citizenship Mattered*, which he coauthored with Michael C. Johanek, and *Dewey's Dream: Universities and Democracies in an Age of Education Reform*, which he coauthored with Lee Benson and Ira Harkavy. His current book project is a coauthored history of Penn's campus development and expansion in West Philadelphia since World War II.

John Saltmarsh is the director of the New England Resource Center for Higher Education (NERCHE) at the University of Massachusetts–Boston as well as a faculty member in the Higher Education Administration Doctorial Program in the Department of Leadership in Education in the College of Education and Human Development. He is the author of numerous book chapters and articles on civic engagement, service-learning, and experiential education, and he is most recently the coauthor with Edward Zlotkowski of *Higher Education and Democracy: Essays on Service-Learning and Civic Engagement*.

Nancy Thomas is the director of the Democracy Imperative at the University of New Hampshire and senior associate at Everyday Democracy in East Hartford, Connecticut. She is the author of numerous book chapters and articles on democratic learning and engagement. Most recently, she edited *Educating for Deliberative Democracy*, the winter 2010 issue of Jossey Bass's New Directions for Higher Education series, and coedited (with Martin Carcasson) a special higher-education issue of the *Journal of Public Deliberation* (2010).

Edward Zlotkowski is professor of English and founding director of the Bentley Service-Learning Center at Bentley University. He writes and speaks extensively on a wide range of service-learning and civic engagement topics and served as the general editor of the American Association for Higher Education's twenty-one-volume series on service-learning in the academic disciplines.

INDEX

Shalala, Donna, 91; "Mandate for a New Century," 91
Shulman, Lee, 69
Simon, Elaine, 73, 75, 76
Smith, Page, 15
Southern Christian Leadership Conference (SCLC), 209; and Student Nonviolent Coordinating Committee (SNCC), 208–209
"Standards of Public Sociology: Guidelines for Use by Academic Departments in Personnel Reviews" (American Sociological Association), 183
Stanford University, 255
State compacts, 36, 37
Stephens, Jason, 67–68, 151; *Educating Citizens: Preparing America's Undergraduates for Lives of Moral and Civic Responsibility*, 67–68, 86
"Strengthening the Foundations of Students' Excellence, Integrity, and Social Contribution" (Colby and Sullivan), 254
"The Struggle Against Positivism" (Boyte), 222
Student Nonviolent Coordinating Committee (SNCC), 208–209; and Southern Christian Leadership Conference (SCLC), 209
Students: civic agency of, 5, 205–206; as colleagues, 211–213; motivation, 206–208; political disengagement of, 8, 29, 30, 40, 155; political engagement, 170–171; practice of engagement, 205–206; role in institutionalization of civic engagement, 200–202, 208–209, 293–294; voice, 203–205
Students as Colleagues: Expanding the Circle of Service-Learning Leadership (Zlotkowski, Longo, and Williams), 212, 217, 218, 232
Sullivan, William M., 254; "Strengthening the Foundations of Students' Excellence, Integrity, and Social Contribution," 254
The Sustained Dialogue Campus Network, 165
Syracuse University, 255–256, 259–260

Task Force on the Institutionalization of Public Sociology, 146
Tenure and promotion, 134, 143–145, 149–151, 178, 180, 182, 188, 190, 191, 194
"The Theoretical Roots of Service-Learning in John Dewey: Toward a Theory of Service-Learning" (Giles and Eyler), 219, 220
Thompson, Dennis, 159, 162; *Why Deliberative Democracy*, 159
Toulmin, Stephen, 223, 226, 235; *Cosmopolis: The Hidden Agenda of Modernity*, 223, 235–236

"Toward Pragmatic Liberal Education" (Kimball), 218, 219, 223
Tucker, Robert, 221, 222; "Biting the Pragmatist Bullet: Why Service-Learning Can Do without Epistemology," 221

United Negro College Fund, 218
Universities in the Marketplace (Bok), 67
University: corporatization of, 15; research, 55; resources of, 50
University-assisted community schools, 4, 57, 59, 60–61, 61–76; challenges facing, 64–68
University of Buffalo, 250–251
University of Chicago, 54, 154
University of Denver, 88–90, 91
University of Hawaii, 165
University of Maryland, 258
University of Massachusetts–Amherst, 209, 212
University of Michigan: Ann Arbor campus, 163, 255; Dearborn campus, 132, 133
University of Minnesota, 249–250, 255
University of Nebraska at Omaha, 245
University of Notre Dame, 165
University of Pennsylvania, 57, 59, 60–65, 69, 70, 149, 212, 252–253, 295; academically based community service course (ABCS), 63; Amy Gutmann, 64–65, 295; community partnerships, 64; International Consortium for Higher Education, Civic Responsibility, and Democracy (IC), 252–253; Judith Rodin, 64; Netter Center for Community Partnerships, 61, 63, 65
University of Richmond, 168
University of Southern California, 258
University of Virginia, 154, 165
University of Washington, 259
U.S. Department of Housing and Urban Development (HUD), 217, 269, 270, 276; Community Outreach Partnerships Centers (COPC), 217, 269
U.S. News and World Report, 189

Vanderbilt University, 165
Viewpoint Learning, 168–169
Volunteering, 34, 210–211

Wallis, Jim, 207
Weber, Max, 206
Weinberg, Adam, 206
West, Cornell, 256, 289
West Philadelphia, 50, 64, 71–72; and public schools, 57, 61–63; West Philadelphia High School (WPHS), 73–76
West Philadelphia Improvement Corps (WEPIC), 57
Why Deliberative Democracy (Gutmann and Thompson), 159